CULT TV

The Golden Age of ITC

CULT TV

The Golden Age of ITC

Foreword by Sir Roger Moore
Afterword by Gerry Anderson

Robert Sellers

Plexus, London

Published by Plexus Publishing Limited
25 Mallinson Road
London SW11 1BW
www.plexusbooks.com
First Printing

British Library Cataloguing in Publication Data

Sellers, Robert
Cult TV : the golden age of ITC
1. Incorporated Television Company 2. Television programs
- Great Britain - History
I. Title
791.4'5'0941'09046

ISBN-10: 0859653889

Printed in Great Britain By The Cromwell Press Ltd.
Cover and book design by Rebecca Martin

Contents

Acknowledgements

Any merits that this book might possess is totally due to the generosity and enthusiasm of some 50 ITC greats, who kindly gave of their time to share memories from that golden period. I thank them all wholeheartedly: Gerry Anderson, Sylvia Anderson, Annette Andre, Jane Asher, Raymond Austin, George Baker, Robert S. Baker, Roy Ward Baker, Martin Baker, Alexandra Bastedo, Richard Bradford, Michael Billington, Ed Bishop, Brian Clemens, Tony Curtis, Lisa Daniely, Clive Donner, Patricia Driscoll, Shirley Eaton, Joel Fabiani, Cyril Frankel, William Gaunt, John Glen, Michael Grade, Peter Hammond, Jane Henson, John Hough, Peter Hyams, Freddie Jones, Burt Kwouk, David Lazer, Valerie Leon, Sue Lloyd, Francis Matthews, Jane Merrow, Roger Moore, Barry Morse, Ian Ogilvy, Nicola Pagett, Conrad Phillips, Shane Rimmer, William Russell, Peter Graham Scott, Marcia Stanton, Robert Tronson, Robert Vaughn, Peter Wyngarde, Michael York, Franco Zeffirelli.

Visually this book owes everything to Jaz Wiseman, who allowed me access to his incredible archive of ITC material. My sincere thanks to him for all his time and effort. It's my pleasure to trumpet his terrific *Persuaders*/ITC website – www.itc-classics.com.

The Muppet Show photos are courtesy of The Muppets Studio, LLC. All rights reserved.

Particular thanks must go to Granada TV, especially Liz Cooper, for permission to reproduce images from all the ITC shows.

I also wish to thank everyone at Plexus who worked on the book, and for saying yes to my manuscript.

ROBERT SELLERS

Introduction

Think back to many of the great British cult/fantasy television shows of the sixties and seventies. Did you wish your own life was exciting as *The Saint*? Or maybe you longed to help prevent disaster with International Rescue and the *Thunderbirds*? Perhaps you puzzled over *The Prisoner*? Or took with you an imaginary (and sometimes annoying) friend in the style of *Randall and Hopkirk (Deceased)*? Were the Mysterons from *Captain Scarlet* your mortal enemy too, and did you laugh along with Kermit and Miss Piggy on *The Muppet Show*? Do you remember the hidden evil in the photographs of *Sapphire and Steel*? Was Moonbase Alpha from *Space 1999* your fantasy habitat? We fondly remember so many shows from what seems a golden age of television: *The Persuaders*, *Jason King*, *Stingray*, *Danger Man*, *Joe 90*, *The Champions* and *UFO*.

The incredible thing about this list, and many more programmes besides, is that they were all the product of one company – Lew Grade's ITC. Can any other independent television company in the world claim such a roster of hits?

This book is a celebration of this long lost golden age of television – long before *Big Brother*, reality TV, garden and DIY shows plagued our screens. In the 1960s TV was colourful, adventurous, controversial, but most of all it was *fun*. ITC encapsulated all of that in their shows. It's for this reason that they still delight and enthral millions today, whether on satellite television or on DVD and video. ITC certainly were unique – it's about time their extraordinary success story was told.

ROBERT SELLERS

SIR ROGER MOORE KBE

I have been fortunate to know a great many wonderful people in my life and career. Right at the top of that list are Lew Grade and Robert Baker.

Lew was, of course, Mr Television. He was a pioneer and a tremendous showman. His handshake was his word. I've never met anyone, before or since, like him. And I don't think there has been a company like Lew's ITC before or since either.

I myself had worked in television quite a lot when the early 1960s came around, and hadn't been too happy if the truth be known towards the end of my Warners contract with *The Alaskans* tv show. After the series, I left Hollywood and went off to Italy to make a couple of films. It was there I first heard from Bob Baker. He had an option on Leslie Charteris' *Saint* stories, with which I was very familiar - having tried to previously option them myself. I thought it could be an interesting show to make, and one – if I was lucky – that might run to a year. It actually ran for seven years and 118 episodes! I directed several too, as well as joining Bob in our own company producing the shows later on. It was one of the happiest periods of my career. I so fondly remember my morning drive to Elstree in the Volvo P1800. It wasn't like going to work … more like going to play!

After I hung up my halo, I was determined that my career would now lie in film. TV had been fun, and very kind to me, but I wanted to move on. I hadn't, however, figured on Lew Grade!

Lew had pre-sold a tv series called *The Persuaders!*. Nothing wrong there you might think. Well, no. Apart from the fact he had pre-sold it with Tony Curtis and ME in the leads! After telling me how much the country needed the money, and how I should think of my Queen, Lew shook my hand. A deal was done.

I spent a wonderful year at Pinewood and on location with Bob Baker and Tony Curtis making 24 episodes in all. Lew occasionally visited, but he instilled total confidence in his producers, and never interfered. He was more interested in the deal-making side.

I miss Lew. Though I will never forget him and ITC as, after all, he paid my wages for eight years!

The ITC story however goes beyond *The Saint* and *The Persuaders!* - here it is in its entirety, I hope you'll enjoy reading it.

Roger Moore

Chapter 1

Glorious Lew

The history of ITC is the history of British television at its most innovative and successful. Although it employed many people ITC was really just one man, and that man was Lew Grade. A Jewish refugee, raised in the East End of London, Lew Grade earned the nickname of 'Mr. Television'. He lived, breathed, slept and ate TV. At home in the mid-1950s, he had set up two television sets playing continuously, so that he could keep up with everything on the BBC and the newly created ITV – then the only two channels on the air. He truly loved the medium he excelled in.

Grade was the creative force behind Associated Television Ltd (ATV), then the largest regional firm in the UK commercial television network. ATV supplied the Midlands with their daily telly diet, and he was the power behind the independent production and distribution company ITC – under whose aegis the classic shows this book celebrates fell. 'Lew was quite simply a gem,' Sir Roger Moore fondly remembers. 'When he was at the height of his powers his energy was enormous. He would get off a plane without any jet lag and just go straight to work. His health regime was, he never had butter and he smoked cigars all day long.'

In today's media climate, research groups and panels of executives spend months exploring the viability of prospective shows. During the ITC era things were far simpler – if Lew liked your pitch, you had a deal there and then. 'Lew always had an open door to his office, he believed that he should be accessible to everybody,' recalls Marcia Stanton, Grade's PA from the early sixties, then executive assistant until his death in 1998. 'Producers would ring up and say, "We've got an idea," and Lew would see them and if he thought it was a good idea, and he liked the people pitching it and felt he had confidence in them, he'd say, "OK, we'll go with it." And it didn't have to go to a panel and a committee and then be talked about forever like now, and no decision made, he knew instantly. He had a sort of gut feeling about things.'

Lew had little time for lawyers and unwieldy contracts, his handshake was usually enough of a guarantee. 'You don't get characters like Lew Grade anymore,' claims legendary *Thunderbirds* co-creator Sylvia Anderson. 'He was a man that could make a decision. It doesn't exist now. What he said went. And he had such a personality and belief. He was a Sam Goldwyn, he was a Darryl Zanuck, he was all of these, like an old Hollywood mogul, but in the UK.' Robert S. Baker, the man who brought *The Saint* to television and created *The Persuaders*, feels much the same way. 'He was the last of the showmen. They don't exist anymore. The suits and

In the mid-1980s, Lord Lew Grade (with trademark cigar) reflects on his momentous career.

accountants have taken over.'

Had Lew's parents decided to head to America after emigrating from Russia, instead of England, he might have run 20th Century Fox or Paramount. If he were alive today he'd probably be head of a media empire. 'Lew was the only television impresario,' insists nephew Michael Grade. 'There had been impresarios in the theatre and in the cinema with [Alexander] Korda and J. Arthur Rank. Lew was the first and probably the only impresario of television.'

Many stories have been told about Lew Grade's colourful career, about his time as an agent, then a TV mogul, and lastly as a film producer. 'There's a wonderful line of Lew's when he was sitting next to a minister of education and talking about educational programmes on ATV,' recalls Roger Moore. 'And he mentioned this *Panorama*-type programme and the minister said, "Well, you hardly call that educational." And Lew said, "Well, you couldn't call it fucking entertainment."'

Grade started out in the business as a dancer, touring music halls, and never lost a chance to show off his old soft-shoe skills. At meetings, when financial matters were getting out of hand, director Raymond Austin recalls the tycoon would often jump out of his chair to jokingly complain, 'You're going to put me in the poor house. You're going to get me back to hoofing.' 'And you'd laugh,' observes Austin. 'And he'd say, "You think I'm joking – you don't think I used to hoof, watch this." And he'd go to the corner of his desk, pull back the carpet and do a little tap dance. And that was Lew Grade.'

Jason King star Peter Wyngarde recalls how, after a meeting with Lew, 'he rolled up the carpet and said, "You do Shakespeare, dear, I don't understand these things, it's not my cup of tea at all. This is my cup of tea." And he did a soft-shoe shuffle – brilliantly. A great character.'

Many of the stories about Lew are apocryphal, but no less entertaining because of that. On one occasion, a beggar is supposed to have approached him in the street and asked if he could spare 50p for a bed, and Lew replied, 'First send round the bed so I can look at it.' Lew's own personal favourite involved Sidney Bernstein, of rival TV company Granada, going into the Rolls Royce showrooms in Berkeley Square and asking for a Rolls Royce just like Lew Grade's, with a telephone. 'Fine,' said the salesman. 'We'll get you one in six months' time.' 'But I'm Sidney Bernstein of Granada,' he replied. 'I can't wait that long.' 'Very well, Mr. Bernstein, we'll get you one in a week's time.' The car was duly delivered to Bernstein, and later Lew was driving along Regent Street when the phone in his car rang. 'Hello Lew, this is Sidney Bernstein. I'm phoning you from my car.' 'Hold on Sidney,' deadpanned Lew. 'I'm just on the other line.'

'There are so many stories about Lew,' recalls Moore. 'I remember Dennis Selinger, who at one time was my agent, got a call from Lew; "What are you doing tonight?" "Nothing," Dennis replied. "Come on then, we're going to the Finsbury Park Empire." There was an act on that so impressed both of them that at the end of the first half they went backstage and Lew said, "You're very good. Who's your agent?" The performer said, "You are, Mr. Grade."'

Hollywood star Robert Vaughn remembers coming over to Britain to star in *The Protectors*, and arriving by ship in Southampton. 'And a lovely, huge Daimler picked us up and we went to the Dorchester. When we arrived, the door was opened by an eager, bald-headed gentleman who got the luggage and carried it in. Finally we realised it was Lew Grade! He was acting more like a doorman than the head of a company. He was a real one-off and the world's greatest salesman. You know, he sold *The Protectors* for a second year all over the world before it was ever aired in the first year. Quite a salesman.'

Lew meets the talent: (top) Rudolph Nureyev, on the set of The Muppet Show*; (bottom) Lew with Franco Zeffirelli, director of* Jesus of Nazareth.

The early years of British television were dominated by just one station, the BBC. Holding a monopoly of the airwaves and insulated by an annual licence fee, the mandarins at Broadcasting House didn't have to worry about such trivial matters as ratings. As a public service provider the aim was first to educate and inform; if the viewers at home also happened to find the channel's output entertaining, this was almost seen as a bonus.

All that changed in 1955 with the launch of ITV – a commercially based television station financed solely through advertising, whose very existence rested on its ability to attract large audiences. From this new world, Lew Grade emerged as a figure of monumental importance and far-reaching influence. 'There are unique attributing factors to Lew's success,' asserts Michael Grade – who has run both Channel 4 and the BBC. 'When he was a vaudeville dancer, pre-war, he got a lot of work on the continent and built up a network of contacts, and began working with acts he thought would do well in the UK. So he made the transition to an agent booking the continental acts that he'd seen. And he'd always enjoyed travelling, he had an inquiring, restless mind about how the world worked and where were the business opportunities. He just thought the world was bigger than Shaftesbury Avenue and Leicester Square, which was where all the agents were, and that if you travelled you'd do business. And as an agent he was one of the first people to go to America, and he booked Bob Hope, his first big coup.

Lew sandwiched between Muppet Show *creators Jim Henson (right) and Frank Oz (the voice of Miss Piggy).*

And he made contacts there and business boomed. And by travelling to America in those early days he saw commercial television and thought, "This is the future." He was a visionary.'

With an uncanny sixth sense for knowing what the public wanted, Grade's brand of scheduling on his ATV network was heavily weighted towards light entertainment, with soap operas, variety and game shows, comedies and imported American serials. These were programmes then disdained by the BBC, but their acquisition irrevocably changed the entire televisual landscape. The influence of Grade's foresight is still reflected on our screens today.

Not content with his dominant role in British television, Grade set his sights on transatlantic success. To a far greater extent than any of his contemporaries, Grade was interested in making programmes for export as well as for domestic consumption. 'None but a fool makes television films for the British market alone,' he intoned. 'Without the guarantee of an American outlet he will lose his shirt.' So Grade fixed his sights on the big guns – the three US networks, NBC, ABC and CBS. That was where the money was. 'Very quickly, it seemed to Lew a natural bit of business that the export market was a big market,' explains Michael Grade. 'He knew people from his days as an agent and he wasn't afraid to travel, cold-call, turn up somewhere. He'd go to Los Angeles just for a meeting and come back. He was a

At the onset of the video age, Lew presents Pope John Paul II with a presentation box of Jesus of Nazareth.

salesman. And that's what he did, whether it was acts or TV shows.'

Besides ATV, Grade also owned a production company called ITC, plus half a million pounds in capital. His most pressing problem was that he had no clue where to go from there. Fate, though, was shortly to intervene.

Chapter 2

Quivering Bows and Clunking Armour

- The Adventures of Robin Hood - The Adventures of Sir Lancelot - The Buccaneers - The Adventures of William Tell - H.G. Wells' Invisible Man -

THE ADVENTURES OF ROBIN HOOD (1955-59)

Shortly after the creation of ITC in 1955, Lew Grade met American producer Hannah Weinstein, a former journalist and publicist, who pitched a series of 39 half-hour shows based on the Robin Hood legend. Lew liked the proposal and asked what it would cost. He was told by Weinstein that it would be about £10,000 per episode and gave the project the go-ahead.

Not until a few days later did Grade realise that perhaps he ought to have consulted his fellow ITC directors, before making such a heavy financial commitment. He called fellow power broker Prince Littler, who was the owner of Moss Empires – at that time the nation's premier circuit of theatres, music halls and variety houses. Grade told Littler to set up a board meeting for 10 o'clock on Saturday morning in his office. At that crucial meeting, Grade stood up and told everyone he'd committed £390,000 out of their capital of £500,000 to make a Robin Hood series. His statement didn't go down very well. How, some of his colleagues wanted to know, could he have taken such a gamble? 'Because I liked the idea so much,' Grade said simply. 'And I honestly believe it can work. We're supposed to be a production company and this will be a good start for us.' One executive asked if Grade had already signed an agreement with Weinstein. 'No,' he answered. 'But I've given my word and I'm not prepared to go back on it.' Grade's saviour turned out to be Prince Littler himself. 'Gentlemen,' he said, 'if Lew has given his OK, that's as good as a contract and we'll support him.' It was a decision that turned out to be one of the shrewdest and most significant in television history.

As played by Richard Greene, ITC's Robin Hood was far removed from the theatrically flamboyant Hollywood version personified by Errol Flynn. But what Greene lacked on the matinee idol front, he more than made up for with his leadership qualities. This Robin Hood was as English as cricket and warm beer. One could just as easily picture him smoking a pipe by the fireplace, listening to the Home Service, as riding roughshod through Sherwood Forest. *Sight and Sound* magazine later described Greene's Robin as 'the archetype fifties English hero'.

Richard Greene became so identified as Robin Hood that he was virtually typecast for the rest of his career.

English-born Richard Greene was a major leading man in 1930s Hollywood – once coming fourth in a poll of the most popular stars, which was topped by Clark Gable. His boyishly handsome looks and stiff-upper-lip gallantry were most effectively illustrated in the role of the young heir protected by Basil Rathbone's Sherlock Holmes, against *The Hound of the Baskervilles*. In accepting the role of Robin Hood – admittedly at a time when his film career was all but over – Greene made television history as the first Hollywood star to film a television series in Britain. 'He was always very nice to me,' Patricia Driscoll, who played Maid Marian, recalls. 'Very helpful and generous as an actor. And extremely professional, there were never any hold-ups with Richard at all. And very good with a bow and arrow too, he did most of his own shooting.'

The huge success of the series resurrected Greene's career, turning him into a global star once more. On publicity tours to the States he needed police escorts to keep avid fans at bay. He also became a very rich man, earning a reported £50,000 a year, at a time when the majority of people earned less than £10 a week. Unsurprisingly, Greene was only too happy to carry on in the role indefinitely. 'I know I'm in a rut,' he said. 'But it's a gold-plated rut and I'd be a fool to get out of it.' When he did finally relinquish his doublet and hose, Greene took his Robin Hood earnings with him to Ireland to escape the government tax sheriff, investing in a 400-acre stud farm. He acted only periodically afterwards in films like *The Blood of Fu Manchu* (as Nayland Smith) and *Tales from the Crypt*, and in a guest spot in cult seventies show *The Professionals*.

The show's first Maid Marian was Irish-born Bernadette O'Farrell, thrust into the limelight only to leave after two years, despite receiving thousands of letters asking her to stay. O'Farrell felt she was becoming too closely identified with her role – shopkeepers were addressing her as Maid Marian. There were rumours that she and Greene did not get on. Her replacement was Patricia Driscoll, who originally wanted the role back in 1955. 'But I never got anywhere and was very disappointed because I thought it was just right for me. And then when Bernadette left I was sent up again and this time got a test and got the part.'

Also Irish-born, Patricia was already a familiar face with younger viewers from her appearances in family favourites *Watch with Mother* and *Picture Book*. Her introduction as Maid Marian is probably the first instance of a regular television character being replaced by another performer mid-run. 'I think the powers that be were worried about my taking over, and so was I. They introduced me rather gingerly to begin with, but people accepted me very readily, it was very nice.'

True to his 'no sex please, we're British' background, Greene was far from a Lothario, and so Patricia rarely got into any romantic clinches with her leading man. 'Richard's attitude to me, whether it was in the script or whether it was the way he wished to play it, was very much a fatherly attitude. So I don't think I ever had that sort of emotional feeling. And in the scripts there was never any closeness required. You barely touched each other.

'It was a children's programme,' Patricia recalls. 'And although I was supposed to be Robin's girlfriend, I think we had two or maybe three little genteel kisses throughout the series. All very sisterly. I do remember after the first one people came up to me and said, "What's going on? You and Robin had a kiss!" You could hardly call it that, not by today's standards anyway.'

In spite of the glamorous leads, the biggest kick out of watching *Robin Hood* today is the host of familiar faces that pop up in supporting roles. In various

Aiming for success: Robin Hood *started the whole ball rolling for Lew Grade and ITC.*

episodes you'll spot future *Carry On* stars Sid James, Bernard Bresslaw, Leslie Phillips and Harry H. Corbett, together with his partner-to-be in *Steptoe and Son*, Wilfrid Brambell. A fresh-faced Richard O'Sullivan (ITV's seventies sitcom king with *Man about the House* and *Robin's Nest*) was young Prince Arthur. And, after suffering a surfeit of dodgy beards and even dodgier accents in a host of different roles, Paul Eddington – the immortal Jerry in *The Good Life* – settled into the regular part of Will Scarlet. Look closely and you'll spot British film stalwarts in the making like Nigel Davenport, Ian Bannen, Gordon Jackson and Lionel Jeffries. Bond baddies Donald Pleasance and Charles Gray appear, as does Q (Desmond Llewelyn), along with future *Dr Who* Patrick Troughton. There's even *Midnight Cowboy* director John Schlesinger, who began his career as an actor. Quite a list.

Child actors would also be gamely employed, usually as forest waifs or filth-ridden peasant urchins. Peter Asher, who later went on to make his name in sixties pop group Peter and Gordon, was used more often than most. He appeared in a couple of episodes alongside his sister, Jane Asher, who'd been a child actress since she was five years old – appearing in Children's Film Foundation productions and, most famously, in the *Frankenstein*-inspired child-meets-monster sequence from *The Quatermass Experiment*. While other kids play-acted Robin Hood in their gardens, Jane lived the dream for real. What she remembers most fondly is the camaraderie that existed on set and the fact that, as a child, she wasn't mollycoddled. 'That was the joy of it really; you felt you were being treated more as an adult. You know, you learn a hell of a lot more by being around actors at that stage than you do by being around normal adults, so certainly one's knowledge of life and sex, you get much earlier if you're in that world. Although we used to call all the actors Mr. this and Mrs. that and Miss whatever, never dared use their Christian names.' Jane was also subjected to having a chaperone with her all the time. 'And some of those were a slightly odd breed of people in those days, again I learnt a lot from them. I learnt to smoke from a chaperone when I was about fourteen.'

Behind the scenes, Grade and Hannah Weinstein also insisted on the best. Sidney Cole, who had ten years experience at Ealing Studios, producing such hits as *The Man in the White Suit* and *Dead of Night*, was called in to oversee the *Robin Hood* series. Hailing from the old school of producers, a man who understood the industry and its personnel, Cole brilliantly decided to set up the production as if it were a cinema feature. He called upon the services of British film industry technicians and, in order to bring a sense of pace and vitality to the episodes, employed a mixture of established and up and coming directors. It was a policy that became a trademark of all ITC shows from then on. The veterans included people like Terence Fisher, who was making a mark with his Hammer horror films, and Bernard Knowles, who as a cameraman had worked for Hitchcock, while the new breed consisted of the likes of Don Chaffey, who went on to direct fantasy classics *Jason and the Argonauts* and *One Million Years BC*, and Lindsay Anderson, architect of the British new wave film movement of the 1960s with *This Sporting Life* and *If*. 'These people never forgot how they got their early breaks,' explains Marcia Stanton. 'When Lew used to go to award ceremonies directors would come up to him and say, "Thank you so much for giving me that great opportunity early on in my career." He didn't recognise half of them, but they never forgot. John Schlesinger, for example, never forgot Lew.'

Lew Grade also insisted on hiring the best writers available, a policy that continued throughout ITC's history. *Robin Hood* utilised the services of several leading Hollywood screenwriters who, at the time, were banned from working in their own country by the McCarthy subcommittee, investigating allegations of communism. Notable among them was Ring Lardner Jnr, who'd go on to pen cinema classics *The Cincinnati Kid* and *M*A*S*H*. These writers worked under assumed names and, consciously or otherwise, lent this otherwise genteel show a slight left-wing political bias: the peasants under the heel of exploitative establishment figures, represented by the Sheriff and King John. This kind of politics-lite went straight over the heads of *Robin* Hood's predominantly youthful audience.

Robin Hood also set the trend for ITC programmes having catchy theme tunes and distinctive credit sequences. In this case, the show was heralded by an arrow whistling through the air then thudding into a thick oak tree. This classic signature tune ('Robin Hood, Robin Hood, riding through the glen') was a big hit in 1956 for Dick James – later to become Lennon and McCartney's music publisher – and subsequently gloriously bastardised by Monty Python as the basis of their song for Denis Moore, John Cleese's highwayman parody.

The diminutive Nettlefold Studios near Walton-on-Thames – very much the poor relation of places like Pinewood and Shepperton – became the production base of *The Adventures of Robin Hood*. Shooting began under the auspices of Hannah Weinstein's Sapphire Films in February 1955. Francis Matthews (who appeared in a number of episodes and later lent his voice to *Captain Scarlet*) remembers Nettlefold – now the site of a shopping mall – well. 'It was tiny and right in the middle of the town of

Robin Hood and sundry medieval folk on the Sherwood Forest set at Nettlefold Studios.

Walton. At the back of some shops and round the other side of the houses there was this studio with a little entrance. There were two small soundstages where you did interiors. And outside they'd bring in plants and artificial grass and you'd shoot there to save you going on location. They'd send a second unit out to do stock shots of riding horses. Most of the time Richard Greene wouldn't be doing those, his double would be, and then they'd do the close-ups in Nettlefold with him bobbing up and down on an artificial horse. A lot of people did their film rep experience there.'

'It was a very nice little studio, very friendly and cosy,' recalls Patricia Driscoll. 'It always seemed to be an early call, so you'd arrive before seven in the morning and, unless you were lucky, you would be one of the last to leave. But I can't think of an acting job that I've enjoyed more. I always looked forward to going to work. And I still look back on it with very fond memories.'

Jane Asher's memories of Nettlefold are equally as vivid today. 'It's so strange, those early memories, it's smells and things like that. It's that lovely smell of the homespun cloth that I used to wear as that little girl, and the smell of the makeup and the lights. And I can remember the wonderful spreads of food, supposedly medieval food, big hunks of meat lying around. Magic times. I loved every minute of it. I absolutely adored it. I think that was the time I began to know this is what I want to do for the rest of my life.'

In order to churn out a complete 30-minute episode every five days, art director

Peter Proud took brilliant and highly innovative short cuts. Instead of building lots of sets, Proud employed stock items of scenery such as a baronial fireplace, a serf's hut, a corridor or entrance hall, all mounted on wheels so they could be rapidly placed into position. In this way, a whole set could be changed in just six minutes. They could be used over and over again too, fooling the viewer into thinking they were watching Robin race into a variety of rooms and corridors, but what they were in fact seeing was the same pieces of scenery rearranged differently. A marvellous ruse.

Such was the hectic work schedule that any kind of cast incapacity spelt utter disaster. Once, when Richard Greene went into hospital and was unavailable for filming, that week's episode went ahead without Robin Hood!

Another gimmick employed by Proud was an authentic twenty-foot high hollow tree trunk mounted on wheels. This, combined with another enormous oak made from wood and plaster, plus assorted hedges and rocks, were all strategically moved around to give the impression of a living and breathing Sherwood Forest. The series' makers prided themselves on its authenticity, with costumes and weapons approved by historical experts. Although the extras playing knights were kitted out in chain mail made of knotted string sprayed with silver paint, some of the leading actors did their bit for realism – refusing to wear false beards and opting to grow their own.

The Adventures of Robin Hood premiered on American television in September 1955 and ran for an incredible 143 episodes, regularly achieving a primetime audience of 30 million on the CBS network. It was the first British show to hit big in the States, temporarily usurping such all-American heroes as Davy Crockett and Superman in the hearts and minds of the nation's youth. Sales of archery sets shot up an incredible 400 per cent. 'Kids love pageantry and costume plays,' explained Richard Greene. 'But the most important thing is Robin can be identified with any American hero. He's the British Hopalong.'

In Britain, the show also proved hugely popular. Like millions of children, Jane Asher never forgot to catch *Robin Hood* in its regular Saturday teatime slot. 'I loved them. They were terrific. I can remember that music right now and the arrow twanging into the tree. I suppose it was the equivalent of a soap, you all waited desperately for them.' An established international hit, *Robin Hood* brought bucket-loads of cash into the virgin coffers of Grade's fledgling company. It was responsible for starting the ITC ball rolling.

Although happy with the show's continuing success, Patricia Driscoll felt she'd arrived slightly after the event, missing out on early promotional tours to America. 'In fact towards the end, the producers were busy financing other series out of the profits of *Robin Hood*, so our show was a bit of a rush job that last year.' It came as no real surprise to anyone when it was finally decided to cancel the show in 1959. 'A lot of the actors felt, "Oh thank God for that, it's gone on long enough,"' reveals Patricia. 'And they also felt that the quality was going and that it was time it finished. I think Richard too was happy to call it a day. I think he felt he'd done enough and would like to do something else.'

After being together for so many years, you'd have thought the *Robin Hood* cast and crew would have thrown a huge farewell party at the studio on that last day of filming. 'No, not really,' Patricia recalls. 'It just sort of fizzled out. Everybody said, "Well cheerio, see you again some time," and that was it. And I never saw Richard Greene again. Never, never met him again.'

Nor was Patricia hired when, in 1960, the Hammer studio made a big screen version of the series. *The Sword of Sherwood Forest* saw Greene don his green tights once more, to battle horror icon Peter Cushing as the evil Sheriff of Nottingham. Certainly, her stint in the show had given Patricia's career a boost, but in the long term it proved more of a handicap. After *Robin Hood*'s cancellation, her career went into freefall as jobs dried up because producers saw her as too firmly identified with Maid Marian. The situation became so bad she moved to America to try her luck there, before returning after two years, hoping people might have forgotten all about *Robin Hood*. But, amazingly, even today she's recognised. 'It surprises me, although I'm a lot older and don't look the same, that people in the street still quite often say to me, "Weren't you Maid Marian?"' It was the same for Greene. He too could never quite shake off his Robin Hood image. In part, he resented this, but was also curiously protective about the character. When invited to do a Robin Hood send-up on a Morecambe and Wise show he flatly refused. When Greene died in 1985, one newspaper headline read, 'Robin Hood is Dead.'

Out of all ITC's 1950s output, *The Adventures of Robin Hood* is undoubtedly the most fondly remembered. So why has the show endured? 'I've got a little grandson who loves to watch them,' says Patricia. 'Children's TV nowadays is miles away from the Robin Hood stories, but they still seem to be enjoyed by children. I think it's because they were good stories. There was the goodie and there was your bad man, your sheriff. It was a bit like watching a cowboy film.'

THE ADVENTURES OF SIR LANCELOT (1956-57)

Over the course of the next few years, the small screen was simply awash with budding Errol Flynns, as other TV companies aimed to copy the success of *Robin Hood* with their own shows – such as *Ivanhoe*, starring a young Roger Moore. The nation's children lapped it up, dashing home after school so as not to miss the latest instalment of their clanking-in-armour heroes. This was an age before mass American TV imports, before cowboy or cop shows won over the hearts of UK audiences. ITC were far and away the biggest and most successful purveyors of televisual swashbucklers. So it was only natural that, following *Robin Hood*, they would look at more historical derring-do for programme inspiration, which they duly found in the Arthurian legend of Sir Lancelot.

The actor chosen to play Lancelot was William Russell. Born in Sunderland and educated at Oxford, Russell began his career in acting by organising entertainments during his national service with the RAF. He achieved even greater cult fame after *Sir Lancelot* as chemistry teacher Ian Chesterton in *Dr Who*, and later continued a successful career mainly in theatre with the Royal Shakespeare Company. 'Initially I went up for the lead role in another ITC show, *The Buccaneers*. There were 24 of us doing film tests for Ralph Smart. Both Robert Shaw, who eventually got the part, and I were waiting for news for weeks. I think as an afterthought they gave me Lancelot.'

As Lancelot's Guinevere, the producers cast Jane Hylton, a product of the Rank Charm School, who went on to make television shows like *Some Mothers Do 'Ave 'Em*, as Frank Spencer's hapless mother-in-law, and *The Onedin Line*. The series chivalrously underplayed any hint of amorous activities within the walls of Camelot, Lancelot only ever indulging in the most innocent of glances in Guinevere's direction.

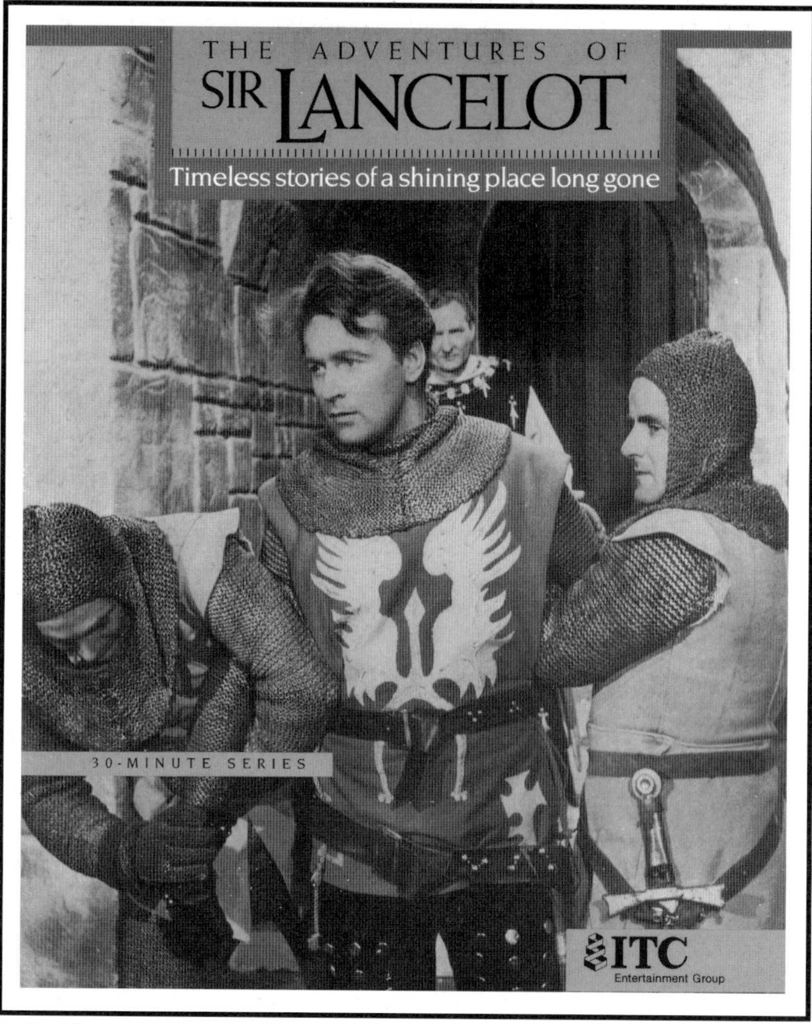

Before becoming the first assistant to William Hartnell's Dr. Who, William Russell found fame as Sir Lancelot.

The butt-naked romps of John Boorman's *Excalibur* were two decades off. 'Jane and I were always trying to have a little kiss,' smiles Russell. 'But we couldn't. They didn't want that. This was a boy's adventure thing. When I look at it today I'm amazed at how innocent it was. It really did seem an extraordinarily innocent world. The total lack of any real violence was amazing because it was all about violence and sword fights. But it was done in a way that didn't disturb anybody. I remember doing a fight and the other actor had a great spear, and he was over me and plunged it down and actually tore the tabard, it went through. A very near miss. But that's what we'd talked about doing, for effect. Oh, they didn't want that at all. It was too much and they cut it. That was the climate of the times. Lew Grade would know he wasn't going to get

Page from an ITC brochure promoting The Adventures of Sir Lancelot.

that kind of thing through at teatime when the whole family are watching.'

As had been the case with *Robin Hood*, amidst the retinue of actors parading past the fake scenery (most of whom justifiably faded into oblivion), there was a smattering of famous faces in their earliest incarnations. Look closely and you'll spot the young Michael Caine, an even younger Petula Clark, an eager Robert Hardy and Patrick McGoohan. Indeed, it was while working on the episode 'The Outcast', directed by Ralph Smart, that McGoohan first met the man who would steer him to global fame years later in *Danger Man*.

Like most of ITC's historical action series, *Sir Lancelot* was clearly aimed at younger viewers, and owed more to the Western genre than it did to Arthurian legend. 'The way the show was presented to me was that he would rescue beautiful damsels every week, and that would be about it,' explains Russell. The scripts certainly expanded upon the original mythos – one episode saw Lancelot press-ganged into slavery by marauding Vikings, while another story had him helping to recover a fabulous jewel given to Guinevere by an Indian Rajah. In keeping with the hiring policy established with *Robin Hood*, several of the writers included those who'd left a McCarthyite America to avoid testifying in the anti-communist witch-hunts.

Once again, Hannah Weinstein's company, Sapphire Films, oversaw production. It was Hannah's American business acumen and drive, combined with the technical skill of British film crews, which provided the foundations for many of ITC's earliest creative triumphs. 'Hannah was a very attractive and intelligent woman, who was very left-wing,' remembers Russell. 'She had a big house called Fox Warren out near Esher and it was here where we did some of the location work for *Sir Lancelot*. We built a fort and there was a stable with horses. She made very good use of the grounds.'

Shot at Nettlefold, *Sir Lancelot* brought more welcome disruption to the staid, middle-class, suburban streets of Walton-on-Thames. Housewives, pausing from their chores, watched and waved from their living room window at the passing cavalcade of actors dressed as bowmen, knaves and knights on their way to work. And if they were lucky they might spy William Russell clanging past, or Richard Greene cruising up to the studio gates in his green Aston Martin.

Filming proved a fearsome slog – particularly for Russell who, every Friday evening, would be handed his script consisting of 60 pages, which had to be learnt by Monday morning when rehearsals began. 'And they were always changing them at the last minute,' he laments. Shot on film, the episodes took five to six days to complete, then it was straight on to the next one with scarcely a break in between. Filmed concurrently with *Robin Hood*, there was little interaction between both shows except during lunch breaks, when the studio canteen would be full of people dressed either in armour or Lincoln green. One assumes bows and broadswords were left at the door.

Unusually for the era, *Lancelot* paid significant attention to historical accuracy, the settings and costumes based on information researched at Oxford University. A medieval village, complete with huts and livestock, was constructed on a soundstage at Nettlefold. An expert in all manner of medieval weapons was on hand too, but his services were quickly dispensed with when it became apparent that fighting in real armour with huge broadswords, though authentic, looked deadly dull on screen. It was far too slow for viewers raised on the rapier-fast swordplay of Errol Flynn. Out went the broadswords in favour of much lighter and shorter swords made from aluminium. The armour was also substituted with rubber and the ubiquitous string chain mail.

Russell recalls that time, rather than budget, imposed the most intrusive limitations on shooting. 'We were conscious of time always. Time was snapping at our heels. Then after making about half of the series in black and white, everybody started talking about colour, we must do it in colour. We had ten days of Technicolor people coming over from the States to do tests. They were spending a lot of money. And the show did go into colour.' This move was purely for the American market, as colour broadcasting in the UK remained several years distant. Inevitably there were problems with this new technology. 'As star of the show I went over to New York to publicise our move to colour, and it was quite a revelation. One of the studio technicians said to me, "It lasts about fifteen miles then it goes all kind of porridgy." Because of some technical reason, beyond New York the colour started to seep out of the picture. I remember someone saying, "Good job you don't live in New Jersey." It was extraordinary.'

No doubt helped by the success of *Robin Hood*, *The Adventures of Sir Lancelot* scored a network showing in America, playing on Monday nights on NBC. Lew Grade certainly led the way for British commercial broadcasters in making these early forays into the US TV market, in the same way that the Beatles subsequently championed British music. For American stations and sponsors, the savings offered by buying in pre-produced programming from the UK were attractive, and for British producers such deals generated much needed revenue for the financing of new ventures. William Russell made some personal TV appearances to promote the series in America. 'We flew in by a Constellation. You went to bed and landed in Newfoundland to refuel, and then came in to Idlewild airport. But I had to appear as Sir Lancelot in his armour, coming off the plane for the press. I said to the airhostess, an hour out from Idlewild give me a nod and I'll struggle into my armour at the back. And I did, and when I came back and sat next to a mother and daughter from New England, who I'd chatted happily with before, they completely ignored me and wouldn't speak to me again. They must have thought I was mad.'

Once on the ground, Russell had to contend with strict hygiene regulations. All aircraft had to be sprayed with disinfectant once the passengers were all out. 'But I was still on the plane, waiting for everyone to get off so I could do my Sir Lancelot arrives in New York bit. And this health authority guy said, "I can't wait, I'm afraid, just shut your eyes and don't breathe." And I got fumigated.' There were also problems getting his sword through customs. One can only wonder about the difficulties he'd have today. 'But I loved that trip. They got me a horse and I had to ride down Fifth Avenue to a studio to get onto the Ed Garoway morning show. Ed had a chimpanzee on his show and when I rode into the studio this chimp went mad and the horse reared up. That was quite a moment. And this was live.'

Though a worthy successor to *Robin Hood*, *The Adventures of Sir Lancelot* failed to emulate the huge popularity of its predecessor and was dropped after only one season. But it was one of the earliest and longest running examples of the Arthurian legend on television, spanning 30 episodes. 'I loved doing that show,' asserts Russell. 'It was, for me, a continuation of the sort of atmosphere I'd had in repertory theatre. There was a kind of lack of seriousness, a cavalier attitude about it all. You never took it very seriously or had the sort of conversations I had later at the National Theatre or now with young actors about, "What's your motivation, what's your target in this scene?" We just got in and did it. It was fun and that's a quality that's gone completely from the business, it just doesn't exist. Everything is so grim now.'

Sadly for Hannah Weinstein, after so much swashbuckling success with ITC her own company, Sapphire Films, was dead in the water by the end of the 1950s. 'Halfway through production on *Sir Lancelot*, Hannah got married to this terrifying character who we all were convinced was the Mafia king of New York,' recalls Russell. 'He was the most extravagantly elegant, tall, but totally dead-eyed man you've ever met. He really was a very creepy person. And he completely changed all of Hannah's ideas.'

At her new husband's insistence, Hannah moved into contemporary drama with *Four Just Men*, an extremely expensive thriller series shot at exotic global locations with top stars (Jack Hawkins, Vittorio De Sica), which failed to attract audiences, destroying Sapphire Films. Hannah left ITC to return to America, where she went on to campaign against racial discrimination in the film industry and helped launch the movie career of Richard Pryor, producing *Greased Lightning* and *Stir Crazy*. She died in 1984.

THE BUCCANEERS (1956-57)

Pirate films had been established as an enduringly popular form of entertainment ever since Errol Flynn's *Captain Blood* hit cinema screens in 1933. ITC identified the genre as a natural progression from *Robin Hood* and *Sir Lancelot*, and set about producing their own tales of high seas derring-do. *The Buccaneers* tells the rousing tale of reformed pirate Dan Tempest, who joins the British colonists in their battles against the Spaniards in the Caribbean during the eighteenth century. The series was notable for two major milestones, as television's first ever pirate series and for introducing the world to Robert Shaw.

In 1956, Shaw – later to achieve stardom in films such as *A Man for All Seasons* and *Jaws* – was down on his luck as an actor and flat broke, so desperate that he even contemplated working in a Heinz factory in London, putting beans into cans. Unbeknown to him, *The Buccaneers* was set to be launched starring Alec Clunes (father of *Men Behaving Badly* star Martin Clunes) as Dan Tempest. But upon reviewing the pilot episode, executives over at CBS declared Clunes 'too British', and wanted him replaced by someone who would appeal more readily to American audiences. Shaw's rugged physique and manner seemed ideally suited to this all-action role, and he landed the casting. Shaw wasted little time in bragging to the press that piracy ran in his blood, gamely bullshitting that 'I'm directly descended from the notorious Cornish pirate Avery, who was put to death.'

Although the role of Dan Tempest represented a real breakthrough for Shaw, it would soon turn sour as the pounding production schedule of 39 episodes over a seven-month period took its toll on his energy and sanity. Almost from the beginning the maverick actor had no faith in the scripts, which he labelled 'a joke'. Aimed at ITC's youthful audience, *The Buccaneers* was deliberately light-hearted and contained very little for him to actually do, save look athletic and bark out the occasional order to his crew of cutthroats. Some episodes did strive for higher ideals, such as when Tempest frees a British slave ship of its cargo of kidnapped African natives. But the bulk of episodes was pretty formulaic, notably one in which Tempest is outwitted by a shipload of nubile young women (including future *Carry On* regular Joan Sims) who have been shanghaied, only to turn the tables on their pirate masters and make off with their ship.

Shaw had to raise himself at 4 am each morning to prepare for work, which began at 6.30 and often stretched into the evening, leaving him little time for home life. But the professional rewards were vast. He was paid £200 an episode, peanuts today, but as the most Shaw had ever earned before was a thousand in a single year, it seemed pretty good. American actor friends told him afterwards that he should have tried for repeat fees as well. (One doubts that Lew Grade would have caved in, even to the demands of someone as headstrong as Shaw.)

Jane Asher – still only ten – appeared in a couple of episodes and found her leading man quite intoxicating. 'I think I was desperately in love with Robert Shaw, he was just magic. And he was the sort of man who would treat you as an adult, quite flirty and wonderful. You know what those feelings are like when you're a child, they're just desperate, and one must never forget, even at the age of five, six, seven, you can fall in love and all those things, and it's very painful and very real. I can certainly remember being very smitten with Robert Shaw.'

The Buccaneers took up two stages at Twickenham Studios, where eight permanent sets provided background for the stories. Exterior sea sequences – undertaken by second unit director Robert Day – were shot off the coast of Falmouth. For Tempest's ship, the producers employed a real schooner that was an already well-established star in its own right, having doubled as the Hispaniola in Disney's *Treasure Island* and the Pequod in *Moby Dick*. For close-up action, a faithful reproduction of part of the vessel was built in one corner of the studios.

In the numerous sword-fighting sequences, Shaw looked utterly convincing – the result of taking daily fencing lessons. He also went on long jogs every morning to keep in prime condition. But Shaw could scarcely conceal his utter boredom with what he considered inane scriptwriting, and the inadequacies of his own character. Sometimes the actor wouldn't even bother to learn his lines. 'How can you go to work without knowing your lines?' his wife would ask, offering to run through the script with him. Shaw later confessed, 'The conscientious actor in television work of this sort learns all

Before From Russia with Love *and* Jaws *made Robert Shaw a star, he first came to the public's attention as TV pirate Dan Tempest in* The Buccaneers.

their lines at night. I didn't bother to learn more than the first two lines and the last two lines; I paraphrased the rest. That was the only way to keep sane.'

Shaw also exercised his penchant for dares as another means of maintaining sanity. On location, he made a bet with some of the cast that he couldn't swim across Falmouth Harbour at three in the morning. Shaw related the sorry event to *TV Times*. 'I was supposed to do it one way and they were to pick me up. But while I was swimming in pitch darkness in an ice-cold sea, the whole bunch were warming themselves with swigs of whiskey. They never came.' Other cast japes included Terry Cooper – who played Blackbeard with a lurid scar down his forehead – travelling home on the train after a day's work in full makeup, enjoying the furtive stares of his fellow passengers.

The Buccaneers was shown on ITV at primetime on Saturday night, following *The Adventures of Sir Lancelot* in the schedule. Shaw and *Lancelot*'s William Russell were neighbours and old friends, who had first met when both appeared in Alec Guinness' stage production of *Hamlet*. 'We both had young families and would go to the seaside for the day and other places, so I never saw the hell-raiser side of Shaw. I learnt all about that later. But he was intensely competitive and easily bored and would say, "I bet a fiver a blonde comes though the door next," that sort of thing, in the pub. He was also very mischievous, that was a side of him I liked very much. There was a sort of naughty boy quality about him. But a dangerous little boy.'

The Buccaneers turned Shaw into a major television star and he began to be frequently recognised in public. He was surprised on one occasion, during a day trip to Battersea funfair, to be accosted by hundreds of school kids with autograph books. This pattern was repeated in America where CBS sponsored the actor to come to New York for a promotional tour – his first ever trip to the States. Scheduled to appear in the famous Macy's Thanksgiving Day Parade, Shaw found himself sharing a limousine with Basil Rathbone and Roy Rogers. Dazzled by his first glimpse of real fame, Shaw never forgot Rogers, then one of the biggest names in America, showing off his guns, claiming the diamonds in his holsters were the real McCoy.

Back home, Shaw bought a set of golf clubs and a 1933 Rolls Royce with the proceeds from *The Buccaneers*. Then, after 39 episodes, word came from Hollywood that Westerns were the new thing, and here was ITC doing a period naval series. So, with no American backing, *The Buccaneers* simply collapsed. 'And I'd spent all the money,' lamented Shaw. 'And there I was unemployed again.'

Though *The Buccaneers* went under, Shaw was still known to the public as Dan Tempest. This was a mixed blessing, as his artistic credentials had taken a dent within the then stuffy theatre community, who looked upon him with disdain for having had a successful TV series. 'After *The Buccaneers* stage producers no longer considered me a serious actor,' Shaw complained. 'And I was equally taboo on TV because of my identification with *The Buccaneers*. As a result I was out of work for over a year.' It wasn't until 1963, and his cold, calculating performance as psycho killer Red Grant in *From Russia with Love*, that Shaw not only equalled, but indeed surpassed, the fame he'd first found as Dan Tempest.

William Russell maintained his friendship with Shaw for years after their ITC experience, but gradually began to lose touch when he attained stardom in the sixties. 'It's always slightly off-putting if you've known someone very well that you ring up and hear, "Mr Shaw's secretary here. Can I get you an appointment?" And I'm thinking, I want to talk to him, I don't want to talk to you or book an appointment. Those are the things that separate you when people become super-successful.'

Ironically, Shaw would later reprise his pirate image for the big screen in 1976's *The Scarlet Buccaneer* (US title *Swashbuckler*), a box office and critical dud. But by then, Shaw didn't care – the sangria and his own private death wish had taken hold and this great actor would be dead by the end of the decade.

THE ADVENTURES OF WILLIAM TELL (1958-59)

Though ITC had enjoyed success with their historical adventure series, none had quite managed to touch the global popularity of *Robin Hood* – the one that started it all. With this in mind, Lew Grade turned his attention to another outlaw figure, William Tell – who, according to popular legend, shot an apple off his son's head with a crossbow and led the Swiss resistance against their Austrian overlords, in the early fourteenth century.

Actor Conrad Phillips was 34 years old when he took on the part of William Tell. A Londoner who served in the navy during the war, lying about his age to enlist, he was subsequently invalided out before his twentieth birthday, after being mined and shipwrecked. Phillips studied at RADA and carved out a career mostly in the theatre. 'But to star in a new international TV series for Lew Grade certainly changed my life,' he claims. 'Almost immediately the organisation began the process of turning a relatively unknown actor into a household name. I was "launched" at a press party given by Lew Grade, who introduced me as his new boy.'

William Tell was saddled with a dreary 1950s nuclear family set-up featuring a wife, son and dog. The dog was swiftly jettisoned, as it required too much studio time to rehearse its tricks. Next to go was the son, played by child actor Richard Rogers, written out chiefly because Rogers rarely made it to the set on time. Jennifer Jayne played the loyal wife, which usually meant appearing at the beginning of each episode to wave serenely at Tell gallivanting off on another adventure, before going back to washing the dishes and cleaning the cave. After a few weeks of being marginalised, Jayne complained and won her argument for greater involvement, to the point of taking up fencing lessons. 'She looked quite formidable,' confirms Phillips. 'From then on she took a much more active part in the action, wielding a sword like a female Errol Flynn.'

The series' other main character was Fertog 'the Bear', played by Nigel Green. One of the great unsung British character actors, Green is famous for his roles in *The Ipcress File* and as the sergeant major in *Zulu*, but he was a complex man and a tortured soul who suffered from depression. He was also a notorious hell-raiser – on his wedding day, Green went on a blinding booze-up that lasted two days. And that was the end of that marriage. Tragically, in 1972 he was found dead in his flat in Brighton. At the time he was separated from his second wife. The coroner put his death down to an accidental overdose of sleeping pills. Green was just 48.

Guest stars were a common feature of the show and Phillips has clear memories of working with many of them. Christopher Lee appeared in the episode 'Mantrap', as a sadistic count who loves to hunt and decides it would provide him with great sport to hunt William Tell. 'I hadn't seen Christopher since my brief time at the Rank charm school in the early fifties. His subsequent fame as Dracula and other creations of the Hammer horror films belied his gentle, civilised nature. I spent an exhausting week filming "Mantrap", running from bloodhounds and galloping horses. I spent some time at the bottom of a river, breathing through a straw, hiding from the dogs. Christopher gave me a run for my money – but I got him in the end!'

Sid James, then a big star thanks to the Tony Hancock BBC series, came down to play a street hawker who is punished for helping Tell and put in the stocks, where he's pelted with rotten vegetables. 'Sid wisecracked all the time and took it all with great humour. It wasn't at all a pleasant experience for him,' recalls Phillips. 'I was slightly overawed by his reputation but I found him very friendly, with great humility as a performer. It was impossible for him to get away from playing the Sid James we all know and love. Although dressed in fourteenth century costume, one felt he should still be wearing his jaunty little pork pie hat from East Cheam. I spent one of the funniest weeks of the series working with him. His soul goes marching on.' Another comedy actor who Phillips remembers clearly is Wilfrid Brambell, later to make his name as the grubby and squalid Albert Steptoe in the classic BBC sitcom *Steptoe and Son*. 'But I was truly amazed when I met him. He was dressed in an immaculate Savile Row suit. A complete dandy. He spoke with a cultivated accent, with just a hint of Irish in it. When he changed into his Swiss peasant costume and started to act, he changed completely, giving a performance of depth and intelligence. There were many facets to Wilfrid Brambell. A courteous and charming man, but remote. A unique personality.'

Other actors – like Warren Mitchell, soon to create the classic Alf Garnett in *Till*

Death Us Do Part – would make return visits to the show playing different characters, carefully made up so that audiences wouldn't realise it was the same person. And like *Robin Hood* and *Lancelot*, count along any row of peasants and chances are the third one down became a major film star. In an episode called 'The Prisoner', filmed in the exotic surroundings of a disused sandpit in Watford, Tell changes places with a slave worker in a labour camp who just happened to be the undiscovered Michael Caine.

And then there was Robert Shaw. Finished with *The Buccaneers* and desperate for work, he was glad of the chance to play a baddie in the show. Phillips had been at RADA with Shaw and so knew all about his competitive nature, how in everything from rugby to tiddlywinks he *always* had to win. In one scene Shaw, in his quest to usurp Tell as resistance leader, challenges him to a fight, which, thanks to the scriptwriter, he ends up losing. 'So we rehearsed it,' remembers Phillips, 'and reached the point where Robert's panting on the ground beaten and I'm waiting for his line, "I've had enough. You win." He didn't say it. He wouldn't say it. He point blank refused to concede verbally that I had won the fight. I made a mock fuss, saying that he ought to stick to the script, but he still refused. As this was typical Robert, I laughed and went along with him on it. At the end of the episode, when I captured him after a treacherous deed, my line was, "Take him away and hang him." Robert suggested we cut this line. Grinning, he said, "Don't you see, boy, I could come back and be a regular character. Be good for you, boy, to have a strong opposition. If I'm hanged, there's no chance." I grinned back at him. "No chance, Robert."'

Another old RADA comrade of Phillips was Lisa Daniely, who recalls the difficulties of acting while simultaneously riding side-saddle. 'There are only two times in my life that I have sat on a horse and one of them was *William Tell*. I had about three lines of dialogue. We were in one of the big studios at the end of the lot and they waved a few branches in front of us and as they said, all right turnover, action, both the horses gave forth. It was like Niagara Falls and I laughed so much I nearly fell off the bloody horse. The whole studio was in tears. If you've ever sat on a horse which is pissing, you've never heard anything like it.'

Location work took place in and around Snowdonia in North Wales. When the crew arrived, unsurprisingly, it was bitterly cold and snowing heavily. 'The prospect of playing a man of the mountains in a costume not designed for such weather extremes did not make the pulse race. Rather the balls freeze,' laughs Phillips. Luckily, when the studio bosses in London saw the rushes, Phillips' flimsy costume of brown tights and jerkin – when filmed in black and white – merged into the grey, granite rocks rendering the actor virtually invisible. The wardrobe mistress hurriedly created a new sheepskin garment that was kept in place by a thick leather belt, handy for Tell's dagger and crossbow bolts. There was also a pouch in which Phillips craftily kept his cigarettes safe.

Footwear was another problem. Rather than using proper mountain boots, fourteenth century mock-ups were created from suede for historical verisimilitude. These had little grip, and Phillips found himself having to move with caution on the icy rocks. Then one day the inevitable happened. 'We were lining up for a simple shot which consisted of my standing on a ledge, a panoramic view of the mountains behind me. There was a drop of about twelve feet below. The cameraman indicated for me to back up an inch or two. Suddenly I felt my feet slipping and tried to recover my balance, but it was too late, I was over the edge and falling. I was standing up when I landed in the snow, which unfortunately was not thick enough to break my fall. My knees received a sickening hyper-extension and I fell forward in the snow in great pain.'

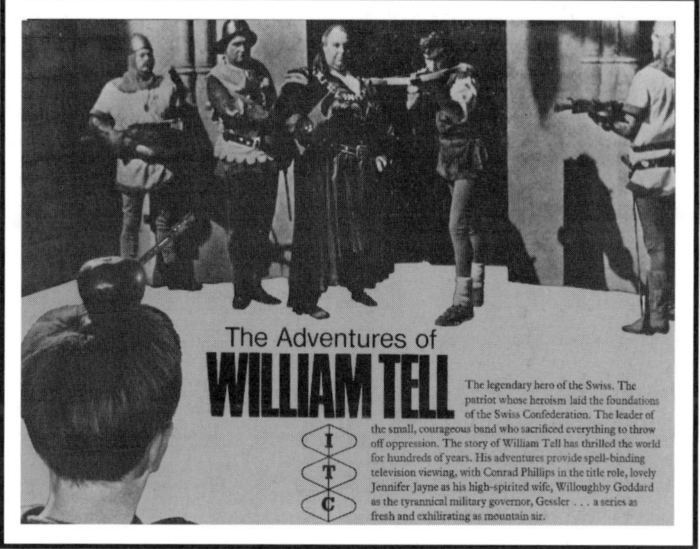

Page from an ITC promotional brochure, extolling the virtues of their latest historical adventure series.

A unit car took Phillips rapidly to hospital and, although X-rays revealed nothing was broken, serious damage had been done. 'I felt very depressed at sustaining an injury so early in the filming of the series, but I was determined to carry on, no matter what. This was my big chance. With both knees wrapped in strong, elasticated bandages, I went up and down mountains, fought Austrian soldiers, rode horses and generally had fun. With the help of those bandages I got through the 39 episodes of *William Tell*. In later life I had to have both knee joints replaced with artificial ones made out of stainless steel and plastic. My second wife, Jennie, used to joke that I had better not stand too close to the fire in case they melted.'

As filming went on, the pressure and pace of it proved gruelling for the star. In almost every episode Phillips had sword, knife and fist fights. Audiences demanded it. 'I threw myself into the role of William Tell with great gusto and enthusiasm. For the most part I did all my own stunts, but I did have a great stunt double called George Leech who was always there if something extremely dangerous needed to be done.' Leech later became a top film stuntman and fight arranger, notably working on all of the Sean Connery Bond movies.

One stunt that could have had fatal consequences saw Phillips sitting on his horse, a noose around his neck, hands tied behind his back, about to be hanged by villainous scum. Feeling a little vulnerable, and knowing that horses were particularly unpredictable, Phillips balked at the idea of his hands being tied for real, insisting instead that he just hold the rope. Before cameras rolled, the clapper boy brought his board down with such a resounding bang that the horse reared up violently. Phillips' hand instinctively came free and, as the horse galloped off, he hung onto the gallows and swung for a few seconds, luckily not by the neck, before dropping to the ground. A very nasty accident had been avoided.

While filming the last ever episode of *William Tell*, Phillips was obliged to do something he'd done numerous times before: emerge from his cave on cue, walk to a rock ledge, and then jump about four feet to the ground. During rehearsals Phillips jumped and broke his ankle. With five days of the schedule left, and a number of sword fights and punch-ups to be filmed, much subterfuge was needed. A wheelchair was produced and Phillips actually sat in it for his close-ups, still managing some crafty swordplay.

Despite his injury and the ignominy of having to bring William Tell to life from a wheelchair, Phillips fondly remembers the series' impact. 'It was acclaimed at the time, the vigour and pace of the production being particularly singled out. It was a great favourite with adults as well as children.' However, Phillips was becoming increasingly concerned at the prospect of being too closely identified with his character, and the way in which this may have affected his future chances of work. In public, he was often greeted by calls of, 'Got any apples on you, mate?' At least he was now no longer an unknown actor, but a TV name. 'A dubious status,' observes Phillips. 'Full of the danger of typecasting and oblivion.'

The Adventures of William Tell was only a modest success, failing to reach the commercial peaks attained by *Robin Hood*. After 39 episodes, Tell was forced to hang up his crossbow. Phillips clearly remembers the last day of shooting, when the final shot was committed to celluloid at 5 pm. It was all over. 'I said my goodbyes. There was no end of production party. I suddenly felt very flat. The harsh commercial reality and realisation of one's expendability hit me. I was no longer needed. The series was over, but if Lew Grade negotiated a second series that would be different. The focus would return, with the smiles, backslapping and congratulations. One would be a valuable property once again. I went up to my dressing room and sat for a while. The studio was silent. I packed my things. The dressing room that had been my home reverted to a series of mirrors, lights and a dressing table. Anonymous. Sterile. I turned out the lights and left.'

Sadly, there was no second series – though rumours emerged about a possible feature film, which interested Phillips much more than a return to television. Along with Peter Maxwell, who'd directed the majority of the episodes, Phillips hoped to form a production company that might oversee any proposed *William Tell* movie. It was a project that never got off the ground. Phillips did, however, return to the William Tell legend in 1989, as part of the cast of an Anglo-French television remake.

H. G. WELLS' INVISIBLE MAN (1958-59)

As the 1960s beckoned, ITC shifted its focus from the swashbuckling genre to attempt a series utterly different from anything that had gone before – its own modern action/adventure show, similar to those seen on American networks but with a distinctly British flavour. Taking inspiration from the H. G. Wells novel, but bearing little or no resemblance to it (or indeed to the classic 1933 James Whale cinematic version), it chronicled the adventures of hapless scientist Peter Brady, whose invisibility experiments go disastrously wrong, rendering him – appropriately enough – totally invisible. Whereas in Wells' narrative the scientist who dared play God, like his gothic predecessors Frankenstein and Dr. Jekyll, goes bonkers and seeks to rule the world, Brady patriotically offers his new-found powers to British intelligence, dedicating himself to thwarting criminals and spies who might threaten dear old Blighty. Dispatched to one mythical country after another, Brady foils all manner of insidious plots such as gun running schemes and attempted revolutions – contemporary stuff that is topical even today. One episode in particular – in which Brady

As a publicity gimmick, the actor underneath all the bandages was never credited.

uncovers a terrorist plot to smuggle nuclear devices into Western capital cities, in order to extort vast sums of money to boost the coffers of communist regimes – reads like Ian Fleming meets *The Avengers*.

As a publicity gimmick, it was decided to keep secret the identity of the man wrapped up beneath all those bandages, neither crediting him on the titles or in TV listings magazines. It was all rather undignified. There he'd be on set, either looking like the Mummy with a hat and sunglasses on, or, *sans* bandages, hidden inside a large raincoat, able only to see his way around through small holes built into the buttons. The secret of who played the Invisible Man was finally revealed in 1965 (the series was still being repeated up until 1966), only to be promptly forgotten again. 'I can't remember his name,' confesses co-star Lisa Daniely, also admitting, 'and he wasn't really a very good actor. And they used somebody else's voice; that was the final insult – poor man. He was quite a nice looking bloke, but not a very dynamic personality.'

That voice came courtesy of unknown actor Tim Turner. Although, in the show's pilot episode, Canadian actor Robert Beatty provided the vocal performance, executives deemed the pilot so poor it was never broadcast and had to be totally rewritten and re-shot. In the process Turner replaced Beatty.

To broaden the show's appeal, ITC's Invisible Man was not the loner of Wells' book, but a family man living in the picturesque English countryside with his sister Diane and daughter Sally, played by a young Deborah Watling (later the companion Victoria to Patrick Troughton's Dr. Who). Cast as Diane, Lisa Daniely found herself questioning why she was playing Brady's sister and not his wife. 'I said to the producer, "Look, this is written like a wife, why isn't she being the wife of the Invisible Man, why does she have to be the sister?" And he said, "Oh well, you know, people might kind of imagine that she would get into a bed with the Invisible Man." That kind of moralistic stance was common back then, it's ridiculous nowadays. I mean the English thought it was ridiculous, but the Americans still stood by their production code, if there was a love scene the man had to keep one foot on the ground, that kind of thing.'

Daniely was also disgruntled by the sheer banality of the role. 'It was just, "That's your frock for today." There was no character at all. I don't know what you could have done with it. There were really only two kinds of women on the TV screen in those days, the good wife or the sexy bad woman. I wanted the meaty parts and the bad girls are always more fun to do than the good ones. So later in my career I got to play quite a lot of those sexy bad women, but it was still very much a cipher.' Honor Blackman's Cathy Gale in *The Avengers*, which revolutionised the role of women on television, was still a few years off.

H. G. Wells' Invisible Man was the brainchild of producer Ralph Smart. An Australian educated in London, Smart began in the business working on scripts for several Will Hay comedies. Returning to his native Australia in 1939, he made several successful films – notably *Bush Christmas*, about a child lost in the outback, which was acclaimed at the Venice Film Festival. 'Ralph was an interesting guy,' recalls William Russell. 'I remember saying to him, "How did you get the boy to eat the beetle?" There's a scene in *Bush Christmas* where an aborigine boy gives him a live beetle, and he had a shot of this thing wriggling in the boy's mouth. And Ralph said, "It was very tricky." I bet it was, but he did get it.'

Back in Britain, Smart learnt that Lew Grade was looking for film people interested in creating British-made TV programmes for the export market. He offered his services and subsequently wrote and directed episodes of *Robin Hood*, *Sir Lancelot* and *The Buccaneers*.

Assisting Smart as production supervisor was Aida Young, who'd blazed a trail for women working in the medium when she took on the production chores for *William Tell*. Aida paid her dues in almost every aspect of production during the early 1950s, before landing a job as an assistant producer at MGM studios. However, it was during the 1960s that she achieved her greatest successes, producing Hammer horror classics *Dracula Has Risen from the Grave*, *Taste the Blood of Dracula* and *Hands of the Ripper*, as well as Hammer's pseudo-epics *One Million Years BC* and *She*.

As series producer, it was Smart's job to choose the writers that would breathe life into *The Invisible Man*. He hired Ian Stuart Black on the recommendation of his wife, who'd read Black's novel *Passionate City*. Black discovered that there were severe production problems on *The Invisible Man*, and workable scripts were urgently needed. 'It was a Tuesday and they had no script for the following Monday,' Black revealed to *TV Zone* magazine in 1995, two years before his death. 'So they said, "Could you get us out of this hole?" They put me in a back room with no windows and I wrote four scripts in five weeks so that they had material. Then there was a break, and they managed to catch up.'

Black looked at the scripts already produced and felt the show was teetering on the edge of schizophrenia, not knowing whether it was a comedy or a thriller. He sensed that the original intention was to go the comedy route, with lots of sight gags and humour derived from Brady's invisibility. It was Black who was instrumental in turning the show into more of a political thriller, as this was an area he had a particular interest in.

Having demonstrated his ability to turn out high quality scripts at short notice, Black was appointed story editor. He was also personally responsible for bringing in another writer by the name of Tony O'Grady. This was actually a pseudonym for the young Brian Clemens – acknowledged today as one of Britain's most important TV writers, later contributing vastly to the success of *The Avengers* and the creative force behind *The Professionals*. Clemens recalls his time on *The Invisible Man* with great fondness. 'Working with Ian was, as always, a delight. He liked the fact that I was a font of ideas and said that, if he could afford me, he would have kept me on contract just to pump out original ideas.' But why the O'Grady pseudonym? 'I used that because I was still, technically, under contract to another company, the Danziger Brothers. I was moonlighting. O'Grady was my mother's maiden name.'

H. G. Wells' Invisible Man *broke ITC's run of historical series, paving the way for modern shows like* Danger Man *and* The Saint. Bottom: *to achieve this effect the actor hid inside the raincoat, only able to see out through the buttonholes.*

What little location work was needed for the show tended to be done as close to the studios (MGM Borehamwood) as possible in order to keep costs low. Lisa Daniely will never forget the filming of one scene where the 'invisible' Brady is driving along a street. 'I was in the back of this large open-top car. And because the light wasn't terribly good, we had some of these huge arc lamps, real monsters, that were raised up to about six foot on huge rostra. We were chuntering down this hill perfectly all right, though I used to feel a little bit queasy with a man lying at the bottom covered in black net trying to drive a car, not seeing where he's going. And one of these enormous lights fell and missed me by inches, it just went *swoosh* down the back of the car and I went *arghh!* I mean three inches more the other way and I would not be here today. That was very unpleasant.'

The bulk of episodes were mostly studio shot, and as *The Invisible Man* developed into a long running series, involving a filming schedule that lasted upwards of six months, the sheer grind took its toll. 'After you've done about a month you get on to automatic pilot,' explains Daniely. And, as is the norm in the television and film world, script changes were not unusual, sometimes shoved into the actor's hand the night before. 'Let's face it, they're not much concerned with words,' adds Lisa. 'I've done a lot of American-backed things and they get carried away and you get about half a dozen rewrites, and you think every one's just as bad as the previous one so you don't know why they bother.'

By today's standards, the special effects in *The Invisible Man* have a made-in-the-garden-shed look about them, but were nevertheless ingenious for their time. This was 1958, after all, and visual effects for television were in their absolute infancy. Puppeteer Jack Whitehead, who'd worked on *Muffin the Mule*, created the illusion of invisibility on objects such as car keys, test tubes and guns floating in the air, using little more than wires. 'It was pretty soul destroying from an actor's point of view, because you were acting to fresh air,' Lisa recalls. Out on location, the 'invisibility' effects hoodwinked the public when, on one occasion, someone attempted to stop what he thought was a runaway motorbike, only to find it was driven by a stuntman hidden in the sidecar.

It was also time consuming to wait for all the effects to be rigged, and then, at the last moment, the actor was expected to get everything word perfect. 'It was, "For God's sake know your dialogue, nobody's going to hang around waiting for you to act, just say the words darling, OK, shoot,"' remembers Daniely. 'It was absolutely a factory. But I had a lot of fun and made some money and learnt how to film quickly and fast as best you could.'

The Invisible Man ran on the CBS network in primetime, and also proved a big hit in Europe and further afield. 'It certainly helped my career along in a commercial way,' explains Lisa. 'I wasn't terribly proud of being in it from the artistic point of view, but it was pretty popular. I remember going to Egypt for an international film and television festival. *The Invisible Man* had just broken over there and I had the most fantastic time staying in a suite at the Hilton. I met the sort of people I never want to meet back home, multi-millionaires who'd say, "Is the servant problem as bad in England as it is over here?"'

In Britain, the show proved mildly controversial when the 'political' and commie-bashing plot lines drew the ire of the Labour Peace Fellowship – an organisation campaigning for world disarmament with links to the Labour Party. Amazingly, they demanded the show be dropped from the schedules, as they considered it was 'calculated to foment hatred against Russia' and 'a danger to East-West relations'.

The Invisible Man was ITC's first contemporary series, and one of the very first fan-

Starburst *magazine singled out* The Invisible Man *as the forerunner to 1960s cult shows like* The Avengers.

tasy secret agent shows. Maybe the stories *were* rather routine cold war potboilers, but at just 30 minutes they were also suitably brief enough to sustain attention. *Starburst* magazine has even gone so far as to call it 'very much a forerunner to those much-loved sixties actioners like *The Avengers*'.

However dated *The Invisible Man* looks today, it was a benchmark in ITC's history, the metaphorical bridge between *Robin Hood* and Ralph Smart's next show, which turned out to be the blueprint for much of sixties cult TV and practically every future ITC show – *Danger Man*.

Chapter 3
The Puritan and the Halo

- Danger Man - The Saint -

By 1960, ITC were going through something of a barren patch. Despite the popularity of their swashbuckler series, they hadn't scored a bona fide smash hit since *Robin Hood*, particularly in the all-important US market. Looking for fresh ideas, Lew Grade approached *Invisible Man* producer Ralph Smart to come up with a new series. The result was to revolutionise television drama and save ITC's bacon. 'It was really *Danger Man* that broke the bad run,' said Grade. 'Since then we have never looked back. Both that and *The Saint* are seen in almost every country that has a television.'

Danger Man and *The Saint*'s success spawned a host of imitators, as Britain and America launched a plethora of playboy TV adventurers and super-cool spies. But none quite matched the brazen originality and impact of ITC's original action heroes.

DANGER MAN (1960-61/1964-66)

Made during the height of the cold war, *Danger Man* was arguably the first television show to translate the elements of the pulp spy novel to the small screen. It was radical, dangerous and a massive gamble. Pre-*Saint*, pre- *Avengers*, and two years before the first James Bond movie, nothing quite like *Danger Man* had been seen before.

Ralph Smart had no particular actor in mind for his spy hero, John Drake, until he saw Patrick McGoohan in a television play and offered him the part. Raised in Sheffield after his Irish parents abandoned their attempt at a fresh start in New York, where he was born, McGoohan worked in a variety of jobs, including chicken farming, before taking up acting. His first big break came when Orson Welles cast him in his West End production of *Moby Dick*. Lew Grade approved the decision to go with McGoohan wholeheartedly, remarking, 'It was the way he moved – like a panther, firm and decisive.' Harry Saltzman would later use almost the same words to describe the reason why he cast Sean Connery as James Bond.

McGoohan so impressed Grade that the TV tycoon later stated that much of the success of *Danger Man* was down to him. Watching today, there's no doubting that McGoohan's strong, understated performance was the show's main virtue. His cool demeanour and underlying intensity made him perfect for the role. During a rerun in America in the late 1980s, *The New York Times* eulogised, 'His performances are

His cool demeanour and underlying intensity made Patrick McGoohan perfect casting as spy John Drake, in Danger Man.

completely devoid of histrionic fat. Here, distilled, is television minimalism at its best.'

Although a respected and highly-strung actor, with various TV, theatre and film credits to his name, *Danger Man* would be McGoohan's first starring role in a major series, and he was tentative about accepting. Becoming typecast worried him, as did the perils of being stuck in a long running show and the difficulties of maintaining high standards week after week. 'It might have turned out to be terrible and trashy,' he told *Photoplay* in 1961. 'But I don't think it has. There are a number of ridiculous episodes which make my blood boil whenever I watch them, but on the whole there have been some pretty fair films in the batch.'

McGoohan was very much the complete professional, and found it utterly unforgivable if fellow actors failed to learn their lines correctly or arrived late. He swiftly gained a reputation for being difficult, edgy and complex. Lisa Daniely appeared in an early *Danger Man* episode and remembers McGoohan well. 'He was rather taciturn and had this touch-me-not quality. Very enclosed. Maybe he was keeping himself in character. But I think that was very much him, and transcribed onto the screen it was always riveting to look at. He kept an aura round him and you couldn't approach him, but quite an extraordinary personality. He didn't have a sense of humour at all, and most actors, out of sheer nerves, are full of fun and giggles, but he kept himself enclosed in this very fierce exterior.'

Actress Jane Merrow, who appeared in a total of three *Danger Man* episodes and became another ITC regular, also retains vivid memories of McGoohan. 'I was frightened to death of him. I was kept so much on my toes. The energy from him was amazing, absolutely astonishing, and that's really exciting to work with, it really brings the whole thing alive. An integral part of a star is energy. And he was very professional. Everybody was on their toes around Patrick, they didn't muck about with him. But nobody felt intimidated, he's not a bully, he didn't throw his weight around, he didn't sulk, he wasn't anything but a consummate professional. He was very pleasant with everyone. But he didn't suffer fools gladly.'

Peter Graham Scott, who directed several *Danger Man*s, found McGoohan to be initially slightly guarded. 'Then he began to realise that perhaps I knew a little bit of what I was talking about and we got on very well. Any idea he had, and some of his ideas were very good indeed, I would somehow use.'

The original concept of McGoohan's John Drake character evoked the stereotypical secret agent: rough, tough, quick with a gun, and equally lethal with women. McGoohan was adamant that he wasn't going to play the part in such a clichéd way and, during the filming of the second episode, under the supervision of director Clive Donner, used his star power to devastating effect. 'There was a scene where Drake got into trouble and had to get out of it,' remembers Donner. 'The stage direction read, "Drake pulls a gun," and Pat said, "I won't pull a gun. I just absolutely refuse." So I rang Ralph and said, "What do we do?" And Ralph said, "He's not going to pull a gun. We're not going to stop and have rows about that at this stage, right at the very beginning of the series." So Pat was extremely clear about the values that he believed in, and if what was being required was something he didn't agree [with] or didn't approve of, he wouldn't do it. I've no idea what was laid down with Ralph and Pat beforehand, but I got the feeling that there was a great deal of pre-production discussion between them, mapping it out. But that was script number two and we were already facing a situation where Pat was directly affecting the style of the film. So the nature of Pat's character was defined and lasted thereafter.

It was his rules which made the series, they set the tone.'

Almost from day one, McGoohan's drive and influence were felt by everyone who worked on the show. 'It was a natural gravitation of people towards a powerful personality,' reasons Jane Merrow. 'If people are very strong, which some stars are, and they are right, you allow them to lead. It's when they're powerful or bullying and they're wrong, then that's when you have problems on set.'

Top*: despite McGoohan's puritanical policy,* Danger Man *played host to an array of glamorous actresses.* Bottom*: a close shave in Tokyo.*

McGoohan wasted little time in laying down the ground rules for Drake, grafting his own individual morality onto the character. 'He is not a thick-ear specialist, a puppet muscle man,' asserted McGoohan. 'I want Drake to be in the heroic mould, like the classic Western hero, which means he has to be a good man.' Always favouring wits over brute force, Drake did end up carrying a gun – though McGoohan made sure it was used only when absolutely necessary, and then rarely shooting to kill. He was also aware that action was vital to a show of this kind, but wanted no gratuitous violence. Each fistfight was planned in minute detail, scripted on paper first and then approved by the actor personally. McGoohan also wouldn't allow doubles to take his place, insisting on handling the stunts himself whenever possible.

Undoubtedly, the most controversial aspect of Drake was his attitude towards sex. Believing promiscuity should not be encouraged on television, McGoohan decreed that Drake must never be involved sexually with his leading ladies. The first script he read contained a romantic interlude in a hotel bedroom, and the actor briskly insisted that the scene was cut and any further scenes of a similar nature eliminated. Sex was not to be introduced into the show simply to provide titillation. Incredibly, the producers acceded to their star's demands. 'Patrick was concerned that we were launching into an age of moral degeneration,' explains Jane Merrow. 'Which I don't think he was actually wrong about. He had some concerns about that and he didn't want to be party to it. And I don't blame him; that was his position, that was his right and his choice.'

Drake poses as a clerk to infiltrate a spy school in a mysterious 'village'. Fans see this episode, 'Colony Three', as the harbinger of The Prisoner.

Certainly, it was made clear that Drake had an eye for female beauty, but McGoohan didn't believe he was the kind of man to indulge in promiscuous relationships. 'Patrick was Roman Catholic and held strong beliefs,' recalls Clive Donner. 'He was also a strange man. I heard this story that he bought a house at Borehamwood near the studios, and he had some young daughters and he surrounded the whole house with barbed wire. I think it was just to protect the children, but there was a certain sense of paranoia, latent paranoia. And I think his not wanting to get involved with his leading ladies all went along with the wire around his house, trying to preserve purity. I think he also would never hit a woman, or behave in any way that was in his opinion not the way to treat a lady.'

McGoohan's rather eccentric behaviour at this time was picked up by another director, Peter Graham Scott. 'He said that the basement of his house was a virtual shelter where he and his family could live if there was an atomic explosion. Whether that was true or not, I don't know, but that's what he told me. He was also very secretive about where he lived.'

McGoohan's puritanism set Drake apart from other spies – notably Bond, who slept around and killed freely without conscience. 'Drake's character was really a spin off from McGoohan's own persona,' asserts Brian Clemens. 'He insisted that he would not kiss a woman, that he would remain a cold, almost ascetic character, creating a kind of mystery of his own.' McGoohan strove to make Drake enigmatic, hoping audiences would remain uncertain about what he was going to do next, an approach that was a hit – especially with kids. 'Drake never kisses the girls, something which has endeared him to the hearts of children everywhere, especially boys who grimace at kissing heroes like *The Saint* or smooching spies such as *UNCLE*'s Napoleon Solo,' *The Guardian* later observed.

Danger Man *was retitled* Secret Agent *in America, where it spawned the now classic theme song 'Secret Agent Man'.*

Aside from his repressed libido, Drake's character was very much in tune with the trends of the early 1960s. He was young, classless, sophisticated and successful. A self-contained upholder of traditional values such as fair play and justice. Though idealistic, he was brutally efficient, getting the job done with minimum fuss and bother. Unlike Simon Templar or Jason King, Drake is a skilled professional rather than a hedonistic man of leisure with a yen for excitement. And yet he set the style for all future TV spies in being chic, resourceful, unflappable and good looking. On sixties television there were no ugly spies, except those hailing from behind the Iron Curtain, whom invariably had nasty beards and worse teeth than Austin Powers. McGoohan's success as Drake lead directly to a boom in spy shows. Who knows if Hollywood would have backed the first Bond film had the popularity of *Danger Man* (notably in America) not clearly indicated that there was public enthusiasm for the genre?

Indeed, such was McGoohan's impact as Drake that he could have been James Bond before Sean Connery. 'Patrick actually would've made a wonderful Bond,' declares John Glen, who edited *Danger Man* and directed no less than five 007 movies during the 1980s. 'Pat was asked but turned it down. He had a thing about kissing on screen and had some hang-ups about the Bond character. I thought he was a wonderful actor. A strange kind of guy, extremely professional, never fluffed a line. He had the same thing that Roger Moore had; this sort of photographic memory.'

Initially, it was agreed the *Danger Man* shows would run for half an hour. Grade wanted them to be fast moving in order to compete with American action series that had similar pace and gloss. This format dictated that the shows were scripted and shot with economy in mind. Each scene contributes directly to the story and there is little opportunity for character development. Invariably, each episode begins with a pre-title credits crime that Drake then solves, with debonair panache to spare. 'This is a job of international importance,' Drake says midway through one episode, handcuffed to a girl. 'I've got half an hour to get it done.'

When Peter Graham Scott crossed over from the BBC to work on some of the earliest *Danger Man* episodes, he found it to be overly formulaic. 'Drake always went to some exotic place or capital and always the situation was the same, his local agent had either disappeared, been kidnapped or murdered, so he had to find out what had happened. He always met a girl who was in some sort of distress. Then he's suddenly set upon by thugs and he knocks them all out. That was the first half. And in the second half he'd find out what the real plot is, and it's quite different from anything he'd expected. The girl turns out to be usually a spy in disguise or something. He has another fistfight and then that's the end. All in 22 minutes. So I did my seven, but at the end of it I felt that, really, this is just digging coal at the coal face.'

In keeping with the 1960s *zeitgeist*, the show was cosmopolitan in its outlook. With a view to international sales, it was decided to make Drake an agent working for NATO rather than some British spy organisation. By 1960, television had begun bringing the world into our living rooms with documentaries and travelogues. Exploiting this new-found public thirst for exotic locales, Ralph Smart employed pictorially interesting backgrounds to compliment the show's exciting story lines. One week Drake might be in New York, the next Rome, or maybe an Arabian desert. He became the most travelled hero yet seen on TV. Locations closer to home were shot partly under the supervision of second unit director John Schlesinger, who later carved out a successful career in Hollywood directing *Midnight Cowboy* and *Yanks*. For the episode 'View from the Villa', the team travelled to a village in North Wales called Portmeirion. Impressed by its beguiling mix of diverse architectural styles, McGoohan made a mental note of the location for future use. Several years later, Portmeirion became the home of Number Six in *The Prisoner*.

After McGoohan, Ralph Smart set the stylistic tone of *Danger Man*. He instigated the series, going on to write, direct and produce many early episodes. 'He really set the stamp,' posits John Glen. 'They were very similar to the Bond style, done on not such an extravagant budget, but we used to be very ambitious and try to do unusual things and try and get exotic locations, even in those days. I think the style was set by Smart in the same way the Bond style was set by Terence Young and Broccoli and Saltzman.'

Writer Brian Clemens takes a lot of the credit too. 'I wrote the pilot, so had a big input in setting the ultimate style,' he confirms. 'We were hoping – pre-Bond – to establish a UK-based spy. We learned quite a bit from Hitchcock, who had already attempted the genre in *The 39 Steps*, *Sabotage*, etc. British literature had already established the ground rules for spy stories, going back as far as Richard Hannay [John Buchan's fictional hero as featured in *The 39 Steps*].'

One of the most intriguing elements of the show was Drake's reliance on tech-

Lew Grade personally singled out McGoohan as the reason why Danger Man *scored such a hit internationally.*

nology. Tie-pins doubled as cameras, cherries contained mini-microphones, an electric razor served as a tape recorder and transmitter. All this a full three years before the much trumpeted attaché case gadget in *From Russia with Love* heralded the film and TV spy craze for such hi-tech gizmos.

Another trademark of *Danger Man* was the plethora of guest stars. Robert Shaw, Donald Pleasance, Warren Mitchell and *Dad's Army*'s John Le Mesurier all made appearances. Landing one of his first jobs on television was recently arrived Canadian actor Shane Rimmer, later to provide the voice of TB1 pilot Scott Tracy in *Thunderbirds*. 'I remember being very impressed with McGoohan. At that time TV was slightly predictable and he was different, and I think a lot of its success was due to him. On set he seemed terribly composed. He was in charge and I'm sure a lot of the direction of the shows had his influence on them. They knew what they were doing and they accommodated his particular talent in the best way possible. I think they gave him a lot of free rein and he prospered; the show certainly did. It was just different. It had a little substance to it which some of the other shows didn't.'

Another relative newcomer to television, Burt Kwouk (later immortalised as Kato in the *Pink Panther* series) was also won over by McGoohan. 'I loved working with Pat, a very powerful actor, tremendous strength. And although this was just basically potboiler stuff, what he brought to it was something that you don't very often find in a television series, something quite extraordinary and fairly unique.'

In spite of McGoohan's puritanical ideals, the female form was well represented by (amongst others) Honor Blackman, Wendy Craig, Jean Marsh (of *Upstairs, Downstairs* fame) and Lois Maxwell. Patricia Driscoll – *Robin Hood*'s Maid Marian – also appeared in several episodes. 'I had nightmares about one in particular,' she remembers. 'We went down to Wales to film on some cliffs, and they got me rolling over and over down towards the edge, with a helicopter hovering up above that was supposed to be firing at me or something. You do these things without thinking. And there was nothing between me and going over the cliff but Pat McGoohan. Only he could stop me. But we did that twice before they said it was OK. I remember going back to the hotel and thinking, my God, I might have gone over the edge!'

Behind the camera, the talent was similarly impeccable. The first director hired to work on *Danger Man* was Clive Donner. Donner started in the business as an editor and as *Lawrence of Arabia*/*Doctor Zhivago* director David Lean's assistant. Out of work at the beginning of the sixties – a decade that would ultimately see his best work, directing the film adaptation of Harold Pinter's *The Caretaker* and cult comedy *What's New Pussycat?* – Donner heard that Ralph Smart wanted him on his new TV series. Like many directors back then who'd plied their trade for Ealing and Rank, Donner had begun making commercials and gravitating towards television as a convenient means of earning a living, as the British film industry was in decline. Donner ended up directing the second ever *Danger Man* episode, Smart having directed the pilot. 'All the production values were extremely high, sets, casting, technicians, right the way down the line,' says Donner. 'I think we all felt it wasn't rubbish, it wasn't crap, we weren't just churning it out, and that made the atmosphere good. And the scripts were reasonably tolerable, well written, so that actors didn't think they were just doing it for the bread and butter, they could actually get their teeth into it. And wonderful, wonderful actors we had. And it was work, in those days with films not providing much opportunity for work, ITC could get the best people.'

Donner approached the series in cinematic terms, as if he was actually making a movie. 'I used to do some very innovative things, a lot of stuff with the camera, moving with the camera, a lot of long scenes that followed the action without cuts. The style was pretty well set by Ralph and Pat, in fact extremely so by Pat, and the scripts had already been approved by the story editor and no doubt by Pat as well, so all one was really was a hired hand. But Pat in no way interfered. He never in any way tried to call the shots in that way, in terms of making the film. There were no rehearsals beforehand either, we just came straight in cold, bang.'

On the writing front, Brian Clemens graduated from *The Invisible Man* to work on the *Danger Man* scripts on the recommendation of Ralph Smart. 'Although I never got a solo writing credit. Ralph always changed a word here and there and then claimed joint credit. I was too wet behind the ears to realise that if Ralph took a credit he also got a chunk of the equity. Which I did not!' Despite this, Clemens and Smart built up a healthy working relationship. 'I remember once we were awaiting a writer of some note to arrive at the office. Ralph reckoned we could get a script from him for about £500. Then, out of the window, we saw the writer arrive in a Jaguar sports car. Ralph frowned and said, "Better make that £1000!"'

Like Donner, John Glen started his career as an editor and worked on the early *Danger Man* episodes in that capacity. 'I met some very interesting directors on that show, Peter Yates and Charlie Crichton, who was pretty old then, a quite grumpy man but a wonderful character. I was editing his episode of *Danger Man* and running the film though the moviola when he said, "Stop!" And I stopped. And he put his head in his hands, and after about ten minutes I wondered whether he'd died or not, because there was no movement. I thought I'd better say something. "Charlie, may I suggest . . . " And he blasted, "Shut up, I'm thinking!" A wonderful man.'

It was when Sidney Cole, who knew the young, eager editor from his days working at Ealing, took over the production of *Danger Man* that Glen really landed his big break. 'Sidney realised that I had a certain talent for doing second unit shots. Sometimes we'd have a troublesome film and we'd have a talk in the office about how we could put things right. I'll always remember one episode called "The Ubiquitous Mr Lovegrove", that was sort of half finished and put on the shelf. And Sidney was quite astute; although we had a deadline when these films had to be aired in a few weeks, you could shuffle the pack a little bit. So he delayed that one and I went out and shot a whole new action sequence with Patrick, and we made the film very watchable and quite interesting. One wonders just what an influence that episode might have had on the series that Patrick went on to do, called *The Prisoner*. It was almost a development of that style of film, rather crazy and well before its time.'

Top: *Like so many ITC series,* Danger Man *worked because the cast and crew approached it as if they were making mini movies.* Bottom: *McGoohan moved behind the camera for the first time in his career to direct episodes of* Danger Man.

Top: *in keeping with previous ITC shows, and those to come,* Danger Man *featured a galaxy of distinguished guest stars such as Denholm Elliott.* Bottom: *McGoohan prepares for a take.*

Often episodes would be left unfinished because the filming schedules were so tight. If, after the allotted ten days, a director hadn't completed all the scenes, tough luck, it was on to the next episode, no standing on ceremony. 'I remember one director, John Moxey, had the breakers pulled on him and he was very upset about it,' recalls Glen. 'He hadn't finished by twenty past five and the producer came on the floor yelling, "Pull the breakers," and all the lights went out. That was it.' Invariably it was the second unit and people like John Glen whose job it was to clean up the episodes afterwards, with insert shots and the like. 'The economics of film-making are very important, almost as important as the creative side,' explains Glen. 'You have to keep one eye on the schedule and one eye on the creative side, you have to weigh up and balance all the various points, spend your money on certain things and other things don't waste time [on], get on with it. That's something you learn on television and I think that was great training for me.'

Danger Man operated under the tightest of schedules – which came as something of a shock to McGoohan. Indeed, it took him a whole month to get into the rigid habit of waking up at 6.30 every morning. Even then, he was forced to take a break in the middle of the first season due to the enormous pressure. 'The pace on these shows is terrific,' he told *Photoplay*. 'By evening you're really whacked.' When the series stopped shooting it was just as big a jolt to the system as it had been when it all started. For a whole week McGoohan continued to get up at 6.30 and drive to the studios as a matter of routine. 'I couldn't break the habit until I fully realised that it was all over.'

Significantly, it was on *Danger Man* where McGoohan first became interested in the technicalities of film production. He even got to direct an episode, 'The Vacation', which he personally considered had the best story out of all the early shows. It concerned a hired assassin that Drake meets sitting next to on a plane. 'Pat was a good director,' confirms John Glen. 'But like a lot of actors who put their hands to directing they realise it's bloody hard work and quickly go back to acting again.'

On set, McGoohan could watch and learn from established pros like Seth Holt and Clive Donner, who found the experience of directing *Danger Man* enjoyable, but at times akin to work shifts in a factory. 'Whatever time of the day it was you finished your episode, another director was standing there waiting to come in to do his episode and the unit just segued.' Nor did Donner attend rushes or oversee editing, that was part of the deal. 'They didn't want me to see them. Once you've shot it, as long as it's alright, get out.' To this day, Donner hasn't watched a single *Danger Man* episode he directed.

Danger Man debuted in Britain in September 1960, four months before *The Avengers*. The success the show enjoyed internationally, playing in countries as far apart as Australia, West Germany, Finland and the Lebanon, turned McGoohan into a global TV star. Letters from around the world, many simply addressed to 'the Danger Man, London', turned up daily at the studio.

But although it began promisingly enough, the story in America was very different. Sold to the Canadian Broadcasting Corporation for a reported £100,000, *Danger Man* played there successfully, achieving a top ten rating. Then CBS bought the show for transmission throughout the United States from April 1961, thereby giving it the distinction of being the first spy drama to air on American television in the 1960s. But ratings were disappointing and within six months the series was dropped.

The last *Danger Man* episode was transmitted in Britain in January 1962. But *The Avengers* and the Bond movies went on to show that there was a massive public thirst for spies, and so ITC decided to revive the show after a hiatus of two years. By 1964 London was beginning to swing, and the producers were keen to exploit the growing perception of the UK as the trendiest place in the world. This meant a change of employers for Drake, who transferred from NATO to M9 – a secret governmental agency whose HQ was situated somewhere in London. McGoohan also reverted to a British accent, as opposed to the transatlantic tones he adopted in the original series. The actor also insisted on driving a Mini-Cooper, a more sensible car for a spy than those preferred by Bond, 'whose cars are fantastic engines of adolescent wish-fulfilment,' scoffed McGoohan. However, the biggest change to the format was the length. The new *Danger Man* was to be expanded to one hour, with the result that episodes carried more complex plots, action and character development.

When McGoohan turned up for work on the first day of the new series, he announced, 'It's an odd feeling to return to a character after such a long break. I'm feeling quite nervous.' He opted not to mention that he'd had to trim off a bit of excess weight to regain Drake's athletic figure. For someone well known for selecting his roles carefully, with particular attention to diversity, critics wondered why McGoohan was back playing the same character. But he saw nothing monotonous in

John Drake – far from it. Every week the setting and story was different, and Drake himself assumed different identities in the course of his job. 'I find the role as stimulating as playing in repertory, with something fresh to tackle in every new production.'

The new Drake hadn't really changed all that much from his previous incarnation. He was still an enigmatic loner with his idealism undimmed. But the one-hour running time did allow for greater insights into his psyche, and it became much more apparent that here was a man of conscience, often unhappy with the violence that occurred in his line of work. Although retaining his sense of duty, we also begin to see him question the judgement of his stuffy superiors and rebel against some of the assignments he's given. According to Ralph Smart, the format was changed to show Drake as a more humane and less calculating person.

However, Drake still eschewed any affairs with women (not even a kiss) and rarely carried a gun. A group of American executives even flew to England on a mission to make McGoohan loosen up a bit, and allow Drake to indulge in the kind of romantic trysts their audiences wanted to see. They wined and dined the star but to no avail. 'I told them that I wouldn't have sex dragged into *Danger Man* and sent them packing with their tails between their legs,' boasted McGoohan. In later episodes, Drake does hint at unexpected regrets that a wife and family were beyond his reach. This was an aspect of his character that would have been interesting to explore more.

There was also a massive increase in gadgets, no doubt influenced by their popularity in the Bond series. McGoohan was against using the fanciful sci-fi gizmos of 007 and *The Man from UNCLE*, so the challenge was always to provide Drake with secret weapons that looked like ordinary objects, so as not to arouse suspicion if found on him. Hence a cigarette lighter became a miniature camera, and a cigar could shoot out clouds of harmless knockout gas. The writers must have had fun dreaming up these things, and even McGoohan couldn't resist getting in on the act. 'I look at the most everyday objects and find myself wondering if they could be adapted for my secret agent's spy kit!' McGoohan did in fact invent several of the devices himself, including a fishing rod which became a high velocity rifle, working by compressed air that fired not bullets, but capsules containing miniature radio transmitters.

Despite this proliferation of gadgets, the series never indulged in the wackier plots favoured by *The Avengers*. A typical episode had Drake out to stop a fellow agent from killing the East German secret policeman who'd tortured her years before. One story, in which Drake gathered together a group of highly skilled friends to rescue a fellow agent held captive in an Eastern Bloc embassy in Switzerland, could almost have been a prototype for *Mission Impossible*. In another, Drake is sent to a self-contained village where agents are being trained to infiltrate the UK. (Shades of *The Prisoner*.)

For the new series, the makers spared no expense to inject each story with liberal sprinklings of action and suspense. McGoohan remained steadfast in his refusal to portray violence for its own sake, and was quick to disassociate Drake from the likes of Bond. Drake was 'As down to earth as good English mutton,' while 007 was 'A sort of cartoon strip fantasy with morals that I find questionable.' Despite this, Sean Connery made an appearance on the set of *Danger Man*, where he and McGoohan happily posed for the camera. They'd previously worked together, when McGoohan was the star and Connery a hard-up actor, in *Hell Drivers*, a late fifties British testosterone-fuelled classic that also featured a pre-fame Stanley Baker, Sid James and David McCallum.

About halfway through production on the second series, *Danger Man* moved

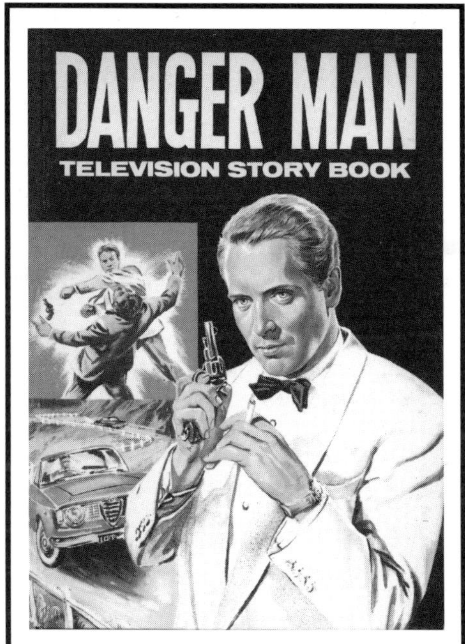

Left: *a rare* Danger Man *annual; his character's demeanour shows clearly why McGoohan was an early candidate to play 007.* Right: *the American comic book based on the series. One doubts today whether the secret agent would be allowed to have a cigarette in his mouth.*

from the MGM studios at Borehamwood over to nearby Shepperton. Everyone concerned was desperate to finish all the outstanding episodes, and start life at their new base with a clean sheet. 'We didn't want to have to carry all the old sets over to Shepperton. So we had a frantic day,' recalls John Glen. 'The whole of my cutting room, all my assistants, we were all on the floor shooting segments. I was delegating all second unit shots to anyone I could find who wanted to direct an insert. And we managed to clean up all the outstanding episodes that were already in the can but needed little bits and pieces done. Pat McGoohan was wonderful. He was really into the spirit of the thing, racing to his dressing room, changing into dozens of outfits, and running back on the set to do all these different shots. I'll always remember there was a scene that required Patrick to climb up this drainpipe and before I could stop him he was halfway up, but it had just been painted and it got all over him. He didn't say anything, he just looked at me and then went off the set and cleaned up, and came back a few minutes later. He was so enthusiastic it was wonderful.'

Once again, McGoohan handled as many of the action scenes as he was able to. Stunt arranger Frank Maher, a former paratrooper, arranged the punch-ups and also doubled for some of the actors. On location in Wales, Maher was obliged to make a spectacular leap from a mountain ledge, but rocks damp from spray off a nearby waterfall caused him to skid and he fell 21 feet, dislocating his neck. Maher spent the next three weeks in plaster, probably wishing he was back in the army.

The new look *Danger Man* hit British screens in October 1964. The public again took to the show, something the crew back at Shepperton derived great pride and satisfaction from. 'We were in competition with the likes of *The Saint* and we always considered ourselves a little bit superior in quality,' says Glen. 'We thought our stories were better and that we had a fantastic actor in Patrick McGoohan.'

Second time around, things in America played out very differently for *Danger Man*. CBS ran the series in a primetime weekend slot, achieving huge ratings. This was partly thanks to the mid-sixties craze for espionage, ironically a trend *Danger Man* had started. Re-titled *Secret Agent*, the US network also used a different theme tune – 'Secret Agent Man' sung by Johnny Rivers. Internationally, the series fared equally well. In France it went under the name *Destination Danger*, while in some South American territories it was known as *El Agente 00*. There was also a boom in *Danger Man* merchandise, with tie-in novels, annuals, a board game, jigsaws, comics and, most collectable of all, a set of 72 bubble gum cards.

Patrick McGoohan as John Drake – along with Roger Moore as Simon Templar and Patrick Macnee as John Steed, were archetypical British heroes; debonair, poised and cerebral. This was in marked contrast to the aggressively virile and ponderously virtuous heroes on American television. The fact that these terribly British characters, in uniquely British series, broke big in the US was a major development for the domestic television industry. *Danger Man* became one of the most important elements in Lew Grade's overseas marketing.

Unsurprisingly, given its Stateside success, a further season of *Danger Man* entered production in 1966. During what could have been the most interesting series yet (with the show heading in a Bond-like direction, with more action and bizarre elements, and in colour for the first time), McGoohan suddenly revealed he'd grown bored with Drake and wanted out. He approached Grade and voiced his dissatisfaction. As a result, filming closed after just two episodes, 'Koroshi' and 'Shinda Shima'. Of these, 'Shinda Shima' is acknowledged as the best, with many fans referring to its similarity with the subsequent *Prisoner* in style, sets and narrative structure. To maximise what they had, ITC hit on the idea of combining these two episodes and screening them as a feature-length TV movie in some territories, with specially filmed linking footage.

Although he had walked out on *Danger Man*, Grade was determined to retain McGoohan's services. Along with Roger Moore, he was ITC's biggest star. McGoohan could do whatever he wanted, he had *carte blanche* to create his own TV show, so desperate was Grade to retain him. What McGoohan was to come up with became television's greatest ever cult show – *The Prisoner*.

THE SAINT (1962-69)

Since his creation in the 1920s, *The Saint* had become a popular figure in books, films, radio and comics, but television had yet to exploit the character. It wasn't for want of trying. As far back as 1952, attempts were made to adapt *The Saint* for small screen consumption, but author Leslie Charteris proved to be notoriously difficult to negotiate with, as he was understandably dubious about how his creation would be treated. '*The Saint* on television might disappoint a lot more readers than it pleased,' he argued. His overriding fear was that the actor chosen might not suit his, or indeed his readers', mental image of what Simon Templar looked like. He'd

Despite his tongue-in-cheek approach to his role in The Saint, *Roger Moore could always play tough if the script required it.*

already expressed disdain about previous screen incarnations of his hero, referring to George Sanders, who played Templar in a series of films in the 1940s, as 'absolutely wrong', lacking as he did the verve that an actor such as Ronald Coleman might have brought to the role.

Charteris was the son of a Chinese surgeon and his English wife. Though born in Singapore, he was a product of the English public school system. Having begun writing fiction while at Cambridge, he dropped out of university to pursue writing full-time, completing his first Saint book in 1928. Charteris' fantasy hero, stylishly righting wrongs in the good old *Boys' Own* tradition, became hugely popular within just a few years, and a steady stream of Saint stories followed. By the mid-forties it was said that the Saint was the most profitable English fictional character since Sherlock Holmes, and by 1951 Charteris' publishers said they had lost count of world sales.

'Leslie Charteris was an extremely handsome man,' recalls Sir Roger Moore. 'He was about six foot four. Very well read. Had wonderful manners. I enjoyed his company very much. He and Audrey, his wife, we'd meet quite often in the South of France, even after I'd finished *The Saint*. I don't know whether Leslie was happy with my casting as Templar at the beginning, but he gradually came around to it when the series was successful.'

The men responsible for finally bringing *The Saint* to television were producers Robert S. Baker and Monty Berman. Baker had been a combat cameraman with the Eighth Army during World War II, where he met fellow sergeant Berman and agreed that, once discharged, they'd go into the movie business together. Capitalising on the late fifties resurgence in horror, inspired by Hammer, Baker and Berman made a number of lurid but effective British Grand Guignol pictures like *Blood of the Vampire* and *The Trollenberg Terror*. By the sixties, Baker realised that the market for his pictures, low-budget programme fillers, was drying up rapidly. 'Television was taking over, so it seemed to me the obvious time to jump off the sinking ship and get into television. I just timed it right because television was at its heyday in the sixties.' To a large extent the second feature, or B-movie, so prevalent in the 1950s became the one-hour TV action series epitomised by ITC's output.

In the autumn of 1961, Baker and Berman were sitting in their company offices in Jermyn Street, London, when a mutual friend, the director John Paddy Carstairs, dropped in for lunch. Carstairs had directed *The Saint in London* for RKO back in 1939, and was also an old friend of Leslie Charteris. 'I told Paddy that we were interested in doing *The Saint* and so he introduced me to Leslie Charteris,' says Baker. 'And I persuaded Charteris – how I managed to do it I don't know – to give me a free option on the Saint books for six months.' Baker took the project to Brian Tesler, head of ABC Television, who considered his proposed budget of £15,000 per episode too expensive and declined.

A week or so later, Baker was invited to a weekend charity function and found himself sitting next to Lew Grade. 'I turned to him and said, "Lew, I've got an option on *The Saint*." He said, "Really?" I said, "Are you interested?" He said, "Yes, very interested. I used to love the Saint books. Come and see me on Monday morning." So I went to his office and I produced a letter from Leslie Charteris. And Lew said, "Where is Charteris?" I said, "He's living in Florida." So Lew said, "Right, go to Florida and do a deal." I left on Wednesday and met Leslie Charteris and spent a whole week negotiating. Charteris was a particularly difficult character and made a pretty tough deal, and also insisted on being paid in Swiss francs, but I had the backing of Lew Grade, who was determined to make the show, and it was all sorted out. And that's how *The Saint* started.'

Now the search was on for an actor to play him.

Charteris' ideal choice for Simon Templar would have been either Cary Grant or David Niven. Grade wanted Patrick McGoohan, fresh out of *Danger Man*. 'We had a meeting with Patrick which didn't go very well,' remembers Baker. 'He was difficult and aggressive. He kind of looked down his nose at *The Saint*. Then our story editor, Harry Junkin, had a private meeting with him to discuss stories and came back saying, "You can't make *The Saint* with this guy." So we went to Lew and said it wasn't going to work with McGoohan. "OK," Lew said, "We'll get someone else."'

The crux of McGoohan's disdain for *The Saint* was that he perceived the character as being far too promiscuous, and while the high moral approach worked for John Drake, it was entirely inappropriate for the debonair Templar. 'McGoohan was ruled out because he was very puritanical,' Charteris observed. 'He wouldn't have any scenes kissing girls.' The producers also felt McGoohan lacked the right sort of panache. Nor did he exhibit much of a sense of humour, as the show was intended to be slightly tongue in cheek.

Also briefly under consideration was American actor Craig Stevens, who soon got his own ITC series, *Man of the World*. Ultimately, it was Roger Moore who was chosen. 'It so happened that Roger was in Italy, making a film called *Rape of the Sabine Women*,' recalls Baker. 'Roger himself wanted to do *The Saint*, he always felt that was the ideal vehicle for him. But his career was actually at that time going nowhere. He had been under contract to MGM and Warners, he did *Maverick* on television and that folded, and now he was in Italy making these awful epics, so he jumped at the chance.'

Indeed, such was Moore's passion for the role that, while he'd been playing *Ivanhoe* during the late fifties, he had made a couple of attempts to acquire the rights to *The Saint*. 'Actually it was my father who said there were two things that would be very good for me. One was a series of books called *The Toff* and the other was *The Saint*. I tried for *The Saint* and didn't have any joy. Charteris was not interested.'

Fortuitously, Moore belonged to London Management, the largest theatrical agency in Europe, which just happened to be owned by Lew and his

Top: *Roger Moore meets the creator of Simon Templar – Leslie Charteris.* Centre: *Moore and* Saint *producer Bob Baker relax off set.* Bottom: *rivals?* The Avengers' *Patrick Macnee shares tea with Moore at Elstree Studios.*

brother Leslie Grade. Keen to use one of his own clients, Lew had no hesitation in approving Baker's choice and a pilot script was sent to the actor, then on holiday with future wife Luisa Mattioli in Venice. 'Next my agent came out to have a chat and I said, "It seems to be an awfully long script. Are you sure it's a half-hour series?" He said, "Yes, Roger." I said, "You'd better make sure because it reads very long to me." And it came back from somebody, who after that never worked in his office again, that it was a half-hour series. So I agreed to do it. I thought we'd do 26 episodes, or at the most 39, and they would be half hours and that it would be all over in quite a short period of time. So when Lew was making the press announcement I was standing there and he said, "We're going to do 39 hour-long shows." I said, "No Lew, it's 39 half hours." Bob Baker got hold of my arm and said, "What are you talking about?" I said, "It's 39 half hours." He said, "No, they're hours." I said, "Oh God, then we have to go back to the drawing board, because as far as I'm concerned the contract I've agreed to do was for half hours, not hours." But that was all eventually sorted out, and what I thought would be 39 episodes turned out to be 118!'

Moore had said he would never make another TV series, but, after separating from his wife, vocalist Dorothy Squires, he was embarking on a new life with starlet Luisa Mattioli, with whom he would have a daughter and two sons. This was an offer he couldn't refuse. 'It was only the fact that it was something that I had tried to acquire before that intrigued me. And actually, even though I thought it was a long script for half an hour, it was a very good story. I think the strength of the *Saint* series was the story-lines.'

Roger Moore was an inspired choice to play Simon Templar, as perfect in the role as Patrick Macnee was as John Steed. Much more than Bond, the Saint was the role Moore was born to play, and much of the success of the show and its enduring popularity is down to his portrayal and his charisma. 'I remember looking at the first day's rushes on the first *Saint* episode we did,' remembers Robert Baker. 'And the second Roger appeared on the screen we knew it was going to work. We all knew we'd got the right man. It was incredible. You saw it – it just gelled so perfectly, it was there.'

The publicity blurb for the TV *Saint* read, 'A roaring adventurer who loves a fight. A dashing daredevil, debonair, preposterously handsome. He lives for the pursuit of excitement.' In many ways, Simon Templar was a twentieth century swashbuckler; Robin Hood or Dan Tempest in modern dress, a romantic buccaneer and a man of worldly experience, with little aversion to breaking the rules or taking the law into his own hands. Always immaculately dressed, Templar exuded taste and élan. A lover of fast cars, and even faster women.

Moore was just the right sort of actor to play Templar; criminally good looking, with a strong personality and a light comedy touch. 'I like to play things for humour, particularly as I was playing a hero, because I consider myself to be devoutly unheroic to the extent of being a sheer coward. I think any heroism I have is the fact that I did things physically that I was absolutely petrified of doing.'

The humour Moore brought to the role was vitally important, as the producers knew they were going to have to drastically tone down the darker elements found in Charteris' novels. The author had conceived his character as a much tougher and more brutal man, with no compunction about maiming or killing his enemies. In one story he toasts the feet of an adversary before an open fire to get information out of him. Putting such acts on television was unthinkable in 1962. Besides, the literary Saint was a character Moore himself could never have played, at least convincingly.

The strict television code of behaviour (upheld by ITV and BBC) decreed that the Saint could not kill or torture, but would rather fight villains cleanly like a proper English gentleman. 'Occasionally you'd get the censor on your back,' explains Baker. 'Mainly on the fight scenes. But we were very careful with the fight scenes, we made the Saint always fight by the Marquis of Queensberry rules; we never had him kick people in the balls or anything like that.'

This new, sanitised Saint allowed Moore to fully exploit what some commentators have unfairly labelled as his pretty-boy, chocolate box charm. Although Moore's Saint is constrained by his very English sense of fair play, his methods occasionally border on the ruthless. In one episode, in an effort to obtain information, Templar plays Russian roulette with two failed assailants he's tied up until, eventually, one of them cracks and confesses all. It's then that Templar reveals his gun was never loaded.

Much has also been made of the similarities between the Saint and James Bond, not least on account of the fact that Moore went on to play 007. Both are adventurers with a flair for violence, which is com-

The Saint had his fair share of glamourous leading ladies, some of whom went on to star in their own ITC series – like Annette Andre (top) in Randall and Hopkirk (Deceased), *and Alexandra Bastedo (bottom) in* The Champions.

Julie Christie, just two years away from her breakthrough roles in Darling *and* Doctor Zhivago.

plimented by a debonair sense of sartorial panache and a taste for the finer things in life. Both heroes have also moved way beyond their original literary existence to become part of the popular cultural landscape. And, like Templar, Fleming's Bond was radically revised and adjusted to fit in with the international climate of the 1960s. Charteris himself acidly labelled 007 as 'Mickey Spillane in an old Etonian tie' and 'A bureaucrat with a gun.'

It was part of the *Saint* formula that Moore would have a leading lady in every episode (not literally, of course), and what leading ladies they were. Future Bond golden girl Shirley Eaton adorned the opening episode, 'The Talented Husband'. 'Because I'd done three *Carry Ons* and *Doctor in the House* with Dirk Bogarde, when I was sixteen,' recalls Shirley, 'I was hot stuff – as it were – then, everybody wanted me to be in their films, so that's probably why they asked for me to be in the first *Saint*. I had met Roger on the set of *Ivanhoe*, and we met occasionally socially and became good friends.'

Shirley would return just eight episodes later, in 'The Effete Angler'. Coincidentally, the previous story, 'The Arrow of God', starred Honor Blackman, who would also appear in *Goldfinger*. Shirley had no inkling she was appearing in something that would later be hailed as a television classic, in fact she can scarcely remember being on the set at all. At the time it was just another job. 'It's like doing my part in *Goldfinger*, little did I know that 38 years later I would still have great loads of fan mail and be invited here, there and everywhere, just because I was in a film painted gold for five minutes.'

Future ITC stalwart Annette Andre (Jeannie in *Randall and Hopkirk [Deceased]*) appeared in no less than five *Saint* episodes that spanned the series' history. 'Roger used to ask for me from time to time, because we just used to have a good time. And Bob Baker liked me. It was like family. It seemed like I did one a year. The scripts were all the same, it was just different names. And occasionally I would have an accent; once I had an Australian accent, another time I had a French accent. And I'd just have a different hairstyle and put on a different dress, but I'd be the same character, really. We'd all laugh about that.'

No longer a child actress, Jane Asher was fast becoming one of the faces of hip London, with high profile roles in *The Masque of the Red Death* and *Alfie*, plus Paul McCartney for a boyfriend. Like Annette Andre, Jane enjoyed her stint on the series and the opportunity of working with Moore. 'He's great, so funny, a clever man and a very good artist. He used to be a cartoonist and I remember him doing lots of drawings on the set. And totally professional. Now he's mocked for the raised eyebrow, but he was very clever at saying a hell of a lot with a whimsical smile or whatever. He'd be the first to say he's not a deep actor, but at that level of acting he's absolutely brilliant.'

One of the episodes Jane appeared in was called 'The Invisible Millionaire', in which she played the daughter of a tycoon who calls on Templar's help when her father is involved in a car crash. 'I enjoyed doing that, but I loathed the way they curled my hair up. Hated it. Absolutely dreadful. Things makeup people did to you, and of course at that age you're far too shy to say, "Oh please can't I have it more like my normal hair?"' Jane was asked back to play another daughter in the episode 'The Noble Sportsman', opposite Anthony Quayle and directed by Peter Yates, who later went to Hollywood and made the Steve McQueen classic *Bullitt*.

Lisa Daniely enjoyed her appearances on *The Saint* to a greater degree than she did her lead role in *The Invisible Man*. 'They were far more fun for me because they were much more interesting parts. In *The Saint* I played an alcoholic film star and I had this lovely line when my boring husband says, "I hate you when you're drunk." And I said, "And I hate you when I'm sober." I had one or two lines like that and that's fun to do, to play witty as well as glamorous. These are the things that you remember as a performer.' She also found Moore the complete opposite of McGoohan, easygoing and charming. 'Although I don't think that you got anywhere nearer the real person than you did McGoohan, but it seemed that you did. That superficial charm Roger could turn on automatically was totally delightful.'

Like Lisa, actress Jane Merrow appeared in both *Danger Man* and *The Saint*, and was ideally placed to compare the two stars. 'Roger was fun to work with and he's a sweet man, but a totally different type of actor from Patrick. I'm not saying that Patrick used to take himself deeply seriously but Roger absolutely was the other way, he didn't take himself seriously at all, the whole thing was a great joke and laugh. He took the work seriously in as much as he didn't muck about, and he took his position very seriously, but he had a very easygoing, life is fun attitude. There was no angst about Roger.'

Jane loved her time working on *The Saint*, largely because of the warm family atmosphere on the set. 'Lew Grade would come on to the set with his huge cigar and say, "Hello my dear, nice to have you in the show," and all of that, and off he'd go again. He was a wonderful man. And Robert Baker was always there, bless his heart. Roger and Robert made you feel really welcome and made sure that every actor felt special on their shows.'

The list of *Saint* leading ladies quickly expanded to read like a who's who of sixties British glamour. There's Hammer scream queens Barbara Shelley, Kate O'Mara and Veronica Carlson, Bond girls Honor Blackman and Lois Maxwell, plus Samantha Eggar, Stephanie Beacham, Nanette Newman, Nyree Dawn Porter, Francesca Annis and Alexandra Bastedo, later of *The Champions*. Not forgetting Valerie Leon, who achieved cult status in the seventies as the leather-clad siren in the Hai-Karate commercials.

Most notable of all the *Saint* women was Julie Christie, arguably the biggest female British film star of the sixties for starring in *Doctor Zhivago* and *Darling*. 'She was totally unknown at the time we cast her in *The Saint*,' explains Baker. 'She used to travel around with a bag and would sleep anywhere; she was a real hippie. I went on set to watch her filming one of her scenes for *The Saint* and she kept fluffing her lines, and the director had to break it down into little sections. Next I watched the rushes, and the second she came on the screen was alight. It's something unexplainable; straight away you knew this girl was going to be big. The same thing happened when we used Donald Sutherland in the show. The camera's got this love affair with certain people.'

Male guest stars, not surprisingly, didn't get so much of a look in, but were no less stellar. The roll call included such luminaries as Steven Berkoff, Oliver Reed, Julian Glover, Ian Hendry, Robert Hardy, Edward Woodward and Ronnie Barker. Francis Matthews, who later became the voice of Captain Scarlet, has particularly fond memories of Moore. 'Roger used to make you come to the rushes. He used to love watching himself on rushes. He was quite unashamed about it. He'd say, "You coming to watch the rushes, Fran?" And I'd say, "What for, Roger?" He said, "Come and have a look, come on, you'll see yourself." I said, "I can't stand seeing myself, Roger." He said, "Oh, I like watching them." And he used to smile all the time watching rushes. He used to think he was great. And then we'd have nice lunches in the commissary. Roger was friendly with everyone.'

Getting a job on *The Saint* also meant meeting up with the same group of actors that people like Matthews would know socially, which always added to the great atmosphere on set. 'In those days there were far fewer actors. Nowadays, with soaps and the like, there are hundreds of mediocre people, but in those days you met the same actors all the time. When they rang you up and said, "Will you come and do a *Saint*?", you'd say, "Oh yes, great, who's doing it?", and they'd say, "Well, Bill's coming," and such and such is in it. We all knew each other. At least 50 per cent of the people in whatever thing you were doing, you would already have met and you'd know them, so it was like getting together with mates all the time. So working on something like *The Saint* was great. But they were churned out. They were formulaic. And also, if you look carefully at any of those shows, the sets are all exactly the same. You would do a *Saint* in a set, you'd come down some stairs, go into a room and stand by a fireplace and three weeks later you'd be in exactly the same set playing a different character. They just guessed that people watching *The Saint* wouldn't notice.'

For many actors appearing in *The Saint*, or other ITC shows, there was never any sense they were making something that, 40 years later, would still be showing

Looks familiar: Oliver Reed guest stars in the episode 'Sophia'.

around the world. 'It was just another job really,' recounts George Baker. 'But you got a *Saint* and you thought, that's very respectable work, it'll take me a week, pay the rent, and won't do me any harm.' Baker later starred with Moore in an episode of *The Persuaders* and played Captain Benson in *The Spy Who Loved Me*.

Baker and Berman made a formidable production team on *The Saint*. Berman looked after the general running of the operation, contracts, schedules and suchlike, while Baker spent most of his time on scripts and casting, occasionally mixing things up by directing the odd episode. An early key decision was to hire as script editor Canadian-born Hollywood writer Harry Junkin, who was serving the same function on another Baker/Berman ITC series, *Gideon's Way* – much to the consternation of director Robert Tronson. 'I remember saying, "Where the hell did they find him? He's useless." Everyone said, "Yes, we know this." Apparently he'd arrived in this country and taken a large advert in *The Stage* saying, "Harry Junkin's here!" And they fell for it. They said, Harry Junkin's here, we must have him. And he had no idea how to script edit this essentially British police series called *Gideon's Way*. It was full of those awful, howling Americanisms, which we had to sort out as we shot. God, it was a trial.'

Junkin also had a reputation for being difficult to get along with. *Danger Man* writer Philip Broadley experienced so much aggravation in preparing his *Saint* episode, 'The Counterfeit Countess', he refused to work on the show again. Neither did Junkin get along with Leslie Charteris. Their relationship got so bad that, according to Baker, it developed into 'a minor vendetta between them. They met but they hardly spoke to each other. Harry found it quite amusing.' Charteris saw Junkin as the main perpetrator of what he perceived to be the TV show's careless treatment of his stories. 'This script is fit for Junkin(g),' asserted one terse telegram from the author about an episode written by the Canadian, who found it so funny he considered framing it.

Numerous writers were employed to work on *The Saint*, many of them very experienced and high-profile. 'But I would say about 80 per cent of scripts were rewritten either by me or Harry Junkin,' reveals Baker. 'We found a few writers that cottoned on straight away to what we were doing. Terry Nation, who was marvellous and also became the story editor on *The Persuaders*, and John Kruse, they were the two best writers, you didn't have to alter a line.'

Charteris' views about the manner in which his books were portrayed on television quickly soured. 'I have been most pleasantly surprised to see how closely they have tried to follow the original stories and preserve the original personality of the Saint,' he said of the first batch of episodes. 'A sincere effort was made to achieve faithful adaptations.' By the second season, significant liberties were now being taken with the stories. In private memos and in public, Charteris never wasted an opportunity to vent his anger and frustration. He felt the show had been reduced to a synthetic and mediocre product, with the sole objective of making it anodyne and inoffensive to any TV sponsor, and therefore saleable anywhere in the world. He lamented that the show 'bears no more relation to *The Saint* that I wrote than *Winnie the Pooh* bears to *Captain Blood*.' He even went so far as to call the series 'an abortive mutation'.

Charteris often wrote to Baker and Junkin, complaining about certain episodes which the producers always sent to him to read before filming started. What peeved him the most was seeing his unconventional stories and unusual plot twists hammered into conformity, to fit a formulaic TV action series. He wrote, 'I have to suffer the humiliation of realising that thousands upon thousands of television viewers who do not read much will justifiably assume that my published stories are as trite and plagiaristic as the televised distortions make them out to be.'

It was strange that Charteris, who for a time plied his trade as a Hollywood screenwriter, failed to appreciate the differences between literature and the visual medium. 'When you transfer from the written word to film you've got to make concessions to film all the time,' says Baker. 'It's very easy in the written word to say what a person thinks, but you've got to express on screen how this person is thinking, so consequently the story's structure is totally different. Most of the original *Saint* adventures were short stories. Consequently, when it came to extending them to one hour, we found that really what we had was the first act, where you set out your problem and then the Saint solved it, we had no middle part to the story. So we had to invent incidents in the first act to see us through the second act, until we come to the resolution of the story. We had to use an awful lot of invention with the *Saint* stories. I can understand why writers seeing their story altered get a bit hot under the collar. And I used to get terrible, stinking memos from Charteris about altering his stories. But it was necessary. He was happy with his bank account, though.'

The one writer Charteris did admire was John Kruse, particularly the way he enlivened the scripts with clever dialogue. But Charteris remained gloomily critical

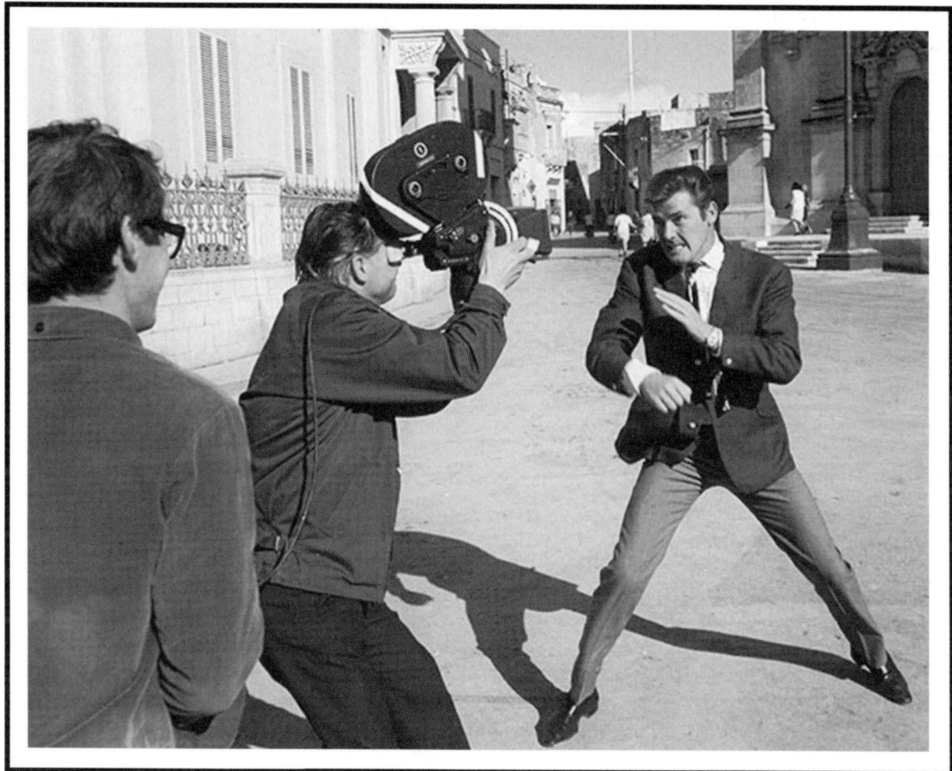

Street fighting man: Moore pulls no punches out on location.

of some of the more cliché-ridden aspects of the episodes. After suggesting changes to one particular episode he wrote, 'With everything fixed up this show may drag itself up from the original trash to the dizzy heights of average TV mediocrity.' When the author learned that the series was to end, he wrote with glee, 'I cannot adequately convey my delight that this is apparently the last of your *Saint* productions, and the last time I shall have to suffer the ordeal of reading the corny abominations which you have lately been perpetrating on my stories.'

The Saint began production in June 1962. During his seven-year tenure as Simon Templar, Roger Moore's work schedule stayed pretty much the same. Every morning he'd drive himself to Borehamwood in the white Volvo Sports Coupe that the Saint used in the series, arriving by 7.30 am. After parking the car he visited makeup and glanced through his lines again, which he would have read and memorised the previous night. It's mind-numbing to think of the thousands of lines of dialogue Moore must have had to remember. Luckily, he was blessed with a photographic memory. 'I once asked Roger how he managed to memorise a page of dialogue just by looking at it,' recalls director Roy Ward Baker. 'And he said, "I don't memorise it really. I just listen to what the other actors are saying and then I think of something to say back and it's usually right." Now, that's a leg pull, but in a funny way it's got the truth in it.'

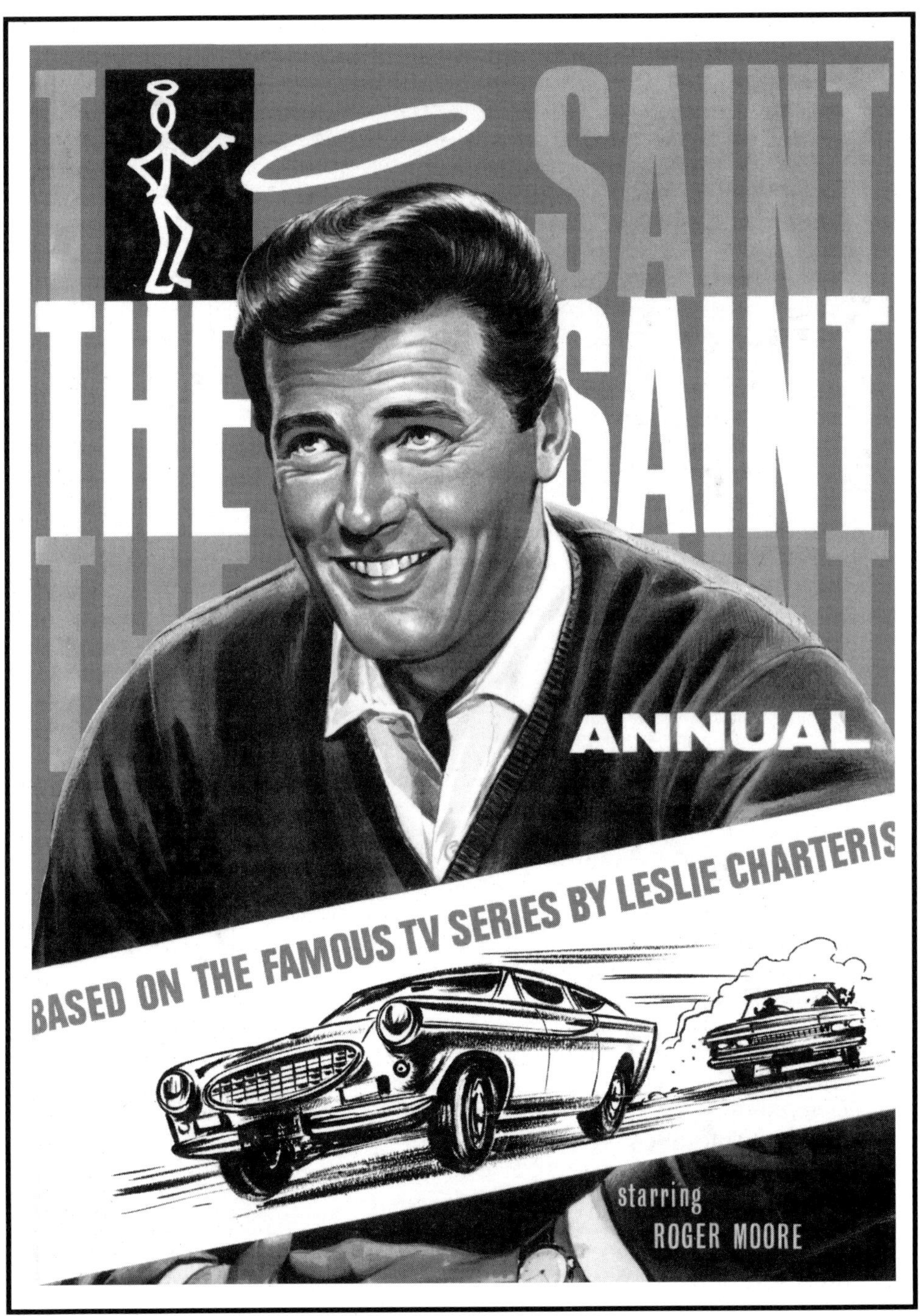

The Saint *1967 annual.*

After his visit to the makeup chair, Moore would be ready on set by 8.30 am. He was always on time. 'Really it was like having a job in a bank, except that you actually got in earlier and went home later,' observes Moore. 'Every week we invariably had a new director. You'd have the same crew, so you were amongst a bunch of friends. And the cast changed too. So it was very interesting, you got to work with a variety of directors and a vast number of actors and actresses. In fact sometimes, when I see an old *Saint* or *Persuaders* and I see an actor that I worked with, I say, "My God, I never realised I've worked with him."'

Moore's famous practical jokes and easygoing manner helped create a genial atmosphere around the studio. He'd often ad-lib a funny line after a scene or, following a tense confrontation with a villain, end it by dancing around the set with him. 'He'd do all sorts of things,' remembers Roy Ward Baker. 'Which was great because it kept the crew in good humour. They used to look forward to going to the rushes because they knew Roger was going to do something funny. Roger was largely responsible for seven years of people enjoying working on the show, not getting bored with it, because he was so pleasant to work with. He has such a great sense of humour.'

It's easy to see why Moore was so revered by those who worked with him, especially the crew. 'At that time the electrical union was very bolshy and, at the drop of a hat, they'd go on strike,' explains Baker. 'There was this rule that if you were in the middle of a scene at the end of the working day, they had the power and discretion to give you an extra fifteen minutes to finish. I remember once asking the shop steward if we could finish the scene, and he "ummed" and "ahhed" and then said, "All right then, but we're not doing it for the producers, we'll do it for Roger." He was so well liked.'

Moore's on-set gags were invariably schoolboyish in nature, like painting the eyepiece of a camera with boot polish. 'And the crew would start moving away if they saw a soda siphon on the set,' he says. '"Oh Jesus," they'd go, "he's going to do it again because he knows that we can't spray him back." If there's a good atmosphere it reflects on everything, it reflects on the speed with which people work. You really don't need a villain around. You don't have to have somebody to hate to work together.' The crew did occasionally get their own back, like this classic jape perpetrated by director Raymond Austin and his cameraman: 'Roger had to come in and search a room,' recounts Austin. 'And we planted notes all over, so when Roger opened a drawer there was a note in there saying, "Roger Moore's a poof." Then there was a note in the back of the closet: "Roger Moore is a great big poof." I said, "Action" and just sat and waited for him to break up. And sure enough we got him on about the last one. "You bastards," he shouted, and cracked up.'

Someone else who got their own back on Moore was actress Sue Lloyd, then filming another ITC show, *The Baron*, on a neighbouring stage. 'Roger and I were always playing practical jokes on each other. He put a condom in my script on the first day of my working on *The Baron*. I opened my script and it fell out on the floor. I was absolutely mortified. After that I put two great big balloons and one sausage balloon on his dressing room door, and they came wobbling down when he walked in with some very important visitors.'

Moore's playacting rebounded on him in other ways too, according to *Saint* director Robert Tronson. 'I didn't get on terribly well with Roger. Terribly affable, but a very unreal sort of person, I thought. He was determined, even then, to play James Bond. That was his goal in life. An awful lot of time was spent doing manipulation and intrigue to get in with people who might help him. For example, I was doing one episode set in the South of France. We shot a scene where he's supposed to be in a speedboat, all back projection with a prop man who kept maliciously flinging more water than necessary. "I'll get you," Roger was saying. He didn't like it at all. A friend of mine was a managing director of some very important company, and his secretary was a deep admirer of Roger's, and we'd arranged for them to come and see us shooting that day. But they were terribly late arriving, and missed everything except the very last scene of Roger behind this bar. And the entire unit knew what to expect. Roger did his look to camera and then up at his halo, and the moment I said cut he darted down behind this bar where he had six fire buckets. Everybody split, except this important financier in his expensive suit and very attractive secretary, standing there soaked. Roger was mortified. He'd absolutely buggered his chances.'

Nor was Moore's japery confined to the set of *The Saint*. Not too far away, Raymond Austin was helming an *Avengers* episode. 'In this scene Linda Thorson had to open a coffin to find some clues. We rehearsed and then broke for lunch. And it was a very tense scene for Linda, because she was so nervous being the new girl and taking Diana Rigg's place on a well-known show. After lunch we went for a take. She creeps all the way over to the coffin, runs her hand along it, moves the lid slightly to the side and suddenly it opens, and Roger Moore sticks up. "Argghhh!" The poor girl jumps out of her skin and the entire crew jump. Roger had sneaked onto the set and sat in that bloody coffin all his lunch hour for the joke. And no one knew. That was the sort of thing he did. You really could have fun with Roger.'

It was largely thanks to Moore that Austin had got his directorial break. He had started in the business as a stuntman out in Hollywood, working on classics like *North by Northwest*. Often Austin would chat with Hitchcock between set-ups, having discovered they shared a common bond; both were Londoners. 'One day I was sitting in the lobby of the Plaza in New York, and Hitchcock was shooting a scene with Cary Grant. We were waiting for the lighting and Hitchcock said to me, "What do you want to do, Ray? You're not going to stay in the stunt business all your life, are you?" And I said, "I want my name on the back of the chair, like you." He smiled and said, "If you want it bad enough, I guess you'll get it."'

But Austin had no idea how he could ever hope to achieve his lofty ambition, and remained for years as a stuntman, earning a reputation as one of the best in the business. It was while working on *The Avengers* as stunt co-ordinator that he got the chance to shoot action scenes with the second unit. Then came his big breakthrough. 'Every time I got a job on *The Saint*, it was to say two lines and then be thrown down the stairs, or four lines and then be beaten up by Roger. But it was a lot of fun. When I'd accomplished three or four good second units, I went to Bob Baker and asked if I could shoot a whole *Saint* episode. And he said, "I'll talk to Roger." And I saw Roger that lunchtime in the restaurant, and he said, "I hear you're coming to direct one of our shows." And I couldn't believe it. I'd got my first whole episode. And everybody was absolutely super to me. And that was it, from that moment on it snowballed, and I was going around that studio like a house on fire, directing *The Saint*, an *Avengers*, *Randall and Hopkirk*, diving backwards and forwards between all these shows.'

Other directors who worked on the series included Leslie Norman, James Hill, Freddie Francis and Roy Ward Baker, who came to *The Saint* with twenty years experience, having served an apprenticeship at Gainsborough Pictures and worked for

Hitchcock. 'The guiding principle was entertainment,' he asserts. 'And none the worse for that. The key to it all was that everything had to be really well organised. It didn't have to be strictly disciplined, although everybody was. Nobody messed about or was self-indulgent. But the successful element of that show was Berman and Bob Baker's handling of the whole thing from the stories onwards. They knew exactly how to handle the material. By the time I got there they'd already done several *Saints*, so I stepped into a fully running machine. And the quality of the production was excellent. Any of the episodes you see now are certainly very well presented, much better than most of the shows on today. And the longevity of these things is unbelievable. And that's because they were done properly. There was no suggestion of, oh this is just a cheapo job, forget it. I dare say a few people did take that attitude, but it was never allowed to show on the screen. For me, it was like making a mini-film. There was no difference as far as I was concerned. I was just making a 52-minute picture.' Roy Ward Baker went on to direct an impressive seventeen *Saint* episodes.

Filming on the *Saint* rarely strayed further than the confines of the studio, or nearby villages like Cookham and Denham. This proved a little tricky, as many of the adventures took place in locations such as South America, Haiti or Athens. Filming in such countries was obviously out of the question due to budgetary constraints, so library footage was intercut with pseudo-realistic studio reproductions. *The Saint* became infamous for sticking a potted plant in a studio and calling it Barbados, or having our hero standing outside a cafe set with accordion music playing, so obviously it's Paris. To some extent that's part of the charm of these shows; they create their own atmosphere, their own world. 'I remember once, we were doing an exterior scene which was meant to be the South of France or somewhere,' recalls Roy Ward Baker. 'And I said to Monty, "I'm not sure we can shoot this. It's raining." And he said, "So it never rains in France?" Which was true. He was perfectly right.'

Car interiors were also shot in the studio, using a big revolving drum with trees, hedges and bushes painted on it to reproduce the effect of scenery flashing past the window. William Gaunt, who later achieved fame in *The Champions*, recalls one incident involving the famous drum on his *Saint* episode: 'There was a scene which I saw in rushes, it was just the funniest gag. Roger gets out of the car and this other actor is at the wheel, doing his best driving acting with the drum going round. And suddenly, what appeared to be Roger was running alongside the car, in fact he was just running on the spot, and he shouts, "My cock is caught in the door!" It looked absolutely so funny.' Monty Berman didn't think so, and wanted to charge Moore for the wasted footage. 'There are lots and lots of stories like that about Roger,' Gaunt continues. 'He was just such a wonderful practical joker. A wonderful schoolboy's humour, very sixth form, but a wonderful character. He was so generous to everybody and everybody just loved him. He set the tone really for those series, for the making of them.'

As star of the show, Moore took it upon himself to make sure everyone working on the set felt at home, from the most experienced actors to the lowliest member of the crew. 'When he had new people on a show each week, he would always go round and introduce himself,' says Raymond Austin. 'I mean, you know who he is when he comes on the set, he's Roger Moore, but he'd come over in the morning and say, "Hi, I'm Roger, how are you, thanks for coming and doing the show." And he always talked to extras and knew many of the extras' names, where other stars would walk straight by them. Also, Roger was never in a bad mood, no matter what may have been going on at home, he never brought it to work, or he never seemed to.'

Although Moore went on to direct a few episodes, generally he didn't have much creative input. If he didn't like a certain line he'd simply change it himself there and then on camera. Nor did his portrayal of Templar change drastically as the years passed. 'Roger played himself, basically,' explains Roy Ward Baker. 'Whenever you watch Roger, when he's himself he's very good, when he tries to act as someone different, it's not very good. That's the definition of a true movie star. James Cagney was always James Cagney. Gary Cooper was always Gary Cooper. Once you took them out of character it didn't work. Roger played Roger, his character happened to be the Saint.'

Such was the pressure of churning out show after show that, at times, the cast and crew could be forgiven for thinking they were working at an assembly plant, at the mercy of a monster that had to be constantly fed. 'You would do thirteen episodes and break for a few weeks and then do another thirteen. It was almost continuous,' recalls Bob Baker. 'The only reason you had a break was eventually you ran out of scripts. The big problem was getting the scripts finished in time. We'd do a show every two weeks, but you don't write a script in two weeks. You've got to do an outline, then a treatment, then a first script, which gets rewritten, you do the final script and when that's done the story editor will go through it again and alter things, adjust the characters and so on. So an average *Saint* script took about six weeks. If you're getting through them at the rate of two weeks, sooner or later you're going to run out. I remember the very last episode of one series, we were writing the script and sending it down to the floor whilst they were filming it. That was right at the very end; it finally caught up with us.'

Some scripts would also be rehashed or, as was the case in at least one instance, recycled verbatim in another ITC series, as Robert Tronson testifies: 'I was directing an episode of *The Baron* and one day Roger Moore, who was on the next stage doing *The Saint*, wandered onto our set and idly took up the script and said, "What's all this about then?" And his face changed as he flicked page after page. "Christ," he said, "we did this as a *Saint*." And they'd only bothered to cross out Saint and put in Baron, but the names of the lesser characters were the same, everything was identical. He tore up to Bob Baker and Monty Berman's office and was clutching at their lapels and shaking them. But nothing could be done, it was in the can. And on one station, I think in Canada, the two went out on the same evening. There was a lot of trouble about it.'

This haphazard and disrespectful approach to scripts was to become *de rigeur* for ITC and Mr. Tronson. After directing various shows, from *The Saint* to *The Baron* (a sort of diet-Simon Templar featuring the American actor Steve Forrest), Tronson finally said he wouldn't do any more because he'd become so pissed off with the poor standard of material. Then he received an emergency call from Monty Berman: 'Please can you do this *Baron* episode?' Naturally flattered, Tronson agreed. 'But I won't do it unless I see the script.' Not an unreasonable request. 'And this rather small envelope arrived and there was not a lot of script in it,' Tronson recalls. 'It amounted to two acts out of three. So I kept ringing, trying to find somebody, but nobody was there. So I went down to the studio and tracked Dennis Spooner and Terry Nation to an office, where they sort of cringed; they were constantly being persecuted.' Tronson confronted the two writers. 'What's this?' he asked. 'This script's not finished,' came the reply. After much heated discussion, Spooner and Nation eventually confessed all. They'd been instructed that the shooting of their episode had to begin on whatever set was left standing on the studio stage, from the previous week. Both reached the conclusion that it was best not to complete their script, so they could insert a new scene in whatever the set turned out to be. 'They were as bamboozled as I was,' explains Tronson. 'Well, the set left standing was a jungle. Now, the whole of Dennis and Terry's script had been set in Paris. So these two geniuses went, right, got it, we'll set it in a disused botanical garden. It was hysterical.'

Another plus in the casting of Moore as the Saint was he looked utterly convincing in his action scenes. Moore's television experiences in Hollywood had taught him the technicalities of screen fighting. 'I would look at a stunt and see how much of it I could do myself. Invariably, I would do the fights myself because it would save time and I'd work with stunt doubles, because they know what they're doing, whereas if you work sometimes with actors they miss punches. I remember doing an episode with Tony Wright, who'd been a boxer, and he laid me out, knocked me straight across the set.' *Saint* fight scenes were as destructive as they were popular with audiences. In the first season alone, some £8,000 worth of studio props were destroyed.

One famous episode, 'The Man Who Liked Lions', also saw Moore come a cropper in an action sequence, opposite guest star Peter Wyngarde, who fondly recalls, 'At the end of the episode I have a sword duel with Roger and I was a very good swordsman, but I got the stunt guys together and said, "Let's have a game with Roger. I'm going to pretend I can't fence." It was outrageous of me. So we went through the moves and I said, "Roger, you're hitting very hard. Have you got to hit that hard?" And I saw the look on his face, he was thinking, "I've got a real one here." And when we came to do the actual shot I let him have it. And the whole idea was that I should fall into this lion's pit, but when we did the take I got him right into the hole and he kept saying, "You're supposed to fall in here. I'm not supposed to be in here." He was great fun, Roger. An awfully nice man.'

To keep their star in trim, ITC built a fully equipped gym at the studio where Moore frequently worked out. But when it came to the more dangerous stunts, Moore was quite happy to leave things to the professionals. 'I was very lucky that I had a wonderful stunt double called Les Crawford, who was pretty good at making me look great. I remember once, Les had a great idea for a stunt. I was being chased in a warehouse and I would leap onto a ladder that was leaning against some boxes, and go from one set of boxes to the next while still on the top of the ladder. I said, "Les, I think the ladder's going to spring back." And he said, "No, no, I'll show you." And he did it. And of course the ladder sprang back and smashed him right in the face, broke his nose, split his lip, blacked his eyes. He went off to the first aid room and came back with bandages all over his head. I said, "Les, you might as well go home because there's nothing you can do." And the minute he walked out of the studio I called his wife, and I said, "Now look, if I catch Les doing what he was doing today again, what I did to him now is nothing." And she screamed, "What the hell have you done to him?"'

To round off Simon Templar's character, the makers had to give him the right car. Initially they approached Jaguar, thinking their E-Type model – which had been launched the previous year – would make for the ideal *Saint* vehicle. This was a wonderful opportunity, so went Baker's pitch, to get free advertising for this new British sports car in a weekly television series. The answer was no. Jaguar insisted that they didn't need the publicity. Next, the producers went to Swedish company Volvo, who also had a trendy new sports car out, the P1800 Coupe. Volvo quickly latched onto the marketing potential. But there was a problem, they didn't actually have a white car (the colour had to be saintly white) in Britain at the time, so one had to be flown in from Stockholm at a week's notice. Moore loved the car so much he actually bought it, resulting in Volvo having to hurriedly supply an identical replacement.

The Saint debuted on ITV in September 1962, just a week before the world premiere of the first James Bond film, *Dr. No*. The sixties had truly begun. It was given the primetime slot of 7.25 pm on a Sunday night – right before the channel's showpiece programme, *Sunday Night at the London Palladium*. With its heady mix of thrills and glamour aimed at popular tastes, *The Saint* was an instant hit. 'The episodes were being shown at the same time we were making them,' says Baker. 'So the crew would come on the set and discuss the previous night's episode. It built an enthusiasm within the crew, they could see their work whilst they were actually doing it.'

By the New Year, *The Saint* had made its way to the top of the ratings – beating stiff opposition from *Perry Mason* over on BBC. Charteris lamented the fact that viewers had to choose between two crime dramas, and in 1965 wrote about his hope that one day someone would invent a device able to tape and play back programmes at the viewer's convenience.

Press reaction to the opening episode was largely favourable. Dennis Potter, writing for *The Daily Herald* and a self-confessed fan of the books, called it, 'A delightfully sleek and promising series. Roger Moore played the Saint with just the right well-tailored dash.' *The Daily Mirror* was similarly impressed. 'Roger Moore made a big impact in the first of ITV's new *Saint* series. He had the right touch of charm and devil-may-care approach. In the past, Mr Moore has never quite made it as a TV hero. This series should put him right at the top.' Prophetic words indeed.

No one, least of all Moore, sensed how big *The Saint* would become. Believing it might last six months at best, it was to take up seven years of his life, turning him into one of the most famous faces on earth and a very rich man – the first British actor to become a millionaire through television. Few actors' careers have been so spectacularly transformed by a single role. As the series grew in popularity, fans often showed up at the studio or on location, hoping to catch sight of their idol. 'I remember when we were on location in Malta,' recalls Baker. 'We had to sneak Roger in through the back door of our hotel because there were mobs outside.'

The Saint became a global phenomenon, sold eventually to 63 countries – including several Eastern Bloc nations. Italy was amongst the last to take the series, after holding out due to one episode ('The Latin Touch') which portrayed the Rome chief of police as a secret Mafia member. 'We felt the series was going to take off,' posits Baker. 'We used to get some snide television critics calling Lew Grade's material "low Grade" and things like that. If you're a television critic, you're right at the bottom of the list of critics because you're a critic after the event, so therefore you have no power to persuade an audience – unless you were foolish enough to show these critics an episode before they were actually transmitted.'

For Roger Moore, fame meant instant public recognition. He was assailed by fans haranguing him on street corners, yelling, 'Where's your halo?' It could have been a lot worse. 'There was a guy who came all the way over from Spain to see me,' recounts Moore. 'And he really believed that I was Simon Templar and a detective and that I could plant evidence on his wife, who he believed was having a lesbian affair. He took a great deal of persuasion to get rid of.'

Left: *in some European territories, the two-part episode 'Vendetta for The Saint' was given a theatrical release.* Right: *the success of the series meant that Moore graced the covers of magazines across the globe – this one is from Portugal.*

Buoyed by *The Saint*'s UK success, Grade flew to New York in 1963 in a bid to sell the show to one of the networks, taking with him two of the strongest episodes. Mort Wener, Vice Chairman of NBC, made a special trip into his office on a Saturday to speak with Grade and to watch the samples. The lights dimmed in the viewing theatre and the first episode was watched in stony silence. The second had barely started before Wener, who could suffer no more, turned to Grade and announced, 'I have never seen so much crap in all my life.'

Undeterred, Grade tried ABC and CBS but both found the show 'too English' and 'too old fashioned'. So Grade had no choice but to deal directly with local TV stations and sell the show for syndication, where it might easily be lost in the schedules at weird hours, or find itself with no regular time slot. But something quite astonishing happened next. Despite these irregular airings outside of primetime, *The Saint* attracted a dedicated cult following. *The New York Times*, no less, rated it higher than the lacklustre dross then being served up by the main networks, mainly comprised of tired private eye shows. 'Then NBC were having trouble at ten o'clock at night, after primetime,' Baker recalls. 'CBS was showing a movie, and whatever NBC put up against them they got beaten. So someone suggested, why not put in this English show that *The New York Times* says is good? They tried it and the first week it beat the movie. And six consecutive weeks it beat the movie every time. Then they tried it out in some of their other stations and exactly the same pattern happened.'

Impressed, NBC wanted more episodes – this time in colour. 'So *The Saint* sort of sold backwards,' observes Moore. 'Normally a show is on network and then it's sold into syndication. *The Saint* started off in syndication and, for the first time ever, a show in syndication was then taken as a network show.'

Now a hit in America, where no new shows were being produced in black and white, Grade made a killer deal with NBC for colour *Saint*s. Having virtually exhausted all the Charteris stories that lent themselves to TV adaptation, renegotiations took place with the author to allow the creation of all new stories. Permission was granted, although, once again, scripts were submitted for Charteris to offer suggestions and criticism. Bob Baker, however, retained final say. Essentially, Charteris became a consultant to the show, and a very highly paid one. Sometimes his views were taken on board, other times not. When they weren't he'd let Baker know in his now infamous memos, such as this one from 1966: 'I note that my constructive suggestions were stolidly ignored, leaving me with a dream-like feeling that the memo might as well have been addressed to Santa Claus at the North Pole.'

After producing some 71 black and white episodes, work got underway on the colour *Saint*s in September 1966. By this time, Baker and his partner Monty Berman had gone their separate ways. 'We parted amicably,' explains Baker. 'We had just started doing *The Baron* together when the colour *Saint*s started, and so I pulled out and gave Monty totally *The Baron*, while I went into the colour *Saint*s with Roger. Actually Roger and Monty Berman didn't get on very well together, and Roger was not anxious to have Monty involved anymore with *The Saint*.' Berman went on to produce ITC classics *Department S*, *The Champions* and *Randall and Hopkirk (Deceased)*. Baker continued his association with Moore, forming a company together. Moore's promotion to a working partner acknowledged his invaluable contribution to the series. 'Roger lived just round the corner to me so we used to see a lot of each other,' remembers Baker. 'We used to spend most of our time in each other's houses. We became very good friends until he left the area and started doing Bond. But he kept in touch. Whenever he's in town he usually gives me a ring and we have a chat.'

More money was lavished on the colour episodes to make them suitable for US network consumption. The team even began travelling outside the country, with location filming in several European cities. The character was also updated in keeping with the swinging sixties, with stories tackling previously unexplored territory like drugs, hippies, private armies, pop radio stations and a community of homicidal students. These later episodes edged closer to fantasy, a natural progression perhaps, or a conscious attempt to widen the show's horizons and keep pace with the escapism pioneered by rivals like *The Avengers* and *The Man from UNCLE*. Charteris himself wasn't averse to including supernatural elements in his books, resulting in stories that dealt with voodoo and the likelihood of the existence of the Loch Ness monster. But 'The House on Dragon Rock' takes the biscuit with its tale of mad scientists and giant ants. This episode fell foul of censors and was removed from the schedules – shown at a later date and time, when a warning was given in TV listings magazines that it was unsuitable for children and may upset people of a nervous disposition. Today, it's more likely to produce guffaws than chills.

Most lead actors appearing in long running series tend to gravitate towards directing the odd episode, if only to relieve the sheer monotony. But for Moore, it was a long-held ambition. 'I always wanted to direct. And I figured it shouldn't be very difficult for me, because I would tell the story from Simon Templar's point of view. Which meant that I could set up a master shot, make the camera come in over my shoulder, and then I was out of shot and could just concentrate on directing. Then at the end of the day I would do all my close-ups. I didn't need the other actors there.'

One of several episodes that Moore directed was 'Invitation to Danger', which featured Shirley Eaton making her third and final *Saint* appearance. 'Roger was a very good director, very understanding. Often actors who turn directors are understanding because they just know what it's like the other side of the camera, more than people who have just directed.'

Moore went on to direct episodes of *The Persuaders*, but, interestingly, never pursued a directorial career after that. 'I was offered a few features, but the problem is that so much time has to be taken up, in preparation and then post-production, that you have to take a year out of your life. And when I was offered projects there was always this little catch that they wanted me to be in it. If I was going to direct a feature, I didn't want the responsibility of directing myself badly.'

In all, 118 episodes of *The Saint* were made. Quite an achievement. No other British series shot on film can match it. Though grateful for the enormous success it brought him, Moore inevitably grew tired of playing the same character. So despite the fact that the series was still enormously popular, it was by mutual agreement that it finally come to a close. 'Maybe I was asking too much money, maybe the shows were getting too expensive,' muses Moore. 'I don't think anybody queried as to why we stopped. I think we all felt we'd gone on long enough.' When production closed down, the first thing Moore did was have his hair cut, removing the old-fashioned quiff that had been Simon Templar's trademark.

On a world-wide sales basis, *The Saint* stands as one of the most profitable television shows of all time. It was a success in much the same way as Bond was, it was fast moving, tightly plotted and good looking. And as the producers had a choice of some 100 Charteris stories to base their episodes on, there was little danger of the series becoming predictable or stale. Though basically a crime series, every avenue of the genre was explored – from normal crime busting to romantic thrillers, from whodunnits to the occasional fantasy edition.

Each episode celebrated a masculine fantasy of luxury and laid-back cool and usually began the same way, with our hero recognised by some hapless damsel in distress, gasping, 'So you're the famous Simon Templar.' That provided Moore with his cue to turn smugly to the camera and, with a wry smile and a cock of an eyebrow, acknowledge the appearance of a white animated halo above his head, as Edwin Astley's legendary theme music kicks in and the credits roll. It's an immortal opening. 'I wanted to make *The Saint* different from other straight heroes,' says Baker. 'So we had him address camera in each episode. So we took it out of reality and put it into a fantasyland, and that worked beautifully for the character. The stories were real, but the Saint played it as if it was a fairy story for adults.'

4
THUNDERBIRD
4

Chapter 4

Puppet Master

- Supercar - Fireball XL5 - Stingray - Thunderbirds -
Captain Scarlet and the Mysterons - Joe 90 -

Gerry and Sylvia Anderson were undoubtedly the greatest husband and wife team the world of television has ever known. Their classic puppet shows have been enjoyed by generations of children and adults alike. Ironically, though, for a man described by *The New Statesman* in 1985 as 'Probably the nearest Britain has ever come to producing a children's myth maker on the level of Walt Disney,' Gerry never wanted to work with puppets. His dream was to make movies, live action movies. The problem was nobody wanted to hire him or his film company, which was spiralling towards bankruptcy. A woman called Roberta Leigh, who had an idea for a children's puppet show called *The Adventures of Twizzle*, saved him. Rather reluctantly, Gerry agreed to deliver 52 fifteen-minute episodes. 'When I learned that we were going to make a puppet series, because we had to in order to pay the rent, I was horrified. I'd never seen a puppet in my life, and when I did I was shocked and I hated them. They were being operated on thick carpet thread, and the puppeteer was standing behind a piece of hardboard with the scene painted on it, and the shadows of the puppet all over the background. It was just a nightmare and I developed a hatred for puppets.'

Originally, Sylvia had joined the company as a girl Friday after answering an ad in a local paper. 'They only wanted me part-time, to keep the company in order, to man the phones, work out the petty cash, but then bit by bit I got more and more involved. We had no money, we existed from hand to mouth, and so all the staff ended up pitching in. And that's how it all started. It was a wonderful training ground. I did voice-overs, worked on the scripts, handled continuity and Gerry directed. We were quite self-sufficient.'

The Adventures of Twizzle turned out to be a rather crudely made puppet show. The models were fairly primitive in design, with wooden bodies, papier-maché heads and thick operating strings. It began on ITV in November 1957. Delighted with its reception, Roberta Leigh commissioned another puppet series, *Torchy the Battery Boy*. 'But after that,' Sylvia recalls. 'We thought, wait a minute, we can do this but we can do it better. Because we'd been actively writing stuff ourselves.' So the Andersons came up with their own show – *Four Feather Falls*, which got backing from Granada; an association that was short-lived, to say the least. 'All I remember about Granada,' says Gerry, 'is that I delivered the last episode to them and they paid for it and I haven't heard from them again to this day.'

Set in the Wild West, *Four Feather Falls* featured the adventures of Sheriff Tex Tucker, voiced by Nicholas Parsons (other voices were provided by *Carry On* actor Kenneth Connor), and his faithful companions Dusty the dog and Rocky the horse. As always, the biggest headache was getting the puppets to walk convincingly. In

Thunderbirds *are go! Two of the classic Thunderbird machines in action.*

Four Feather Falls, Gerry tried to disguise it by providing a horse for his cowboy characters to ride, only the horse proved just as difficult to move as the human puppets. Then the perfect solution was found. 'Little by little, we were getting the puppets to do most things that we wanted them to do, but the one thing we couldn't get them to do, and it looked as if we would never be able to conquer the problem, we couldn't get them to walk. So I came up with the idea that if we made a series using a special car, we could get a lot of action and movement without the puppets actually walking. That's the reason we made *Supercar*.'

***SUPERCAR** (1960-62)*

The idea to feature a space age car as the hero of a TV series was an ingenious one, but securing backing proved difficult. With mounting bills to pay, the Andersons were facing catastrophe. 'We'd taken a lease on a big new studio and mortgaged ourselves to the hilt on new equipment to make *Four Feather Falls*,' recalls Sylvia. 'It was a bit naïve of us really, on the strength of just one contract, but we thought we'd really arrived. Then Granada turned round and said, thank you very much but we don't want any more shows from you, we'll just keep repeating *Four Feather Falls*. So we were about to go out of business. I rang a production manager we all knew called Frank Sherwin Green and said, "We all need jobs." He came over, and we sat round this empty studio. He said he'd introduce us to Lew Grade. Well, we'd never heard of Lew Grade at all. So a meeting was arranged. Lew saw *Four Feather Falls* and said, "What have you got next?" And I'd just written a children's book called *Supercar*, so we rushed to get the manuscript and he said, "Go ahead and make it."'

That meeting would assure the Andersons' future, and provide the kind of financial security and creative freedom that is rare in television. But it wasn't quite as straightforward as Sylvia makes it sound. Lew was never less than the shrewdest of operators and unwilling to spend more money than was absolutely necessary. When the Andersons pitched *Supercar*, he wanted to know exactly how much it was going to cost. 'And when I told him,' remembers Gerry, 'he literally exploded and said, "I can't spend that sort of money on a children's show, it's ridiculous. I'll tell you what, go back to your studio, come back here half past seven tomorrow morning and tell me you've cut the budget in half, and I'll give you a contract for 26." Well, we couldn't cut it in half, and I came back the next morning in tears and I said, "We just can't do it." And he said, "OK," and gave us the contract for 26. And that's how *Supercar* was born.'

Supercar was the brainchild of Professor Popkiss, the archetypical doddery professor with white hair, thick wire-rimmed glasses and cod-European accent, and Dr. Beaker, an occasionally absent-minded technical genius who spends the series dreaming up new hi-tech gizmos for Supercar – the precursor to *Thunderbirds*' Brains. The incredibly courageous Mike Mercury was Supercar's pilot. Tall, blue-eyed and firm of jaw, he was the first of the classic Anderson heroes – in his wake followed Troy Tempest, Captain Scarlet, et al. 'My shows are all based on very simple formats really,' explains Gerry. 'Good guy versus bad guy and bad guy loses. Mike Mercury was one of the early characters. I wouldn't say that he was going to win an Oscar for the sculptor. But we had very little money and we were shooting very fast and we did our best to create a hero figure.'

Completing the Supercar team was a young boy called Jimmy (voiced by Sylvia Anderson) and his pet monkey Mitch, both rescued by Mercury when they were spotted adrift on a raft in the ocean after a plane crash. Together, they encounter a host of baddies, from gangsters and international spies to mad scientists. But the show's central villain is a character called Masterspy, who resembles rotund forties Hollywood cad Sydney Greenstreet, and was aided by creepy assistant Zarrin. This evil duo were more comedic than formidable, as their incompetent plans to steal the secrets of Supercar for their own nefarious ends were thwarted at every turn.

Located at a secret research station in the Nevada Desert, Supercar – in the words of the title song – 'travels on land or roams the sky, through the heaven's stormy rage. It's Mercury-manned and everyone cries it's the marvel of the age – Supercar!' Plot lines ranged from crime thrillers to daring rescue missions and comic adventures that took the team to Europe, the Middle East, the jungles of South America, even the frozen wastes of the Arctic. *Supercar* was the first of the Anderson shows to introduce technology and to use it in a way that benefited mankind – such as the episode where Supercar rescues scientists trapped in an undersea lab, a plot reminiscent of subsequent *Thunderbirds* rescue missions. Other episodes had the team tracking down a gang who have planted atomic bombs across the United States, or a canister of experimental rocket fuel tested in the outer atmosphere that fails to self-destruct, and must be shot down by Mercury before it falls to earth. (Shades here of the climax to *Moonraker*, where Bond in his space shuttle must destroy poisonous globes before they enter earth's atmosphere.) There were also some bizarre episodes, such as a mad professor's plan to miniaturise everyone and take over America.

The series entered production in September 1960, at the Andersons' brand new studios in Slough. 'Our first three productions were made in a mansion on the river Thames where we used to film in the ballroom,' reveals Gerry. 'When we got the deal from Lew Grade to make *Supercar*, I wouldn't say it was a huge increase in budget, but we did have more money, and we moved to the Slough trading estate and took over a small factory. We all worked together to build the studio. We formed the offices out of wood and hardboard. I had a little office with no windows in it. I had a little fan at the top because I was a very heavy smoker. We also had a control room rather like a television studio. I used to sit in there, quite high up, and talk to the puppeteers over a PA system.'

The amount of collaborative effort that went into making these shows was truly inspirational. 'Right from the beginning I was the major shareholder and chairman of the company,' says Gerry. 'And the main creativity came from me. I invented the shows and I steered the shows. And I controlled the shows. Now, having said that, I had some wonderful support. Reg Hill was a very talented man, wonderful storyboard artist, and a wonderful engineer. John Read was really the guy who lit the shows. And whatever we were doing, the fact is that we used to roll up our sleeves and sweep the studio and clean the toilets and everything else. It was a real collaborative effort in every sense of the word.'

It was a production team of technicians, artists and model makers who'd remain with the Andersons for the rest of the decade. A superb collection of incredibly talented people who by design, or sheer luck, all arrived at the right time and place, and together went on to make television history. Newcomers on *Supercar* included directors like Alan Patillo and Desmond Saunders, while Bob Bell came in to assist Reg Hill in the art department. The biggest recurring problem faced by Bell was the

Supercar *was the first of Gerry Anderson's futuristic puppet shows.*

incredible attention to detail required on even the smallest elements of the series. Whereas on live action shows you merely hired the props you needed, here everything from furniture to clothes had to be made from scratch. Among the three puppeteers hired to work on the series was Christine Glanville, who eventually assumed the role of chief puppeteer on later shows. 'We worked very hard,' explains Sylvia. 'We had people in from the local art college and we were working with puppeteers who'd never done anything like this before. But it was all a lot of fun.'

Stuck with making puppet shows, Gerry was determined to make them look as realistic as possible and brought in innovation after innovation. 'The thing about *Supercar* was that we had been experimenting with putting the puppeteers on a bridge over the stage, so their legs wouldn't get in the frame. The reason for the stage, which was about eighteen inches high, was for the camera to be low enough to get low angle shots on the puppets. The problem with the overhead bridge was that the puppeteers were looking down on the characters and they couldn't see their faces. So when I used to say, "Get Fred to turn to George when he says that line," the puppet would turn and walk and go straight past the eye line and talk into fresh air. And we came up with the idea of using a cine-camera, so that the puppeteers could see their puppets on the television screen as the camera filmed. I claim to be the inventor of video assist, which is used all over the world now. The pictures were terrifyingly poor quality, but it did the job.'

As the series developed, Anderson employed a wider and bolder range of film techniques, not least in the use of special effects. 'We had an assistant, a very bright boy called Derek Meddings,' Gerry remembers. 'He used to come over in the evenings when we were making the first three shows, painting the backdrops. And then on *Supercar*, we took him onto our payroll. We had a sequence where Dr. Beaker was playing a piano, it was a very strident piece and he's getting carried away, and at a given point he hit the keys and the piano fell apart. Derek said to me, "I've got an idea, Gerry." I said, "What's that?" He said, "Why don't we blow the piano up?" I said, "How do we do that?" He said, "Don't worry, I'll do it. I'll buy some fireworks and I'll use the black powder." I said, "Are you sure nobody will get hurt?" He said, "No, it'll be all right." So we prepared it and then the music started, and when Beaker put his hands down, Derek detonated the charge and the piano went up in flames in a bloody great bang. It was a wonderful shot and I said to Derek, "I think we'd better start a special effects department."' Meddings went on to supervise the effects on many of the Andersons' future shows, before making his name on the Bond films and winning an Oscar for *Superman*. He died in 1995 after working on the miniature effects for *GoldenEye*.

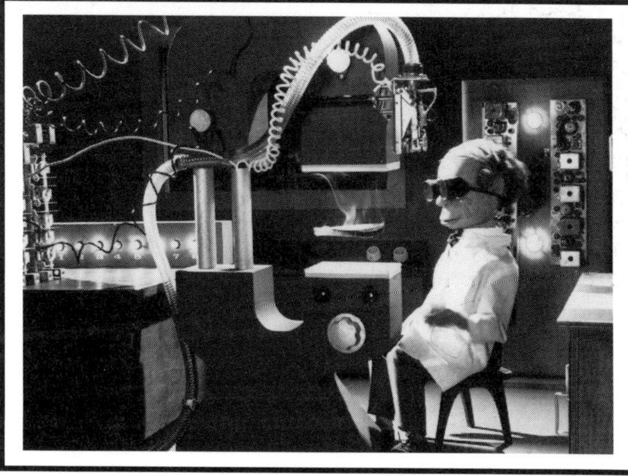

Top: *these crudely caricatured models are a million miles away from the brilliant puppet creations of* Thunderbirds *and* Captain Scarlet. Bottom: *hi-tech gizmos and barmy inventions were very much a feature of* Supercar.

Supercar was the first of the hi-tech craft that proliferated in the Anderson universe, vehicles that became almost characters in themselves. Powered by rocket engines, Supercar could reach speeds in excess of mach one in flight. To aid navigation it was fitted with a video map system, four decades before such technology was introduced into the cars of today. Supercar could also be flown by remote control, and came complete with a range of additional devices including an ultrasonic gun,

Jimmy (voiced by Sylvia Anderson) offers his pet monkey Mitch a banana.

a high powered drill and a clear-view system linked to its forward video camera, which enabled the pilot to see clearly through cloud, fog and smoke. It also had a periscope which was brought into use when underwater. Added to all this was a magnetic grab, that in one episode lifts Masterspy's car off the road, dumping it on top of a television transmitter mast. (Shades here of *You Only Live Twice* – when a helicopter lifts an enemy car off the road and drops it in Tokyo bay.) Another pre-Bond gimmick was the use of an ejector seat. 'All the gizmos were not designed right at the very beginning,' reveals Gerry. 'It was just as each story was written another gadget was born; just push a button, something came out.'

The actual design of Supercar was down to Reg Hill, who also personally undertook the construction of a seven-foot mock-up for the lab sequences (at a cost of around $3,000) and a variety of miniatures for the flying shots. For the underwater scenes, Gerry and Derek Meddings employed a technique used later to even greater effect on *Stingray*. This involved suspending the craft above a model seabed and placing a glass tank between the camera lens and the set, creating the illusion that Supercar was zooming gracefully beneath the waves.

The series first aired in January 1961 and was a huge hit, effectively launching the Andersons' unique style of tele-fantasy. It was also the first of the Anderson TV shows to generate significant merchandising, a common enough concept today but relatively unique back then. There was a *Supercar* fan club where members received an I.D. card, a code breaker, magnifying glass and badge, while books on the series regularly sold in excess of 250,000 copies. In America, tie-in items such as cut-out books, dolls, mechanical toys and comics went on sale. It was the beginning of the mass marketing that reached its zenith with *Thunderbirds*, and still thrives today.

In comparison with the Andersons' later series, *Supercar* looks understandably tame and a little infantile today, but there's still much to enjoy thanks to appealing central characters, story lines that gently zip along, and quaint sets ranging from jungles and ancient temples to modern offices and laboratories. Sylvia herself thinks the show has aged comparatively well. 'I did a lecture at the Bournemouth film school and had a compilation tape made up of effects from all the shows. And I said to the students beforehand, "Now look, you can laugh because some of these even I think are funny, but bear in mind it was a long time ago." But they didn't laugh at all. They were so intrigued. And I was forced then to sit and look at it myself and I felt, well, it was the beginning. The puppets were a bit clumsy. But it was just fun and charming. And it was something different, something original that's never really been copied. If you tried to make it today it would all be computerised.'

Although much mileage remained in the *Supercar* format, it was decided to create a brand new series after production ended on its second season in December 1961. Techniques that Gerry and his team had developed would be improved upon and put to more dramatic use on their next project – *Fireball XL5*.

FIREBALL XL5 (1962)

After the success of *Supercar*, it was only natural that the Andersons would take the concept one step forward and go into space itself; at a time when space travel was still in its infancy. 'We weren't very heavily involved in the UK with science fiction,' explains Sylvia. 'So I think, after *Supercar*, we were looking for subject matter which we couldn't afford to do with live actors and all the effects involved. So we were picking subjects that we could easily do in miniature scale.'

According to Gerry, the choice of science fiction really had more to do with the limitations of the puppets themselves than any genuine love for the genre. 'Because we had characters who couldn't stand properly without their knees sagging, and characters who had no expression, it was very difficult to play a love scene and impossible to have a fight. And so it seemed the way to go was anything that was fast moving and had a lot of excitement, so it seemed that science fiction was the best option. When *Supercar* went on air, friends of mine in the industry, when they met me, said, "Oh hi Gerry. I see you're in science fiction now." And I remember thinking, am I? So it wasn't a conscious move at all.'

The idea for *Fireball XL5* was conceived as production wound down on *Supercar*. 'After its success Lew said, "We'd like you to make another series,"' Gerry recalls. 'I'd hoped he would say that as I'd prepared *Fireball XL5*. And this time it was more expensive than *Supercar*. And we got the same old business from Lew of, "Oh it's too much," and all the rest of it, but he said it a bit tongue-in-cheek this time. And in the end he said, "OK, fine." So we had a better budget.'

Set in the year 2067, *Fireball XL5* centres on the adventures of Colonel Steve Zodiac and his crew of space explorers. The story lines were more advanced than *Supercar*, genuinely exciting and fast moving, though you still had the occasionally bonkers episode like '1875', in which the crew are accidentally sent back in time to a Western town and Zodiac becomes the sheriff. Supporting Steve Zodiac, Fireball's handsome, tough, heroic and fearless commander, is Venus, the beautiful medical expert, Matthew 'Matt' Matic, the standard scientific boffin, Zoonie, Venus' space pet, and Commander Zero, who's in charge of Space City, the futuristic earth base from which Fireball is launched.

One of the more interesting characters was Robert the Robot, Zodiac's co-pilot, who was voiced by Gerry Anderson himself. Gerry's search for a suitably robotic-sounding voice took him to Edinburgh University, where they'd designed a vibrator pack for people who'd had their larynx removed because of cancer. The idea was that you put it under the chin, switched it on and it produced a vibrating noise that, when you spoke, would modulate it into something like normal speech. 'Today of course, you'd just press a button on a computer which reads robot,' observes Gerry.

Robert the Robot was the only character voice Gerry ever attempted, being inherently shy and possessing not an ounce of thespian ambition. This was in complete contrast to Sylvia, who lent her voice to numerous characters, including *Fireball*'s Venus – the first 'leading lady' puppet in an Anderson show. It was puppeteer Christine Glanville's task to construct the face of Venus, but Sylvia couldn't decide on the right type of features. Glanville's Plasticine models would be sculpted, painted and tested, but always rejected. This situation continued for almost five weeks, until Glanville's father astutely suggested his daughter model the face on Sylvia herself. And it was that puppet which got the thumbs up.

Fireball was just one of a fleet of XL vehicles that make up the World Space Patrol, keeping the galaxy safe in the 21st century. This was the first of the Anderson shows to introduce the theme of world organisations. Subsequent series almost always featured some form of uniformed force dedicated to saving the world from various perils. Named after a popular advertisement at the time for a motor oil called Castrol XL (Gerry merely added the 5), Fireball featured all mod cons: a lounge, crew accommodation, a prison and a medical laboratory for Venus, plus a navigation bay. The spacecraft had a detachable nosecone, Fireball Junior, which was also a landing vehicle that allowed the crew to explore alien worlds while the main section of XL5 remained in orbit. 'Fireball Junior was my contribution,' says Gerry. 'Because we were already learning from the various moon landings that one part would go down and one part would stay in orbit. I also came up with the idea of the revolving skyscraper in Space City, which was really just one move on from revolving restaurants.'

Other gizmos included thrust packs, which strap onto a crew member's back, enabling them to manoeuvre in space, and oxygen pills which allowed a person to go into space without the need of a breathing suit. On the surface of planets the crew used jet mobiles, motorcycle-type vehicles which hovered above the ground. An ingenious ruse, as these were merely another device the Andersons employed to overcome the problem of making the puppets walk convincingly.

Scriptwriters for the series included Dennis Spooner, one of the great TV writers. Spooner started out in showbusiness aged eighteen, when he was sent to Egypt as part of his National Service and, in a bid to escape guard duty, volunteered to organise the camp entertainments. After a stint as a stand-up comedian, he turned to writing full-time, providing scripts for the early Honor Blackman *Avengers* as well as *Coronation Street* and Tony Hancock, before commencing his association with Gerry Anderson – who later used him on *Stingray* and *Thunderbirds*. Spooner would also work on numerous ITC shows, as well as *Dr Who*.

Another recent recruit to the Anderson team was composer Barry Gray, whose distinctive military style themes became something of a trademark. His *Thunderbirds* theme, for example, is one of the most instantly recognisable in television history. People like Gray and all those working behind the scenes fitted easily into the Andersons' creative machine, becoming vital cogs that helped churn out product of the highest quality at breakneck speed. 'Our shows were conducted

The crew of Fireball XL5, *including Robert the Robot, the only puppet character ever voiced by Gerry Anderson himself.*

almost like a family affair,' says Sylvia. 'We had the same crew and so on, which is nice and it does generate something on the screen, I think, a warmth and a familiarity, and we could do that because we were a small company. It was really a big family atmosphere. We had talented people, and they were young talented people, and we were able to train them in what we were doing because we couldn't bring anyone experienced on board, because nothing like what we were doing had been done before. So that gave us almost a school of film, if you like.'

With demand for more spectacular stories growing, Derek Meddings found himself in charge of a rapidly expanding special effects department. He enlisted the services of a young technician called Brian Johnson, who later worked on *2001: A Space Odyssey* and *Space 1999*. For added realism, miniature rocket-firing devices were used for Fireball's various motors. Sound effects were also specially recorded for the series, using a stationary jet engine at a nearby airfield. Meddings even went so far as to cannibalise household items such as toothpaste caps and old cooker dials, for use in the ship's control section. Watching today, of course, a lot of the model shots look seriously dodgy, but in good old black and white they're almost convincing – especially when one considers how old these shows are, and the limited technology available then. 'Derek was such an important part of the success of those shows,' asserts Sylvia. 'Actually, if I had to pick any one person out of our team, it would be Derek Meddings.

Sylvia Anderson with her puppet alter ego – Venus.

It was very sad in many ways, because one of the things I think should have happened was that Derek should have been more a part of our company, not just an employee.'

The biggest SFX problem was getting Fireball to lift off. As in George Pal's classic *When Worlds Collide*, Fireball took off horizontally from a long launch pad. 'The effects guys had Fireball on three wires,' Gerry recalls. 'One on each extremity of the tail and one on the nose, and they had a long piece of wood which they'd hold. The rockets would be fired by remote control and then they would run along the gantry above the stage, building up speed, and when it got to the ramp it went up and out of picture. Of course, you try running and keeping your hand steady. They used to rehearse like crazy. It was a hell of a job.'

Fireball XL5 hit British screens in October 1962, and was a worthy ratings successor to *Supercar*. It also had the distinction of being the first, and the last, Anderson series to be networked coast to coast in America. 'It had the most amazing success imaginable,' recalls Gerry. 'At the time British shows were an absolute no-no in America, apart from the fact that they were considered to be lousy, and a lot of them were, to be fair. For any company their dream was to get their series on network, because with network they pay a huge sum of money and then every year for ten years, if they ran it again, the money was doubled and tripled, just a wonderful thing to sell. And Lew got us on NBC.'

Fireball's success also did much to bolster ITC's American profile. 'Lew Grade had opened a subsidiary of ITC in New York,' says Gerry. 'They had very flash offices, a lot of very expensive people working there and they were losing money hand over fist. And Lew decided to close it. And they were about to shut down when they got *Fireball*, and *Fireball* took off and they just couldn't believe it. We went over there to see them and they were all frantically busy typing contracts. So *Fireball XL5* saved them. If it hadn't been for *Fireball* ITC would never have existed, not the American arm.'

Fireball XL5 also sold well around the world, making pots of money which didn't necessarily filter back to the Andersons and their team. 'Back then we were very green,' explains Gerry. 'I knew how to direct, knew how to cut, knew how to dub,

Fireball *was the first, and last, Anderson show to be screened coast to coast on US network TV.*

hadn't got a clue about broadcasting and ratings, audience reactions. All we knew was that we got our money from Lew every week, yippee, and we paid our wages. And we were working hard. We were very ambitious. The deal was that we would get ten per cent of the profit. I'm not criticising Lew Grade here, I loved the guy, but the fact was that we never received any profit. And it may seem odd to you, but we really didn't care, because when we finished *Fireball* Lew bought our company, and in today's money he paid a lot of money. So we became wealthy people overnight. And from then on we'd say, "Can we build a new studio, Lew?" And he'd say, "Yeah, sure – go ahead." "Oh, we need to buy five cameras." He'd say, "Fine." "Lew, I want to go to America." "Don't ask me, just go." It was such a wonderful relationship that it never occurred to us to say, "Where's our profit?" because we were doing so well and being treated so well. I don't think it ever entered our minds.'

Merchandise for *Fireball* was a step up from that tied in to *Supercar*. Items ranged from slippers through to bendy toys, jigsaws, lunch boxes and books. There was also a weekly cartoon in *TV 21* that became one of the comic's longest-running strips, plus a construction kit of the spacecraft itself, sponsored by Lyons Maid ice cream – today a highly prized item among Anderson devotees.

Fireball XL5 established a style that the Andersons refined and improved on with each successive series. In many ways it was the blueprint for *Stingray* and

Thunderbirds. 'A lot of people talk to me and say, "I love *Fireball*,"' says Gerry. 'And I don't understand why. I really wouldn't look at it today, because I would just see bad puppets and strings and shaky craft flying in space when they should be gliding perfectly smoothly. Having said that, if somebody says I enjoyed it, I'm chuffed.'

STINGRAY (1964-65)

After the international success of both *Supercar* and *Fireball XL5*, Lew Grade knew he was on to something very special with Gerry and Sylvia Anderson, and astutely decided to buy them out, lock, stock and barrel. 'I was very proud of our company,' declares Gerry. 'We started it from scratch and here we were making successful shows. I went to see Lew one morning and he just blurted out, "Gerry, I've decided to buy your company." And I thought, "What a bloody cheek – I've decided to buy your company – who is this man?" Not, "Gerry, I'd like to buy your company," or "Gerry, would you like to sell me your company?", no, it was, "I'm going to buy your company!" And I sat there seething. And he said, "You don't look very pleased," and I said, "Well, what sort of money?" And he mentioned this sum and I thought, "That's a bloody good idea."'

Not content to allow the Andersons to sit on their laurels, Grade placed huge pressure on them to come up with ideas even more exciting and commercial than any that had gone before. 'One of the things that maybe one can criticise Lew Grade for was that whenever we came up with a successful show we only did it for a year, and then he wanted a new idea. Which in a way was good for us because it made us think harder,' explains Sylvia. 'So in the middle of what we were producing at the time we were always thinking, "What are we going to do next?"'

Gerry had the answer – and it was to make television history. 'I was always, and still am, anxious to do something different each time. And I thought, "We've done space, we've done flying in earth's atmosphere, we've done a Western, let's go for underwater."' So *Stingray* was born.

Stingray is set in the year 2065, when the surface world is at war with alien races that inhabit the oceans. Chief among these is Titan, a despotic ruler intent on destroying the World Security Patrol, an international organisation set up to preserve global peace, rather like the UN. One of its affiliations is WASP (the World Aquanaut Security Patrol), an ocean police force that patrols the seas. Its most powerful asset is Stingray, a deadly underwater craft. The headquarters of WASP is the aptly named Marineville, located somewhere on the West Coast of North America; its exact location is a closely guarded secret. An entirely self-sufficient community, its most famous feature is that, when under attack, the entire complex is lowered beneath the surface to the safety of an underground emplacement by use of enormous hydraulic support platforms.

'That was my idea,' says Gerry. 'Tremendous compliment to Derek Meddings for making it happen. At the time, the Americans and the Russians were building bloody great intercontinental rockets carrying atomic warheads and these were housed underground. And a lot of them had innocent things like a thatched cottage over the top that would then slide back and the top would open. It was that sort of thing that made me think of it.'

Stingray was populated by some of the most fondly remembered Anderson puppet characters. Chief among them was Troy Tempest, the strikingly handsome hero and skipper of *Stingray*. Gerry reveals how the character's distinctive physical appearance came about. 'We wrote the first script and it went to every department and the sculptors came in and said, "How do you see Troy Tempest?" Well, I had zero education and I don't have a great command of language, and I was stumped, how do I see Troy Tempest? I said, "Well, he's a hero, blue eyes, square jawed." And the sculptors were looking at me like, "This guy's crazy, what's he talking about?" And finally, in total exasperation I said, "You know, something like James Garner." And they said, "Oh right, we know what you mean, OK." Well, they went back and obviously got hold of a film magazine, tore out a page and copied it, or were inspired by it, and then when the series aired people started saying, "That's like James Garner!"'

Helping Tempest aboard Stingray was his co-pilot and best buddy, Phones. Laid-back and cool, he was almost the equal of Tempest in the bravery and resourcefulness-under-pressure stakes. There was also Marina, one of the great Anderson characters and the spitting image of Ursula

Top: *Phones and Troy Tempest take the wheel of Stingray for another ride into danger.* Centre: *the lead characters of* Stingray *at WASP HQ.* Bottom: *poor old Phones never got a look in when it came to Marina's affections.*

Andress. (Perhaps another case of the puppeteers being overly inspired by film magazines.) Rescued by Troy after being captured and made a slave by Titan, Marina is a hybrid, equally at home underwater or on land, but sadly mute. She is, of course, utterly devoted to Troy. 'Marina was very much my creation,' claims Gerry. 'She had to be a very good looking, sexy girl, but not cheap. I was interested that she should have big jugs, because I thought that would be attractive. And also be sensuous and dumb. I thought, what a great idea, it's the perfect woman, all these looks and dumb. Of course you'd never get away with that today. But it worked very well, it made her sympathetic and made men want to help her, me included!'

Aiding Stingray on land was Commander Sam Shore, Marineville's tyrannical boss. Shore is the show's most bizarre character. Entombed in a hover-chair, the result of being crippled in combat, Shore whizzes round the control tower, barking out orders like a demented Dalek. His daughter, Atlanta, is assistant communications officer, part of whose job is to supervise the launch of Stingray. Like her father, she is strong-willed. And like Marina she is also desperately in love with Troy. Poor Phones never gets a look in. Voiced by Lois Maxwell, Atlanta's unrequited love for Troy mirrored her role as Miss Moneypenny in the James Bond films.

Stingray also featured a host of baddies. Titan is the series' sub-Blofeld/Fu Manchu figure, ruler of the undersea kingdom of Titanica, his dreams of dominating the land people constantly thwarted by Tempest. Doing his bidding are an army of slimy green fish people called Aquaphibians. Very stupid, but loyal, they communicate in gurgling noises supplied by a constant looped tape of bubbling water. Titan also employs a surface spy, agent X-2-Zero, to keep up with events at Marineville. This creepy, bug-like individual was obviously modelled on Hollywood villain Peter Lorre.

Despite this plethora of characters, the real star of the show is *Stingray* itself. This atomic powered submersible is arguably Gerry Anderson's most famous hi-tech creation. It was fast, travelling at 600 knots underwater, with a surface cruising speed of 400 knots. Stingray came armed with sixteen Sting Missiles, equal to 1,000 tons of TNT, which could be guided by remote control to their target. The vessel's pressurised hull was able to withstand tremendous underwater pressure, allowing it to submerge to previously unexplored ocean depths. Whenever danger called, Troy and Phones could be in Stingray and launched within minutes. They sat on designated chairs that slid down a pole straight into the submarine, waiting in a flooded pen beneath the Marineville complex. Gerry got the idea because of the way Cold War American and Russian pilots used to sit in their bombers day and night, so if and when they got the call they could be away in seconds.

Selling his company to Lew Grade after *Fireball XL5* enabled Gerry to move to a larger studio, with extra room to allow for the construction of a prop department, several cutting rooms, a scenery building department, a carpenter's shop and a wardrobe department where hundreds of miniature costumes were made. 'It was great,' he remembers. 'We were in this brand new studio with all mod cons. We even had a dirtying down department where new models would come in and be made to look used. For example, if it was an aircraft they would put burn marks on the cowlings and put dirt round the doors where the pilot got in, all these things made the model look more realistic.'

There was definitely a sense that the company was moving in the right direction, and new techniques that were being brought in all the time were heightening the

Stingray, the pride vessel of security agency WASP.

dynamism of what they were producing. 'As each show was made we really streamlined the art,' says Sylvia. 'Each time we made a series we improved slightly. And we all worked together. There was no such thing as finishing at five. Sometimes I'd be at the studio all night working on sets.'

All the underwater scenes central to *Stingray*'s plot were imaginatively filmed using an aquarium made of double-walled, armoured plate glass. The same company responsible for the fish tanks at London Zoo specially constructed these after a disastrous early test. Bob Bell never forgot the day the first tank, made originally of tempered plate glass, was test filled and exploded under pressure, flooding the studio floor.

Originally, Gerry wanted a tank that was the size almost of a living room, with port holes in the side for cameras and people swimming underwater to move the models. 'Reg Hill and John Read came to see me and said, "Look, this is totally impracticable, we have another idea." Their idea was an aquarium measuring eight feet long and four feet high, the distance between the front and back panels being only six inches. Small tropical fish were introduced and vegetable dye was used to make the water appear murky. Rocks, sand and seaweed were placed on the floor, while a light shone through a rotating piece of board with different size holes cut into it, to create the illusion of sunlight reflecting off the surface. Behind the aquarium was a large cyclorama on which Derek Meddings painted a realistic seabed to give the impression of depth of field. 'And then we would fly Stingray through the shot on wires behind the tank,' says Gerry. 'It was a marvellous idea and we made the whole show like that, and Stingray very rarely got wet. The only time it was in the water was when it was on the surface, then it would be on one of our shallow tanks. And also when Marina was swimming, that was done in the same way.' Ironically, in the episode 'Tom Thumb Tempest', Stingray itself is reduced in size and ends up in . . . a fish tank.

There were also improvements with the puppets themselves. *Stingray* was the first of the Anderson shows to make extensive use of multiple heads for one puppet character, enabling a wider range of expressions. Sculptors even used real human hair to give a more lifelike appearance, while a leading optical firm manufactured special glass eyes on which reduced photographs of the iris and pupil could be printed. There were also improvements when it came to the ubiquitous puppetry problem of the wires showing. 'We originally started off with carpet thread, then fine twine. We even experimented with fishing lines,' recalls Gerry. 'Eventually we started to use tungsten wire, which was drawn to 5000th of an inch thickness. The trouble with that was it glinted, so we painted it black, but the paint made it thick again. Then the company that made the wire found a way of turning the wire black photographically. They didn't tell us how they did it, but we finally ended up with very, very fine wires which hopefully people didn't see too much of.'

Besides becoming a memorable fixture of countless childhoods, *Stingray* also made history by being the first British TV series to be filmed entirely in colour, a move precipitated by a trip Gerry and Sylvia made to the States. 'We saw all the network Saturday morning programmes, which was wall-to-wall children's stuff, but it was all in colour and we were just stunned. It was wonderful,' says Sylvia. 'So we came back and said to Lew Grade, "We've got to move into colour." And he was fine with it. He was always receptive to our ideas.' Colour broadcasting had been a regular feature in America for nine years. Britain would have to wait until July 1967 for the official launch of colour TV, leading to the crazy situation of the Andersons having to print separate black and white negatives for the UK screenings (which began in October 1964), while the colour prints all went to America.

The reason why Tempest and the rest of the cast all spoke with American accents was another conscious decision made on the part of the Andersons. By the early sixties, some 60 per cent of their entire world revenue from programmes came from the US. It didn't take an Einstein to work out that their shows needed to be marketable first and foremost to American audiences. It's why Sylvia recruited almost a repertory company of mainly American, Canadian and Australian actors, names like Ray Barrett, Paul Maxwell, Ed Bishop and Shane Rimmer. Sylvia also handled the directorial duties during the many recording sessions, always held over weekends as the actors were invariably working in the theatre or on radio during the week. 'They were fantastic to do,' Sylvia recalls. 'We'd all arrive and each of the actors would talk about what work they'd done the previous week. For instance on *Stingray*, Lois Maxwell would tell us what she'd been up to on the Bond films. So we had a bit of fun first. And then I'd say, "OK, you've all had a little bit of a play, now we've got to get into it." It was like a nursery school if you like. We'd do a read through and somebody might say, "I don't think I can do that line," and we'd have a discussion. Then we'd do a couple of rehearsals and then put it on tape. It was a very enjoyable experience.'

Even today, Gerry expresses his disappointment over *Stingray*'s obvious merits as entertainment. 'I don't really think I was particularly happy with it. The fact that the puppet's faces were made of fibreglass and therefore expressionless. The fact that their mouths weren't always in perfect sync with the dialogue they were speaking. But again, everybody seemed to enjoy it.'

Again, Gerry is being unnecessarily hard on himself – as *Stingray* represents the first truly classic Anderson show. Despite being created more than 40 years ago, it is often repeated and the effects have stood the test of time remarkably well. And yet in spite of its huge success, nothing could have prepared the Andersons or Lew Grade for the phenomenon that would come next.

Aquaphibians, Troy Tempest's underwater nemesis.

THUNDERBIRDS (1965-66)

The inspiration behind this all-time great show came from a radio broadcast that had Gerry hooked for days, as he drove into work nearing the end of production on *Stingray*. A group of German miners were trapped underground, and the world waited with bated breath as a massive, long, drawn-out rescue attempt was mounted. Gerry was seized by the notion of a fictional team armed with the most sophisticated equipment, able at a moment's notice to go anywhere in the world to rescue people in dire peril. It was a premise of dazzling genius.

Aware that any day soon, Lew Grade would want to hear his ideas for a follow-up series to *Stingray*, Gerry began formulating what eventually became *Thunderbirds*. Gerry's meetings with Grade were always scheduled for half past seven in the morning. 'And I had to be very careful to get there exactly on time, because if I got there before him, although he wouldn't say anything, I knew he was upset because he prided himself in always being the first person into ATV. And equally I didn't want to be late. I used to get in the lift and if I could smell cigar smoke I knew that he was in.'

Grade made a habit of coming into work early. It was a hangover from his days as an agent, when he made some of his biggest deals with overseas clients before his rivals had even gotten into their offices. 'And it became a lifelong habit,' says

Waiting to be brought to life by Thunderbirds' *brilliant team of puppeteers.*

Marcia Stanton. 'He just always got up very, very early and was usually in by 6.30 in the morning. So by nine o'clock, when most of the rest of the staff came in, he'd really done most of his important work, he'd rung Australia, Japan and America, looked at all the telexes. He was extremely bright and absolutely firing on all his cylinders at six in the morning.'

On this particular morning, Gerry feared what Grade's decision might be. 'On the way up to Lew I was thinking, "This is going to be a hell of a thing to film, it's going to cost a lot of money." So I go into Lew's office. He poured me a coffee and gave me one of his giant cigars. Then he sat back in his chair and said, "All right Gerry, what have you got for me this time?" I said nervously, "Well Lew, I have got a new idea but I'm not sure you'll want to back this one." He got up out of his chair, came striding round his desk, grabbed me by the scruff of the neck, I thought he'd gone mad, dragged me into the centre of the office and pointed to the ceiling. "Gerry," he said, "if you want to make a television series about that electric light bulb, I'll back it." So I sat down and told him the basic idea of *International Rescue*, which is what it was going to be called. Lew thought it was terrific. I had no script, no synopsis, no illustrations, no nothing. We simply chatted about the idea for about twenty minutes and then he said, "OK, go ahead." And in today's money he made a commitment for the equivalent of £50m. Amazing man.'

Even at that early stage, Gerry Anderson sensed that he'd latched onto a one in a million idea. 'As a matter of fact I went out of Lew's office and I closed the door, made sure it was shut, and then went, "YEAH!" And I got into the lift, and as it went down my spirits sank too, because I thought, "What have I let myself in for?" Back at the studio my partners wanted to know what happened. "He said OK." And they asked, "Why are you so bloody miserable? It's marvellous." I said, "I know, but now we've got to make it."'

Set in the year 2065, and operating from a secret island base somewhere in the Pacific, International Rescue was the brainchild of former American astronaut and self-made millionaire Jeff Tracy. Jeff's five extraordinary sons piloted each of the incredible Thunderbird rescue machines. Thunderbird 1 – a faster than sound rocket plane – was piloted by Scott to the disaster area, where he could assess the situation and lead the rescue. Second in command was Virgil, pilot of Thunderbird 2 – a heavy transport vehicle designed to carry rescue equipment installed inside a variety of interchangeable pods clamped to its interior. It was Gerry's idea for the craft to be concealed in a cave with a rock face that lifts up, and for the palm trees to fall down as it taxis before take-off. 'But I had support,' he says. 'For example, it was Derek Meddings' idea to have the pods as a separate unit. I'm not an artist, so all my ideas are in words. And Derek would be the guy who would take the words and then draw the craft.' Alan was the pilot of the scarlet Thunderbird 3 – a rocket capable of travelling into space, where John commanded the orbital space station Thunderbird 5 – which monitored the world's SOS messages, intercepting them at will and responding in cases of extreme emergency. Jeff's fifth son, Gordon, captained Thunderbird 4 – a yellow mini-submarine.

Adding a shadow of menace to the show, scriptwriters installed in Jeff Tracy the overriding fear that, in the wrong hands, his Thunderbird craft could be used for destructive purposes. So enter our villain, the Hood – he of the Kojak haircut and Christmas tree-light eyes, who will stop at nothing to learn the secrets of International Rescue. Other regular characters were Brains, the bespectacled and vocally challenged genius behind the *Thunderbirds* technology, Kyrano, the Tracys' loyal housekeeper, and his daughter Tin Tin, and Jeff's doddery old mother.

But quite definitely stealing the show from everyone else was the double act of Lady Penelope, *Thunderbirds*' glamorous London-based agent, and her butler-cum-chauffeur Parker. These are immortal characters, and were employed by Gerry to offset the heavy American influence on the show provided by the Tracy family. 'In those days, getting English television shows to play in the States was almost impossible. I thought, "If we make it like an American programme we can probably break into the American market." So we used American voices and we used to print our scripts on American paper as opposed to A4, so if they asked to read a script it felt to them like an American script. We also used American spellings. Then I thought, "I've got to do something for the home audience." Now we British can laugh at ourselves, so therefore we had Penelope and Parker as this comedy team. And in America they love the English aristocracy too. So it balanced the show perfectly.'

The shocking pink Rolls Royce (number plate FAB 1) was a stroke of genius too. Officially approved by the Rolls Company, it contained six wheels with retractable studs for snow and ice, tyre slashers to disable enemy cars, an oil slick, a retractable machine gun, hydrofoils for travelling over water and a top speed of 200 mph. As a final precaution, the glass canopy hood was bullet proof. Obviously influenced by

Bond's trick Aston Martin from *Goldfinger*, the main seven-foot long model of FAB 1 was constructed at a cost of £2,500.

Although significantly involved creatively in all the shows, one must single out Lady Penelope as Sylvia Anderson's greatest and longest-lasting contribution. Instinctively, she knew American audiences would go for an aristocratic character. 'I actually based her on the Scarlet Pimpernel, which was always my favourite character. Who would you least expect to be the London agent for International Rescue, certainly not the lady of the manor?' It was also a reaction against too many women on television who said nothing but 'Yes, dear' or 'Of course dear.' Here was someone who, beneath that cool exterior, had all the derring-do of 007. Certainly, Lady Penelope was following in the liberated footsteps of Cathy Gale and Emma Peel, which presented its own special problem. 'Because we had an all-male writing team, they didn't quite know how to handle this first woman puppet character who actually had an identity of her own,' explains Sylvia. 'So at the beginning, they didn't really know how to involve her, and in some of the early shows you only see Lady Penelope in a couple of scenes. But by this time we had a marketing division and they decided to have a magazine devoted to Lady Penelope, and I did a column in that called "Lady Penelope Investigates". And they came back and said, "Look, we've got this fantastic magazine for her, but we're not seeing enough of her on the screen." So we had a hasty meeting and she was written into more episodes.'

Again, it was Sylvia's voice that gave life to Lady Penelope, and her face that became the model for the puppet, just as earlier she'd inspired the look of *Fireball*'s Venus. Incredibly, Lady Penelope is as famous an icon now as she was back in the sixties. Together with Parker, she ranks amongst the most popular and recognisable TV characters ever created. Quite an achievement when one remembers she's only a puppet! She was also a firm favourite with her boss, too, according to Marcia Stanton. 'Lord Grade did say that Lady Penelope was his favourite female artist, because she was always smiling, she never asked for a raise and she never answered back.'

As for Parker, Gerry unashamedly ranks him as his favourite *Thunderbirds* character. 'When I first saw the model of Parker, I thought it was terrific. And then of course I thought, "Well, a character that brilliant needs a really good voice." And I used to go to a pub in Cookham called the King's Arms for lunch every day. And they had a waiter by the name of Arthur who had this ability of dropping his H's and putting them all back in the wrong place. And I thought his voice would be marvellous with Parker's face. So I sent David Graham, who played the voice ultimately, down to have lunch there every day for a week – at my expense of course – and he chatted to Arthur and at the end of the week he'd picked up the mannerisms, and that's how he got the voice. The interesting thing is that Parker was a star overnight. And then we had a meeting at the studio and said, now do we tell Arthur? And we thought, "No, we can't really," because although he was a cockney really, he had elevated himself in life and thought he was a bit of a toff. And I said, "If we tell him that this guy's based on his voice, I think he would be mortally offended." So we didn't tell him, and he went to his grave never knowing the truth.'

At the time, *Thunderbirds* boasted the biggest ever budget for a British TV show at £40,000 per episode, an incredible 60 times more expensive than an instalment of *The Adventures of Twizzle*. Almost from day one, there was a vibe going round that this series was going to be something special. Sylvia remembers feeling 'a buzz' when reporters came to the studio to watch the early stages of shooting. As usual it was Grade that cottoned on first. 'Originally Lew had commissioned it as a half-hour series,' recalls Gerry. 'And when I took the first episode for him to see, the lights came up and he didn't say a word, and I thought he didn't like it. And he got up and he walked very thoughtfully all the way down to the screen, and then he turned, came right up to me and looked me straight in the face and shouted, "Gerry. This is not a television series! This is a feature film." He then said I had to change it into an hour. The fact that they were an hour was one of the big contributory factors to its success, because we had time to introduce a new set of characters to the kids each episode, get the kids to like them and then drop them in the crap. It was a very good format.'

With its hour running time, *Thunderbirds* necessitated a massive hike in expense, technical know how and manpower. The Andersons now employed some 250 people at their studio, as they had to deliver two *Thunderbirds* episodes every month. It was a mammoth undertaking, and when asked now what the toughest obstacle to overcome

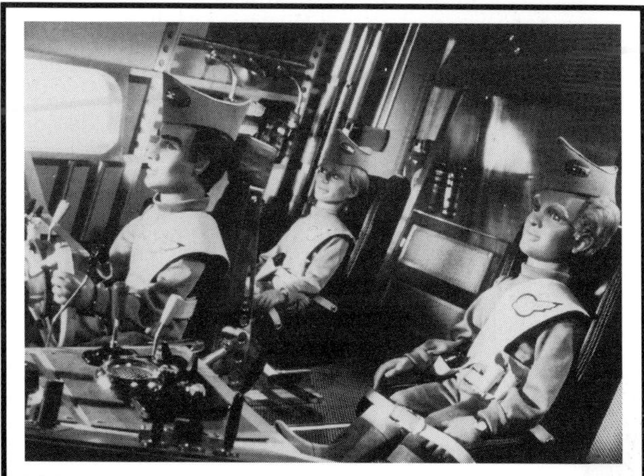

Top: *Lady Penelope's indomitable chauffeur, Parker.* Centre: *behind-the-scenes shot of* Thunderbirds. Bottom: *the crew of Thunderbird 2 blast off to yet another disaster zone.*

was, Gerry says (not in jest), 'Every shot.' The only way it could be done was to have two puppet units shooting simultaneously with duplicate puppets and sets and three special effects units.

More than most, it was Derek Meddings who benefited from the bigger budgets, able to indulge his passion for blowing things up. A feature of *Thunderbirds* is the inordinate amount of pyrotechnics and mass destruction on view. Despite this, Gerry was still wont to economise. 'We hardly ever blew a model up. We would put a model in shot and film it and then we would take it out and put in a bag of explosives filled with all different bits and pieces. Say if it was a car – there'd be wheels, mud guards and steering wheels and so on, and that would explode and all the debris would fly towards camera, and then we would cut the two together and it would look as if the car was exploding.'

One of the most famous *Thunderbirds* episodes is the one where the Tracy brothers come face to face with giant alligators. 'All we did was bring in real alligators, some were twelve foot long, and alongside the miniature sets they looked absolutely enormous,' recalls Gerry. One afternoon the girl on the studio reception desk phoned her boss and said, 'Mr. Anderson, there's an inspector from the RSPCA who says that he's received anonymous telephone calls saying that we are giving the alligators electric shocks.' Nonplussed, Gerry asked for him to be sent in. Confronted by this figure of authority, Gerry said, 'Look, I've nothing to hide. I'll take you straight onto the stage and you'll see exactly what's going on.' After being introduced to Meddings, the RSPCA guy asked, 'Is it true that you're giving alligators electric shocks?' And Derek said, 'What our problem is . . . ' Suddenly, the inspector cut in. 'Isn't that Lady Penelope over there? And isn't that Parker? This is my favourite show. *Thunderbirds*. Good Lord. I bet you wouldn't show me round the studio.' 'Sure,' said Gerry. The man from the RSPCA was totally enthralled by it all. But after a while Gerry said, 'Look, do you want to deal with the complaint?' He said, 'Oh yes.' So Meddings continued, 'You see, we put the alligators down on the set and they won't do anything, it's like they're carved out of stone. So when we want them to move we give them electric shocks.' The inspector asked, 'What sort of voltage are you using?' Meddings said, 'Only twelve volts.' The inspector said, 'Twelve volts! Twelve volts! Do you realise these animals have got very thick skins? Try turning it up to 60. Ah, that's better, that's made them move.'

Along with Sylvia's husky Lady Penelope, Shane Rimmer is really the voice of *Thunderbirds*, providing as he did the vocal talent for Scott Tracy. Hailing from Toronto, where he sang as well as acted, Rimmer arrived in Britain at a propitious period. 'I sort of snuck in when nobody was looking. At that time, they were doing a lot of made-for-America series like *Danger Man*. All those kinds of things were going on at quite a rate and doing very well. I was actually doing a cabaret tour, I think up in Leeds, when I got a call about the *Thunderbirds* job. And I remember weighing it up, I said, "God almighty, it's a hell of a trip down to London, will I be able to make it back up again to Leeds in time for the first show?" Anyway, I went down and they just gave me a few things to read. Later I got an offer to do it.'

Although he'd done voice-overs back in Canada, Rimmer had not done this type of work in Britain and it was all a new and bewildering experience. 'The Andersons had the characters in vision, they'd made rough facial representations of them – so it was just a matter of the voice matching up with how they conceived the character to be. Also they had Peter Dyneley as Jeff Tracy there I think first, and he had this

A new super satellite is in orbit. A trouble-spotter for the world's most exciting organisation, International Rescue. A warning signal from the

THUNDERBIRDS

satellite and the sleek Thunderbird machines roar into action, gliding silently beneath the seas or out into space in a constant battle to save the peoples of the world from impending danger. Filmed in breathtaking Supermarionation. Introducing the fabulous Lady Penelope and the remarkable Tracy family—man-made actors with more appeal than many humans. Puppets with a purpose in adventures that zoom into the future.

A Thunderbirds *promotional brochure.*

incredible basso profundo voice, so anything that was lighter or probably a little more excitable than that would probably register OK.'

The actors used for *Thunderbirds* had to be well chosen by Sylvia. Many in the entertainment business exploit their own personality and physical appearance, but here it was only the voice that had to work. 'You just let the words talk,' says Rimmer. 'We're not talking about Tolstoy, but the characters were very firmly written.' Rimmer remembers the recording sessions for the series well. 'It was just like a BBC radio show, you know, the pictures you see with this huge bloody microphone and everybody grouped around it. That's more or less what we did, reading through the script like a radio play. We did it at the Slough Trading Estate. I mean, what an exotic place that is. It's just one-storey buildings and about 25 feet away from the Mars bar factory. We'd go in on a Sunday afternoon and did two or sometimes three shows. We never saw any footage; the soundtrack was the first thing to get put down. And that was great because it allowed you the freedom to more or less fantasise the whole thing. You weren't tied down to whatever was on the screen; you just did it. And there was a nice feeling amongst everyone. About five or six of us were there every week. Other people came in periodically to do other characters, Peter Bowles and Bob Monkhouse, people like that, but the original batch were very comfortable with each other.'

Amazingly, Rimmer remembers only being paid £20 an episode. And no residuals (payments made to a performer on a recorded television programme for repeat showings). Which came as something of a shock, particularly when the show started reaping untold millions. 'It took us the best part of fifteen years to get our residuals. There was no clause in the contract that said that residuals were not allowed. So two of us out of the original cast took ITC to court and finally got a concession from them. And we ended up rather nicely. Unless you sign a clause saying that you're not entitled to residuals, it's always in contention. And certainly, a few years after our case that clause was in print, because they knew what they were giving away.'

Despite critical acclaim and huge audiences in Britain, where it debuted in September 1965, *Thunderbirds* failed to get an American network showing. 'The States was our main market,' confirms Sylvia. 'So we were disappointed it didn't get shown on any of the main channels over there, but it sold all around the world. It was particularly big in Japan, as all our shows were. But strangely there were certain areas that were no go, like France and Germany, who didn't take to it at all.'

The reason for *Thunderbirds*' failure in the States is bizarre. 'I have never said a bad word about Lew Grade because he was such a wonderful man,' says Gerry. 'But he made a tragic mistake with *Thunderbirds*. He took the show to America. And to get a British show onto American networks is like climbing Everest without using ropes. But NBC and CBS both said, "We'll take it." Lew flew back to London and there was a tannoy announcement at the airport: "Will Mr. Lew Grade come to the telephone?" It was ABC, who had turned it down, but now wanted to take it. This was television history; all the main US networks wanted it. And then Lew got quite excited and asked for, I don't know, 44 billion dollars an episode or something, and it was too strong. And one of the networks said, "That's too much." And then the other two networks said, "Why did he back out, what do they know we don't know?" So they backed out. So *Thunderbirds* never got the showing in America it should have,' languishing as it did in regional syndication.

Then, at the height of its popularity, Grade announced he wanted to cancel *Thunderbirds*. 'When we were getting towards the end of production I went to see Lew,' recalls Gerry. 'And I said, "There's not much to discuss is there, so let's go straight on with making *Thunderbirds*." And he said, "I've been thinking, Gerry. I honestly think I could sell a new show quicker than more episodes." And because I had such a respect for him I didn't argue too much.'

Still, it was a massive shock. Neither of the Andersons was expecting it, nor did they have much say in the matter. 'In America, if you've got a successful show you go on for five years,' asserts Sylvia. 'Most of our shows could have gone on longer, but we didn't really resent it at the time, and in retrospect I think it was a good thing because it meant we were always doing something new. But I do think we could have, and should have, gone on and made more *Thunderbirds*.'

Aware of the Andersons' disappointment, Grade suggested *Thunderbirds* live on as a series of cinematic features. In January 1966, backed by United Artists, *Thunderbirds Are Go* entered production, and was to feature puppet versions of Cliff Richard and the Shadows. A second movie, *Thunderbird 6*, followed in 1968, but neither attained the heights of popularity enjoyed by their TV counterpart. In the mid-eighties, Gerry even dabbled with the possibility of bringing the show back. He theorised that the Tracy family could no longer base themselves on an island, as vehicles couldn't now be launched undetected. So his idea was to have all the vehicles housed in a huge atomic submarine which moved around the ocean bed. Inside, the Tracys enjoyed artificial sunlight and a beautiful olde-worlde oak-panelled cottage, complete with garden and pool. Upon receiving a call the sub would surface, launch all vehicles and disappear again underwater.

Then, in the mid-nineties, rumours emerged about a live action movie. The tabloids had fun speculating over whom to cast in any prospective film, with Bob Hoskins favourite to land Parker and Joanna Lumley as Lady Penelope, a role Sylvia herself saw as being more suitable for Kristin Scott-Thomas. After many false starts, 2004 finally saw the release of the much-mooted *Thunderbirds* movie, with the (admittedly inspired) casting of Ben Kingsley as the Hood. Unbelievably, it was a project that neither Gerry nor Sylvia Anderson had anything creatively to do with. And it shows. The movie stiffed at the box office.

Since its demise, the cult of *Thunderbirds* has grown to near mythic proportions. The show's enduring appeal for both young and old is perhaps the equal of other cult hits like *Star Trek* and *Dr Who*. 'And a lot of credit goes to Gerry,' insists Rimmer. 'He got the thing together and he made it work. All the TV companies do now is put the show on the shelf for seven years and then bring it down and the whole business starts again. It's amazing. I don't know of anything like it. And I don't think I've quite come to terms with the fact that it's still going on. Obviously you're rather grateful that you were part of a show that seems to endure. When I do the odd convention the fathers are coming up with the sons, it's a sort of perpetual motion that's going on, which is quite extraordinary.'

Part of *Thunderbirds*' enduring appeal could be that kids know they're not looking at computer images processed by some nerd in an office, but real models lovingly crafted, and almost always lovingly obliterated. For his part, Gerry has his own theory as to why *Thunderbirds* continues to fascinate and enthral successive generations. 'It is a sad fact of life that kiddies want to see death, destruction and jeopardy on the screen, and if you don't give them that they will flip to another channel. Now I am very anti-war and anti-violence, so the last thing that I want to do is to pander to the kiddies just to get ratings. *Thunderbirds* gives them what they want – death and destruction – and yet the underlying story is about saving life, not destroying it. So I think it has parental approval and is looked upon as a responsible programme, but not a boring responsible programme, but a very exciting one.'

CAPTAIN SCARLET AND THE MYSTERONS (1967-68)

With the world-wide popularity of *Thunderbirds*, Gerry Anderson had assumed they'd go on making the show for years to come. All that changed one late summer morning in 1966, when Lew Grade told him *Thunderbirds* was being axed and he wanted a totally new puppet series. 'It never crossed my mind that this would happen. I really just went to Lew's office for confirmation that we should continue with *Thunderbirds*, and it was like a bombshell when he said no. And I had to say to him that I hadn't got a new show this time, and that I would have to go away and think about it.'

Captain Scarlet was born out of the 1960s sci-fi obsession with alien forces infiltrating society, reflecting perhaps anxieties about the spread of communism and the Cold War – although Gerry had a strict policy when it came to any of his show's villains being coloured by politics, in addition to the moral aspect of good always triumphing over evil. 'I never allowed the villains to be Russian, as everybody else was doing. Every goddamn show at the time, every villain, every spy, every murderer was Russian. The reason being, I lived through the war and the bombing of London. And I had a brother who was a pilot who was killed in the war. There was fear of an atomic war, and at a very early stage I made up my mind that I'm not going to brainwash children into hating the Russians, and I'm not going to do anything which will encourage kids to become murderers, rapists or drug addicts. I felt a huge responsibility.'

Like *Thunderbirds*, it was a current news event that caught Gerry's imagination. 'At the time, astronomers were looking at Mars and they could see these very straight lines on the surface, and they were convinced that they were canals, and canals don't make themselves, and so there was speculation that there was life on Mars. And I thought, it would just be my bloody luck if we make a story about Mars to say there's nobody there and then they'll find that there are beings out there. I know what I'll do. I'll make the aliens invisible so we can't be caught out. It was just a very practical decision, and this was how the Mysterons were born.'

Able to conquer death, the Mysterons – who declared war on Earth after their base on Mars was mistakenly attacked and destroyed – could create an exact copy of a human being that is indestructible and programmed to do the evil bidding of its masters. Such missions included assassinating world leaders, hijacking airliners and driving trucks laden with explosives into buildings – all very redolent of today's terrorist activity. Only one man could stop them – Captain Scarlet, top agent for Spectrum, and a man the Mysterons have made indestructible.

Supplying one of the most distinctive voices ever to grace an Anderson show was Francis Matthews – who won the role of Captain Scarlet by a lucky fluke, when Gerry heard him on the radio impersonating Cary Grant and decided that was the voice he wanted. Previously best known for appearances in the classic Hammer horror films *The Revenge of Frankenstein* and *Dracula – Prince of Darkness*, Matthews emerged as a TV star in the late sixties thanks to the BBC's mystery serial, *Paul Temple*. He was also good friends with Roger Moore, appearing in episodes of *The Saint*, as well as Moore's ill-fated big screen spy romp, *Crossplot*. Indeed, Moore playfully believed he was the inspiration behind the *Captain Scarlet* puppet. 'Roger always said that they've got your voice and my face,' says Matthews. 'He thought they'd modelled it on him. But Gerry asked his sculptors to make the puppet of Captain Scarlet look like everybody's ideal of the really handsome man, with film star good looks. So it wasn't modelled on either Roger or me at all. I wish I did look like that!'

Like *Thunderbirds* before it, *Captain Scarlet* featured a large supporting cast of characters, mostly agents for Spectrum, a world security force operating out of Cloudbase – a huge headquarters located in the stratosphere. Cloudbase was another brilliantly innovative idea. 'During the war, one of the biggest problems with Spitfires was getting an early enough warning so they could get enough height to intercept the enemy. So I thought if we launched from an aircraft carrier in the sky, if the Mysterons were to send any ships to Earth we could very quickly get aircraft onto the fringe of space. And then we needed a highly dedicated and trained force, the equivalent of the SAS. And by this time I'd made a lot of series, so I thought, "What are we going to do about names?" Then suddenly came the idea of Captain Scarlet. I said, "Wait a minute, Scarlet, and there's another guy called Captain Blue, let's call the force Spectrum and the commander will be all the colours put togeth-

He's indestructible, he looks like Alan Hansen, he's Captain Scarlet!

er, which is white – Colonel White." And that's how it came about.'

Given Gerry's penchant for formulaic good-against-evil scenarios, it's not surprising that the main villain was called Captain Black. Formerly a Spectrum agent, Black was the first Mysteron victim and was originally to have died in the pilot episode, but his puppet was so vivid and menacing looking that Gerry decided to keep him on as a regular. And there was a step towards female emancipation, as the pilots trained to protect Cloudbase were all women. Nicknamed Angels (before Charlie got the idea), their monikers of Symphony, Destiny, Rhapsody, Harmony and Melody do sound a bit like a collection of FM radio stations.

Scarlet's closest friend was fellow Spectrum operative Captain Blue, voiced by American actor Ed Bishop. In 1967, Bishop was an underpaid actor working for Joan Littlewood's Theatre Company at the Theatre Royal, Stratford East, when the offer to do *Scarlet* came up. 'There was an actor in *Scarlet* called Cy Grant,' Bishop recalls. 'And Cy and I had the same agent, and I think Sylvia called up for Cy and the girl on the desk was bright – which is very unusual in an agent's office – and said, "By the way, I know you use a lot of American accents and we've just taken on this new American actor called Edward Bishop. Would you like to meet him?" So Sylvia said, "All right, send him along." It was that capricious, as it often is in this business.

So I met Sylvia and Gerry, auditioned, and got the part of Captain Blue.'

It was a godsend for Bishop – not only did it mean bigger bucks but, as the recording sessions took place on Sundays, it wouldn't interfere with his theatre work. 'We'd get together twice a month and record two episodes in each session, that's four a month. And we did 32, so that's just about eight months of employment. We'd just had our first child, and I was working with Joan Littlewood and making something like £5 a week with her, but I was making my real money with those two days. I was buying Heinz baby food and paying the rent on *Captain Scarlet*. So I've always had an affection for it.'

To put down their dialogue, the actors made their way to a small recording studio in Denham, where – according to Bishop – it was only then that they were handed the scripts. 'And the first thing that you did was leaf through to the end of the episode to see if your puppet got killed, because then you were out of a job. Matthews, he could sit there nice and cool because he was indestructible, he knew he was back next week.'

After some friendly banter and numerous cups of coffee, everyone got started. The recordings were executed in similar fashion to the way Sylvia handled those on *Thunderbirds*. 'Usually, you'd take probably the morning doing one script,' says Matthews. 'And then we'd go and get stoned in the pub across the road and come back and do the second script. It wasn't a very hard job. Doing the voice of Captain Scarlet wasn't difficult at all, I can't pretend it was difficult. In fact we fooled around an awful lot because it was sort of silly, saying lines like, "Look – Captain Blue, it's a Mysteron!" I mean you can't really go into great depth. But it was jolly, and they were a great gang. Ed Bishop and I became great mates. It was in the pub we had the best time, having the Guinness, oiling our throats. "Why don't we go oil the tubes?" Ed would say.'

Bishop also recalls the playful and relaxed nature of those recording sessions. 'The Andersons created a wonderful atmosphere to work in and we never had any problems whatsoever. Once there was a bit of tension between two actors. Donald Grey, who did the voice of Colonel White, only had one arm, [the other of] which he'd lost in the war; a charming man. At that time Rhodesia was declaring independence from the Commonwealth, and Donald had a sticker on his car which said, "Hands off Rhodesia," because a lot of people felt [Prime Minister Harold] Wilson should go in with troops. And Cy Grant, who was black and played Lieutenant Green, said, "Donald, I'd like to have a talk with you about this." So there was a little bit of tension there. But apart from that it was just wonderful.'

For the most part, Sylvia directed the recording sessions herself – one of the most important duties that she took responsibility for. As a rule, the way the Andersons worked was for Gerry to concentrate on technical matters and company management while Sylvia, who'd done a bit of acting in the past, naturally gravitated towards the creative side, working with actors, supplying voices and helping Gerry formulate new show concepts. 'Another of my functions was to get the characters right,' she explains. 'For me you had to make these characters as real as possible. The effects and sets were brilliant, but you had to make it come to life with all the shortcomings of puppets, wooden characters basically. So the effects and music all contributed, but you had to have characters which audiences immediately recognised and responded to. And I felt with *Captain Scarlet* there was very little setting up of the characters. It was all action, basically. I thought the puppets looked fantastic, and it's a great show, but I look upon it more as a comic strip show. Very, very good, but I think it lacked humour.'

As with *Thunderbirds*, the dialogue was the first element captured. The actors had no footage to guide them in their roles, nor did they even know what their characters looked like. It wasn't until almost half thc episodes had been recorded that the cast was shown paintings of the individual puppets. 'Actually there wasn't a great deal of direction necessary, because we were experienced actors,' says Bishop. 'Occasionally you might query the writer, you know, that doesn't sound like a Blue line, no pun intended. But it wasn't a Chekov play. It was *Captain Scarlet*! It was just technical delivery, timing and the kind of positive energy that you had to give these guys. I don't mean to trivialise it, but you had to keep a sense of balance otherwise you'd sit around for hours discussing your motivation, which was not called for.'

Shane Rimmer also came in to do a few peripheral voices, but his biggest contribution to *Captain Scarlet* was a creative one. 'I got together with the screenwriter Tony Barwick and wrote a couple of episodes. I wanted to get into writing. I'd written in Toronto, mainly radio. Writing for *Captain Scarlet* was fine. Like *Thunderbirds* it was still adventure and the same sort of themes were still more or less persistent, good against evil. It was the white hats against the black hats. I think that was always a prerequisite of what you were going to do. But *Scarlet* was a little more shadowy. It had more of an edge.'

Often Rimmer visited the set, still friendly with a lot of the studio technicians who had worked on *Thunderbirds*. 'Those shows were created by a lot of young guys obviously wanting to make their way in the business. The atmosphere on the floor depends very much on what the director's putting out and about his ability to make the atmosphere as convivial and as productive as possible. And good pictures always have a director who can handle that. And this was a bunch of very young guys and they were loving what they were doing, and it was coming out on screen.'

The remarkable feature of the series was the acutely realistic puppets. Gerry, always the frustrated filmmaker, had felt trapped in having to churn out puppet show after puppet show. 'We became typecast. So, knowing it was the only thing I could get finance for, I desperately wanted to make the thing look as close to live action as possible. And I think it was that that drove me on to bring in all the improvements and techniques. The puppets up to that point had oversized heads, and this was because they needed the room to put the automatic mouth movement in. People thought they were caricatures, and I suppose they were, but not by design. And because I was desperately trying to emulate live action, all the electrical components had now been miniaturised, and we were able to put the gubbins in the chest and operate the mouth with a valve and cable up the neck. And therefore we were able to produce a smaller size head and a more lifelike puppet.'

Gone were the caricatures of yesteryear, to be replaced by something close to what Gerry had been striving so long to achieve. 'Sometimes on the set you'd pass a monitor and not know whether you were looking at somebody real or a puppet,' remembers Rimmer. 'I remember being absolutely caught a couple of times – "Am I looking at somebody or is this a puppet?" Because they were beautifully engineered.' Critics also picked up on the technical brilliance on view, with *The Daily Telegraph* noting, 'The puppets are so life-like and well manipulated that one almost accepts them as actors after the first five minutes or so of viewing them.'

Such was the convincing nature of the puppets that Gerry formulated a plan to have Hollywood guest stars (Dirk Bogarde was mentioned) come in and lay down

The Angels: these female fighter pilots were Gerry Anderson's nod to women's emancipation.

their voice, and then for the sculptors to reproduce the actor in puppet form. The team even went so far as to write into the pilot script an appearance of *Danger Man*'s Patrick McGoohan. But the whole intriguing idea was scrapped due to time and money concerns.

Once the shows were in the can and ready to go out on television, producer Reg Hill invited Francis Matthews and his two sons – one five, the other just three – to the studio for a private viewing of the first episode. The idea was to gauge the reaction of children. 'And of course, when the film started and Captain Black's voice came on, "This is the voice of the Mysterons," my eldest son screamed and jumped up and ran out of the studio. I had to run after him and calm him down. But the other one just sat there quite happily. So he was all right, but the eldest boy was badly affected. He used to have nightmares about Captain Black.'

As for Ed Bishop, his first exposure to the show was at a special premiere in a cinema in Soho. 'But I had lost my admission ticket and they wouldn't let me in. I said, "Could you please go down and get Gerry Anderson?" So the doorman went into the audience and Gerry came running up the stairs, because Sylvia at that time was in hospital having their first child, and he thought that this was the message that she'd given birth. It was only just a poncy actor who had lost his invite. And he said,

"I thought my wife had a baby. Yeah that's Ed, let him in." That was the first time I saw it. I was knocked out.'

Top: *Captain Blue and Captain Scarlet, SPECTRUM's top agents.* Bottom: *ITC brochure for* Captain Scarlet and the Mysterons.

Captain Scarlet made its debut on ITV in September 1967. Reviewers at the time, though impressed with the visuals, found the scripts dramatically lacking; a criticism that can be thrown at most Anderson shows. 'Separated from its technical brilliance the style is that of any American strip cartoon of the past 50 years,' asserted *The Daily Mail*.

From the earliest days, Gerry Anderson was keen on merchandising his shows, and Captain Scarlet toys literally flooded the market in time for that year's Christmas. 'Unashamedly we used to exploit merchandising as much as we could. We never created a crappy vehicle just for the sake of selling it, whatever we created we really made well. But we used to go in for merchandising, because the shows were so expensive that we had to merchandise like crazy, otherwise we could never have afforded to make them.' Some of the show's impressive cars were released as superb, and now highly collectible (and expensive), Dinky toys – the blood-red Spectrum patrol car and metallic blue SPV, Spectrum's tank-like pursuit vehicle. This had a neat little door mechanism that opened sideways to lower a mini-Scarlet to the ground, and became one of the biggest selling Dinky toys ever. Also available were Action Man-type dolls, a Scalextric-inspired car-racing game, wallpaper, jigsaws, annuals, records, ice lollies, sweets; it was endless.

And it's still going on today. 'I was recording a commentary with Gerry for the DVD of *Scarlet* in 2000,' says Matthews. 'And while I was in there they said, "Oh, before you go would you mind doing these few lines for this new doll?" And I said, "I'm not being paid for that." They said, "We'll send you some money." They did, but not very much. And of course it sold all over the world. My son said to me, "Why on earth did you do that? You should have got a residual, a percentage." I said, "Listen, if I hadn't done it they'd have just got somebody to imitate me, imitating Cary Grant."'

After a few repeat showings *Captain Scarlet* went back into the vaults, emerging in the eighties on video and on cable TV in the States. Its true rebirth came during a highly successful re-run on BBC2 during 1993. Such was its new found visibility that it caused a minor political storm, hilariously accused of political incorrectness by the Commission for Racial Equality. According to newspaper reports, the commission claimed it perpetuated racial stereotypes, as the hero's superior was Colonel 'White' while the nasty, 'orrible villain was Captain 'Black'. One Labour MP even called for the BBC to disown the series. What these twits failed to realise was that, if anything, *Captain Scarlet* was actually ahead of its time in respect to race relations. Lieutenant Green, Cloudbase's communication controller, was a positive black character, for example. And few other shows of the period had women cast as heroic fighter pilots, one of whom was black. The introduction of two leading black characters was a deliberate move on Gerry's part. Years earlier, on *Supercar*, he'd written an episode featuring black characters, only for an American advisor for ITC to order their removal and replacement by characters of white origin – otherwise they couldn't hope to sell the series to stations in America's South. By the time of *Captain Scarlet*, such rabid discrimination no longer applied, and Gerry was anxious to go ahead and promote racial harmony in all his shows.

Although *Thunderbirds* undeniably remains the Andersons' most high-profile series, many fans cite *Captain Scarlet* as their favourite. Little surprise then that, in 2005, Gerry decided that of all his shows, *Captain Scarlet* would be the one to remake as a new, computer-generated animated series. One of the reasons for *Scarlet*'s popularity is that it portrays a much harder edge. Gone is the two-dimensional comic book action of previous shows, replaced by heavy doses of realistic violence. People are shot, blown up, burnt to death, crushed, you name it. Gerry claims that the move towards an all-round tougher show wasn't a deliberate move on his part. 'At the time I was still pursuing my quest to go into live action, and so realism was the order of the day. And this business of people now saying to me, "It's a dark show," when we hadn't even heard of the expression "dark". A lot of people say that it's dark. It's quite funny, because we showed a clip of the new CGI *Captain Scarlet* show to the BBC, and they sat there going, "Oh my God, you can't do that. Oh look, there's blood." Now, on CGI you build up an image on the computer in layers, until finally you put the whole lot together and produce the finished picture. Well, the last thing we're putting on is blood. The BBC said. "You can't have that amount of blood, rub it out." We go to Japan they say there's not enough, so we splatter blood all over the place. Crazy.'

Perhaps *Captain Scarlet*'s greatest triumph is that, coming so soon on the heels of the phenomenal *Thunderbirds*, it didn't turn out to be an anticlimax. Who can forget the immortal opening sequence of Scarlet cornered in a dimly lit alleyway, shooting his invisible assailant, and the ominous Captain Black standing zombie-like in a misty cemetery? For Gerry, the pressure of having to top *Thunderbirds* was no different to that which he self-imposes upon himself and his team on each successive project. 'Every time I start a new show I try to make it look more real and more exciting. And today nothing's changed, because we're now working with CGI. It's now called "hyper-marianation". Because again it's trying to do something better.'

There's also *Scarlet*'s enduring appeal to consider. 'When it's re-shown, a whole new generation pick up on it. And kids are fascinated by it,' says Matthews. 'I don't know why. I hardly ever watch it now, but when I do see it I don't understand its compulsion. I think it looks a bit stiff. But that's just me. In my opinion it doesn't touch *Thunderbirds*, but there we are, people seem to like it.'

Perhaps Matthews is perplexed at the show's cult status because, for him, *Captain Scarlet* was just another job and has since, he feels, disproportionately taken over from what he considers other, more important, aspects of his career: movies, theatre and playing Paul Temple. 'The puppet is famous, not me,' he argues. 'I don't think it would've mattered who did the voice. I just happened to be the one who did the voice, it could have been anybody.' Fans and conventions also get Matthews scratching his head in mild bewilderment. 'I've only done two conventions. I did one in the early nineties. I thought I'd never do another one. I said, "It's ridiculous." I felt a bit of an idiot. But then I did this Fanderson convention because Ed Bishop – who lived near me, I used to see him occasionally – he said, "Come on Francis, why don't you come along? We have a great time, we eat well, we get lots of booze and we meet a lot of nice people." So he was going and I thought I'd go with him and we had a great time, it was very nice. But there are some very strange people who go to these things. They really are anoraks. They're just strange. Their enthusiasm is overwhelming. They dress up as Captain Scarlet and they stare at you when you're signing the autograph as if you're some kind of extraordinary god!'

JOE 90 (1968-69)

Today, this puppet series can be seen as a departure from the more traditionally epic heroics of *Thunderbirds* and *Captain Scarlet*, in that it follows the adventures of a bespectacled nine-year-old schoolboy called Joe McClaine. This being Gerry Anderson, however, the boy also happens to be a secret agent, a sort of pocket-sized James Bond. As the ITC publicity brochure hailed it – 'There has never before been a special agent like Joe 90 and television has never before presented such an original, imaginative and intriguing series.'

The inspiration behind *Joe 90* was the invention of magnetic tape recording, which made it possible for people to wipe tape and re-record on it. Gerry Anderson began thinking that one day it might be possible to record an individual's brain activity and put it into another person's brain. Even better, you could take on the experiences and skills of that person to become the best driver in the world, a daredevil pilot, anything. 'And of course all these ideas came to me when I was driving home, narrowly missing death because I was a million miles away. Or lying in bed not being able to sleep.' Once again Gerry was ahead of his time, predating such films as *The Matrix*.

Such a concept lent itself perfectly to the spy genre, as who would suspect a nine-year-old Chris Evans look-alike? 'The idea of introducing the boy was very simple,' says Gerry. 'Why transfer the expertise of that man over there to this man over here, why not use a boy? So the idea was to transfer the expertise into somebody who'd be the last person in the world that you would imagine could, for example, steal an MIG.'

Again, Gerry took his idea to Lew Grade. By this time, these meetings between two of British television's greatest talents followed a very well worn pattern. 'I'd go in the office and Lew would open this big box and give me a cigar. We'd both light up and then he'd sit up in his chair and say, "OK, tell me about the new show." I had no script, no designs, I'd just tell him. And he would think, maybe ask a couple of questions, and then he'd say, "OK, fine." The usual thing of him asking how much it was going to cost followed, and I got to the point where I would add on the extra amount that I thought he was going to cut off, so it was a little bit of horseplay. So I would say such and such an amount. "Christ!" he'd yell. "That's too much, Gerry." "Well, I dare say, Lew, we could do it for this." "Yeah," he'd say, "that's better."'

Joe is the adopted son of brilliant electronics genius Professor Ian McClaine, creator of BIG RAT (Brain Impulse Galvanoscope Record and Transfer), a hi-tech device which records the brain patterns and special talents of a person and can transfer those to anyone else. Recognising its potential, the professor is persuaded by Shane Weston, deputy head of the World Intelligence Network, or WIN, to keep the machine a secret and allow them to use it for special missions. As a guinea pig, McClaine subjects Joe to BIG RAT and successfully transfers to the boy the specialist knowledge and attributes of an appropriately highly skilled adult, thus making him WIN's most special agent.

Although essentially children's shows, devising and then writing episodes for *Stingray* or *Joe 90* was a far more complex job than anyone ever gave credit for. 'Every time we would start a series,' explains Gerry, "ITC New York, who we saved with *Fireball XL5*, then became a pain in the arse because they were forever telling Lew that they understood the American market, and you tell Gerry this, that and the other. So we got a lot of interference from them. And they were saying things like, "Gerry, you need at least a dozen writers." I'd say, "How's that?" And they'd say, "Because we want all different ideas." So I'd get eight writers and they used to fall by the wayside one after the other, because they wrote crap, because this was a very specialised form of writing. I remember one writer came in with his script, and I read it and it said, "Fade in, the surface of the moon, a hundred horsemen gallop across . . . " I'd rip it up because clearly he hadn't got a clue what we were doing. So we would usually end up with three writers and I would tell the Americans to get stuffed, because there were very few people who could do it, very few people who could get into my mind. One of the best writers we ever had was Tony Barwick. And Alan Fennell was another key writer.'

The voice of Joe 90 was courtesy of fifteen-year-old Len Jones. 'One of the problems of the show was selecting a kid to play Joe 90,' reveals Gerry. 'I hate hearing adults playing children's voices. Also, young actors are always a bit precious, as well as being bastards to handle. So we took somebody literally off the street, and the recording sessions were done with me playing the role of Joe 90, but line by line. So I would say something and he would repeat it.'

At the outset of each mission, Joe was placed in a special chair that rose up into a circular, revolving cage. (You can hear the theme tune now in your head, can't you?) Then the BIG RAT tape containing the chosen specialist's brain patterns was run and fed directly into the boy's mind. Joe had only to don a special pair of electrode glasses to trigger the new knowledge housed within him. Over the course of the series, Joe's missions called for him to adopt the personas of such diverse experts as an astronaut, a computer boffin, even a brain surgeon! Would you let a nine-year-old pimpled schoolboy anywhere near your cranial region?

As usual, Gerry and his effects team introduced highly imaginative innovations in

When connected to BIG RAT, Joe can take on the brain patterns of anyone from surgeons to jet fighter pilots.

the field of model work. For instance, they'd sprinkle talcum powder on the set of a road, so that when a car travelled along it, with a fan hidden underneath, the powder would blow around like dust coming up from a real vehicle. Yet the sheer drudgery and toil that went into producing just 30 minutes of television was often backbreaking.

'These films were such hard work to make, incredibly difficult,' recalls Gerry. 'From morning to night we were forever having problems trying to keep on schedule. If a puppet wire broke it was half an hour to replace it. And if one of our cameramen were ill the production manager would hurriedly phone for a replacement, and in would come a movie cameraman. I remember someone came in who said he'd worked on *Doctor Zhivago* and other big pictures. I said, "OK, I'll take you on the floor and explain how we do it." And he said, "You don't need to do that, leave it to me." Well, an hour later I went back and there was this bloke, sweat pouring down his face because he had 24 shadows all over the set. It was so specialised that these movie cameramen couldn't light our shows.'

Adding to the pressure was Gerry's own notorious perfectionism. 'I would go to rushes and sit there in agony because I'd see a bad movement; can't let that go.

Rare annual based on the short-lived Joe 90 *series.*

On the odd occasion when I saw a good shot I used to think, "Oh, that's wonderful." Then I used to spend my time in the cutting room, almost every night until eleven o'clock, trying to cut away from the bad movements, putting the mouth movements into sync as best as I possibly could and making the bangs sound as loud as possible. And then, in the dubbing theatre, using Barry Gray's wonderful music to good effect.'

Joe 90 is clearly the most kiddie-orientated of the Andersons' post-*Stingray* ITC shows. Teenagers and adults who'd been captured by *Thunderbirds* found it hard to relate to a character whose balls hadn't dropped yet. It's still enjoyable and technically accomplished, although the puppets themselves are a bit of a letdown after the brilliant near-realism of *Captain Scarlet*. As vitriolic TV critic Victor Lewis Smith in the *Evening Standard* wrote of them, after the show was re-run in the mid-nineties, 'The puppets all wear miniature ill-fitting suits presumably made by a blind seamstress to the pixies and with faces so expressionless that you knew they were all either stroke victims or else Mogadoned to the eyeballs.'

Overall, *Joe 90* ranks as one of Gerry Anderson's lesser creations – it was especially disappointing coming right after the dark and edgy *Captain Scarlet*. Although at one time Disney were in negotiations to turn it into a feature film, *Joe 90* also proved to be the last significant puppet show Gerry ever made. It was followed by the bizarre *The Secret Service*, which was inspired by Stanley Unwin, a favourite comedy actor of Gerry's, famous for his use of gobbledegook language.

Unwin's character was a parish priest and undercover agent for B.I.S.H.O.P, carrying out dangerous assignments using a miniaturisation device that can shrink his assistant. Sounds good. But few people on earth actually saw it. And for this reason it remains Gerry Anderson's forgotten show. 'And there's a very good and simple explanation for that,' he quips. The series' running gag was that no one could understand what the Unwin character was talking about when he went into his gobbledegook, or 'Unwinese'. That was the whole point. 'I showed an episode to Lew Grade, and Stanley Unwin went into Unwinese, and Lew stood up and said, "Put the lights on." And he turned and said, "Cancel the show." I said, "Why?" He said, "They'll never understand him in America." I said, "But they're not supposed to!" So the show was cancelled. We finished thirteen only. Lew put it out on his transmitter in the Midlands and it was never shown again.'

Despite its monumental failure, *The Secret Service*, in blending live action with model footage, was the way that Gerry particularly wanted to move forward. It was a long cherished dream that would, in the seventies, thanks to Lew Grade, become real-

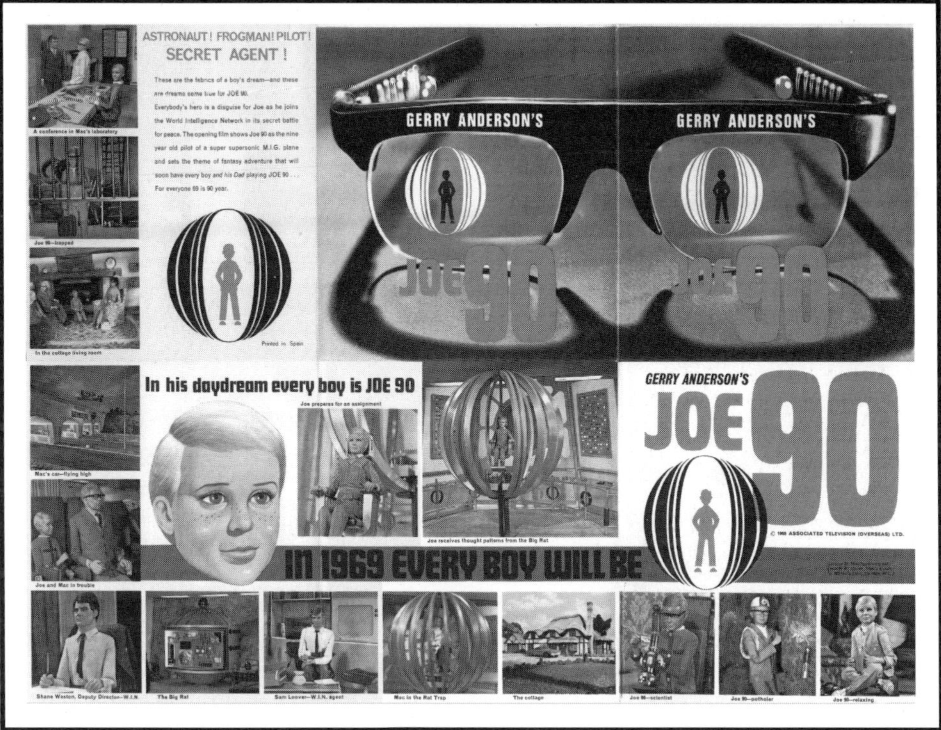

Elaborate promotional brochure for Joe 90.

ity and spawn further cult TV hits. But Gerry never quite succeeded in escaping his puppet past, and it is those shows which largely underpin his legacy to the entertainment world, and for which he will always be remembered – something that deeply rankled with him. 'Following every puppet show I made, I wanted to go onto live action, so I never had too many kind things to say about the shows in the past. But the years roll by and suddenly *Thunderbirds* is back, toys are selling like crazy, new generations are watching the shows, so I've become respectful. Now I feel OK about them. But I never watch any of the shows today because it would just depress me.'

Chapter 5

Ghosts in the Machine

- Man in a Suitcase - The Prisoner -

When the massively popular *Danger Man* series ended early in 1966, the production team split into two separate units to embark upon new projects. One faction went with star Patrick McGoohan, while producer Sidney Cole, previously involved with the best of ITC's historical shows like *Robin Hood* and *The Buccaneers*, headed the other.

The two shows that emerged from these two disparate groups, though different in both style and content, paralleled each other in terms of theme – two solitary men in an alien environment, railing against a system they hold to be unjust and oppressive. Ironically, one of the shows was destined to become an all-time classic, while the other's fate was to languish in near TV-oblivion.

MAN IN A SUITCASE (1967-68)

Though it would never cause the sensation that *The Prisoner* managed to, *Man in a Suitcase* is a fine example of the action thriller TV genre. Many commentators have championed the show, like the trendy *Uncut* magazine, who wrote, 'You can leave your *Avengers*, *Star Trek* and *Dr Who* to the anoraks. If you want real cult television look no further than *Man in a Suitcase*, the most criminally ignored of all Swinging Sixties TV dramas.'

Writers Dennis Spooner and Richard Harris devised the format for this bold series, about a CIA agent called McGill who'd been drummed out of the service and forced to make his living as a freelance private investigator, working out of London. Strangely, Spooner and Harris had no further connection with the show as, according to one of the directors, Robert Tronson, both were, 'Immediately rode out of sight and an American script editor, Stanley R. Greenberg, was brought over instead. He was very peculiar and didn't know any British writers, and didn't have a very clear idea of what the subject was at all.'

The basic concept was not too far removed from previous ITC series, in that it featured a lone hero getting into scrapes and assorted adventures, but this time with a far harder edge to mirror the increasingly violent nature of the late sixties. Richard Bradford, an American actor with distinctive prematurely greying hair, was cast as McGill. No one quite like him had ever been seen on British TV before. In 1965,

Kicked out of the CIA, McGill becomes a tough private investigator working in London in Man in a Suitcase.

he'd landed his big break when Arthur Penn cast him in *The Chase*, alongside Marlon Brando. In the film's most notorious scene, Bradford beats Brando's small-town cop to a pulp, aided by his redneck cohorts. It was this role that brought him to the attention of the makers of *Man in a Suitcase*.

Texan-born Richard Bradford was heavily influenced by his cinema idols, James Dean and Marlon Brando, even enrolling at the mecca of the method – Lee Strasberg's Actor's Studio. And he brought this mean and moody method acting style to the show, with controversial repercussions. 'They kind of looked down upon the Actor's Studio in England,' explains Bradford. 'Kind of made fun of it, I think. And I probably took it a little too far at times. There were times when I went kind of far out. But I wanted to be real. I wanted to be as honest as I could.'

Being 'real' did have its problems, however. 'Richard had this thing that he wanted to be a real person,' says director John Glen. 'He wanted to do everything for real. Well, if you're a good actor you don't have to do everything for real. On the episode I directed, there was a scene where McGill confronts someone at the entrance to a house. Richard starts pulling and shoving at the door, and suddenly the whole set collapsed, and both actors were framed in the open doorway with the whole set completely obliterated. As the dust cleared they were just standing there. Fortunately, no one was hurt. But that's an example of how he liked to do everything for real. He didn't realise that we just stick sets up with nails in the floor, we don't expect anyone to try and wrestle it down. He was a bit odd. A very nice man but completely Brando-fied. He was a method actor and had worked with Brando and was trying to copy him. Unfortunately, he didn't have Brando's talent. But he tried to imitate the way Brando behaved on screen, great, thoughtful, long ten-second pauses between lines – which on television doesn't work, not when you've got to get the whole damn show done in 55 minutes on the screen. So there was a lot of editing involved.'

Also, if McGill was out of breath in the story, Bradford insisted on working himself up into a state of near exhaustion himself, much to the amazement of Robert Tronson. 'It transpired that he needed to have a long run to get out of breath to start this scene, so we had to open the big studio doors and he pounded outside, got out of breath and was ready. But then we had to shut the doors, ring bells, do the lights, roll camera, and by this time he'd regained his breath and wasn't ready, so had to run outside again. This went on for hours, and he was getting more and more exhausted as he was running further and further. There are certain good elements about the method, but a lot of it is crap, and Richard was right up to his neck in that crap.'

Another acting ploy Bradford used was behaving to his fellow actors in a way that mirrored their on-screen relationships. 'I didn't go out of my way to be real friendly with actors if they were an adversarial character. And I figured if I don't go schmooze with them, maybe they won't like me a little bit for that, and maybe it will have a little edge in the scenes that would be good for the show. But if I was friendly with them in the show, then I was friendly with them on the set.'

Akin to fellow methodologists like Brando and Dean, Bradford tended to mumble his dialogue, which frustrated the sound guys, who pleaded with the directors to get him to speak up. 'I was just trying to be as real as I could,' argues Bradford. 'I remember one director, Pat Jackson, came up to me one time and said, "Richard, you're right to underplay like that, because when you explode it really has an effect."'

Tronson believes that the crew assigned to the show were too old-fashioned and set in their ways for what was, for its time, something new and innovative. 'We could've done with a much better camera and sound unit. They weren't really geared to someone like Richard, who did act in a peculiar way. Getting Richard to stand in the same place and do the same thing twice running was pretty hard. The cameraman we had was an old Ealing guy, a perfectionist who took his time. We really wanted someone who could shoot quickly and move about on the set, so he wasn't right for this. So there was a lot of tension on the set which was sad and unnecessary.'

An atypical publicity image: McGill was more used to seedy bedsits and drab hotels than villas with swimming pools.

As originally conceived, McGill was your bog-standard action man. That was until Bradford approached the character in the method style, injecting large doses of his own personality and acting technique and turning him into a vulnerable human being, a man of complex, hidden frustrations, his nerves constantly on the edge. Or, as *Uncut* put it, 'Forever being beaten with life's shit end of the stick.' 'Stanley Greenberg was the writer and it seemed to me he was writing Mickey Spillane, kind of a wise arse, wisecracking guy, and I didn't want to be that kind of guy. I wanted to be the opposite of that. I wanted to be a guy that didn't use his gun unless he had to use his gun. I didn't want to have it out all the time, ready to kill people. I wanted to be more sensitive, more aware and more compassionate, all the things that are [the] opposite of the wisecracking bullshit artist. I just saw the part differently and I just kept fighting in that direction. I'd change my lines. I'm no writer, and some lines I changed badly. But I just couldn't get Stanley to write what I was trying to do. He just wouldn't do it.'

Watching it today, *Man in a Suitcase* works brilliantly, largely on account of Bradford's intense, brooding presence. 'It wasn't bad to have this method style of Richard's on the show,' says Tronson. 'Compared to other actors it was refreshing to have someone who was that concerned, but it did go too far. He was bizarre. I got on with him very well, though not many did. For some reason I could cope with him. He was difficult, there's no other word for it. He would keep everyone waiting for hours.

Top: a *self-professed fan of Marlon Brando, Richard Bradford's method acting brought him into conflict with his directors.* Bottom: *before her fame in* The Good Life, *Felicity Kendal enjoyed numerous TV guest star roles.*

You couldn't get him on the set. He played up. There was quite a lot of mischief in it really.'

Certainly, English crews and English directors hadn't come across an actor like Bradford before – so conflict was almost inevitable. 'I didn't have a lot of conflict with directors,' Bradford asserts. 'Only with Charlie Crichton did we scream and holler. I'd question things. I wasn't just a robot that did anything they said. We did an episode where the CIA used me and put my life in jeopardy. At the end one of the guys says, "Let's go have a cup of coffee," and he starts going off to the left, and I head off to the right, which is what my character would've done. They said, "No, no. Go with him." I said, "No, my character wouldn't do that, why would I go with him?" So they said, "Well, let's just shoot one going with him." And actually that's what they used. So they did those things to me that just burned my ass.'

Old school directors like Crichton, who in their Ealing heyday were used to being called 'Sir' and getting their own way when it came to actors, took the most offence at the way Bradford conducted himself on the set. 'Charlie kept saying, "Do this. Do that. Stand over there,"' recalls Tronson. 'And Richard would always say, "Why do I stand there? Why do I do this?" And they'd have a terrible row and it would end up with Charlie yelling, "Because I'm the fucking director!" Which is what Richard was aiming for. He

It doesn't take a genius to work out the symbolism – but it's a nicely executed piece of publicity art, all the same.

loved to hear him say that. He thought it was terribly funny.'

Irrespective of these clashes, when Bradford was asked to nominate three directors to work with for the last batch of episodes, he chose Crichton. 'I'm sure he was surprised, but I loved the guy. He was rough, that was his reputation. I don't think he cared for me, but I really liked what he did and really liked him, and we did some good shows.'

Bradford's relations with producer Sidney Cole were also strained, according to Tronson. 'Poor old Sid was terrified of Richard. Physically, Richard was enormous and very strong. And he was dangerous, because every now and then it did seem that Richard might suddenly turn on Sid.'

Again, like his perceived enmity with Crichton, Bradford insists that relations with Cole were fine. 'I had a room at Pinewood Studios where I had a little shower and a changing area. And there was a bag I used to punch, and they said I put Sidney Cole's face on it and beat the hell out of it. I mean, I don't remember doing that! I liked Sidney, certainly better than I did our American producer, Barry Delmaine. So the word is that

I didn't like any of them. To me that's a little bit of an exaggeration. And they said I was late all the time. So either they're exaggerating a bit or I'm just completely out of it.'

Despite the problems surrounding its production and the treadmill schedule – Bradford only had about three weeks off during the year and a half it took to make *Suitcase* – the actor enjoyed his stay in England. 'There were times when it was infuriating, but mostly I really enjoyed it. I stayed in a great house near Highgate that had Henry Irving's foils that he used when he played Hamlet over the fireplace. It was fantastic. I felt at home in England, strangely enough. Supposedly, my relative William Bradford came over on the Mayflower, and became one of the first governors of one of the colonies. So maybe that's why I felt at home there. But I've never been back to the UK. I just figured I'd be back, so I didn't go to all the tourist places I should have gone to. I didn't have a brain in my head, number one. Number two, my wife and I are at Harrods and I hear this scream of girls, and I turn around and they come running, "There he is! There he is!" I don't thrive on those situations so I quit going to those places.'

Behind the credit list of established directors who worked on *Suitcase*, like Tronson and Crichton, came the little-known name of John Glen. Having done so well on *Danger Man*, Glen was personally approached by Sidney Cole to work on second unit and be supervising editor on *Suitcase*, from where he could (to some degree) influence the style of the show. 'It was an action-based series, but we tried to be a bit different. I brought the same kind of style from *Danger Man*. Quite frankly, we were trying to do a Bond thing with it.' It was on *Suitcase* that Glen finally got his longed-for directorial break. 'We used to go into Sidney Cole's office in the evening and discuss the day's work, and how the schedule was going. Really it was a good excuse to have a drink. I remember once Sidney was pouring the whiskey out, and I asked, "Who supplies the whiskey?" And he said, "I supply the whiskey and Lew Grade supplies the cabinet it sits in." The old Ealing crowd would be there sometimes, people like Charlie Crichton. They all liked their drop of whiskey and used to fight over the bottle sometimes. So I enjoyed all that. Anyway, one day I said to Sidney, "How about giving me an opportunity to direct?" And he paused for a moment and looked at me and smiled, and said, "Oh, you want to join those other 350 out of work directors in my book, do you?"'

Cole left it pretty late in the series before giving Glen his chance behind the camera. 'And it was a tough one as well, it was full of action and very difficult to do in ten days. I remember I was shooting a car chase in Black Park, and halfway through the shooting we got mixed up with horsemen from a Robin Hood film they were making there. Those sorts of things used to happen all the time. Great fun, but it was a learning curve for me. I realised then that I had to take full responsibility, not sit there and be a nice person all the time, that in actual fact you've got to crack the whip and ride over people if they're obstructive.'

Unfortunately, Glen was a couple of days over schedule on his episode and they never asked him back, ending his association with ITC. It was really only in the 1980s that Glen came to the fore as a major filmmaker, helming no less than five consecutive Bond movies, including Roger Moore's last (*A View to a Kill*) and Timothy Dalton's debut (*The Living Daylights*), surely a record that will never be broken.

Man in a Suitcase is undoubtedly the toughest and grittiest series ITC ever made, perhaps even an influence on the violent cop shows of the seventies like *The Sweeney* and *The Professionals*. Sixties TV audiences were used to heroes like Simon Templar and John Steed, defeating villains with nary a scratch or hair out of place. Then along came McGill, who was regularly used as a punch bag. Bradford particularly wanted to show the effects the physical violence had on his character. 'Most guys, when they got knocked out on TV, just got up, shook their heads and then ran straight ahead like nothing happened. I wanted to still have the effect of that fight. I'd try to walk but fall and flop over things. But I found that I'm falling and bouncing my head on the floor, literally bouncing my temple on the floor, and I think they're getting this on film, but they're not, they're letting me fall out of frame. What does it take to follow the guy? I didn't know they weren't following me. I'm crawling though glass, cutting myself, nicks and bruises all the time, and half of it's not even in the frame. And I was totally unaware. I wasn't watching what the camera's doing; I just assumed the camera's following you. Why not, what are you doing it for?'

An episode usually wasn't complete without McGill enduring at least one heavy beating or, in the case of the fan's favourite episode, 'Web with Four Spiders', being shoved out of a speeding car. This, coupled with the character's own chain-smoking death wish, combined to create one of British television's first anti-heroes. 'The most difficult thing about Richard was his attitude to the violence,' says Tronson. 'We got into a lot of

Up against Star Trek *on US TV,* Suitcase *failed to find an audience, but has since acquired a loyal fan following.* Bottom: *before stardom with the film version of* M*A*S*H, *Donald Sutherland was still a regular ITC guest star.*

trouble. He insisted on doing his own makeup and putting on hideous scars and scabs. Usually we had to shoot on the other side of his face because it was so revolting. It was almost pathetic in a sense. He just loved it. He was also out of control in a fight. Stuntmen, after a bit, wouldn't work with him. He'd rehearse the fight for hours, but when it came to actually shooting it he'd just go mad. And he was as strong as a bloody ox. He did frighten people. He was always sort of angry, Richard. Which comes over in his performance. That worked very well for what we wanted, of course, but it wasn't entirely acting.'

In his youth, Bradford had been a keen athlete and duly enjoyed the physical aspects of the role. 'I loved the fights. Although, in the very beginning, I did tear into this guy. I barrelled into him with just abandon; I really hit him hard. And I think a couple of stunt guys backed out of wanting to work with me because of that kind of thing. Someone said I broke somebody's nose. Maybe I did, but I don't remember. I think I would've remembered that. So they were afraid to work with me, a lot of stunt guys.'

The series is also notable for its high number of sour and downbeat endings. The bleakest was 'Burden of Proof', guest starring John Gregson as Henry Faversham, aide to the president of some fictional African republic. Bravely volunteering to set himself up to obtain proof that one of the president's henchmen is killing people, Faversham is held prisoner within the republic's London embassy. McGill forces his way in and overcomes the bad guys – too late to save Faversham, who has already died from injuries sustained under torture. Powerful stuff, and not what the viewer was expecting, the build-up having implied Faversham would be saved. *Jason King* this ain't.

Indeed, compared to other ITC action heroes, McGill really did come out of leftfield. There are no smarmy quips a la *The Saint*, he never gets the girl, and is frequently drugged, interrogated and double-crossed. And if that's not bad enough, he drives a Hillman Imp. As for his dress sense, there was no super-spy white tuxedo here, but bottle green zip-tops, brown cords and turtleneck sweaters. If the occasion called for it he might wear a suit, though a pretty drab one at that. This was as close as ITC got to *noir* realism. McGill certainly lives in the real world and, unlike Simon Templar, who we never saw haggle for his fee, is utterly mercenary and single-minded when it comes to professional matters. This is no knight in shining armour; he's all about being paid.

In one episode, a client refuses payment and orders his bodyguard to throw McGill out. A fight ensues, during which the American emerges victorious, forcing the man to pay up. As he does so, he's quick to compare McGill's tactics to his own: 'McGill, in what way is your blackmail different to mine?' McGill's answer is simple: 'Mine worked!'

Liberally sprinkled among the hardcore action was the usual constellation of guest stars. Heavyweight acting talent was provided by the likes of Bernard Lee and Ray McAnally, there were future film stars in Donald Sutherland and Edward Fox, plus a few familiar faces too, like Jane Merrow, who was drawn from a stable of performers who did the rounds of ITC's shows. 'It was a bit like being in a little repertory of actors,' she observes. 'I was in the episode with Rodney Bewes jumping off Albert Bridge. We were all clambering around Albert Bridge on a Sunday morning with this very egotistical star, Richard Bradford. He was an all-American, real star, and he behaved like he would in Hollywood, and frankly most of it just washed over us. He was all right, he wasn't unpleasant, but he was very much larger than life. I think it was fine for the show, but at the end of the day I thought it was a bit over the top.'

Although she looks back fondly on those ITC shows, Jane considers her work on numerous BBC dramas in the sixties as far more creatively fulfilling. But, unlike ITC, who shot everything on film, the Beeb still used videotape, and that whole aspect of Britain's golden age of television has been wiped and lost to posterity. 'People still ring me about things like *The Saint* and *Danger Man*, which is wonderful and I deeply appreciate those shows, but they were the entertainment and the rest was the créme and it's lost, gone. Those taped BBC dramas were just binned, or they reused the tapes, it's really a travesty, a disgrace actually. The ITC stuff was slightly better paid, we got to wear prettier dresses and the filming part was a luxury, they were like mini-movies, and I absolutely adored filming. The scripts weren't all that great, I have to say, but they were written to a sort of formula. They weren't writing Shakespeare and they weren't expected to write Shakespeare, they were just good old adventure stories.'

Nicola Pagett, who'd done a *Danger Man* as well as a *Suitcase* episode, feels much the same about the quality of ITC's scripts. 'I remember saying that the script didn't make any sense, but that I'll say it anyway. I'm just glad I did a lot of theatre. I mean, it was fun doing those shows, but you didn't really learn very much about acting. At least on the stage you get stuff that makes sense. Half of that stuff didn't make any sense at all. Maybe that's why people liked it.' Even the thrill of making a glossy TV series was missing for Nicola. 'I remember having to get up really early to catch the number 27 bus. They didn't give you any money for a taxi, you had to get to the studio by public transport.'

Once it began its run in Britain, in September 1967, the critical response to *Man in a Suitcase* ranged from the average to much worse. Under the heading, 'Low Grade nonsense', the TV critic of *The Sunday Times* really let fly: 'McGill looks to me like any other of the American actors, apparently made of concrete, whom ATV [ITC] have hired during the long and shameful history of pandering to supposed American tastes which recently won them a Queen's award for industry.'

Although a moderate ratings success in Europe, the show fared less well in America, although it got a network showing on ABC from May 1968. 'A lot of people liked it but it was up against *Star Trek*,' Bradford recalls. 'And ABC just let it die, they didn't back it at all.' Alas, only one series of 30 episodes was made. Not that Bradford wanted to have anything to do with the show anymore. 'By the end I just wanted out. The scripts seemed to get worse and worse and the situations my guy was in were less interesting. Nobody asked me to make any more. I think they knew I didn't want to. Then I did a stupid thing. All the clothes I wore in the series I took on purpose without asking, because I wanted to punch back some way, to get back at them a little bit. But that was a stupid thing to do. I've never felt good about it.'

After *Suitcase*, Bradford returned to the States and pretty much sank into obscurity – apart from the odd appearance in TV shows like *The Waltons*, as a daughter-beating, drunken religious nut who burns down John Boy Walton's school, or in a *Cagney and Lacey* episode. Bradford's most notable post-*Suitcase* achievement was his role as the corrupt police chief in the 1987 big screen version of *The Untouchables*. His best scene was a back alley brawl with Sean Connery, a moment not lost on spy fans: McGill and Bond slugging it out. So, does he now maybe regret leaving the role of McGill too soon? 'If I knew what I know now I would've done more, because I was really free to do what I had in my head, much more free creatively speaking than you are on American television. If I had a brain I would've done more. But I would've only done more if they had tried to make it good. To be helpful in that direction, not spiteful, which I felt they were being. But I didn't realise until later that everybody was so pissed off at me. I had no idea.'

As for producer Sidney Cole, he decided against pursuing other shows in a similar vein to *Suitcase*, instead returning to his love of historical series – producing such seventies classics as *The Adventures of Black Beauty* and *Dick Turpin* with Richard O'Sullivan.

'Sid was a man I had tremendous respect for,' Robert Tronson recalls. 'It was lovely to work with him. At the end of a day's shooting, a few others and I would be expected to go into his office and sit and drink. And there was an associate producer called Barry Delmaine, who was a pain in the arse, and every night he'd get up and put the tops on all the bottles and Sid would be taking them off again. One great trouble was that Sid was a very strong union man, a socialist, crypto-communist even, so therefore he was in a terrible position as a producer; nobody was ever sacked or disciplined. We had a bloody awful union really, and they just got away with practically anything, simply because Sid was in a terrible sort of dichotomy and nothing was done. But I have to say *Suitcase* was the nearest I got in those ITC shows to ever feeling I was directing something, as opposed to just standing there saying, "Action!" and "Cut!" There was much more scope there, and that was largely Sid's doing. He had a large respect for directors.'

Although it is established as a cult favourite today, Bradford looks back on the series as a lost opportunity. 'I really wanted that thing to be special. It was a pain in my ass that I felt like I was the only one that cared that much. And it was a pain in my ass that the scripts weren't really that good. I think they were retreads from other shows. I haven't seen any of them for so long. I like "Brainwash". But some of them were just badly written, and there's not a hell of a lot you can do. I felt they didn't take the time necessary to do that kind of show. They were always in a hurry, always trying to get onto the next one without finishing what we just did. And then later you have to go back and shoot one of the shows you did two months ago. That's weird. I just felt that they cheaped it out and just didn't care like I cared. I really loved it, I had a good time, it's just that I thought we should all be trying to do the best we can possibly do, not just eke it out and make it work a little bit. Why not do it right and do it really well? And I felt like I was the only one that cared that much.'

The character of McGill, an existentialist loner in a corrupt, greedy, hostile world, was perhaps too out of step with mass audience taste at the time to be a big mainstream hit. Although, had the makers got their way, the show would have been even grittier. 'We tried desperately to get even more of an edge into the show,' claims Tronson. 'But outside forces wanted it bland, wanted another *Saint* figure. It was a bad time because ABC, the American backers, were going through various boardroom crises, and quite often a new raft of men in suits would appear off the plane, having taken over from the last lot, and wanting everything different. And so every now and then we'd have to re-shoot scenes and change things. The show was originally called *McGill*, which I think was a better title, and I had an argument about them changing it. The American executives sent out this questionnaire to housewives in the Midwest saying, "Would you watch a show called A) *McGill* or B) *Man*

Left: *this postcard, featuring a greeting from Richard Bradford, was sent to fans of the series.* Right: *sheet music to the now classic theme tune, later reprised by Chris Evans for his* TFI Friday *chat show.*

in a Suitcase? Please tick." So it was never as hard edged as was intended. [Writer] Richard Harris wanted it to be much tougher. I think Lew would've liked it tough but the Americans softened it, the ABC lot. They interfered enormously.'

For much of its existence, the biggest criticism levelled at ITC was this pandering to the US market. But their shows had to be as populist as possible, with particular emphasis on appealing to tastes in America, which was where the money was. In many ways this enhanced the shows, as each ITC series had to be of a very high standard to win a network showing. On the negative side, the networks had certain rules which had to be obeyed, like not seeing dead bodies with eyes open or running blood – but, as ITC were generally family-orientated, that didn't prove too restrictive.

Like Bradford, John Glen feels that the show somehow missed its target, and lacked the sheer quality of, say, a *Danger Man*. 'We were always trying to do better than what really the material was worth, trying to make a silk purse out of a sow's ear. But we were learning our craft, most of us, we were young people trying to emulate some of the successful American shows. It was kind of a mediocre series and wasn't a huge success, though knowing Lew Grade he probably made a few bob out of it. But funnily enough, as time has gone by it's got its fans, and a lot of people write to me about it. I suppose it depends how old you are when you start looking at these series and how impressionable you are. I used to watch the John Wayne films when I was a kid, and I used to come out feeling about six feet tall when I was about four feet tall at the time. It's the effect a film has on you. Its not so much what's on the screen, it's what your imagination does with it, and it has a lasting effect on you and you remember it with affection.'

THE PRISONER (1967-68)

Actor and ITC veteran George Baker tells a story about how *The Prisoner* came about. 'The director Don Chaffey had a little cottage down in Hampshire somewhere. Twelve o'clock one night, bang, bang, bang on the door, and it's McGoohan. "I've got an idea!" And Don said, "Do you know what time it is?" McGoohan went, "Look, I've got a really good idea." "Well you'd better come in, I suppose," Don relented. And Pat talked his idea through and a couple of days later they sold it to Lew. That's how *The Prisoner* happened.'

Much has been said and written about *The Prisoner*. With the obvious exceptions of *Dr Who* and *Star Trek*, it's probably the most analysed television show in history. Its tale of a British agent who resigns his commission – only to be kidnapped and to wake up in a superficially cheerful village, whose sinister purpose is to extract or protect the valuable knowledge of its inhabitants – is a brilliant mix of Orwell, Kafka and Ian Fleming.

The Prisoner really came about through sheer boredom on McGoohan's part. After 86 episodes of *Danger Man*, he'd had enough and wanted to do something else. Grade wasn't at all happy, but was prepared to listen to any new ideas. At a Saturday morning meeting McGoohan came along with a prepared format, even photographs of the main location he intended using: Portmerion in North Wales. Grade looked at it and said, 'I don't want to read the format.' Grade's preferred reading matter was accounts. 'Just tell me what it's about.' McGoohan's pitch lasted ten minutes, after which Grade said, 'I don't understand one word you're talking about. But how much is it going to be?' McGoohan told him. 'When can you start?' Grade asked. McGoohan thought for a while, before answering that he could start on the scripts that Monday. 'The money will be in your company's account on Monday morning,' said Grade. And it was. *The Prisoner* had begun.

Incredibly, from that moment on, there was no written contract between Grade and McGoohan; Lew's handshake was guarantee enough. Michael Billington, who guested on the show before making his name with *UFO*, had his own theory as to what prompted McGoohan to do *The Prisoner*. 'Pat told me that he only did it on the strength that Lew Grade would finance him to do a movie production of Ibsen's play *Brand*, which he'd had a big success with on stage and TV. But the film never got made.'

Neither did Grade interfere in how McGoohan made the show. 'I can't conceive of anybody else in the world – then or now – giving me that amount of freedom with a subject which in many respects was, you might say, outrageous,' observed McGoohan in 1995. It was all to do with trust. Grade knew that his star would deliver. 'I'll never forget *The Prisoner*,' says Marcia Stanton, Grade's loyal assistant. 'Because we never knew what the next episode was going to be. And I remember the head of production for ITC, Bernard Kingham, was absolutely terrified because he had to deal with McGoohan. But Lew said, "Look. He's writing some of them and he's directing some of them, just let him get on with it."'

At one point, the President of CBS came over to England to meet with Grade about *The Prisoner*. He'd seen four episodes and didn't understand what on earth

This publicity brochure hails the arrival of the granddaddy of all cult TV shows – The Prisoner.

the series was all about. Soon, he wouldn't be the only one. After spending two days in Wales, at Grade's suggestion, watching some of it being filmed, the TV executive returned and said, 'I don't understand that Patrick McGoohan. Do you have problems with him?' Grade answered, 'I never have any problems at all with Patrick McGoohan. He's wonderful.' 'Well, how do you do it?' To which Grade replied, 'Always give in to what he wants.' Much of what works and doesn't work about *The Prisoner* can be traced back to that statement.

Basically, McGoohan ran a creative dictatorship on the set. *The Prisoner* was his baby. Not only was McGoohan the star, but he produced, wrote and even directed some of the episodes. It's one of the most staggering achievements in the annals of British television. Certainly no individual before or since has ever had such freedom and power to indulge his imagination on so major a TV series. Not one actor was cast without McGoohan's agreement and he personally vetted every script. Morris Farhi, who later wrote for BBC's *The Onedin Line*, was asked to submit an episode in just a week, only for McGoohan to turn it down flat. The reason? In one scene Farhi had him perspiring under torture. 'Heroes don't sweat,' asserted McGoohan. After episode thirteen, George Markstein, the series story editor, resigned in protest, saying, 'I think McGoohan would like to be God.'

Years later, McGoohan did confess that he perhaps wielded too much power on

The Prisoner. 'The hardest thing to hold onto was perspective. I got spoiled because I had complete control, down to every last nut and bolt.'

George Baker, one of many actors to inhabit the crucial role of Number Two, personally saw the creative autonomy the star enjoyed. 'He had a lot of control on the set. He was very helpful, courteous, but he was actually working himself to death.' Baker didn't need a whole lot of persuasion to do the show. 'I did it because Pat was a wonderful actor and I knew him quite well. He rang me and said, "We've got this idea, would you like to come and do it?" And I read the script, which was marvellous, it was a complete culture shock and quite different to anything one had seen before. You didn't understand what was going on, but mind you, I don't think you understand what's going on now. I've had a look at it once or twice and I thought, very clever really, very clever hokum, because you never knew who Number Two was or what they were doing there, but there was a sort of fear hanging over the whole place. It all looks so like a holiday camp, but in fact, what's going on underneath?'

Jane Merrow, who'd appeared in three episodes of *Danger Man*, was also asked personally by McGoohan to return for *The Prisoner*. 'I loved working with Patrick, it was so exciting, you never quite knew what he was going to do next or how he was going to play it. I think I was a good partner for him, we'd spar and spark off each other. I have to be honest; he wasn't always comfortable working with actresses. He liked working best with actors. Some of the actresses he cast he didn't seem to have a good communication with.'

In the case of Annette Andre, that was an understatement. Just two years away from her big break as the female lead in *Randall and Hopkirk (Deceased)*, Annette was cast in a *Prisoner* episode and found the experience among the worst of her career. '*The Prisoner* I hated with a passion. I disliked McGoohan so much I can't tell you. He was a madman, an absolute madman. And very cold. I wanted to get off that. I actually phoned my agent to ask her to get me off it, but she couldn't. He was a dreadful man. I had no clue what I was doing. I read the script and I didn't have a clue what it was about from beginning to end.'

Perhaps because McGoohan was wielding so much power on the set, his actions could sometimes border on control freakery – or was it something much deeper and more personal? 'He was also drinking,' insists Annette. 'He used to drink vodka. And when he was really drunk he would be abusive. I hated the man. I thought he was an absolutely dreadful man. I tried to talk to him at one point, and all he would do would be to put you down. He didn't like actresses anyway. He made everything unpleasant. And he was very unpleasant to various people, including our director Bob Asher. I was very upset about that, because Bob was a very nice man and didn't deserve what went on. I have no respect for people who treat people badly. He was vile to me and he was vile to Bob, and I thought that was unforgivable. So I hated *The Prisoner*.'

Whether a fierce drinker or the ultimate control freak, the truth is McGoohan defied categorisation, a man prone to contradictions and fluctuating moods. 'You couldn't say what Pat McGoohan was like,' says Raymond Austin, who worked as a stuntman on both *Danger Man* and *The Prisoner*. 'It was what he was going to be like that day, which no one ever knew. He was crazy. Sometimes he'd play the dialogue, sometimes he wouldn't. You just had no idea what Pat was going to do. One of the most difficult people for directors and writers ever. Especially when he got a bee in his bonnet about something. Patrick wouldn't do things unless they did it his way. I mean, he really would sulk, he wouldn't come out of his dressing room. And people started to let him go that way on *The Prisoner*, and so it went completely out of control.'

And yet Peter Wyngarde, another guest star that played Number Two, was inspired by the way McGoohan took charge of *The Prisoner*, and put a lot of what he learnt into practice when his own TV showcase came along, *Jason King*. 'I have enormous respect for Patrick McGoohan. I believe that the leading player makes the series. The others help, of course, the producer, the director, but the main guide, the guru if you like, is the leading character, and watching Pat on that series, I knew then that was the way to deal with a series. But you get no thanks for it; in fact it kills you.'

McGoohan asked many old friends onto the show. Leo McKern, later the legendary *Rumpole of the Bailey*, came in at short notice for the episode 'Once Upon a Time', one of the most bizarre of the series. It was mainly a two-hander, where McKern tries to brainwash Number Six only for our hero to turn the tables. It was eight days of shooting and, for much of the time, both actors were head to head from morning to early evening. 'It was pretty intense,' McGoohan observed. 'It was psychiatrist couch time.' There's some very strange dialogue too, consisting largely of bursts of 'Six, Six, Six.' One lunchtime, McGoohan caught the rushes and went to

Top: *for some, McGoohan's latent paranoia and ove-bearing personality spiralled out of control during the filming of* The Prisoner. Bottom: *behind the camera, McGoohan takes control of*The Prisoner*'s notorious final episode.*

McGoohan wins the Village's staring competition hands down.

McGoohan with Randall and Hopkirk*'s Annette Andre, who confessed to hating her time on* The Prisoner.

see McKern in his dressing room to compliment him on them. What he found was McKern curled up in the foetal position on his couch, screaming, 'Go away! Go away you bastard! I don't want to see you again.' Perturbed, McGoohan asked what he was talking about. 'I've just ordered two doctors,' McKern announced. 'And they're coming over as soon as they can. Go away!' He had too – they both arrived that afternoon, and McKern didn't work for three days. It emerged that he'd had a breakdown of sorts. 'He'd cracked, which was very interesting,' as McGoohan later sympathetically put it. 'He'd truly cracked.'

It's an amazing story, and one that is confirmed by director Robert Tronson, who was a friend of McKern's. 'Leo had to go into treatment because he had a breakdown. That's absolutely true. And of all people, Leo was pretty tough. But it drove him potty, McGoohan and the piece. McGoohan was a brilliant actor. I saw him in *Brand* and it was the most extraordinary performance I've ever seen. It really was electric. That brought him lots of publicity, and why I think Lew Grade pushed him into *Danger Man*. And that show developed a massive profile, and he became a psychopath, no question. I think he was always an odd man, but that success developed it and it screwed him up. And he would only do *The Prisoner* if he had complete control, and Lew agreed and so they wrote all the producers and everybody out of it, and there was nobody, nobody in charge at all. He was driving everybody mad.'

Top: *shooting on the streets of London.* Bottom: *Location shooting in Portmerion, the Welsh coastal village discovered by McGoohan, whose décor and atmosphere contributed so much to the show's success.*

Another face from the past was *Danger Man* director Peter Graham Scott. At the time, Scott was producing a BBC series called *The Troubleshooters*, about oil moguls. 'It was a big show. We shot all over the world, Libya, Malta, Thailand, Hong Kong, India. We were in Beirut when the Six Day War started, which was not very funny. So I was preparing the next season of that when one Friday night the phone rang, and a voice went, "This is Patrick McGoohan. I want you to come and start directing on Monday." I said, "Directing what?" And he said, "It's a series called *The Prisoner*. Haven't you heard about it?" I hadn't. So he said, "A script will arrive by motorcycle tomorrow morning." I said, "Wait a minute, I'm under contract to the BBC." And he said, "Who do I have to talk to to get you out of it? It's just for two weeks." I told him it was Sydney Newman, head of drama, but I thought there wasn't a chance in hell of Sydney agreeing to my going. But Sydney did agree. So the script arrived on the Saturday and I read it and I felt, either this man is mad or there is something here that I've missed. Then I had another look at it and I said, "Oh I see, yes. Very clever."'

Scott encountered a McGoohan more or less identical to the one he'd left behind on *Danger Man*. 'Patrick could be aggressive. Once, on the set of *The Prisoner*, an actor came up to me quite late in the afternoon and said, "I just can't understand this bit of dialogue." And I said, "Oh, think of the money and just speak the line." And this voice from behind yelled, "You haven't done your homework, Peter!" And it was Pat. Otherwise he was super. He was a taskmaster, there's no doubt about it. He wanted results. He wanted interesting shots. He wanted everything that I could give him.'

Only much later did Scott discover that McGoohan had hired him because his original choice of director had backed out at the last minute. Producing the 1985 TV movie *Jamaica Inn* in Cornwall, Scott would cast McGoohan in one of the principal roles. 'Along with some of the crew, I met Patrick at the airport and we all went for lunch. And my cameraman very bravely said, "What I can't understand is why did you have old Peter to direct one of your *Prisoners*?" And I felt, Patrick will come to my rescue, he will say, "Because Peter has studied all the great playwrights, because he understood motivation," and all that. Instead Patrick said, "Because he was quick. And he was cheap."'

Much of the charm and endearing appeal of the show comes from its distinctive location. Portmeirion, an Italianate resort village in North Wales built as a folly by Sir Clough Williams-Ellis, was discovered by McGoohan himself during location work on an early *Danger Man* episode. And it was here that filming on *The Prisoner* commenced in September 1966, on a budget

Top: *the bizarre set designs contributed greatly to the series' unsettling atmosphere of paranoia.* Bottom: *another behind the scenes shot taken on location in Portmerion.*

nearing a million pounds, a huge sum for the sixties. Some actors, like Jane Merrow and George Baker, never set foot in Portmeirion. For instance, all Baker's scenes took place on a huge, pseudo-Bond control centre housed at the MGM studios in Borehamwood. 'That was an extraordinary set, with that great big chair. It was terrific fun to make *The Prisoner*. You knew you were doing something special. And Patrick believed in it so much, he knew he was onto something good.'

Poor Annette Andre, already unnerved by her leading man, found the sets equally threatening. 'You were stuck in this awful set which was very depressing. It wasn't a good set to be in. And you were in these uniforms. It was a bit like being in a real prison. I guess that was the atmosphere he wanted to create, in which case he did a very good job of that, of making one feel very enclosed. But it was unpleasant to work in.'

As production continued, McGoohan upped and left for Hollywood to make the Cold War thriller *Ice Station Zebra*, resulting in one *Prisoner* episode being made virtually without him. On his return, a *coup d'etat* of sorts had taken place behind the scenes. With the production getting increasingly more expensive and bewildering, Grade decided McGoohan's number was finally up, and that episode seventeen would be the last ever *Prisoner*.

Thrown into disarray, McGoohan had just one week to tie up all the loose ends of the series into a climactic episode that has entered history as the most controversial television denouement ever.

After Grade's decision to cancel *The Prisoner*, McGoohan decided to go down in flames. According to Raymond Austin, the actor insisted on going ahead with the final episode without a script – essentially, to improvise as he went along. 'And they said, "You can't do that, we don't know what clothes people are going to have, what make-up, how much film we're going to need, you can't do something without a guideline." But he wanted to do it without a script. And they started the thing off with Pat sat on a chair, and he said, "What you do is you squirt shaving cream all over my face." And that was it. Lew Grade got this message about what was happening and said, "Hold everything! I'm not going to carry on with this because it's got crazy."'

Since the series hit British screens in September 1967, it had become a huge smash, hooking the public almost from day one. Few programmes before or since have had the nation talking quite so much, as George Baker recalls. 'The next time that I noticed a public reaction quite like the one *The Prisoner* got was with *I, Claudius*, because it cut right across social barriers. You had an intellectual audience, a sort of middle ground, and then the dustman used to come up and say, "Cor, that was a good episode last night." It was the same with *The Prisoner*; it just caught the imagination of the whole nation.'

A big fan of the show was Lew's nephew, Michael Grade. 'I loved *The Prisoner*. That was really exceptional. Don't know what it was about, load of old cobblers really, but it was very groundbreaking. Lew was thrilled with it at the start and wanted more episodes, and Pat McGoohan said, "I'm stuck. I don't know what to do with it. I've run out of ideas." It was a very clever, unusual show.'

McGoohan revelled in the fact that many of the allegorical aspects of the show totally flummoxed audiences, who kept watching out of a sheer morbid fascination with finding out just what the hell was going on. 'I think there was some degree of frustration because nobody quite understood it,' observes Jane Merrow. 'I didn't

McGoohan makes for a great cowboy in this episode, set in the old West.

understand a word of it. Nobody explained it to me, but I just went along with it and it was terrific fun. And I think, to be perfectly truthful, Pat McGoohan didn't totally understand it himself. And I think he'll admit to that. But it was so much ahead of its time and it's still ahead of its time in a way. It's such an extraordinary piece.' Raymond Austin confirms Jane's suspicions. 'Lew Grade told me this story once. He asked Pat, "What's this show about?" And Pat said, "I don't know." And Lew says, "Well I fucking well don't know myself either, so I'd better find out what it is, as I'm backing it."'

McGoohan enjoyed brandishing one particular letter he got from a member of the public, an old duffer of a colonel, Order of the British Empire and all that. 'Sir,' it began, 'I've watched all of them now and I've never seen such an utter load of tripe. I wish to say unreservedly that if nothing worse happens to you, I hope the taxman gets you.' McGoohan wrote back, thanking him for his interest and hoping he'd stick it out for the last few shows.

Who knows if he took McGoohan's advice, but millions did keep watching, and, when the final episode was broadcast, television switchboards were jammed for days. Viewers felt cheated by the failure of the concluding episode to explain the myriad puzzles the series had thrown up, especially the discovery of the true iden-

Not just the show's star, McGoohan also acted as producer, writer and director – a staggering achievement.

tity of Number One, the controller of the mysterious Village. The press besieged McGoohan's London home and, according to the star himself, he was physically attacked in the street. 'When the last episode came out in England it had one of the largest viewing audiences,' McGoohan told Canadian TV in 1977. 'Because everyone wanted to know who Number One was. They thought it would be a James Bond-type of Number One. When they did finally see it, there was a near riot and I was going to be lynched. And I had to go into hiding in the mountains for two weeks until things calmed down. That's really true!'

The real thrust of the show is McGoohan's quest to find out the identity of Number One. All inhabitants of the village are assigned numbers; there are no names. When McGoohan arrives he becomes Number Six. Constantly at war with his captors, refusing to reveal the reason behind his resignation, Number Six is determined to escape and uncover the truth behind the Village and the man who runs it, Number One. In the final episode he meets his nemesis face to face, pulling off his mask only to reveal his own features staring back at him.

McGoohan has claimed that, when he first came to write the outline for the series, the concept of his character also being Number One was nowhere in his thoughts. It only came to him when he was forced to quickly conceive the final episode. Certainly, his team of writers were taken aback. Ever since the series started they used to frequently ask him, 'Who's Number One?' To which McGoohan always replied, 'It's a secret.' Having Number Six also be Number One was a very clever conceit; we are our own prisoner and prison guard. But the public saw it as the biggest anticlimax in TV history, and ultimately McGoohan had to flee the country because of the fall out (ironically the title of the final episode) and a crippling run-in with the taxman. Settling in America, his career was never the same again. It was an utter tragedy, for here was a man easily the equal of Olivier, with the potential to be a screen giant. (Though arguably he never quite had the right ingredients to be a Connery, a Caine or a Burton.) 'Patrick was perhaps a little bit too closed off to ever be a major star,' posits Jane Merrow. 'Because nobody quite understood him, which makes it difficult. You've got to have the audience completely on your side, and if they're not quite sure where they are with you they'll never be completely on your side.'

McGoohan was perhaps his own worst enemy. In America, he landed his own big network show called *Rafferty*, but the wayward temperament so in evidence on *The Prisoner* again reared its head. 'They did a few episodes and then one day he never showed up,' says Raymond Austin. 'They phoned his house and said, "Patrick, what's wrong?" And he said, "I'm not coming in. I don't want to do them anymore." And they said, "What do you mean, you don't want to do them?" He said, "I'm not going to do any more." And they said, "We have a contract. We'll sue you for everything." He said, "Sue me. I haven't got anything. So sue me. I couldn't care less." And he just put the phone down. No one sued him or anything, because they knew they were on a loser with this man. And the sad thing about it for me as a director is, he is a bloody good actor. But he's just completely irresponsible when he wants to be.'

At the time of its demise, rumblings were heard about a possible second *Prisoner* series in which Number Six escapes to engage in adventures elsewhere, yet always remains shackled to the Village. It was a more straightforward concept that McGoohan felt had too many echoes of *Danger Man*. Since then there have been various attempts to resuscitate the series in the form of a movie, particularly during the 1990s, at one time with Mel Gibson in the lead. Even McGoohan wrote his own screenplay. And it was announced in 2001 that British director Simon (*Con Air*, *Tomb Raider*) West was at the helm of a mega-budget movie version. Nothing materialised and perhaps it was for the best, considering Hollywood's weak record of adapting British cult TV shows to the screen (*The Avengers*, *The Saint*).

Despite numerous false dawns for a new *Prisoner*, the series continues to justifiably maintain massive cult status, owing in large measure to its aggressive pop art sensibilities, liberal use of 'swinging London' iconography, and the fact that, to this day, fans still argue over exactly what it was all about. Fans regularly make the trek to Portmeirion in order to pay homage; university courses have been set up in order to dissect the apparent multi-layered concepts behind this complex series, bemusing the likes of Marcia Stanton. 'We used to have letters for years and years afterwards from obscure universities in America. People were doing theses on it, reading all sorts of incredible motivations into all these crackpot ideas. They really did take it tremendously seriously. And it was very clever, so original. But you see they'd never do anything like that now, because nobody would ever green light it. They'd be too afraid.'

One of the most intriguing debates concerns whether or not McGoohan's Number Six is in fact *Danger Man*'s John Drake. There are striking similarities: the file photograph seen during the classic credit sequence is the one that was used for *Danger Man*, while the catch phrase, 'Be seeing you,' popularised in *The Prisoner*, crops up repeatedly in *Danger Man* episodes. McGoohan has always contested the fact that Drake was Number Six. If he had admitted it, his old *Danger Man* boss, producer Ralph Smart, might have sued, seeing that he and he alone owned the rights to the character.

McGoohan was genuinely surprised, irked and secretly pleased about the fuss his pet project caused, and that the interest in it has never dwindled – although a little mystified that some observers burden it with far heavier philosophical and hidden meanings than was originally intended. After all, despite the social message McGoohan undoubtedly wanted to convey, that of the individual striving to maintain his identity in an increasingly totalitarian world, *The Prisoner* was meant as pure escapism. McGoohan did the Western episode, for example, simply because he'd never played a cowboy before. Most famous of all is 'Rover', the white spherical balloon that pursues and smothers escapees. Much has been made of its significance, though it came about purely by accident. The Village's main weapon was to have been a hovercraft prop that crawled onto the beach, climbed walls, the lot. But on the first day of shooting it went into the water and stayed there, and, so far as is known, remains there today. The craft was in every scene scheduled for that particular day, and the crew stood around scratching their heads, wondering what the hell they were going to do. Just then the production manager, Bernard Williams, saw something in the sky, a meteorological balloon. Both McGoohan and Williams looked at each other, sensing what the other was thinking. McGoohan broke the silence. 'How many can you get within two hours?' Williams thought about it. 'I'll see,' he said, and raced off to fetch a hundred of the things. And thus one of the series' most indelible images, later even satirised on *The Simpsons*, was born.

Everyone has their own theory about what *The Prisoner* was ultimately about, from die-hard fans, critics, and academics to those who actually worked on the series. Peter Graham Scott had just three days to prepare the ground in order to direct his sole episode, 'The General', and went to see McGoohan in the hope of

Left: on the beach – filming the famous weather balloons that act as the Village's security force. Right: publicity material in tune with the bizarrely surreal nature of The Prisoner.

advice. 'But he wasn't very forthcoming, "Just get on with it," he said. So I got hold of George Markstein, who was the story editor, and we both had a long talk and he was very helpful, and gave me some clues. He said, "This show is about a man whose mind is so full of terrible secrets and things that he's encountered that he's trying not to go mad. So he was attempting to escape from the Village because he's really trying to escape his past, and forget his past." My own private theory about *The Prisoner* is that Patrick shut himself into a box with *Danger Man*. He started to live in the studio. He certainly spent nights in the studio and I think he probably spent some weekends there, away from his family. He literally became a prisoner in that MGM studio and was fighting a sort of demon, of having worked so long on one series. And I thought that was what he was trying to express with *The Prisoner*.'

Chapter 6
Fairy Stories for Adults

- The Champions - Department S - Randall and Hopkirk (Deceased) -

In 1967, Lew Grade's company won the first Queen's Award for Industry to be awarded to the British entertainment business. The following year it was presented to the Hammer horror film studio. Proudly, Grade announced that, in their first twelve years, ITC had sold overseas TV programmes worth $101 million. But by 1968, the TV spy craze, begun by *Danger Man*, was starting to wane. Critics were bemoaning the saturation of our airwaves by spies, whisked off by M15 to the inevitable Iron Curtain country with a name not found on any map, and populated by British supporting actors with dodgier accents than Dick Van Dyke in *Mary Poppins*.

It was producer Monty Berman who brought fresh blood into the tired genre, by combining espionage with science fiction. Largely influenced by the surreal nature of *The Prisoner*, ITC's next batch of shows became increasingly bizarrc and fantasy-orientated. As well as mirroring the swinging sixties as never before, they also proved groundbreaking in their use of multiple lead characters, rather than the solitary hero that hitherto had been ITC's trademark.

THE CHAMPIONS (1968-69)

When Monty Berman's occasional collaborator Terry Nation left for America, to attempt to sell a proposed Dalek series to the networks, it was Dennis Spooner that he turned to for ideas for a new show. Spooner came up with a superhero concept, but with the emphasis on everything being visually believable. His heroes would posses incredible physical abilities – but not of comic book proportions. Drawing on Berman's interest in Tibetan philosophy, a pilot episode was devised in which three agents returning from a mission near the Chinese/Tibetan border (that bit of Red China often featured in sixties TV that looks awfully like Hertfordshire) crash-land in the Himalayas. There, they are rescued from certain death by mysterious robed figures, inhabitants of a forgotten civilisation who administer medical care that results in the three agents attaining special powers.

The trio of agents were Craig Stirling, Richard Barrett and Sharon Macready, who worked for Nemesis: a Geneva-based, top-secret international agency dedicated to law, order and justice. The enjoyable plots pitted the Champions against typical ITC

The Champions: Sharon Macready (Alexandra Bastedo), Richard Barrett (William Gaunt) and Craig Stirling (Stuart Damon).

villains in the form of would-be world conquerors, traitorous scientists and revived Nazis. Though never fully defined, and kept hidden from their colleagues and superiors, their powers included the heightening of the senses and improved strength, agility and stamina. As the series progressed other skills surfaced, such as ESP and telepathy, manifested in the sudden awareness of danger, not only personally but also when other members of the trio were in imminent peril. These abilities also included photographic memory and instant recall. *The Guardian*'s TV critic mockingly classified the character's powers as, 'The ability to lift huge papier-mâché rocks and hear ridiculous dialogue from a ridiculous distance. Unfortunately, one detects no improvement in their acting ability.'

In the role of Richard Barrett was William Gaunt, already a TV veteran by the time of *The Champions* with roles in *The Avengers* and *The Saint*. Most importantly, he'd starred in *Sergeant Cork*, which ran on ATV in the early sixties. 'Lew was very supportive of that series because Ted Willis wrote it,' says Gaunt. 'Ted was a very experienced writer; he'd done *Dixon of Dock Green*, and told me the story of *Sergeant Cork*'s commissioning, which I thought was wonderful. [In] Today's television they go to focus groups, and commissioning is a terribly tortuous process for producers and writers. But Ted Willis went to Lew about another project, and Lew wasn't interested and said, "Have you got anything else?" And Ted said, literally off the top of his head, "What about a thing about a Victorian detective and his assistant; Jack the Ripper, music halls, foggy London streets and all that." And Lew took a big puff of his cigar and said, "We'll have 26." And that was the commission. Incredible man, Lew.'

Several actors were in the running for Richard Barrett, including a young Ian McShane, but Gaunt was always Lew's favourite for the part. Barrett was the group's thinker and strategist, although the scope for delving deep into the characters was limited due to the tight production schedules, according to Gaunt. 'It was really just a question of trying to learn it and get on and do it. We didn't really have any time because we could never rehearse. We'd go through the lines in the makeup room and then get on the set, go through it once and then shoot it. We had one or two episodes where there was a little bit more character development, but basically it wasn't really much to do with the actors. You just did it and relied on your own personality to try and carry it through.'

After *The Champions*, Gaunt moved into the theatre as his appearance in the series proved a double-edged sword. 'The trouble was, because everybody thought it was pretty frightful, it didn't do any of us any good from a future employment point of view. I had to wait two or three years to really get back into mainstream television. So it never really helped my career at all, at the time.' In the eighties Gaunt enjoyed a long run in hit BBC sitcom *No Place Like Home*, and has since alternated between theatre and TV.

Lew Grade had managed to obtain desirable amounts of cash up front from NBC, on the strength of the format and some persuasive salesmanship, so it was essential that one of *The Champions* be an American. They found their perfect Craig Stirling in the shape of New York-born Stuart Damon, then living with his wife in London, and whose TV work had included guest spots in *The Saint* and *Man in a Suitcase*. At the time, Damon was appearing in a West End musical portraying Harry Houdini, and it took some careful negotiations to release him from his theatrical obligations in order to make the series.

Stirling was the action man of the team. 'We tried to get a relationship going

Promotional material for the series highlighted the three main players.

between the three of us, but particularly between Stuart and myself,' Gaunt recalls. 'A joshing sort of relationship, and the writers picked up on that a bit. And if you look at the episodes, usually either Stuart or I had the most to do. And as the series developed they gave me more dialogue to do than Stuart did, because Stuart was better at the action. Stuart was very brash, he was from the Bronx, and he was a very big personality, an awfully nice fellow, very hard working, quite serious, but good fun. He was a bit like Roger Moore in that way, he was very relaxed about everything and made a very nice atmosphere on the set.' Following *The Champions*, Stuart Damon had guest spots in other ITC shows before returning to the States in the mid-eighties, to win huge popularity with regular appearances in daytime soap *General Hospital*.

Several people were auditioned for the pivotal role of Sharon Macready. In the end, model and actress Alexandra Bastedo had the exotic look the producers were after. This was despite her comparative lack of acting experience – which amounted to fleeting roles in the Morecambe and Wise film *That Riviera Touch* and Bond spoof *Casino Royale*. 'I remember when I got the part, Lew Grade said to me, "I see you covered in dollars,"' Alexandra recalls. 'Which presumably meant that I was going to help with the American sales.'

It was Cyril Frankel, the director of all the screen tests, who particularly favoured Alexandra. 'I just felt she was the next Grace Kelly. She was so beautiful.' Frankel had been the one to first bring Alexandra to the producer's attention, having heard about her through a German director who'd seen her on a poster for Shell petrol. 'They tested us all in groups,' Alexandra recalls. 'I did tests with Stuart and William. So it was almost as though our group got through, because other actresses tested with another two fellas. I guess they liked the combination.'

In *The Champions*, Sharon Macready's male colleagues regard her as something of

At Nemesis HQ.

a younger sister, though she's quite capable of defending herself. There was no sexual tension between the group whatsoever. 'It was very *Boys' Own* as far as that was concerned,' remembers Gaunt. 'Alexandra was very inexperienced and very, very nervous of it all. I think you can still detect that. She was quite a reserved girl, but very, very nice. I'm sure she would be the first to admit that she wasn't very experienced. Stuart and I had done a lot more. But I think we all worked very well together.'

They also looked good together. Perhaps too good. *The Daily Mail*'s TV critic complained that they had, 'The look of brimming health and lightness of step of the characters in the commercials when they've got hold of the right laxative or shampoo.'

Like Gaunt, Alexandra found there was little time and no great desire for too much character background. 'It wasn't very in-depth because it was mainly an action series and a lot of it was, "He went that way," and, "Stick your hands up." And you might be working on three scripts at the same time on different sets. For example, if there were three submarine scripts you would be doing all of those at the same time, and it was quite difficult to work out which one you were working on. So the pressure of work was such that there was no way you could learn a script ahead of time, you just learnt what you had to learn the night before.'

Alexandra was just twenty at the time she landed the role, and the series provided her with a massive learning curve. But she wasn't so naïve as to be unaware that the contract she'd signed was a fairly punitive one. 'I got paid £100 an episode, plus

£50 for the foreign buy-out. And when you consider it was shown all through South America, North America, Canada, all around the world, and I never got a penny. That was very bad. Lew Grade had been an actor's agent, and he was very clever and made a lot of money for his company, but he actually kept the actors very poor. Any of the actors you speak to were all living extremely modestly, whereas had we done the same amount of work in America it would be a very different story.'

The series' other permanent character was Lawrence Tremayne, the crotchety and short-tempered head of Nemesis, played by Anthony Nicholls. The noted Shakespearean actor underwent an extensive transformation, having hairpiece additions and a false beard to alter his looks. 'Actually, Douglas Fairbanks Junior was going to play Tremayne initially,' reveals William Gaunt. 'But he eventually decided he didn't want to do it. Tremayne's stuff was all very self-contained in the office, he was very rarely seen outside the HQ of Nemesis, and so Anthony Nicholls only came in once every couple of weeks to do his few scenes.'

For Alexandra Bastedo, one

Top: *relaxing at London Zoo.* Centre: *Alexandra and Stuart Damon pose outside the north London office block that stood in for Nemesis HQ.* Bottom: *ITC stalwart director Roy Ward Baker instructs Alexandra between takes.*

Top: *one of the rare instances of the usually studio-bound crew out on location, note director Sam Wanamaker, crouching.* Bottom: *a scene from the pilot episode where the* Champions *prepare for a crash landing.*

of the pleasures of the series was the chance it afforded her to work with old hands like Nicholls, as well as rising stars. 'I remember doing one episode with Jeremy Brett. And I had seen him as Hamlet when he played in Brighton and I went there with my school, and I had the most enormous crush on him. So to actually find myself starring opposite Jeremy Brett was for me just wonderful. And then the other person who absolutely sticks in one's mind is Donald Sutherland. And about a week after he finished *The Champions* he went on to *The Dirty Dozen*. And I thought then that he was absolutely extraordinary, quite, quite different. They were really a training ground, those shows, for a number of actors. Kate O'Mara became a huge friend after she appeared in one episode. I know Maureen Lipman did one, Paul Eddington and Colin Blakely. I suppose they probably got through 30 actors a week.'

On the writing front, Dennis Spooner had gathered together an impressive team, commissioning scripts from old friends Terry Nation and Brian Clemens. 'The writers were not given too much time,' Clemens recalls. 'I would be invited to contribute a script, would pitch an idea to Dennis or whoever, we would kick it around for an hour or so, then I would go away to write it – usually in a week.'

This time around, Clemens' problem was writing for a trio of characters rather than a solitary hero. 'It is harder, you have to keep them separate yet active, and bring them all together for the climax. In whatever I'm doing I always look for the fault in the character – or the strength. So I wrote one episode in which a Champion had amnesia, thus limiting his powers. And then an episode where I set them against each other, thus testing their powers.'

Also on board were Tony Williamson and Ian Stuart Black, who penned just the one episode. 'If I'd had more time I would have enjoyed doing more,' Black said in 1995. '*The Champions* was quite a good idea. It was sufficiently nutty. It was the best of the ones ITC did, I think.'

While Spooner drafted in top writers, Berman handpicked a number of noted cinema directors to work on the show, including, Freddie Francis, Roy Ward Baker and Leslie Norman – along with lesser known talents like John Moxey, who'd made several horror movies before cutting his teeth on Berman's ITC shows. (Moxey later moved to America where he worked mostly in television, helming the pilot episodes for both *Kolchak the Night Stalker* and *Charlie's Angels*.)

But it was Cyril Frankel whose creative input would be felt the strongest. He was working on a sub-standard Hammer chiller, *The Witches* with Joan Fontaine, when Berman came to see him about the show. Frankel immediately latched

Top: *Alexandra Bastedo looking suitably glamorous, with her mobile makeup room, on the Nemesis HQ set.* Bottom: *publicity shot of Stuart Damon, emphasising his action man status within the group.*

onto the Eastern mysticism elements of the premise, given his interest in meditation, and assumed the post of creative consultant, in effect helping to set the style of the show. He also had a major hand in casting and became *The Champions*' in-house director, taking charge on nine episodes. It led to a close association with Berman and Spooner that lasted for the next few years. Henceforth, Frankel would be brought in at the development stage of numerous other ITC series.

Production commenced in February 1967, and the schedule was murderous. 'They started a new episode about every eight or nine days,' Gaunt remembers. 'There was no gap between them; it was like a production line. We were in every morning at about seven and we never got out of the place before eight or nine in the evenings. We worked under such pressure, and often shot on three or perhaps even four episodes in a day, using second unit, because they'd be picking up bits and pieces of stuff all the time from other unfinished episodes. I don't think we ever finished a complete episode in the scheduled eight days, and some were very much incomplete. I remember Sam Wanamaker directed one and he only got about half of it done in the time.'

The speed at which the episodes were churned out left little or no time for the actors to hone a performance. 'Sometimes the acting was the least regarded of the elements when it came to saying, "That's the one, move on to the next shot,"' says Gaunt. 'Often, providing sound's happy, camera's happy, continuity are happy, the director's happy, if it isn't a good take for the actors, hard luck. You weren't popular if you said, "I'd like to have another go at that one." That really wasn't an option, particularly if it was a big set-up. Once they'd got the one that they thought was technically right, you just hoped it was your best effort. Often it wasn't.'

There weren't many holidays either; the cast worked Monday to Friday, and only got weekends off every fortnight. 'It was incredibly tiring,' recalls Alexandra. 'Once a producer said to me, "You're looking tired. Are you having late nights?" And I wasn't, that was the point. By the time we finished and spent two hours getting through the traffic back to London, had something to eat and washed your hair, you were ready for bed. The pressure was on the whole time. I remember one morning my alarm didn't go off, I jumped into my car and raced to the studio with my hair in curlers and I was stopped by the police for speeding. And I've always said it's the one time when I've never been able to talk myself out of a speeding ticket. With curlers in your hair you can't talk yourself out of anything.'

The entire series of 26 episodes were made in something like eight months. 'We worked unbelievably hard,' explains Gaunt. 'One day, me and Stuart unexpectedly finished on the main unit early, like six or something, but they were still shooting second unit with our stand-ins. And the first assistant came up and said, "Right, now you're available you've got to go to the backlot and take over from the stand-ins." And we both said, "No. We're absolutely knackered, you just continue shooting with the stand-ins." And we both got into our cars and went home. When we arrived in the morning there was a terrible atmosphere, and we were both called into the office and told that if we ever refused a call again they would sue us. We were given a right old bollocking and told we weren't allowed under our contracts to refuse a call unless we had a doctor's note. Fair enough. But Monty was very tough when it came to something like that. Monty and people like Bob Baker, they were tough guys because Lew was very tough with them. There was no leeway to do anything except get on with it. And unlike today, where it's a much more collaborative process, a lot of directors were quite authoritarian in those days, their word was final and everybody jumped and you called them "Sir".'

Although a brilliant concept, Berman knew he was going to have to use all his ingenuity and resourcefulness to get *The Champions* on screen without spending an absolute fortune. Half the story-lines involved foreign locations: European countries, more exotic places like Australia, Antarctica, South America and Burma, all of which had to be realised without stepping a foot outside of Britain. This problem was mainly overcome by the use of stock footage: ready-filmed inserts of snow-capped mountains, aerial views of world capitals, aircraft carriers at full steam. Berman became notorious for buying scenic and hardware footage from film libraries for inclusion into scripts. Sometimes plots would be altered just to accommodate the footage. 'They bought up everything that was usable,' says Gaunt. 'If they saw a piece with a red helicopter flying over the Arctic, they'd buy it and then we'd get a red helicopter flying over the Arctic sequence. We'd have a little red door, not even the full helicopter, we'd get in through the little red door and we'd have a few scenes looking through the frosty window. Monty was quite a famous cinematographer, he'd worked for Michael Powell, and if anything happened locally, like a fire, we'd see him running out of the studio with an Aeroflex on his shoulder and he'd get a lot of fire footage with fire engines arriving. And then we'd see this stuff come up in rushes and know that we'd have a fire sequence coming up in one of the stories. He did a lot of that. If there was anything that was usable, they'd either buy it or try and shoot it.'

One particular piece of stock footage attained near-legendary status at ITC. It was a shot of a white Jaguar saloon spectacularly careering off a cliff. First used in an episode of *The Baron*, it was considered so exciting that future writers fought tooth and nail to get the footage into their episodes. Scenes would be dreamt up merely as an excuse to replay it. Consequently, that same poor white Jaguar is seen hurtling off the exact same cliff not only in episodes of *The Champions*, but also in *The Saint*, *Department S*, *Randall and Hopkirk*, *Jason King* and *The Adventurer*, until it was respectfully laid out to pasture.

Even with such verisimilitude, the producers were obsessed about conserving their budget. 'There was one time when I did this episode which was almost entirely Stuart Damon in one set,' remembers Cyril Frankel. 'Monty Berman said, "Look, the series has gone over schedule and we've gone over budget, so we've got to make the thing in one set in six days." So I was faced with a tremendous challenge. But it turned out to be one of the best episodes.' Called 'The Interrogation', it's certainly a favourite among fans, and concerns Craig going missing after completing a mission in Hong Kong. Unknown to Sharon and Richard, he is in fact being held against his will somewhere in the Nemesis building, under interrogation by the organisation's security chief. They suspect Craig is a security hazard, as anyone who is constantly successful in so many different fields of operation must be a double agent. Craig escapes and confronts Tremayne, understandably bitter about his unjust treatment. The inspiration for this story probably stemmed from the fact that, at that time, Spooner was sitting in on production meetings for *The Prisoner*.

Another penny-pinching exercise was to film in and around the soundstages at Elstree, which could easily be made to resemble warehouses, docks and utility buildings. And when the producers bought a submarine mock-up, they used it in no less than four episodes to make the most of their purchase. 'Because of the way it was set up and shot, we did the show in bunches,' explains Gaunt. 'We did three jungle pictures to start with, we then did the opening Himalayan episode, and two others set in the snow. We then did the submarine episodes. Most of it was done in the studio. They were making what were basically mini-movies in eight days! You hadn't got time to go on location. We went out to the odd sort of local pond and ruined mansion where we'd do a bit of leaping about in the garden. And then we'd be back in the studio again. I shouldn't think there was more than a day an episode outside the studio.'

Though the stars each had stand-ins, the show was about as physical as anything ITC ever made, so they were constantly obliged to handle a lot of the action personally. One of their special powers was the ability to jump higher than mortal man, a trick achieved using a trampoline. 'But because Stuart was bigger than I was, and he was much more gung-ho and athletic than I was,' admits Gaunt, 'if we had to jump over a wall or a hedge, the likely outcome would be that Stuart would clear the hedge and I'd land in the middle of it.'

Considering the show's tight schedule, had any of the actors injured themselves the producers would have faced a catastrophe. 'Looking back on it now, I think they were tremendously lackadaisical about all that,' observes Gaunt. 'The stunt-men were really responsible for us not getting hurt. But we did a hell of a lot of running and jumping about and we could easily have done our ankles. Fortunately, apart from a few bruises, we were fine. We all had stand-ins. Unfortunately my stand-in looked quite like me from the front, but from the back he had a bit of a big bum and a bit of a bald patch. So I can always tell, if I ever look at an episode, which was my stand-in.'

Each episode opened with a 007-style teaser, a dramatic, action-packed scene to entice viewers to keep watching. Then came the titles, accompanied by Tony Hatch's theme. (Hatch never worked on another ITC show, but went on to compose the main themes for *Crossroads* and *Neighbours*.) The titles feature our three heroes standing in front of the impressive Lac Leman fountain in Lake Geneva, home of the Nemesis HQ. In reality, the Nemesis building was Barnet House in Whetstone, North London, located about 25 minutes from the studio. The impressive office structure was filmed from a certain angle in order to avoid telltale surrounding buildings, while the Lac Leman fountain was later optically imposed into the picture. 'That opening sequence Monty went and shot himself,' explains Gaunt. 'He just went to Geneva and shot it. We never went. All he had was the fountain, and then we stood in front of the bluescreen. We'd no idea what was going to be behind us.'

British transmissions got underway in September 1968, but the series suffered due to the fact that it wasn't shown nationwide at the same time – rather in piecemeal around the regions. Thames in London even went so far as to withhold the series until November 1969, when colour broadcasts on ITV got underway. Viewers everywhere else saw it first in black and white. Ironically, the show was never that popular in the capital, more so around the regions, particularly in the Midlands. 'I remember making a personal appearance in Birkenhead,' recalls Alexandra. 'And I had to be rescued by the police, because so many people wanted one's autograph and they hadn't organised it in a safe fashion. There were 30,000 people there and I was nearly crushed to death.'

Out of the three *Champions* stars, it was Alexandra who received the most press and public attention. Unsurprisingly, as she was then arguably the most stunningly beautiful woman on television. 'The downside of all of it was the stalkers. One was a woman who left her husband and came over to England, and ended up on my

Left: *a rare paperback novel tie-in.* Right: *before video, fans of the series had to make do with expensive 8mm colour film copies of selected episodes.*

doorstep in London. She found out where I was and had to be removed by the police. Then I had somebody else who wrote letters to me practically every day. So one was a bit vulnerable. So immediately after *The Champions* I started having Doberman Pinschers as my dogs, which helped. Once a person wrote and said, "I was going to come up to you but you came out of your house with your Doberman Pinscher." Even today, if I go touring I have a Doberman with me. I had a stalker as recently as the late nineties.'

In global terms, *The Champions* was one of ITC's biggest hits, showing in something like 60 countries, where invariably it was dubbed. 'In France, as well as dubbing it, they put a lot of quirky music with it and made the whole thing more spoofy,' says Gaunt. 'I saw one episode in France and it was much camper and more knowing. And I think it worked better than it did over here, and it was very successful in France.' Across Europe and South America the show was massive. 'It was huge in Spain,' recalls Alexandra. 'And I got an award there as best foreign actress, and ended up making about ten films there after I finished *The Champions*.'

But the actors didn't benefit financially from the international popularity of the show, as they were not entitled to any overseas profit. As Gaunt explains, 'Because of the contractual arrangements which we had with the great Lew, we never got a penny. It went nine times on the full network in Japan; it was huge in France, [but we] never got a penny. When the series was shown on BBC2, fifteen or twenty years after it was made, we got a reasonable fee for that. And then eventually some money appeared from France for something that Lew had forgotten to cover. And we get the odd video and DVD rights, but very little, it's been minimal over the years. For the entire series I think I earned £400 an episode, that was the fee. So it was about twelve grand for the entire series. And that show's made millions! But I was happy to do it, I signed the contract, I've never complained about it. Also Lew wasn't the kind of mogul who would then say, let's pay these guys something out of the profits. No, they've been paid, and they'd signed the contract, and that was it. But it happened with all those shows. Bob Powell in *Jesus of Nazareth* signed the same sort of contract, and that plays all over the world, all the time! But I have nothing but tremendous respect for Lew.'

Although the public took to the show, newspaper critics were not amused. '*The Champions* work for Nemesis,' wrote *The Daily Sketch*. 'Which my dictionary says means retribution. I trust it comes swiftly to the people who devised this super silly show.' *The Sunday Telegraph* thought it, 'Quite unbelievably bad. Dennis Spooner is the story editor. His illustrious namesake, the Rev. W. A. Spooner, who invented the Spoonerism, would have had a phrase for such cupid strap.' The *Guardian* said, '*The Champions*, like say Miss World, reaches a peak of pure awfulness which is downright enjoyable if you are in the mood for it.' And as for *The Daily Telegraph*, 'Once puppet series used to imitate human beings. Now with *The Champions*, human beings can give a striking imitation of puppets.'

In America, *The Champions* was given a summer primetime slot on NBC. But its action-adventure format was something US audiences were increasingly growing tired of, and, after a tepid response from viewers and hostility from critics, it was dumped. So, despite its popularity elsewhere, without a network slot it was financially impractical to do a second season, and *The Champions* were quietly retired. 'I think there was talk of a second series,' recalls Gaunt. 'We were only contracted for the one. I think what happened was they were waiting to see how it went in America, and then it didn't, so it was dead.'

Alexandra was more than happy for the series not to continue. 'I was too exhausted to want it to go on. I wanted a life. I know that I was quite ill by the end of it, and ended up going into hospital and having my tonsils out. I'd had to carry on working regardless, even though I was getting more and more exhausted because the poison from the tonsils was affecting my health. There was no let up; too much money was at stake. So it was something of a relief when it stopped.'

Like so much of ITC's 1960s output, *The Champions* was stylish and hugely influential, paving the way for other multi-character series like *Department S*, *Randall and Hopkirk* and *The Protectors*. It was also television's first superhuman show, five years before *The Six Million Dollar Man*, which Spooner always considered to be just a bigger budget clone of *The Champions*. With exciting scripts, incorporating solid action and the occasional bizarre situation, *The Champions* still makes for good, escapist TV.

Amusingly, when the series was repeated in the early 1970s, scenes that hadn't been a problem previously caused censorship concerns. In 'The Fanatics', Richard escapes from a room by placing two fingers into a light socket and blowing all the fuses. His super powers protected him from the shock, but Welsh regional station HTV saw it as potential inspiration for a tragic domestic accident and cut the scene completely. Another TV station, Central, took offence to a scene in 'The Experiment', where genetically created superhumans attack Craig and Richard with scalpels, which they throw with unnatural accuracy. Considered excessively violent, Central (though none of the other regions) removed all shots of the scalpels flying through the air and sticking into the inhuman assailants.

Despite the frantic shooting schedule and the critical drubbing the show received, the cast's recollections remain, for the most part, positive. 'It was like being in the movies,' declares Gaunt. 'We had chairs with our names on the back. We made it at a movie studio, and so therefore we were in the big soundstages. While we were there, Bette Davis did *The Anniversary*. That was literally next door, and I used to wander in and watch her working. Yul Brynner did a movie while we were there. So I look back fondly on the making of it. And never a week goes by without somebody talking to me about it. I did this Channel 4 drama called 40, and I'd been working on it for a couple of days when one of the producers came up to me and said, "I've got to tell you, you meant such a great part of my youth. When *The Champions* was first shown I was ten and it was just the best show ever." And I get that all the time now from people who were that age.'

'The interesting thing about *The Champions*, and indeed the other ITC shows made at that time,' muses Alexandra, 'is that the reason they've lasted and still go on is because they were done on film, the quality is always there, whereas stuff that was done on tape has long ago faded or been destroyed.'

Because all of ITC's shows were made on film, not videotape, on DVD today they look as fresh and sharp as when they were first produced. But it was a practical, not creative, decision. By the late fifties/early sixties, American viewers had grown accustomed to the production polish of filmed TV series, so Lew Grade knew his shows had to look good to sell abroad, which meant costs sometimes three times as much as a taped show. The risks were big, but the rewards were high. 'The use of film was obligatory,' says director Roy Ward Baker. 'Because if you wanted to have a foreign version of your show and screen it in a territory which had different television standards, the only way to translate it was to have a filmed negative that you could then put into their machine, and it would turn out a television copy of the right standard for their network. I don't know whose decision it was originally to shoot all those shows on film, but it was a decision which paid off handsomely.'

Wherever in the world *The Champions* is playing, Alexandra is quickly made aware – for a heap of mail suddenly arrives from, say, Germany, Latvia or Singapore. As for the fame the series brought her, 'It was interesting having it that early, because as a result I find it totally unimportant now. I know what it's like, I've experienced it, and it's not a situation, like we've had with the Beckhams, that I would want. I wouldn't want to have my public ability to walk around and be normal impaired by fame. I think it is quite a high price to pay.'

Though he doesn't watch the series now, does William Gaunt have a favourite episode? 'It's probably "Autokill". And I also liked the one that was set in Australia; all done in the studio, of course, where we had to diffuse a bomb near this bar in the outback. But I never watch them now. When my children were very young we had a look at a couple of episodes. I remember my boy, he was about six at the time, and he watched it for quite a long time and said, "Which one's you, Daddy?"'

DEPARTMENT S (1969-70)

Seen by some as almost a precursor to *The X-Files*, this intriguing series mixed espionage with way-out plot lines, and centred on an elite organisation within Interpol who inherited cases that baffled other police forces: like finding out why a plane vanished in mid-air for six days, the identity of a man found wandering the streets of London in an astronaut suit, or tracking down a mad scientist with a container of

Stylish promotional material for Department S, *a show considered to be a forerunner of* The X-Files.

deadly bacteria (an episode that guest-starred a young Anthony Hopkins). Principally though, *Department S* is today famous (or infamous) for launching the character of Jason King – one of the inspirations behind Mike Myers' Austin Powers – upon an unsuspecting populace.

The search for an actor to play King, the hedonistic maverick within the group, who wrote mystery novels and solved cases by projecting himself into the mind of his own fictional hero, Mark Caine, was a convoluted one. Kenneth More was an early candidate, before Cyril Frankel suggested Peter Wyngarde. The director had previously worked with the hugely flamboyant Wyngarde and been impressed with him: 'He was a very fine actor, but unfortunately a difficult person.' When Frankel suggested to Monty Berman that Wyngarde would be the perfect choice for King, the producer replied, 'Don't you think he'll overdo things a little?'

Wyngarde was already a well-established actor appearing in numerous television shows, most famously in the S&M *Avengers* episode, 'A Touch of Brimstone', where he controversially made Diana Rigg wear bondage gear and whipped her for good measure.

Less well known was an appearance in an episode of ITC's *The Baron*, where he played an actor impersonating a monarch. 'And I decided to play it as John Gielgud,' says Wyngarde. 'Unfortunately the producer was illiterate and didn't know who the fuck Gielgud was. So he couldn't understand why I was playing him as a poof. So he didn't like it and dubbed me, and I got very angry. However, it impressed the director, who was Cyril Frankel. And that's how I was chosen for *Department S*.'

At the time, Wyngarde was about to appear in London's West End in Chekov's play *The Duel*, when Berman approached him with the offer, which was received with muted enthusiasm. The last thing Wyngarde wanted to do was become tied to a long-running TV series. But he invited Berman to his opening night. 'And I gave a dinner party afterwards. And the notices came in about four o'clock that morning and they were terrible. I'd said to the cast, "Don't ever let me read the notices because it affects my performance." So I went to the loo when the notices came in, and when I came back and saw their faces I knew it had gone down the drain. In fact it didn't, we ran for nine months. So I wrote on a napkin – "I, Peter Wyngarde agree to do your television series *Department S* on condition that you drive me back to the theatre in the evening." And that's how it started.'

On the page, the Jason King character was nothing like what Wyngarde ultimately turned him into. He didn't even, as yet, have a name. That was solved over a weekend break Wyngarde took at fellow actor Michael Bryant's home. 'I said, "Look, I've got to find a name for myself for this television series I'm doing. Do you have any ideas?" We bandied a whole lot of names about. I thought of Jason and his wife thought of King. Then we started talking about what car he should drive and Michael said, "There's no doubt you've got to have a Bentley." And I said, "Oh, I like that."'

Incredibly, early scripts had envisaged Jason King as an ageing Oxford don in plus fours and tweeds. Wyngarde thought that wasn't him at all. He wanted to play King as much more of an extrovert, with a kind of Carnaby Street masculinity, and in the end was given virtual *carte blanche* to invent his own screen persona. 'I was very lucky. I think it had a lot to do with Patrick McGoohan. I think Lew

Top: *co-star Joel Fabiani revelled in Peter Wyngarde's flamboyant approach to the whole series.* Bottom: *Jason King was totally at home in this particular undercover outfit.*

It was Peter Wyngarde's ultra-chic Jason King *character that the public latched onto; his co-stars didn't stand a chance.*

Grade and the producers realised that actors are pretty creative people, and if you give them their way you get something out of it.' In the end, Wyngarde created one of British television's most fondly remembered characters – which, in reality, was merely an eccentric version of himself. 'Wyngarde had his own conception of what he wanted to look like and it began with the clothes,' remembers Frankel. 'He had a session with the wardrobe mistress and said he wanted this, that and the other. And the decision really was Monty Berman's, who said, "Yes, we'll go along with that."' King/Wyngarde would become notorious for his outrageous wardrobe sense. Late sixties fashion has never been so disastrously exhibited. And yet his taste in clothes did catch on. When high street stores started bringing out their own 'Jason King' ranges, Wyngarde and the producers fired off numerous furious letters threatening legal action.

Co-credited as the brains behind *Department S*, along with Monty Berman, was Dennis Spooner. Intrigued by who would investigate mysteries like the Marie Celeste in a contemporary setting – along with WWII tales about Churchill enlisting the help of Dennis Wheatley and other authors to dream up madcap schemes to win the war – Spooner arrived at the idea of a team of super sleuths, each with a different approach to solving bizarre cases. 'I was amazed to find out that *Department S* was largely based on Ian Fleming,' offers Wyngarde. 'It was a real department run during the war, with MI5, and Fleming was the naval side of it. He was the head of this department. And that gave me the idea of Jason King being a writer, like Ian Fleming, who wrote about his hero, only my hero was Mark Caine, which I took from Michael Caine.'

Backing up King was Annabelle Hurst, the scientist of the team, played by Rosemary Nicols, then appearing in the West End musical *Fiddler on the Roof*. Relations between Nicols and Wyngarde were cool to say the least. Wyngarde found the actress totally aloof and incommunicative. In fact the two hardly spoke for the entire shoot.

Next, Berman and Frankel went to New York to cast the obligatory American. Unlike many ITC shows, where the American lead seemed grafted on purely to facil-

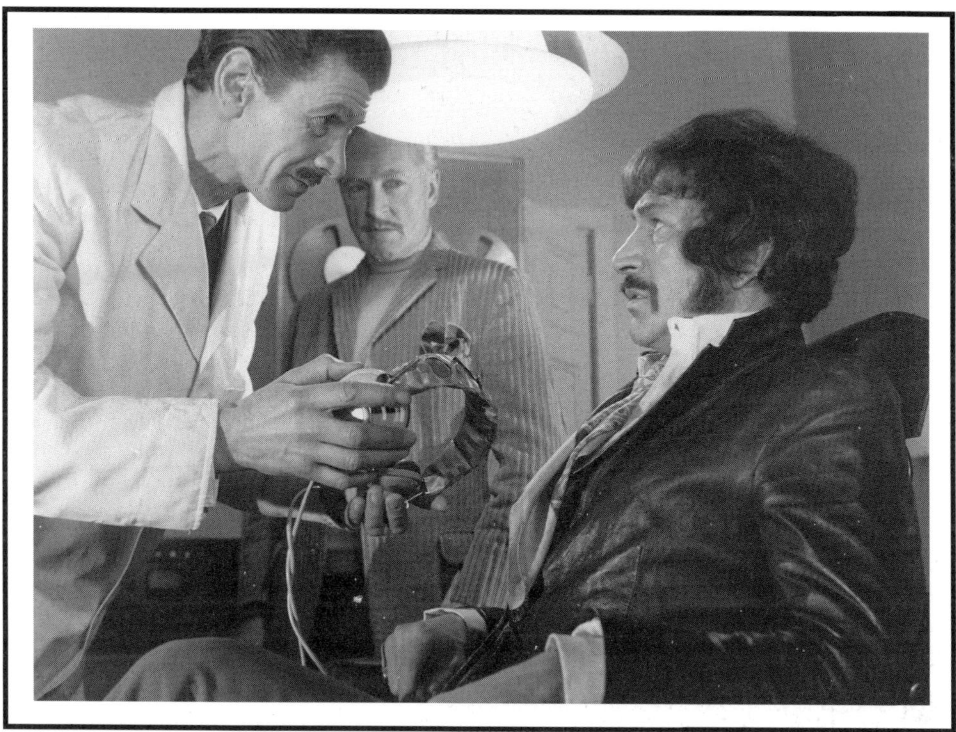

Trapped: Jason King is prepared for torture, as long as it doesn't affect the line of his suit.

itate international sales, as *Department S* was a specialised offshoot of Interpol one could logically accept that a member could be American. And Stewart Sullivan was the muscleman of the group, as down to earth as Jason King was extravagant. Frankel and Berman met various hopefuls during their trip, including a young actor by the name of Joel Fabiani, who'd worked mainly in the theatre (at one point understudying Robert Shaw and Alan Bates during the Broadway run of Harold Pinter's *The Caretaker*). 'They asked me if I had any film to show them,' Fabiani recalls. 'I hadn't done that much except a very splashy commercial for a cigarette, and I was dressed in a tuxedo. I've never been lit so well in my life, and I was around these gorgeous models. So they looked that over and said, "Yeah, that's kinda what we were looking for."' Fabiani was then invited to England for tests. 'They shot some footage of me jumping over boxes and being very athletic. And then I went back to New York and a week later they said, "You've got the job." So I flew back and within a couple of weeks began shooting the show.'

Relations between Wyngarde and Fabiani were much closer than was the case with Nicols. 'Joel was wonderful. He saw the play I was in and came into my dressing room, and was wearing little granny glasses, jeans with holes all over them, and a sweater that had more holes than the jeans. He was really kooky and funny. And I said, "For God's sake don't let anybody change your appearance, because that's exactly what we want. We've got a piss elegant Jason King, and what we want is you as a wonderful contrast." And he agreed, but said, "I don't think my wife's going to

Wearing shades indoors is not cool – unless, of course, you're Jason King.

like that." And I said, "Well, bugger your wife." But she won in the end and he went to Lew's bloody tailor, who made suits for the royal family, and ended up wearing these really drab clothes.'

Before settling on the authentically American Fabiani, London auditions had taken place in the hope of snaring either a British-based American actor, or some suitably debonair Brit who was cheap, and could put on a reasonable accent to play Sullivan. One young hopeful who attended that audition was Michael Billington, later to find fame in *UFO*. But this early bid for fame turned into a complete disaster. 'I had a girlfriend at the time, a young model, and she gave me some of this sponge-on tan, and by the time I went into this meeting with the casting director I was totally canary yellow. And later this director told my agent, "I don't know who his image advisor is, but he mustn't show up for auditions looking like a squeezed lemon!"'

With the cast now assembled, Lew Grade organised an elaborate press reception for *Department S* at the Cumberland Hotel in Marble Arch. Wyngarde remembers it only too well. 'Lew stood up to introduce me and said, "I want to introduce you to my star, one of our greatest Shakespearean actors. Ladies and gentlemen it is my great honour to introduce you to Paul Scofield."'

Further indignity was to follow when, just a few weeks into production, Wyngarde was almost axed from the series on Grade's orders. A bunch of American TV executives were due in London to see the show with a view to buying it, and Grade asked to see an episode. 'It's fantastic,' he told Berman. 'But you've got to get rid of the one with the *Viva Zapata* moustache. I mean those clothes and that hair. The Americans won't like all that, they'll think he's a faggot.' 'So I was actually sacked,' Wyngarde reveals. 'Lew told the producers to write me out. And I was playing the lead! It was ridiculous.'

The reason for Wyngarde's now legendary droopy moustache and leonine mane of hair was because of his role as a Russian in *The Duel*, which he was doing concurrently with his filming commitments. 'I said to them, "I can't play Jason King any other way, he's got to look like this because I'm performing in this play at night." It had to be the same look.'

When the Americans duly arrived, the top executive sang the show's praises to Lew. 'And hey, that guy's just incredible and those suits are fantastic. Who's his tailor?' Pleased as punch, Lew replied, 'I'm so glad you like it, and his tailor is my tailor too.' Meaning, of course, Fabiani. Quick as a flash, the American ordered 25 suits all in the same style. Not long after they'd been shipped out to the States, Lew got a phone call from him. 'What the hell are these goddamn suits? These aren't like the ones the guy wore in *Department S*.' Bemused, Lew explained they were exactly the same suits as those worn in the show by Joel Fabiani. 'Not Fabiani!' roared the executive. 'The other guy, with the *Viva Zapata* moustache.' Immediately, Lew was on the phone to Wyngarde, desperate to find out where he got his suits from and to tell him he was back on the show.

Remember, it's the 1960s.

Overseeing production on *Department S* was ITC veteran Monty Berman. 'I remember when you went into Monty Berman's office, the chair that you were made to sit in was always considerably lower than the one that he was in,' recalls Alexandra Bastedo. 'And I made some comment about this at one point, and he said that it was like that on purpose because it actually put you at a disadvantage, that you were sitting in a low chair and he was there like a kind of king behind the desk.'

According to director Raymond Austin, the likes of Berman were old school producers from the very top drawer. 'There aren't producers like that anymore. In America I did a show called *Jag*, about Navy lawyers, and you've got fourteen producers on that! But in those days Lew Grade, Bob Baker, Monty Berman, these were producers, they were the ones with the ultimate power, who took responsibility and made the decisions. If things weren't working out they'd say, "Do it this way, he's fired, replace so and so," or whatever. In America it goes through maybe twenty people to get a decision, and then they chicken out, saying, "Don't upset the star." If the ratings are high they'll keep the person working forever. On some of the American shows I've worked on, people did ridiculous things. On *Charlie's Angels*, some of the girls used to turn up some mornings four hours late, and they'd get away with it. You couldn't get away with that with Lew Grade or Monty Berman, they'd be on that set saying, "What the hell do you think you're playing at?"'

Another vital contributor to *Department S* was Cyril Frankel. Today he ranks the series as his all-time ITC favourite, believing the balance between the three principals was just right. 'Basically, my role on those shows was to endeavour to lift the level of the making of the television series to that of a feature film. It was the challenge to use the experience you had gained on making other things to do it in the nine or ten days you were allotted, and to endeavour to lift the quality through the performances if the script wasn't quite right.'

As he'd done on *The Champions*, Frankel was brought in not just as director but to be involved on a creative level right from conception. 'And I had another very good collaboration with Monty Berman. He was very funny and charming and would always come on set and see the first shot in the morning. We used to travel together in the car to the studio, and it was on those journeys that we would discuss casting the next episode. You had to know your *Spotlight*, the actor's directory, through and through. I remember on one occasion saying, "I just don't know who we can cast for this part." And Monty said, "Well, how about so and so?" And I said, "But Monty, you told me you'd never work with her again, that she was always late." He said, "Well, what I meant was I wouldn't work with her again unless I had to."'

From day one, Frankel realised that in Peter Wyngarde he had a brilliantly gifted, though temperamental actor. 'My job was to control him from going too far,' the director claims. 'Occasionally he might say to me, "Oh, wouldn't it be good if I had a falcon on my arm?" And I would say, "No." "Oh," he'd say, "you're so mediocre."'

Director Raymond Austin also had his run-ins with Wyngarde, over his off-the-wall interpretation of the role. 'Peter was a bit of a prima donna sometimes. He really wanted his own way. But I think he did a good job on that show. I remember doing a scene where Jason King turns up to look at the body of a girl found dead on a beach. I look up from the camera and Wyngarde's standing there with his cuffs rolled back over his white linen jacket, a cheroot in his hand and a glass of scotch. And I said, "Cut! Peter, where'd you get the glass of scotch?" He said, "I always have a glass of scotch on the show." I said. "I know, but where did you get it? I mean, you're on a beach and you've got a glass of scotch." "I just always have it," he said. And he was bloody well determined that he was going to have this glass of scotch. He didn't win in the end, because he saw the error of his ways when everybody looked at him to say, "Ray's right, where did you get the scotch?" But Peter was a guy who always wanted to do that sort of thing, and he got into a fad about it and nothing was going to change it. Also, he was that character. He used to come in the studio in the morning, put those clothes on, and he was the character all day.'

Allowing Wyngarde to fly off on wild tangents, but bringing him back down to earth whenever he went too far, wasn't a case of Frankel and Austin being party poopers. After all, it's the director's job to keep the production on schedule, and to do this means sticking to the script. Creativity is fine, but if a director goes along with the whims of their lead actor they can quickly lose control. And because the director has ultimate responsibility for a show, if it goes wrong it's him, not the ego-obsessive actor, who gets the blame. 'In the business, it was well known with Peter that you had to really keep your eye on him, because he would do his damn level best to upstage you,' says Fabiani. 'I don't know that there's anything wrong with that, but that's the

Jason King shows his disdain for the more mundane aspects of detective work.

way he was. It never offended me because I thought the work that he did was very good. Maybe I was too stupid to say, "Hey, stop that, this is my scene, stop farting around." But it never bothered me. I could see what he was up to, but I was as fascinated as the crew. But I think from Frankel's point of view, and Monty's, they had to put the wraps on him once in a while or the damn thing would've gone way off the rails. But who knows whether that wouldn't have been a more interesting direction to go in anyway.'

Fabiani found Wyngarde 'a wonderfully exotic kind of performer'. At the same time, the American was struggling with his own role in the series, and the kind of insecurities that were natural for an actor new to television and working in Britain for the first time. 'I was always trying to get my character revved up and developed in such a way that he would be interesting and compelling throughout the show. I don't know what they thought of me. Maybe the powers that be, like Cyril and Monty, felt that they wished they'd had somebody a little more dynamic. I know I worried a lot about the role. I felt I did some good work, but there were times when I thought I should have been better or maybe brought something more to it. And I think maybe they felt that too.'

Made at Elstree, the 28 episodes were shot between April 1968 and June 1969. 'I loved the English way of shooting,' declares Fabiani. 'They worked ten days on an episode and from eight to five in the evening. It was very civilised. In America they knocked out those hour episodes in six days.' At the time *Department S* came into the

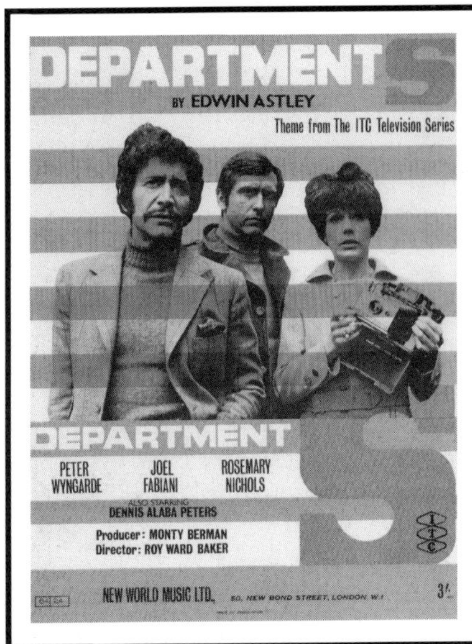

Left: *sheet music to Edwin Astley's theme tune.* Right: *this super 8mm film is today a collector's item.*

studio, *The Saint* was winding down, and Roger Moore came onto the stage before work began on the first episode to present the cast with a bottle of champagne. 'Roger's dressing room was just down the corridor from mine and we used to often talk,' Fabiani recalls. 'He got me into the Curzon club and invited my wife and I to dinner. He couldn't have been more charming.' Meanwhile, at the nearby MGM studio Stanley Kubrick was shooting *2001*. Magical times indeed. And an experience Fabiani still treasures and rates as the highlight of his career. 'London in 1968/69, those years were just phenomenal. I did, however, make something of a fool of myself when Monty and Cyril and I were driving out to the studios, and we passed this castle and I said, "My God, is that Norman?" And Monty said, "No, that's on the MGM lot." It was a big castle they'd built for some picture. And I said, "Oh Christ, there you go."'

Sadly, *Department S* never really took off with the public, and also flopped badly in the States. 'It wasn't ahead of its time,' observes Wyngarde. 'It was of its time. The problem was everything else was out of its time, it was behind. There was a lot of rubbish on. *Department S* had something that I think a lot of programmes don't have now, and that is that it had style. And people want style.'

For his part, Fabiani wasn't too disappointed that no more episodes were commissioned. 'When I came back to the States from England, I was full of beans and piss and vinegar and everything and wanted to go out and conquer Hollywood, which is what I immediately set out to do – and didn't – but I had an awful lot of fun trying.'

Like so much of ITC's output, since its demise *Department S* has achieved cult status. 'I've even developed, for some odd reason, a fan club from Japan,' marvels Fabiani. 'Two poor little ladies send me notes saying, "We're very pleased with your vigorous work in *Department S*." And I'm thinking, "Jesus, this is 35 years ago, if they think I'm 30 now they've got another thing coming."'

RANDALL AND HOPKIRK (DECEASED) (1969-70)

After working on *Department S* and *The Champions*, the brilliantly inventive Dennis Spooner came up with the even more bizarre idea of a series about a pair of rather seedy private detectives, one of whom happens to be dead! During a routine investigation, Marty Hopkirk is killed in a deliberate hit and run incident. After the funeral he reappears as a white-suited, wisecracking ghost, and rounds up those responsible for his death, but misses the sunrise deadline by which time he must return to his grave. His punishment is to remain a ghost wandering the earth, visible only to his bemused partner, Jeff Randall. What a premise!

Yet Lew Grade was sceptical, perhaps because he saw little or no opportunity for the use of an imported American star, and he also felt that the casual way the show treated death bordered on the tasteless. Luckily Ralph Smart, then very much seen as a father figure at ITC, was impressed with the proposal, so much so that he wanted to write the pilot episode. It was that which persuaded Lew to go ahead with the series.

Again hired as a creative consultant, director Cyril Frankel played a major hand in casting the show. At first it was suggested that comedian Dave Allen play Randall, a down-at-heel gumshoe, but instead London-born Mike Pratt, previously famous for writing the song 'Little White Bull' for Tommy Steele, landed the part. 'I had used Mike in another project,' explains Frankel. 'And when his name popped up I said that I liked him and thought he was right.'

Once described as having the weather-beaten features of a mountainside, Pratt was a veteran of numerous ITC shows, usually playing the heavy, duffing up both Simon Templar and John Drake in episodes of *The Saint* and *Danger Man*. After *Randall and Hopkirk*, Pratt alternated between stage and television. He enjoyed small roles in later ITC shows, and the classic seventies series *The Brothers* and *Arthur of the Britons*. Tragically, Pratt died of lung cancer in 1976. 'There was an unfortunate man,' observes director Roy Ward Baker. 'He once fell out of a window and into a sort of basement area and broke both his ankles. An extraordinary thing. And he died very young. Very sad. Sad man.'

Director Robert Tronson has happier memories of Mike Pratt. 'I was a great chum of Mike. And it was he who persuaded me to do my one episode. He was a very self-destructive bloke, but brilliant. A very clever musician. He had all sorts of talents. I was very fond of him. But so self-destructive it wasn't true, in every way, but drink in particular. Halfway through the episode I did, Mike got into a fight in a pub and came in with a huge black eye. The makeup woman was quite good and did him up, but you couldn't possibly shoot him in close-up except at a very funny angle. But he was so sweet. He was so apologetic about it. But I think he was pissed most of the time.'

Drink certainly played more of a routine role in the day to day life of television and film production back in the sixties than it does today. 'It's hard to imagine this,' admits Tronson, 'but we all drove and drank, taking terrible risks. Some people drove around incapable. We all did. Pinewood especially had a very efficient system of getting leading actors and important people off charge. They had the police all squared.'

With Jeff installed, the search was on for his 'dead' partner, Marty Hopkirk. 'We didn't know who to cast,' Frankel remembers. 'And it was only by chance in a restaurant I saw Kenneth Cope and I thought, "Ah," and went to Monty Berman and

With its quirky humour, Randall and Hopkirk *proved to be one of ITC's most popular shows.*

said, "I think I've found our Marty."' Cope was given a screen test, directed by Frankel, and got the part.

Born in Liverpool, Cope conned his way into television after years of touring in rep, by telling prospective directors he'd done loads of TV in Canada, despite never even stepping foot in the country. To which they'd usually reply, 'Yes, I think I've seen some of it.' Early roles saw him playing opposite Richard Greene in *The Adventures of Robin Hood* and Roger Moore in *Ivanhoe*. Later a huge success on *That Was The Week That Was* and as a regular on *Coronation Street*, following *Randall and Hopkirk*, Cope would appear in a couple of early seventies *Carry On* movies – *At Your Convenience* and *Matron*. Then, after a lean period, he would come back to prominence with a regular role in Channel 4 soap *Brookside*.

When a casting director called him up with the *Randall and Hopkirk* job, it seemed the most preposterous of offers. 'Kenny,' went the pitch, 'we want you to star in a series – you get killed in the first episode!'

As Marty, Cope famously wore an immaculate white suit, of which there were five, all made of silk and bought very expensively from Savile Row. After each take, the jacket and trousers would be whipped off the actor to prevent coffee stains or marks getting on them. Cope also wore a wig in the show, although for the first two episodes had the thing on back to front accidentally. 'I looked like the middle one of the Three Stooges!' he later joked.

Completing the cast was Jeannie, Marty's widow, who wasn't in Spooner's original outline for the series but was created to conform to ITC's policy of including, wherever possible, a female lead. Perfectly cast in the role was Annette Andre, who'd

The delightful cast of Randall and Hopkirk*: Kenneth Cope, Annette Andre and Mike Pratt.*

actually been an early candidate for the Sharon Macready role in *The Champions*. 'I wasn't enthusiastic about *Randall and Hopkirk*,' Annette admits. 'I wasn't enthusiastic about any series. You were scared of being typecast. In those days it was great to have a series, but people always said, "If you're in a series, you can forget about working for the next couple of years after you've finished." And actually it was true, I don't think I worked for a year after I did that series. So you were a bit wary about doing it. But they explained a bit about it and I thought it sounded like fun. And I liked the idea of the ghost; it sounded more attractive somehow than *The Champions*. And I think they were right, because Alexandra was far better in *The Champions* than I would have been. And I'd worked with Mike before and liked him, and I think that had a bearing on my decision, so I just said, "Alright, I'll do it."'

Annette came to the show with great experience, appearing in ITC classics like *The Saint* and *The Prisoner*. But it was her guest spot in *The Baron* that brings back her most vivid memories. 'I had to go through a skylight in a roof, which they'd rigged up. I was probably wearing a mini skirt. And I got through it and it was rough wood, and I got all these splinters in my arse and they had to get them out. So I remember *The Baron* because of that. I don't remember the part, but I remember the splinters.'

On paper, the Jeannie character Annette was being asked to play was minimal in the extreme. 'Apart from *The Avengers*, in those days women in series were very limited. They were thought of as second class citizens really. At first Jeannie was a very ordinary part, she didn't do anything. I only had the husband for half an episode and didn't have any length of time to form any affinity, so for the whole series I was a single girl who'd had this husband who I couldn't even see, but was there, so I had no relationship with anyone. Then I figured Jeannie was someone who'd want to be more involved in the detective business, and organise Jeff better. I played her with that aspect, because that's how I felt she was getting her confidence back after losing her husband. And I felt that she would eventually, had we gone on further with the series, have become a detective, that's what I had in mind when I played her. And come another series that's possibly what might have happened. That's what we were aiming for, because we were talking about a second series and we were putting in ideas about it.'

Special mention must also go to Ivor Dean as Inspector Large, who popped up occasionally throughout the series. Dean's bloodhound features typified the stereotypical notion of Scotland Yard duffers in 1960s television, and he had played a similar role, that of Chief Inspector Teal, in *The Saint*.

Backing up the wonderful trio of Pratt, Cope and Andre were regular ITC guest stars like Jane Merrow, who particularly enjoyed her stint on the show. 'That was lovely to do, such fun. Mike Pratt was such a sweet man, and I'd worked before with Kenneth. That was a nice show. And much better than the BBC remake, because the secret of so many of these shows is their light touch, they didn't go overboard and they didn't try and get too hot and heavy with it. It's like *The Avengers*, it was fun, it was complete fantasy rubbish nonsense, but it was still very appealing and had great humour.'

Another guest star was the glorious character actor Freddie Jones, who has made something of a career out of playing misfits and eccentrics, notably in films like *The Elephant Man* and Hammer's *Frankenstein Must Be Destroyed*. But Jones has bad memories of his *Randall and Hopkirk* episode, directed by Cyril Frankel. 'I couldn't bloody bare him,' declares Jones. 'I've loved most of my directors, but he was so awful and dismissive. It's the only reason I remember that episode. I mean, darling Ken Cope and Mike Pratt were friends to me. Anyway, Frankel gave them both a note and then threw at me, "Keep it real." Keep it real! I mean, of all the bloody insults. The last thing I wanted to be was real. I wanted to be super real. So, sod him. As Joseph Conrad called it, all art is a kind of super truth. And I believe darling Ralph Richardson said once, "The performance has about it the boredom of reality." I mean, for Christ's sake, it's about entertainment.'

The biggest headache on *Randall and Hopkirk* was striking the correct balance between drama and comedy. Monty Berman and Frankel sought more of a traditional detective show, while Spooner and the cast wanted to play it with a touch of whimsy. This clash of styles caused considerable friction behind the scenes. 'I saw it very much as in the mode of Raymond Chandler,' says Frankel. 'And the first episode has that. And then I went back to work on *Department S* and when I returned Kenneth Cope said, "Oh, we're doing it differently now. We're making it more comic."'

Cope instinctively knew that what would give the show its charm and prove most appealing to viewers was the comedy element, so he was always looking for the humour in most of the scenes he played. Some of the directors allowed him the freedom to add little comedic touches, others did not – notably Frankel – and the two often clashed head-on. Cope would say, 'Cyril, you're stopping it being funny.' Frankel's reply would always be that the series had to be realistic, and strike a balance between the serious and the comic.

Cope also wanted more fantastical elements brought into the series, such as showing what happened to Marty in ghost limbo. (Something the 2000 BBC update dwelled on perhaps too much.) Some of Cope's ideas were truly inventive, like wanting to get stock footage of Bobby Charlton scoring for England, and show it was Marty who blew the ball in the net using his special ghostly powers, and then superimpose him celebrating with the players. A great idea, it was rejected for being too costly and too wacky. Another discarded idea was having Marty leave white footprints everywhere. 'As a pair, Mike and Kenneth worked very well together,' recalls Frankel. 'Mike was a very instinctive player and Kenneth was more of a comedy actor, but he also could be serious. The only problem I found was that Cope was inclined to broaden my concept, and then I would have to try and bring him back.'

Just how much influence the actors could exert on set or during the scriptwriting process is debatable, though. 'We could have our own ideas,' explains Annette. 'Ken and Mike used to throw them to Dennis and the writers. I don't think they took a whole lot of notice of me, because I was the woman. It really was very sexist. But there wasn't a lot of room to change stuff. The powers behind the scenes wouldn't allow too much change.

Top: *the most prolific of all ITC directors, Cyril Frankel puts Mike Pratt through his paces.* Bottom: *which one's the dummy? Mike Pratt and Kenneth Cope fool about off-set.*

Especially when it came to comedy. We would have liked to have done a bit more humour, but they were a bit cagey about it, because everybody was into this detective thing with fights and stunts.'

Director Raymond Austin was certainly on the side of Cope and the actors, and is today adamant that *Randall and Hopkirk* would have been a bigger hit had the comedy been played up. 'The only problem with that show was Monty Berman wanted to do it serious, to play it straight. Kenny Cope was a riot as that ghost. In rehearsals he and Mike Pratt had us in stitches. It should have been tongue-in-cheek comedy, but to play that in such a serious vein, it didn't click for me. If only they'd played it as a comedy it would've been brilliant.'

The early episodes are true to Spooner's desire for a quirky thriller; lots of haunted houses, eccentric mediums, ghost hunters, etc. In the episode 'Murder Ain't What It Used To Be', Marty even gets to meet a ghost gangster, complete with white machine gun. But word got back that the American network were not happy with this approach, so the series began to adopt a more straightfor-

Top: *the cast relax and learn their lines between takes.* Centre: *Mike Pratt auditions for an American TV cop show, while Ivor Dean's Inspector Large looks wearily on.* Bottom: *Kenneth Cope and Mike Pratt made for one of sixties TV's best duos.*

Stuck down a well, even Marty's supernatural powers may not be enough to rescue his partner this time.

ward detective format with stories about protection rackets and the like.

In the end, Spooner and Cope's stance was vindicated, as today the series is remembered most fondly for its comic element. 'Of course the comedy had to be there,' concedes Frankel. 'I just felt that with Hopkirk's wife you had an emotional situation there, and I maintain that every film has to have an emotional moment. If you take that away it gets a bit like drivel. I had to have the emotional moment; OK, have the comedy, but look at Chaplin, he always had the emotional moment, or two or three.'

In addition to his role as creative consultant on the series, Frankel also directed six episodes, including the all-important pilot that went before the cameras in mid-June 1968. 'I was involved because Lew Grade said to me, "Cyril, if your name comes up on the screen as director I know I don't have to worry, I can sell it." Which was nice of him.'

Along with Monty Berman and Dennis Spooner, Frankel was on a percentage of the profits in addition to his regular salary. In fact, he was the only director working on those ITC shows that Grade ever put on a percentage. As such, he was supposed to receive two per cent of the profits from *Department S*, *Randall and Hopkirk*, *Jason King* and *The Adventurer*. Not a penny came his way, however, and when he pressed the company for his monies the director was told, rather inconceivably, that none of the series he worked on ever went into profit, despite the fact that they still play all over the world.

On *Randall and Hopkirk*, Dennis Spooner was given the grandiose title of executive story consultant and brought in tried and tested writers Tony Williamson and Donald James, who between them accounted for twenty out of the 26 episodes. ITC regular Edwin Astley composed the main theme, which was notable for its use of a harpsichord. Astley was after something so distinctive that, if someone had the telly on in the next room, they'd know immediately that the programme had started. The composer knew it had to be something unique in the orchestration or the tune, and so used a harpsichord with its unique and haunting sound.

Behind the cameras were notable directors like Roy Ward Baker, Leslie Norman and Raymond Austin, whose memories of working at Elstree remain vivid even today. 'It was a family there, everybody knew each other. You'd go in in the morning, go to the canteen and have a bacon sandwich or a sausage roll, sit around and chat and then go to the set. And you would be able to wander from stage to stage on the different shows and everybody knew you. Knowing I was a part of that is wonderful, because no one will ever have that kind of experience again, that family of technicians and artists will never happen again. Those days will never, ever come back.'

It took roughly fourteen months to make all 26 episodes, with each one shot on a two-week turnaround. The majority of filming took place at Elstree at a time when the studio was a hive of activity, with *The Avengers*, *The Saint* and *Department S* all in production. Kenneth Cope's dressing room was next door to Linda Thorson's, who left him her kettle when *The Avengers* closed down. Productions would also regularly borrow each other's sets. The *Randall and Hopkirk* crew used to often nick library sets from *The Saint*. Indeed, the writers would deliberately incorporate a library scene into an episode, knowing they wouldn't have to build their own.

Director Robert Tronson, however, has less than idyllic memories of the studio. 'It was awful. I hated it. It had a very bad atmosphere, but very suited to that sort of factory work. There were hundreds of security men. And if you went in or out everything was logged, so they always knew where you were. I had a first assistant whose joy was to leave the studio and go across to the pub, and that would be logged. Then he'd get a lift back in a car and lie under the back seat, and so he hadn't officially returned, and he'd set up this pandemonium as people tried to find him, but he'd actually be on the stage floor doing his work. It was not a nice studio. Like all those places, there was a terrible snobbery. There was a restaurant, a private dinning room and a cafeteria. Directors, cameramen, leading actors could go into the restaurant, a camera operator couldn't, but he could if his cameraman accompanied him. Things like that. It was like apartheid! I used to go in the worker's canteen, because it was the only thing open first thing in the morning, and it was awful, with a concrete floor, freezing cold. And it actually had two great vats, one of red sauce and one of brown sauce, with ladles with chains attached so they couldn't be stolen. And a bell would go at eight o'clock and a security man would arrive and yell, "Come on all you ignorant workers, out of here." And I used to think it was a joke, but it wasn't. He was practically manhandling them out!'

As usual, location shooting was done in and around the Elstree area. 'Mostly, I remember, in graveyards,' recalls Annette Andre. 'And it was usually terribly cold and wet, and we'd be in this little caravan trying to keep warm, and Mike would be saying, "Why don't we get a proper caravan with a proper heater?" They had this tiny little heater in there and we were all crowded around it. It was dreadful.'

The schedule was punishing too. 'We never had a break,' recalls Annette. 'In today's world you do so many episodes and then you have a break. In those days we just went straight through the whole lot. It was a tough routine. From half six in the morning I'd be there in the makeup room, and we wouldn't get away till perhaps seven at night. And you're doing that every single day, every week, every month, you need a break. So by the end of the series everyone was starting to get a little bit on edge with each other, and that made it a bit tough.'

The team celebrate the end of filming in one of the cramped location vehicles. Ah, the luxury of it all!

Annette was taken ill at one point and had to miss two episodes, briefly replaced by an invented sister who came in as Jeff's temp secretary. Most famously of all, Mike Pratt's balcony fall resulted in one episode having to be hastily altered to accommodate the incapacitated actor. It was Pratt's 38th birthday, and he'd perhaps had a little bit too much to drink by the time he arrived back at his London flat. Searching for his keys, he realised he'd left them at the studio and was locked out. Luckily his stand-in was there. (Both Cope and Pratt had stand-ins. Pratt even used to have regular fistfights with his to keep in trim.) So the stand-in climbed a drainpipe up two floors, got in, came down and opened the door. 'I can do that,' said Mike. His confidence proved misplaced, and he fell twenty feet into the basement area and smashed his legs. With filming duc to start on the final episode, Spooner called screenwriter Gerald Kelsey and asked him to rewrite it. What Kelsey did was to reverse the parts. So, with Pratt laid up in a hospital bed in the studio, with a real-life nurse in daily attendance, it was Cope as Marty that did the legwork in that episode, and it rapidly became a fan favourite.

Despite the pressure of filming, the atmosphere on set was genial and good-natured. 'We all liked each other and got on very well,' reveals Annette. 'Because in some of the series, my God, the cast were at each other's throats all the time. I remember Joel Fabiani from *Department S* used to come on our set and say, "I've just come over to sit with you for a while, because it's all so tense over there on our set." We had a lot of fun and laughs. And Ken would make you laugh. In the story you're not supposed to know he's there, and then he'd do something and we'd all end up in peels of laughter and have to do the whole take again.'

Robert Tronson especially remembers the light-hearted atmosphere that pervaded the whole set. 'Again the scripts were absolutely abysmal. It was an extraordinary atmosphere, because Mike and Kenny, and to a smaller extent Annette, they didn't care, they had a marvellous don't-give-a-fuck attitude to Monty Berman and everything else. The set was awash with champagne all the time. And Monty wouldn't pay them any more, so they made a deal to have their dressing rooms done up. Mike had a piano in his, and a sort of secret passage he could hide in if the assistants were trying to call him. So it was great fun, unlike some of the others that were pretty deadly serious. It was quite extraordinary. Even Monty, who didn't like any wasted money, when Kenny was so pissed he couldn't say his lines and was rambling on at the rushes, even Monty had to laugh.'

Cope was the joker in the *Randal and Hopkirk* pack. Perhaps his greatest gag during filming was the time he put a lubricated condom inside Annette Andre's script. 'The crew thought it was hysterical, usual lavatory humour,' recalls the actress. 'But it progressed. At lunchtime I went into the restaurant, and my great friend Roger Moore was sitting at a table with a couple of people that obviously he was doing business with. I filled this condom with water and I put it on a plate, and asked the waiter if he could put a silver salver over the top and deliver it to Roger, which he did. And Roger smiled when it arrived and took the silver salver off, and this thing is sitting on the plate wobbling around, and he slams the top back on it and looks around the room and sees me, and knew immediately I'd done it. He glared at me and then he started to laugh. Then Roger sent it to Peter Wyngarde, who was in the bar. Well, it got passed around. It went all through lunch, and you'd hear these roars of laughter. It was hysterical.'

The show proved a big hit with the public – so much so that, not long after its initial run, a fan club was formed which, according to Cyril Frankel, urged the makers to turn the series into a spin-off movie. Like the majority of ITC's output, *Randall and Hopkirk* sold world-wide in something like 35 countries, as diverse as Mexico and Ghana. And it continues to be shown today. Cope once joked that every now and then he'd get a royalty cheque for 43p, from somewhere like Tahiti. Syndicated in America in 1972, where it went under the title *My Partner the Ghost*, the show floundered, with audiences preferring to watch *Hogan's Heroes* on another channel.

While the public took to the show, the critics gave it something of a pasting. '*Randall and Hopkirk* just shouts American from the musical soundtrack down to the obvious breaks in the action for commercials. As a money spinner it may do well, as watchable English entertainment it can go jump in a lake,' moaned *The Daily Mail*. And this from the *Evening Standard*: 'The fact that there has been no massive protest against the sheer silliness of this series indicates to what depressing depths the tolerance level of the TV public has now been pushed.' The same critic was equally scathing of the two leads. 'Mike Pratt views every situation with the enthusiasm of a bankrupt bloodhound. Kenneth Cope wears the perpetual worried look of a soul that realises his purgatory is having to come back and appear in a series like *Randall and Hopkirk*.'

Despite the occasional hostile review, Lew Grade never lost his regard for the critics, nor they of him. 'Every Christmas, Lew was the only television executive who ever entertained all the press,' explains Marcia Stanton. 'And he knew everybody's name and they were all friends, and he did this every single year. They all used to come, Alexander Walker, Barry Norman, every critic you can think of, television and film, from all the papers. And one time they said to me, "He's done it for so many years that we want to surprise him. We want to do the party for him." But Lew always said to me, "Never, ever do anything to surprise me," because he hated being [taken] unawares. So I secretly told him, because it just was not worth my while not to. And we got to the restaurant and he went in the door, and they were all standing there and all clapped and applauded him. And he was really overwhelmed by it, because they were all genuinely fond of him. So even though sometimes they wrote lousy reviews, he never held it against them.'

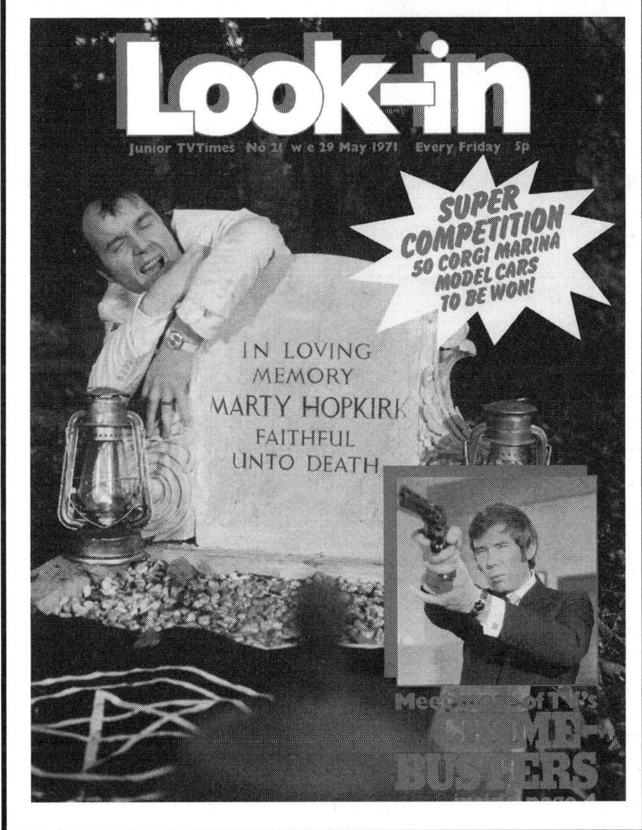

Randall and Hopkirk make the cover of 1970's kid's magazine Look-In.

In keeping with well-established ITC custom and practice, the decision to go ahead with any second series was based purely on financial matters. 'In those days, unless you got sold to the States and went network they wouldn't do anymore,' says Annette. 'And that was stupid. And unfortunately *Randall and Hopkirk* didn't get networked, we were syndicated, and so they said, "That's it, no more." They just didn't look to the future, because I think *Randall and Hopkirk* was a cut above a lot of the other ITC shows.'

The cast were bitterly disappointed at the prospect of not doing more episodes, as ideas had already been mooted about where to take the series and the characters. 'Some of the ideas we were talking about were to try to get more interesting locations, and locations abroad,' reveals Annette. 'And that it would be fun to have more ghosts coming in, and that Jeannie would become more involved, a partner with Jeff. Dennis Spooner liked our ideas, and I think it could have been fun. I really think it could have expanded the show. I think it was a terrible shame we didn't go on and do a second series.'

Spooner was similarly disappointed at the show's demise and, according to

Mike Pratt, embracing the counter culture of the early seventies perhaps too enthusiastically, meets his co-stars again after the show's success.

Raymond Austin, for a while he was keen to get it back up and running as a US-based comedy series, but couldn't get the rights from ITC.

Randall and Hopkirk brilliantly fused the well-worn private eye drama with the comedy of Noel Coward's *Blithe Spirit*. It was a neat gimmick that also borrowed from successful American shows of the period like *Bewitched* and *The Ghost and Mrs Muir*, where the main leads dabbled in flirtatious affairs with those beyond the grave.

But what really makes the series a joy to watch is the obvious screen chemistry shared by Cope and Pratt. Hopkirk's occasionally schoolboyish sense of humour is the perfect foil for Randall's gruff machismo. Marty actually seems to revel in being a ghost, and much of the comedy springs from his supernatural abilities and frailties. He can't touch anything or be seen, but he can materialise where and when he pleases and, poltergeist-like, is able to move objects or blow doors shut to trap escaping villains. But such gags tended to be repeated rather too often, like Marty's habit of intruding into his partner's conversations with clients, and Jeff suffering acute embarrassment at appearing to talk to furniture or thin air.

It is this quirkiness and undeniable sense of fun that has made *Randall and Hopkirk* one of the most beloved of ITC's shows. It's undoubtedly the company's funniest series, as opposed to many of those that were unintentionally funny. 'I used to go to some of the conventions and it's incredible, all these people turn up and they're all enthusiastic and know more about the show than you do,' marvels Annette. 'It's really extraordinary. But lovely that it's got that sort of life. We had no idea when we made it that it would do that. The fans are just wonderful. A few years ago I went to a sporting event with friends, and, coming out, a whole group of young people ran up to me and said, "Oh my God, you're Jeannie Hopkirk." This was when the BBC was repeating it back in the early nineties. And I looked at them and said, "My goodness you're so young." And they said, "We're all watching it and we love it. We think it's great and really cool." I've no idea why it's endured, but it seems to appeal to young people, even today. I was very surprised.'

Cope has also experienced the fan convention circuit, which is notable for bringing all the obsessives out of the woodwork who ask the nerdiest questions, like, 'What sort of mugs did the crew drink out of?' Cope believes part of the reason for *Randall and Hopkirk*'s enduring popularity is the nostalgia factor. He once said, 'A show like *The Darling Buds of May* harked back to better days and made everyone feel good, and I think this is the same. They were happier times when that show went out, and you get comfort from it.'

However, the cast didn't initially feel the benefits of their popularity. Annette Andre particularly had trouble getting work afterwards, and couldn't understand why. Jeannie hadn't been a part so singular that it would be hard for audiences to accept her in other roles. Yet casting directors didn't want to know, and before finding a satisfying career in the theatre, the actress, who now lives in America, was unemployable for over a year. 'So I can't say that *Randall and Hopkirk* had a great impact on my career. I think it was probably a negative rather than a positive. But I don't regret it at all. I'm absolutely delighted to have done it.'

The show was even resurrected in the late nineties, with comedians Vic Reeves and Bob Mortimer. Critical reaction to the BBC make-over was mixed, to say the least, but from the original cast and crew it was a uniform thumbs down. 'I watched part of the first episode and turned it off,' says Frankel.

AE 2

Chapter 7

No Strings Attached

- UFO - Space 1999 -

In 1969, after a virtual conveyor belt of hit shows, Gerry and Sylvia Anderson took their boldest career step yet – one that Gerry particularly had been yearning to make: to wave goodbye to their puppet heroes and concentrate on a live action series.

Amazingly, in the end, it wasn't an artistic decision, but a purely practical one. 'What happened was we were producing show after show after show, and then some clever dick invented repeats,' quips Gerry. 'And we were literally drowning in our own product. And one day I went to see Lew Grade and he said, "Gerry, we can't go on with puppet shows, everyone's repeating them. So you're going to have to go into live action."' It was what Gerry had been waiting almost ten years for somebody to say. The results would prove to be groundbreaking, and rank amongst the most polished and popular sci-fi series of all time.

UFO (1970-71)

The basic premise of *UFO* mirrored *Captain Scarlet* – that of a secret organisation defending Earth from alien invasion. The aliens, clad in red spacesuits and breathing green liquid, raid the Earth to harvest humans for body parts. It was a pretty unpleasant idea to present the public with at tea-time, and one inspired by the groundbreaking heart surgery carried out by Dr. Christian Barnard, which was the beginning of organ transplants. 'Because I got this name for science fiction, if I spoke to anyone, including Lew, about anything that wasn't science fiction, they didn't listen,' laments Gerry. 'So I'd get an idea and the second thing was, now how can I turn it into science fiction? So that's really how all those shows came about.'

As ever, to sell the series to a US network it was deemed essential to cast an American in the lead. It was Ed Bishop's voice work on *Captain Scarlet*, and an appearance in the Andersons' first live action movie, *Journey to the Far Side of the Sun*, that helped him win the plum job of his career – Ed Straker. New York-born Ed Bishop arrived in England in the early sixties and found work pretty easy to come by, particularly from ITC, for whom he became almost their American actor in residence. '*The Saint*, for example, I did six of those. Once you got in with them you were OK. And it wasn't that you had to be Laurence Olivier. If you could learn your lines and

The influence of Kubrick's 2001 *can clearly be seen in the costumes and hardware of* Space 1999.

hit your mark, that was a good plus. And if you could look fairly interesting in addition, that was a double plus. The money wasn't all that terrific though. But they were great little things. You simply played the same character in a different costume and the plots were more or less the same. It was like a factory. One week you could be playing a whacking great big part and the next come in just for a couple of lines. But the turnaround was so fast, that was the all-embracing thing. If they went beyond three takes on any of those things, boy, they were looking at their watches and flicking through *Spotlight*.'

From playing supporting roles, *UFO* thrust Bishop into the role of a leading man, with the responsibility of an entire series resting on his shoulders. 'But it didn't start out that way,' says Bishop. 'Straker's original role was to be the guy in the office banging on the desk saying, "Get me this, do this," goosing the plot along while other people were out fighting the bad guys. But I think that the writers got fascinated with this Frankenstein monster they'd created, and wanted to take that character and put him in more different situations. So the emphasis changed.'

Straker was head of SHADO (Supreme Headquarters Alien Defence Organisation) – a stoic and stalwart figure, an automaton almost. 'I thought of him mainly as a guy whose world was composed of black and white,' Bishop reveals. 'There were very few greys in his life, and this is why he was very good at his job because you had to make instant decisions. He was a man of intellectual action and a man who was answerable to virtually nobody in an entirely secret organisation. And we have lots of people like that all over the world in positions that we don't even recognise, but they have absolute power. The politician is maybe upfront, but these guys are the power behind the throne. I thought he was an interesting guy, although you wouldn't want to have him as a dinner guest necessarily.'

This ruthless dedication to his job was a character trait Bishop borrowed from a documentary he saw about the regimented mentality of American missile silo workers. 'These two guys would go down to the bowels of the earth, into a vault like Fort Knox, and they'd be locked in there, and the right chain of command would push the red button and send this missile off to wherever it was gonna go. And they each carried pistols and the interviewer said to one of them, "Why do you carry a gun? You're inside a bank vault, nobody's gonna get in," and he said, "That's to kill him in case he goes crazy." The reporter then asked, "You press that button, you don't know where it's going, you could incinerate a couple of million people, and you don't have any qualms?" He said, "No qualms." And that really was the nucleus – that little bit of a hook I hung Straker on.'

But beneath Straker's cold exterior and shocking blond wig, Bishop's performance hinted at a tragic man whose marriage had fallen victim to his ruthless dedication to his job. SHADO was Straker's total existence. When a colleague suggested he go home and get some rest, Straker bitterly replies, 'What home?' And the episode 'A Question of Priorities' deals with the tragic death of Straker's young son. For what was ostensibly a kid's show, this was powerful stuff. 'I was delighted when the kid died,' admits Bishop. 'Because I thought that was a wonderful, courageous thing to do in a TV series like that. That's the kind of thing that would go on in *The Sopranos* or *The West Wing*, the very sophisticated programmes of today. There was no soppy Hollywood ending. I thought it took great courage for them to do that.'

Backing up Bishop was a large supporting cast. George Sewell, a well-known TV character actor best known for police dramas and, later, the BBC comedy series *The*

Eye-catching cover of a super 8mm home movie.

Detectives, played Straker's right-hand man, Alec Freeman. But the American backers found Sewell, with his pock-marked face, less attractive than second leads on US TV shows customarily are. 'I'd cast George,' Sylvia Anderson recalls. 'He was a good actor, and I felt it didn't matter if he didn't look like a Greek God. But after a few episodes, word came back; "Sylvia, we've got to recast." So he was recast with Michael Billington, who was like a Greek God.'

As Paul Foster, Billington proved to be one of the series' most popular characters. 'Sylvia saw a photograph of me which my agent sent in,' he explains. 'She thought there was something interesting and called me in for a meeting, and we hit it off. Then I disappeared to the Cannes Film Festival, sleeping on boats and things, hanging around trying to make contacts. One day I got a message from Sylvia, can I get back as quickly as possible because they want to screen test me? So I drove back and I was totally tanned and looking gorgeous. No fake tan needed this time, like on *Department S*. I looked like the pages of an ancient medieval manuscript.'

Billington tested alongside four other actors, all completely different physical types. In the end it was the actor's physicality that won him the role. 'When I was spruced up, I did look a little bit Bond-like. I think they felt that could be an influence. Foster was a veiled attempt to introduce a Bond-type character.' After *UFO*, Billington became a hot contender for the role of 007. 'I think I was the unanimous choice of both [Bond producers] Cubby [Broccoli] at one point, and Harry [Saltzman].' Billington ultimately had to settle for a role in the pre-credit sequence of *The Spy Who Loved Me* – he's the guy who gets killed in the ski chase.

Billington believes that Gerry Anderson, along with co-writer Tony Barwick, largely modelled the character of Foster after his own personality. 'Both of them were writing how they thought I was as a person. I think they'd gleaned little bits of tittle-tattle about my private life. I was going to the King's Road partying. I was probably the actor who had the least sleep of anybody on the unit. And I think Gerry particularly found that tantalising, and felt he could weave it into the story. I would venture to say that Gerry felt my character was what he would have liked to be, but knew he couldn't fulfil that ambition himself. It was, at the same time, a fulfilment to him, but also a threat.'

That threat manifested itself towards the end of production when, while out on location, Anderson decided not to use or pay Billington's stand-in. 'So I decided to pay him myself,' says the actor. 'Which was foolish on my part because that meant I had a stand-in and Ed didn't – which made Ed look silly. And from that point on, Gerry never really forgave me, because he thought I was in some way being disrespectful. And from then on he started to write me out as much as possible.'

Writers on the show have since told Billington that episodes meant for Foster were turned into Straker storylines. Perhaps this animosity from Gerry was because Billington was a creation of Sylvia's. After all, she'd found him, she'd cast him, and battle lines were beginning to be drawn in the Andersons' marriage. For years, the couple had been sailing pretty close to the divorce courts. As early as the production of *Thunderbirds*, the Andersons' marriage had been under strain – so much so that Gerry had considered finishing it, only to change his mind when Sylvia announced she was pregnant. Their son, Gerry Anderson, Jr., was born in 1967. Now the cracks in their marriage had reappeared, and the frictions caused by it almost demanded that people take sides. 'Ed took me aside one day while we were filming,' Billington remembers, 'and said, "Mike, you know what's going on here, don't you? This marriage is going down the tubes, and we mustn't become pawns in this game that's being played." It was like we were both gladiators, but operating in different corners. It's not like who's got custody of the children, it was who's got custody of these TV stars? To this day, I still talk to Sylvia once a week. We're still very close after all these years. But Gerry did give me one good bit of advice. I'd just done several scenes and ended up shouting a lot, and he said, "Mike, I like what you're doing in the series, but internalise your anger rather than shouting it." And I think I did that from then on. The only real compliment Gerry ever gave me was on a documentary. He said, "Mike Billington was a good looking guy, he always knew his lines." So if he could've found an excuse to fire me, he would've done.'

The female characters in *UFO* were curiously stranded between a vision of future equality and the leering sexism of the late sixties. Thus, the women who controlled SHADO's Moonbase so efficiently did so dressed in skin-tight leotards and swathed with mascara. Not forgetting those fetishistic purple wigs. Sylvia hit upon the idea of the wigs. 'Well, we should do something different with the hair,' she mused. 'I know, we'll dye it purple.' Always determined to include strong women characters as opposed to mere set decoration, Sylvia was a lone feminine voice at executive level, and by no means always happy with the results of the all-male writing team. 'The only thing about *UFO* I object to now is that some of the lingering shots of girls walking down corridors, and men peering at them, seem a bit out of place today. I suppose in their way they were right for the time, but it does root the show very much in the seventies. It's very old fashioned.'

One woman who did have a big impact was Wanda Ventham. 'They wanted to bring in another actor to be my sidekick,' explains Bishop. 'And I said, "Look, instead of having another actor why don't we have another actress?" And they thought this was a great idea. I claim the credit for putting that to the executives, but it's to their commendation that they did something about it. So they brought in Wanda as Colonel Lake, and I thought that relationship worked very well. And it was kind of groundbreaking to have a strong female lead in a popular series; now it's all over the place you think it's been there forever, but in those days it was a bit of a breakthrough.'

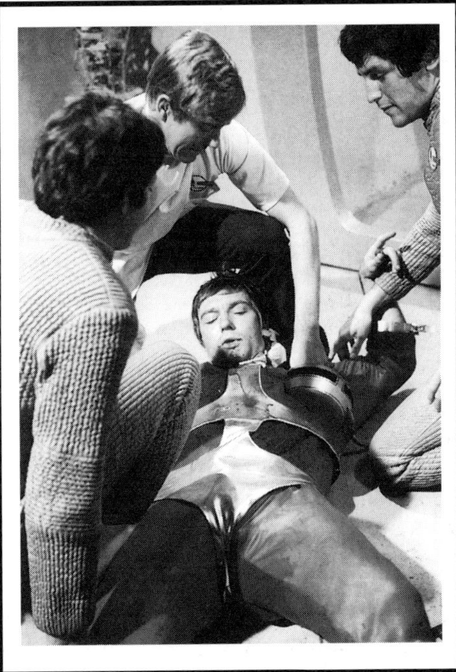

Left: *Wanda Ventham as Colonel Lake and Ed Bishop as the one and only Ed Straker. Right: Paul Foster (Mike Billington) finds the going tough on Moonbase.*

Working in partnership again, Gerry and Sylvia Anderson gave every indication of being the perfect professional couple, despite the frictions that existed in their personal life. As a team, their different talents contributed vastly to the creative success of projects. 'Gerry rarely came down onto the set, he'd breeze through occasionally but was mainly in his room watching the monitors,' recalls Billington. 'But Sylvia was up and down all the time, she'd be behind the camera, and if there was something slightly not right she'd step in front and sort it out. Sylvia never let a thing go through the camera she wasn't happy about. She was much more meticulous than Gerry was. Gerry was always studying budgets and rough cuts, but Sylvia was very much involved in the casting, the look of the thing, keeping everybody happy. If ever we had a problem we'd go to Sylvia first; you certainly wouldn't go to Gerry. You couldn't find two more different people. Why they ever got married in the first place is extraordinary.'

But not everybody found the Andersons easy to get on with. One of the guest stars on the show was Jane Merrow. 'I have to say *UFO* was probably the least happy experience of the ITC shows I made, because although I got on with the Andersons, they didn't get on with me. Because I'd been in Hollywood they thought I'd learnt some Hollywood tricks, and that I'd want more close-ups and things like that. And that's so far from the kind of person I am, and such nonsense, that I was really tight-lipped about it to say the least. I enjoyed it, it was fun, and Ed Bishop was very sweet. But the whole experience was soured a little bit by this idiotic lack of understanding. They'd probably worked with puppets for so long they didn't understand real actors. I shouldn't say that, but that was the impression I got.'

Among the many directors on *UFO* was the ever-reliable Cyril Frankel, who was hired after Gerry saw his work on *The Champions*. 'There was one episode called "The Invisible Man",' recalls Frankel, 'which Gerry and Sylvia Anderson thought was the best television episode they'd ever seen, and they asked me to come and direct for *UFO*. And that was very enjoyable.' Following his stint on *UFO*, Frankel went on to develop his own TV series about a group of scientists who make a robotic man. 'Lew liked it very much,' the director recalls. 'And he went over to the States and sold the idea to ABC. Then he told me and Dennis Spooner to go over to America and meet these guys, so we did and they seemed enthusiastic. I came back and, with Dennis, worked on the script and went and did a reconnaissance of Cyprus for the locations. We then went back to the States to present the photographs, but got a rather cold reception. Things had changed and they were not interested anymore. Later, they made it themselves and called it *The Six Million Dollar Man*. And Lew just said to me, "Look, Cyril, I can't do anything about it, because these are the people that I have to sell things to."'

David Tomblin, who went on to become one of the industry's most respected assistant directors, working on the *Star Wars*, *Superman* and *Indiana Jones* series, also came in to write and direct some episodes – purely on the strength of the one *Prisoner* episode he'd helmed. 'I think Lew told Gerry that he should use this guy,' explains Billington. 'Because he thought he had the dynamic quality which he thought that the series was missing. Which was the last thing Gerry wanted to hear.'

Bishop feels that the introduction of these two directors was a big boost to the show. 'One of the difficulties about our series was that some of the episodes we shot at the beginning were very slow, the audience worked it out before you had, and that's a danger sign. Then Gerry got in the likes of Dave Tomblin and Cyril Frankel, who'd worked on these ITC series, and they could look at two or three pages of dialogue and just shoot. All the editor had to do was join the ends together from where one take stopped and the other one began. There was no nonsense.'

Although *UFO* had a good, solid premise, the main weakness was its lack of scope. Every week the aliens came, SHADO went on red alert, and that was essentially it. 'It was too narrow,' says Bishop. 'Take *Star Trek*, Kirk says at the beginning of every episode its mission is to seek out new worlds, that gives you everything under the sun. But this was, in they come, we scramble; it was too limited.'

The majority of *UFO*'s 26 episodes are straightforward action, but occasionally, in an effort to make the series as innovative as possible, it touched upon more adult themes such as drug use. So despite the superficially lightweight premise, many plots had a remarkably adult subtext, sometimes without the knowledge of its creator, Gerry Anderson. 'I would never have anything to do with gratuitous violence, and drugs are absolutely out of the question. But I was still very naïve in some things. I didn't go to night-clubs and didn't know one drug from another. David Tomblin was without question a brilliant filmmaker. And he'd come to me with ideas and sometimes I thought, that's a bit bizarre, but quite interesting. And I tell you, I made those more "adult" episodes in all innocence. And it wasn't until the TV companies rejected a number of episodes, and I said, "Why?" and they said, "Because of the drugs," and I said, "What drugs?"'

UFO certainly improved as it went on, breathing life into its rather limited format with some almost surreal episodes such as 'Mindbender', where Straker finds himself in a nightmare world where SHADO is merely a TV show. Today it's a huge fan favourite, as it provides an intriguing behind-the-scenes look at the *UFO* sets and studio. Bishop also felt these more fantastical episodes were the way the show should go. 'Actually I think *UFO* could have gone further in that direction, it might have broken us out of that mould we were stuck in.'

The series also relied heavily on special effects to make its impact. Dozens of spaceship models were built just so they could be blown up. Ultimately this became rather expensive, so the effects crew learned to rely on quick editing, and to insert shots of exploding magnesium rather than destroy more ships. Despite all this paraphernalia, Billington believes the *UFO* stories were largely character-driven. 'They dealt with race issues – why one character couldn't be promoted because he was black – and they dealt with marital infidelity. I think the Andersons saw this as a stepping stone to doing more adult and adventurous material. Gerry used to call it "kidult". It was aimed at the kiddie audience in an early viewing slot, but he hoped that the adults would catch onto it.'

As for the look of the show, more than three decades on it's still visually extremely impressive. 'And the two people who are most responsible for that, in my view, are Bob Bell, who did all the sets, and Sylvia Anderson, who did all the costumes,' insists Billington. 'There's no way Gerry can deny that. Bob Bell and Sylvia really created the look of that show. It's quite stunning even today.' Bishop agrees that the main strength of *UFO* was the visual presentation that Sylvia, in particular, brought to it. 'It was her eye for design, colour, and harmony and balance. She used to hand cast all of the extras in the background. She had a wonderful eye.'

Like all previous ITC shows, the pressure was enormous to get the episode in the can within the allotted time. Gerry made a point of directing the pilot, just to prove that it could be done in ten days. A lot of responsibility fell upon the actors not to cock up their scenes and hold up filming. 'I can't remember ever doing a re-take because the acting wasn't right,' Billington recalls. 'I don't remember ever fluffing a line or getting it wrong, because we were really under scrutiny. We were so on edge all the time; knowing that the budget was of prime importance. I thought Ed Bishop was phenomenal. I can't remember a time when he blew a line, and he had an enormous amount of dialogue. The only thing they ever went back for was any technical hitches. Three takes and they started blowing a fuse. The main thing Gerry required from any actor was they showed up knowing their lines.'

The cast also felt somewhat intimidated by Gerry's practice of watching them on TV monitors from his office. 'We always knew he was watching,' says Billington. 'And the one thing you didn't want to do was screw up your lines. Another thing was you didn't look as though you wanted to laugh or enjoy it, because it might suggest that you were in some way poking fun at it. The one paranoia he had was that we weren't taking it seriously.'

Despite this tense atmosphere, the cast got on extremely well. Bishop recalls the male crew perking up when actress Gabrielle Drake walked onto the set every morning, wearing her skin-tight latex Moonbase costume. 'It just made you feel good to be alive to see Gabrielle.' Gerry also enjoyed working with the cast, notably Bishop. 'Ed was nothing short of outstanding. Here was a guy that never complained about anything and was always in the studio on time. I can't speak highly enough of him, and I thought he was going to be a great star. As for Mike Billington, he was a good-looking hulk. End of story.'

The first seventeen episodes of *UFO* were shot from April 1969 at the MGM stu-

Mike Billington was deliberately cast to bring a bit of Bond-like style and action to the series.

dios, Borehamwood. 'The only time I really felt physically uncomfortable on *UFO* was shooting my first episode,' recalls Billington. 'But I got through it with a lot of grit and determination. I was shuffling around on a dusty moon surface in a moon suit. And it happened to be the hottest day ever in the world. They had to keep giving me salt tablets and I was sweating like a pig. In some shots you can see my face looks like a beetroot. And that was the first one I ever did. I thought, "God, how many am I doing of these?"'

As the series' action man, Billington was often required to don spacesuits or engage in physically demanding activities. He enjoyed these elements of his work, as well as the opportunity to do his own stunts. 'Any actor enjoys stunts. When you've been bound up by lines for three or four days, it's nice to jump through a window. So any opportunity I got to do it myself, I would. I'd be a little disappointed when they said, "We have to use a stuntman because insurance won't allow you to do it."'

Though made at Borehamwood, the establishing shots of SHADO's headquarters were in reality the main administration block of Elstree Studios. Gerry's idea of having SHADO secretly operating beneath a film studio was actually born out of practicality, rather than creativity. 'If you want to make a television series and all the sets have got to be science fiction, forget it, it's just impossible to afford it. So I came up with the idea of having SHADO under a film studio, with Ed Straker being accepted as a movie producer, with an office just like any other office, except that it went down into the bowels of the earth. It also meant that we were able to shoot around the film studio because, even 40 or 50 years later, a film studio's a film studio.'

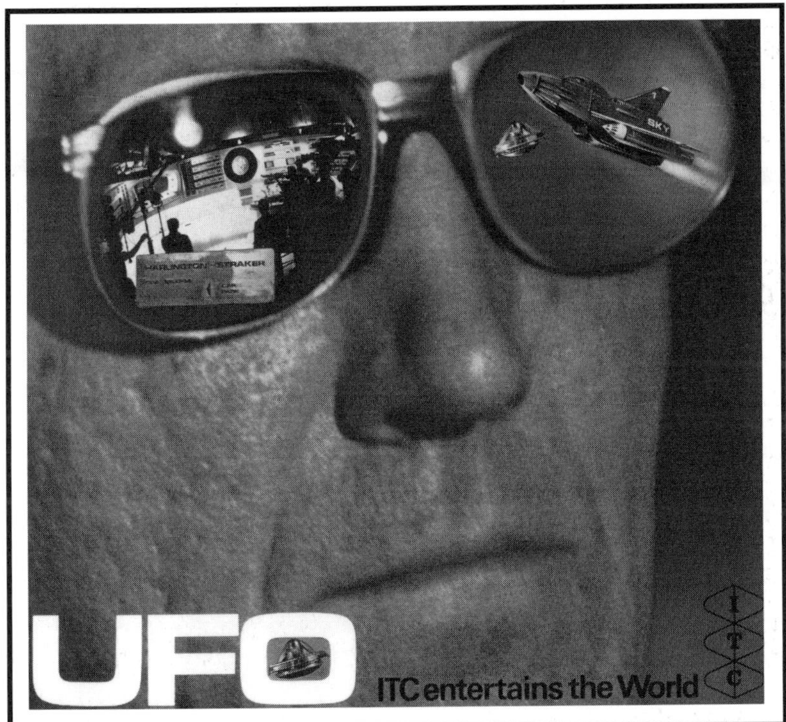

Simply stunning publicity brochure.

As production neared its end, the *UFO* team were forced to relocate to Pinewood, as the Borehamwood site was closing down after many years as one of Britain's premier studios. 'Looking back on it now, it was a very puzzling place to work at,' recalls Billington. 'There were these huge soundstages which seemed to be under-utilised. We seemed to be the only thing that was on for any length of time. And we did the last filming that was ever done at MGM, which was a few pickup shots on the episode "The Dalotek Affair", with myself and Tracy Reed spinning around with all these psychedelic lights. And then they pulled the plugs, and we all got drunk in one of the green rooms and that was it. And I remember this old sound guy came up to me and said, "Do you realise you're the last bit of filming done in this studio? And I was here when they did the very first film, *Edward My Son* with Spencer Tracy." And I thought, "Good God, there's a whole canon of film production ended with me spinning round with Tracy Reed."'

UFO made its UK TV debut in September 1970, and received a mixed critical response. Billington has particular cause to remember one of the poorer notices. 'One of the critics said of my performance in *UFO* that it was a character built out of the shavings of Captain Scarlet, and probably that's right. I don't think I really grew as an actor until later in my career.'

Initially, the series looked like being a hit. 'We were still filming one of the last episodes when Gerry came up with some good ratings results, and I was very pleased,' recalls Bishop. 'But later on I was absolutely devastated. The *TV Times* totally ignored it – they didn't even list the bloody actor's names when it first came up. And they stuck it on Saturday afternoon, opposite *Dr Who*. But all the kids on the block would come into my house to watch it with my own children and me. That was great fun.'

UFO's scheduling was erratic, to say the least. TV executives expecting another *Thunderbirds* were more than confused to find this heavy, adult-orientated show on their desk. As a result, they just shoved it out there to sink or swim, and ratings were generally poor. Some episodes were even broadcast in late evening slots, to protect younger viewers from their intense themes. Arguably, *UFO* is the most atypical of the Anderson shows, which, by and large, have all followed a similar pattern. 'There was a formula to these shows, although at the time I wouldn't have called it that,' says Gerry. 'I was given some great advice early in my career. I was the sound editor on a picture called *They Who Dare*, starring Dirk Bogarde and directed by Lewis Milestone, who'd made the classic *All Quiet on the Western Front*. He took me aside one day and said, "Now listen carefully, because I'm going to give you a bit of advice, and I want you to remember this for the rest of your life. Don't ever, ever try and second-guess your audience, because if you do that you're going to be a failure. You do what you want. Of course, if the audience don't like what you want, you're going to be a failure anyway, so you do what you want." Well, that was the formula. I never had focus groups. I'd simply read a script, liked it or didn't like it.'

Billington has his own take on why the series never quite captured the public imagination. 'When *UFO* first came out, 99 per cent of people watched it in black and white. Can you imagine *UFO* without the purple wigs? That's the thing everyone remembers. But most people couldn't afford colour TVs. So consequently the whole lustre of it, the extraordinary imagery, was lost. I mean, there's no reason to have purple wigs, but why not, it adds an extra lustre, an extra dimension you can't do in *Coronation Street*. There's no way it could have succeeded in black and white. It was probably three or four years too early. It did better in New York and LA, because there were more people out there who had colour televisions. So in places where they had colour, it probably had a better impact.'

As for the cast, *UFO*'s less than successful run did nothing for their careers. 'The show was almost totally ignored and I couldn't get arrested,' laments Bishop. 'My phone gathered cobwebs. I think a lot of people thought, "Oh well, Bishop used to be a very reliable jobbing actor, you could get Eddie to do anything, radio, TV, stage." And then they said, "Oh wow, now he's done a big TV lead and he's with a big agent, he's not interested in coming down and doing a school's radio broadcast." So, for about a year, nothing was happening. That's why I decided to go back to America. And nothing happened over there either!'

To supplement his Stateside acting income – which notably included voiceovers for the cartoon version of *Star Trek* – Bishop undertook some painting and decorating work in the New York area. One job in particular remains fresh in his memory. It was a Saturday morning, and a couple wanted the kitchen in their Bronx apartment wallpapered. 'I got there at about ten o' clock. It was a swine of a job. But I'm very good at it, actually. I can hang a pretty mean piece of wallpaper. About six o'clock, this couple and their teenage daughter went to watch TV in the living room. And I'm hanging my wallpaper and I hear, "ba-ba-ba-ba-baba-ba," and I stuck my head around and there it was, they were watching *UFO*. I didn't know whether to laugh or cry. I

Straker on the film lot that acts as an ingenious front for SHADO.

think I did both. They would have been apoplectic if I'd said, "By the way, that's me, mind if I sit down and watch?" I guess its all part of life's rich tapestry as an actor.'

Although not shown in America until the autumn of 1972, three years after its production, a second series was highly anticipated. A lot of the props had been stored and most of the cast voiced interest in returning, although some were busy elsewhere – notably Billington, who had a regular role on BBC's *The Onedin Line*. Alas, despite the initial encouragement driven by American audience response, when the ratings started to slump, CBS backed out. 'We literally came within half an inch of making more episodes,' Bishop reveals. 'They got into advance production, but at the last minute the numbers didn't work out in America, and they pulled it. It was too bad, because we had some scripts prepared. And I've read since that those scripts became transmogrified into the first episodes of *Space 1999*.'

It wasn't until the mid-eighties that *UFO* started being rerun sporadically, generating legions of new fans. Ed Bishop attended many of the fan conventions, and was gratified at the show's sustained popularity. The reaction he got from fans made him ponder the possibility of a *UFO* film. 'There's still a lot of mileage in old Straker.' And there have repeatedly been rumours of a big screen version. But how much validity you ascribe to them depends on your level of gullibility. 'Although there is this German multi-zillionaire,' reveals Bishop. 'The series was the centre of his childhood, and now he's made a zillion dollars, got a lot of film companies in his group, he wants to make a feature film of *UFO*. But he said he would only make it if I would

Back in the good old days when kid's annuals were cool.

play Straker, and I said, "My God, is the Pope Catholic?"'

For Gerry, however, the memories of *UFO* are inexplicably linked with a breakdown in his private life, which was to have even more of a dramatic impact on his next show. 'At the time, I probably was quite happy with the series. But I wouldn't say it was the happiest show I've ever worked on – and that was because of the problem with Sylvia and myself. The trouble between Sylvia and myself was getting worse by the minute, and that made the work somewhat unpleasant. In theory you should not let personal circumstances impinge on your work, but in reality it's terribly difficult.'

Out of all the episodes, Bishop's own personal favourite is 'Sub Smash', in which Straker struggles to survive in a capsized submarine after a UFO attack. 'I always promised myself that if Straker was ever in a life or death situation, I would call upon every intellectual, emotional resource, experience, training, to convey that I actually believe I'm going to die. That there wasn't [going to be] a look in my eye that said, "I'm back next week." And I think I went a long way to succeed in that episode. Straker thinks, "This is it, the oxygen's gone," so it was my idea he write in this diary something from *The Burial at Sea*. And I thought that was brilliant as an intellectual exercise. Here's this guy who, all his life, has been led according to dictums of technology, right and wrong, black and white, but at the end he converts to some kind of spirituality. There was a great controversy on the set, because some people thought it was mawkish and sentimental and false. I think people practically came to blows. But it's still there. Unfortunately, Des Saunders, who was the post-production guy, he hated it, and I think he drowns it in music. I think you can just about pick out the dialogue – "We now therefore commit ourselves to the deep and we shall wait for the day of resurrection."'

Despite a distinguished TV and film career, appearing in everything from James Bond films to *The Professionals*, Bishop will forever be remembered as Ed Straker. 'A few years back I had a minor operation on my eye, and I was wearing a Fedora, a Philip Marlowe-type trench coat and a black patch over my eye. I drove in to get some gas, and went in to the clerk and was paying with my credit card, and he said to me, "You're Ed Bishop, aren't you? You were in *UFO*." And I looked up at him with the hat, the trench coat with the collar up and the eye-patch, and said, "Man, you ought to be with the police, you have wonderful powers of observation!"'

It was much the same with Billington. 'I go to Italy quite frequently, and as Paul Foster I can go into any bar or restaurant, anywhere, and the guy I go with only has to tell the manager who I am, and I suddenly get a free meal. It's like you're giving something back to them which is part of their childhood.' *UFO* was particularly popular in countries like Italy and Spain. 'Because when we did them James Bond was very big,' Billington continues, 'and the Bond movies in Italy played in the big theatres, but the small theatres couldn't afford them, so what they used to do was cut together two episodes of *UFO* and put Bond music over it.' Also a hit in Japan, Billington was invited to go out to Tokyo to make *Godzilla*-type monster films, but decided instead to stay in England and try for more creatively rewarding work. 'I could have gone over there and lived off sushi for the rest of my life.'

In an appallingly tragic coincidence, both Ed Bishop and Michael Billington died within days of each other, early in June 2005: Bishop of a fatal chest infection, Billington of cancer. TV fandom mourned them both.

SPACE 1999 (1975-77)

In 1972, Gerry Anderson was in the process of obtaining funds for a new series of *UFO*, when word reached him that the sci-fi show had been cancelled. Entitled *UFO* 2, later changed to *UFO 1999*, prospective scenarios had the SHADO team taking the fight to the aliens in outer space, and an enlarged Moonbase with advanced weaponry to defend mankind against the alien menace.

It had all started so promisingly, with Abe Mandell, ITC representative in the USA, raving over *UFO*, which was leading the ratings in Los Angeles and New York, while Gerry was hard at work on the new episodes at Elstree studios. 'Then Lew phoned me and said, "I hate to tell you this, Gerry, but I'm cancelling the new series of *UFO*." I said, "Why?" He said, "Because the ratings have dropped off." I said, 'Well, maybe they have dropped off, ratings do, don't they, and then they come back again." He said, "No. Abe's phoned me and recommended that we don't make it, and I can't go against Abe because he understands the American market." Like hell he did, but anyway. So *UFO* was cancelled.'

Determined to make something out of this ungodly mess, Gerry had a brainwave and went to see Lew. 'I said, "Look, we've done a lot of work on this, spent a lot of money. What if I change the story and make it into a brand new show." And he said, "You think you can do it?" I said, "Yes." And he said, "OK, sounds like a good idea." So we started switching the story into *Space 1999*, which was going to be based on the moon.' Then Gerry hit a stumbling block. In *UFO*, there had been a story where Ed Straker's son was killed. It was Gerry's own idea, and when he saw the finished episode he loved it. Abe Mandell hated it, and phoned Gerry to complain; 'You're making a science fiction show, what's all this business about doing a domestic story?' So when Lew Grade informed Mandell of the idea to switch *UFO* into a new series, Gerry got a red-hot call from the American. 'Gerry, in the new show you're gonna do, I don't want one single story to take place on Earth. Got it?' Gerry agreed. Mandell continued, 'How can I be sure that you won't do it?' Gerry said, 'Right here and now, I promise you I won't do it.' He said, 'That's not good enough. I'm going to give you until tomorrow morning. If you ring me and tell me how the show's going to be pitched, in such a way that it will be impossible for you to make an episode on Earth, I'll tell Lew I'm backing the show.' So Gerry phoned the next morning and said, 'Abe, what if we blow up the earth?' That was too drastic for

Bold explorers hurtle through the galaxy on a toxic moon
SPACE
1999
AN ADVENTURE THAT KNOWS NO BOUNDS
60-MINUTE SERIES
MARTIN LANDAU
BARBARA BAIN

ITC
Distribution

Left: *advertisement selling re-runs of* Space 1999. Above: *the original and best line up. Barbara Bain, Marty Landau and Barry Morse (right) left controversially after the first series.*

American primetime consumption. 'OK, what if we blow the moon out of orbit?' Mandell yelled, 'Fantastic – you're on.' One of the biggest cult TV sci-fi shows ever had just been born.

The idea of a scientific research colony on the moon that also oversees the dumping of Earth's nuclear waste quickly evolved. When a massive radiation surge causes an explosive chain reaction, the moon is catapulted out of Earth's orbit into universes unknown, and encounters with, as Gerry put it, 'life, as we don't know it.'

Such an expensive project was obviously going to need Stateside appeal, as it wouldn't hope to recover its cost in the home market alone. Mandell insisted that American stars play the two leads, necessitating a casting trip to Hollywood. Under consideration were Katherine Ross and *I Spy*'s Robert Culp, who Sylvia Anderson particularly favoured. But at a meeting, Culp revealed his intention to also write and direct for the series, and Gerry was having none of that. In the end, it was decided to go with the husband and wife team of Martin Landau and Barbara Bain, who'd achieved huge success with *Mission Impossible*. Fraught negotiations went on for a week, before a deal was struck that the stars' agent could agree with. 'But then he came back and said, "We've just got one more thing,"' Gerry recalls. 'And it related to money. And Abe said, "We can't lose these people now, not after what we've been through. We've got to get hold of Lew. Oh Christ, it's half past eleven at night in London and Lew goes to bed at half past nine, and if I phone him he'll go bloody berserk." So we're sitting in this hotel and Abe suddenly goes, "Gerry, come on, we can't let this deal go." So he storms into his room, picks up the phone and starts dialling. And I'm thinking "This guy's got some guts after all." And he's standing there with the phone, and I'm standing next to him and I hear, "brr, brr, brr, brr," and I can just hear Lew saying in a groggy voice, "Hello." "Lew," Abe says, "I've got Gerry for you." And he slammed the receiver in my hand. Bastard! But Lew was always very nice to me, and he agreed and we had a deal.'

Both Landau and Bain had never worked in Britain before, but their pedigree was impressive. Bain had been a successful model in New York before studying at Lee Strasberg's prestigious Actor's Studio, and was the first woman in television to win three consecutive Emmys, for her role in *Mission Impossible*. Landau was also a protégé of Strasberg, one of only two people among 2,000 that applied to the Actor's Studio and were accepted that year – the other was a young nobody called Steve McQueen. Landau's other claim to fame is that he turned down the chance to play Spock in *Star Trek*. Mighty credentials then, but to some on the *Space 1999* team they arrived with a little too much Hollywood baggage. 'Barbara especially was very Hollywood,' observes director Raymond Austin. 'Martin actually was as good as gold. At the beginning none of the cast and crew knew Martin, but I did, I'd doubled him on *North by Northwest*. I did the fall off Lincoln's nose for Martin and he's a great guy. And they had these adjoining dressing rooms. Martin, if he'd had his way, would've had his dressing room at the other end of the block to Barbara's. It wasn't that great on the set with those two. It was a bit of a pain.' At the time, the Landau and Bain marriage was navigating choppy waters, and they eventually separated in the early eighties. Barbara's career never again reached the peak of her *Mission Impossible/Space 1999* days, while Landau, after a long lean period, leaped to prominence again with his Oscar winning portrayal of Bela Lugosi in Tim Burton's *Ed Wood*.

Over the course of the series, Barbara Bain gained an unwanted reputation and the on-set nickname of 'Barbara Pain'. 'I did an episode in which Joan Collins guest-starred,' Raymond Austin recalls. 'And Joan came on the floor with a very short skirt, and Joan Collins had great legs, absolutely great legs. Now Barbara Bain had a short skirt as well, and she's got good legs, but you could see from the moment she walked on and had to play a scene with Joan, she didn't like it at all, and tried like crazy behind the scenes to have Joan's skirt lengthened. But Sylvia didn't let her get away with it. But there was such feeling there that Barbara didn't want to be on the same set as Joan Collins. It was so funny.'

On screen, Landau and Bain also came over as rather aloof and detached. Landau's portrayal of John Koenig, commander of Moonbase Alpha, is shot through with tension, anxiety, and bursting with controlled nervous energy, while Barbara's Dr. Helena Russell, head of the medical unit, is cool to the point of arctic conditions. 'Barbara did a journeyman's job all the time,' says Raymond Austin. 'Martin was always more adventurous and wanting to do more things with his character. But a lot of the other artists never liked playing scenes with Barbara at all; they'd rather play with anyone else than Barbara. They always said to me, "I'm not getting anything back from her at all."'

Much more personable was Barry Morse as Professor Bergman, astrophysicist extraordinaire and Alpha's father figure. Morse had just finished the ITC show *The Zoo Gang* when Grade phoned him up with the offer. 'There's a thing I'd really like you to do. Gerry and Sylvia Anderson are putting together a science fiction series and there's a part in it that we'd like you to play.' Interested, Morse replied, 'That sounds fine, get them to send me along some scripts and I'll have a look and see what it's like.' 'Ah,' said Grade, 'that is a bit of a problem because they've only got one script.' Morse stood there dumbstruck. 'Lew, you're kidding me aren't you, I thought you said you only had one script?' 'No, that's true,' admitted Grade. 'Lew, you've been in this trade longer than most of us, with more success than most of us, and you're thinking of embarking on a television series, a science fiction project, for which you only have onc script?' 'Well, yeah,' Grade carried on, 'but these people, Gerry and Sylvia Anderson, they know what they're doing.'

Almost convinced, Morse asked to at least see this solitary script. 'Well,' recalls the actor, 'even this one script wasn't completely finished, and there was no indication in it at all as to what the characters were, further than their names. Nothing about what their backgrounds were, what their natures were, nothing at all. It's rather as if Shakespeare should have agreed for the first production of *Hamlet* after he'd only written the first four lines. "Who is this guy called Hamlet?" we'd start to say. Well, that's what we all started to say about our characters. Now people come in white coats and lock you up for such lunacy, don't they?'

The series became renowned for its famous guest stars, such as Christopher Lee.

Morse's worst fears were immediately confirmed at a pre-production meeting he attended with Landau and Bain. 'Our two so-called producers, Gerry and Sylvia Anderson, were raving on about these wonderful moon city costumes that were being created by this popular designer, Rudi Gernreich. They were saying, "You know, he was the first person to pioneer topless dresses." And I, always the troublemaker, said, "Gerry, Sylvia dear, before we get into all this about the glory of the uniforms, could we spend perhaps a minute or two talking about who we are?" "Ah, well now, about the boots," they said, going on to talk about who was going to design the boots. I don't think that Gerry and Sylvia Anderson were the best producers I've ever come across, and I've come across a good many in the four corners of the earth during my 70-year career.'

In the end, Morse took matters into his own hand, writing a potted biography as to the kind of life someone like Professor Bergman might have led before he arrived at Moonbase Alpha, coming up with some character traits and little eccentricities to add flesh onto an all too bare skeleton. 'Bergman was a man of science, so let's look at outstanding men of science within roughly our time, and one of the characters that presents itself to us is, of course, Einstein. Let's take Bergman as being somewhat like Einstein. One of the first things about such a character is he's totally unworldly, and so the first battle I had was to try and resist wearing those dreadful uniforms, because such a man wouldn't be bothered with all that. I wanted him to go round in an old cardigan with holes in the elbows, and tennis shoes without any laces in them, and odd socks and all of that, make him a real character and rather eccentric. But they never made any advantage of it. I must do justice to the writers, however, mostly they hadn't the time because they were trying to get enough pages ready for us to shoot tomorrow, or next week, all the way through that first series.'

In a bid to sort out the scripts, science fiction writer Christopher Penfold had been recruited as story consultant; he in turn brought on board poet and novelist Johnny Byrne. As was usual in an Anderson production, it was husband and wife who sat down to write the pilot episode. Originally conceived as a half-hour show, there was a radical rewrite which boosted it up to 90 minutes, followed by further tinkering that reduced the show's duration to just under an hour. But the general consensus was that the pilot script wasn't working, and there were more rewrites. Titles came and went too. *Menace in Space* became *Space Probe* became *Space Journey 1999*, with a story that had malevolent aliens reducing the moon's gravity to zero, causing Alpha to drift helplessly out into uncharted space.

Despite the fact no human being had set foot on the moon since 1972, Gerry believed that lunar colonisation was a distinct possibility by the end of the century, and deliberately set the show in the not too distant future. As with the Enterprise craft on *Star Trek*, Moonbase Alpha had a multinational crew and was a completely self-contained environment, with a control centre, interconnecting corridors, a transport system, landing pads and a shuttle service to Earth.

Production got underway in December 1973, and already technical and teething problems looked like scuppering the entire enterprise. 'Our shooting schedule was nine days per episode,' explains Morse. 'That first episode took 27 days. So something had to be done about that, otherwise the whole project would be bankrupt within its first couple of months. So we were forever fighting the clock. We worked immensely long days in order to try and keep up with the schedule, and eventually, with great credit to the crew, who were very experienced, we managed to shoot each episode within, or not too far outside of, the nine-day schedule.'

For a while *Space 1999* looked like it was going to be made in Hollywood, but eventually the makers saw sense and based operations at Pinewood Studios, taking over two soundstages. Much of the budget was consumed by the impressive set design. Sleek and futuristic, they were created by production designer Keith Wilson, who'd worked with the Andersons since *Fireball XL5*. 'Some of the stuff Keith used to come up with on those stages, you'd think you were in Hollywood,' remembers Raymond Austin. 'The sets and everything were so good. But it used to get very claustrophobic at times in those confined compartments Keith designed. Sometimes you'd find that you'd got a whole day's shoot in just the one room, and you'd be going round the bend by the end of the day with the damn thing.' There was a definite feeling amongst the cast and crew of acute claustrophobia, as everything was filmed indoors. 'We were never out of the studio,' says Morse. 'Except for one episode that was shot near Pinewood in Black Park, and by sod's law it rained almost every day.'

Even by today's standards, the production values on *Space 1999* were impressive, and few shows have ever matched it. But all this came at a cost. For its time, *Space 1999* was the most expensive series ever made in Britain, at £3.5m. And even that wasn't enough, as towards the end of the first series the budget was stretched to near breaking point, and the Andersons were forced to beg Grade for more money. Seeing footage of what had already been achieved, Lew had no hesitation in giving them the extra cash.

Take me to your leader.

The state-of-the-art effects didn't come cheap either. Based at Bray Studios near Windsor (once home to the Hammer horror films), the model work and visual effects team was supervised by Brian Johnson, who'd started out under Derek Meddings on *Thunderbirds* before working on *2001: A Space Odyssey*. Johnson was also responsible for the design of the Eagle fleet of versatile spacecraft, which were constructed of durable materials to withstand the constant crash landings they suffered on the show. In all, four different scale models existed, the largest at 44 inches, costing £3,000. Inevitably, paper cut-out Eagles would be substituted for the real thing when explosion shots were required.

The effects on *Space 1999* turned out to be superior to anything yet seen on television, and received some of the show's best notices – like this from *The Financial Times*: 'Visually the quality of *Space 1999* approaches and sometimes even reaches the standard of *2001*. How unfortunate though that the stories show so few signs of achieving the level of expertise to be found in the wonderful sets and effects.' Barry Morse couldn't have agreed more. 'A lot of credit for the success of *Space 1999* must be given to the special effects people, because the range and variety of the effects was considerably greater than the range and variety of the human relationships.'

Backing up the main stars was a group of personable supporting characters. There was second in command Paul Morrow, played by Prentis Hancock, Australian Nick Tate as the easygoing Alan Carter, Alpha's chief pilot, and data co-ordinator Sandra Benes, played by Eurasian actress Zienia Merton. Despite being full of potential, these characters scarcely developed as the series went on and ended up with very little to do. The reason was that, before he signed, Landau insisted on a stipulation in his contract assuring him of a high percentage of screen time per episode. Barbara Bain also had an unwritten agreement that more or less stated that, for every three minutes screen time her husband had, she'd have two. All of which inevitably meant less screen time for other characters. 'They had big heads, basically,' asserts Sylvia. 'And, of course, Lew allowed them that. They wanted to be in every scene. We had good actors in supporting roles that could take a scene on their own, but they were never allowed to. For instance, Martin Landau would never allow anyone to make a decision on the screen, it always had to be his character giving the commands. And I felt that was wrong.'

Gerry, on the other hand, was nothing less than impressed by his two stars. 'They were very good to work with. I can't tell you how good. Nice people. And they supported the show. Eleven out of ten.'

Adding to the production woes was Morse, still exasperated over what he deemed to be a lack of dramatic content in the scripts. 'Over and over again the episodes were passed back to the people in the special effects, to construct sufficient explosions and model collisions to make some drama out of it, because there was very little drama passing between us as human beings. Martin and I got a little bit impatient about the quality of the material. We knew, of course, that our so-called producers had come to prominence with puppet shows, and during a scene we shared together I said to Martin, "Look, as a little message to Gerry and Sylvia, in take one of this next scene why don't we play it as if we were puppets?" I told the cameraman that, no matter what we did, just to keep rolling. We arranged for it to go through with the rushes the following day to Gerry and Sylvia, and they laughed indulgently, as if we were having some mischievous joke, and paid no attention at all.'

But pressure was mounting on the producers from other sources. Despite the acquisition of Landau and Bain, and scripts being vetted by ITC's New York office for their appeal to the American audience, Grade was unable to secure a US network sale and had to look elsewhere for finance. The Italian television station RAI had been interested in co-financing the series from the outset, but as production got underway they still hadn't committed. And so a lavish reception was held at Pinewood for a delegation of their executives, who were given a guided tour around the sets. Impressed, RAI agreed to invest, but there was a catch – the Andersons had to use a number of Italian guest stars. Sylvia was immediately dispatched to Rome to begin casting. In the end, most of these performers had to be dubbed, as their English was so poor.

Other, more familiar faces, like Christopher Lee and Peter Cushing, were brought in to lend the series additional gravitas, along with distinguished stage performers such as Richard Johnson and Margaret Leighton, who Raymond Austin has cause to remember particularly well: 'She was very ill at the time, and on the third day she said to me, "Raymond, how much more do I have to do?" I said, "You've got about five more minutes screen time." And her part was sitting on a throne, all dialogue, because she couldn't walk. She said, "Can you shoot it all today?" "I doubt it, Margaret. Why?" She said, "I don't think I'm going to be with you much longer." I knew she was ill, so I took it for granted she meant that she was going to die. So I went to Gerry and Sylvia and they said, "OK, let's not do anything else and just shoot her until it's done." So we sat her down, and she had reams of nonsensical technical dialogue, the gyration of the earth is so and so, with the permutations of this and that. And when I said cut she'd say, "Did that make sense, because I don't know what

I'm talking about. It's coming out of my mouth, but I don't know what it means." I said, "Nor do any of us, it's all mumbo jumbo, just keep going." And we got her stuff done, and sure enough she died not long afterwards. But God – what a super lady.'

ITC regular Shane Rimmer came on board for one episode, but found the atmosphere at Pinewood disagreeably tense. 'I didn't enjoy that one as much as the other shows I did for them. It might have been the Hollywood factor, although Martin was fine. I think Barbara was a little "Hollywood". Martin was very amiable, very easy to get along with. And there was, not acrimony, but a little disagreement between the production office and what was going on on the floor. It just wasn't the same atmosphere that you were used to.'

What only a handful of people knew at the time was that, behind the scenes, the Andersons' marriage was falling apart. Although in the studio they tried to keep things as professional as possible, and not allow their personal traumas to affect the show, inevitably the strains showed. 'You would very rarely see them in the same room together,' says Rimmer. 'When two people have been very close and been so integral to each other for a long time, any sort of variation of that comes to your notice. It wasn't quite as amicable as it had been previously. And thank God I didn't get torn into this one. You had to choose whose side you were on, and that is really ugly stuff.'

The inevitable split came at the close of *Space 1999*'s first season. 'We had an end of shooting party,' says Gerry. 'And I said to Sylvia, "Are you going to the party?" And she said, "Why do you ask?" And I said, "Because if you're going, I won't." She said, "I don't want to go." "OK, fine." So I went. And then she turned up. She also invited a mutual friend back to the house afterwards, and then the argument just flared up. And I'll never forget this poor guy sitting there. And he went over to the piano and started playing as if he was in a hotel bar, with us thundering away at each other. It was almost like a scene out of a bad picture. And it was at that point when I said, "That's it, I'm leaving." Not for anyone else, I might add, but just simply because I couldn't stand it any longer. As a result of that I went to pieces. I didn't have a nervous breakdown, but I just lost every ounce of courage I had.'

The divorce was equally devastating to Sylvia. Not only did she cease her personal association with Gerry, but also any hint of professional association, and so was forced to leave their film and TV company, and also *Space 1999* – a series she'd helped launch. 'I was very hurt,' she says. 'It's a funny business that we're in. Martin Landau and Barbara Bain, who I'd had into my home and helped while they were over here, never called me or anything. So I was out in the cold for a while. But I had a small group of friends who stayed loyal to me, and eventually I got a job, which I needed because I didn't come away with a lot of money.' The offer that resurrected Sylvia's life and career was a position with American cable giants HBO, as a production consultant and their British representative. 'HBO saved my life,' insists Sylvia. 'No one else came forward to say, "You're a fantastic person, here's a job." And I've been there ever since.'

So the creative partnership, which had gone from the obscurity of primitive children's puppet shows to international co-productions watched by millions around the globe, had reached its sad and destructive conclusion. 'Not only was it a personal tragedy that they parted,' observes Ed Bishop, 'because it's sad when a long term marriage comes to an end, but it also brought to an end a great professional relationship. They worked absolutely in tandem with each other. And Gerry depended a great deal on Sylvia. I think they would have gone on to do some really good work.

It's a sad loss.' Raymond Austin feels much the same way. 'Gerry and Sylvia were a great team, a bloody marvellous team. Because Gerry could really put a story together, his concept on storytelling was absolutely superb, and Sylvia was great on those costumes and the look of the show. It was a great combination.'

Yet the legacy of those incredible shows will always remain. 'I think Gerry is still regarded as somebody who created a television franchise that is just going to go on forever,' says Shane Rimmer. 'And I think people in the business, maybe not the general public, they know that Sylvia was an integral part of all that.'

Sylvia herself is justly proud of what she and Gerry achieved. 'I think it's fantastic. You only have one life, and if you're remembered for something that's an achievement in itself. I'm terribly proud. I'm just terribly sad that some of it has to be negative. There are certain times when I read things that are not true, but then, what do you do? And Gerry has since tried to denigrate my contribution to those shows, and me. Also, however much I've tried to distance myself from all of that, people still know me basically as the *Thunderbirds* girl, whether you like it or not, it's there. And I don't run away from it anymore. I used to, but not anymore.'

Gerry is less magnanimous when it comes to he and Sylvia's past. Their protracted and very public divorce hurt him deeply, as did the bitter custody battle over access rights to his son. 'If anybody says to me, "Gerry would you like to bring one of your old shows back?" and it was a very attractive proposal, I will say to them, "Look, I'm very proud that I live in a democracy, and as far as I'm concerned Sylvia Anderson is a free agent, she can do whatever she likes, and I would never dream of trying to prevent her doing anything. Having said that, if I am to walk within 100 yards of her, forget it. For the last 30 years I've never spoken to her. And nor will I."'

When the first season of *Space 1999* finished production, another high profile casualty was Barry Morse. The actor confirms that in his contract was a clause stating that, if there should be a second series, he had the choice of continuing or leaving. 'And so I went along to see Gerry Anderson, I remember it well, with great pleasure. I said, "Gerry, dear, I wish you every conceivable kind of success with the next series, but if it's all the same to you, I'd like to go and play with the grownups for a while." Because I could see that, in the year and a half it had taken us to shoot this first series, there had been, in my view, all too little improvement in the quality of the dramatic writing. And so they went on to do a second series, which I've seen hardly any of. Though the viewers, whether they're trying to be kind to me or not, most of them tell me that they considerably prefer the first series to the second.'

Happy to walk away, Morse was left bemused and angry that no logical reason was presented for his character's disappearance. 'Every time I go to one of these conventions, scores of people ask me, "Whatever happened to Victor Bergman?" And I always say, "They never offered any explanation as to what happened to him, so you must assume that he fell off the back of the moon." The character disappeared without any attempt at an explanation at all. Typical of the kind of insulting attitude that such mindless, stupid people as Gerry and Sylvia Anderson have towards their customers, the people who pay their wages. They offered no explanation at all!'

Space 1999 was seen by many as Britain's answer to *Star Trek*, a group of scientific boffins operating from a central base who fight hostile aliens and discover new planets. The Andersons are adamant that the American show had no influence on them. Indeed, when the show debuted in the autumn of 1975, the science fiction genre was in decline, so a big budget TV space opera was a major gamble. But Martin Landau sensed that it was the perfect time for a show like *Space 1999*. 'I felt it in my bones. That this type of entertainment format was about to be popular in the near future.' He was right; *Star Wars* was just around the corner.

With the three main US networks having passed on the series, Abe Mandell launched what he claimed was 'the most intensive marketing and merchandising campaign ever seen in the history of our business,' in a bid to get *Space 1999* shown on local TV stations up and down the country. He even roped in Landau and Bain, who estimated they gave 89 press interviews. The strategy paid off, and the series sold to 155 cities and made a solid impact on the ratings. 'Lew Grade hasn't had a US series invasion like this since *The Saint*,' trumpeted *Variety*. Other critics weren't so kind. *American Film* magazine called it, 'Another example of how producers can spend perfectly good money to achieve perfectly dreadful results.' The critic also drew unkind parallels with 2001. 'The stylish hardware, the pretentious musical background and the cast's stiff-faced, witless dialogue. But while Kubrick was trying to make a point with his wooden actors, *Space 1999* merely has wooden actors. Barbara Bain looks as if she's just stumbled out of electric-shock therapy.'

Acclaimed science fiction writer Isaac Asimov also criti-

Top: *Moonbase Alpha's Commander Koenig and Dr Russell's search for a new world to colonise.* Bottom: *Barry Morse was often driven mad by the lack of emotional depth in the scripts.*

cised the show for the inclusion of unscientific details, to which Gerry Anderson retorted that, dealing with deep space, no one had complete knowledge, but that everything that took place on the moon was based on fact. In other words, up yours, Isaac.

In Britain, *Space 1999* suffered an even worse fate than befell it in the US. ITV never fully networked it, chucking out the show at different times around the regions. Landau complained that, in London, it was given little chance by being put up against the BBC's ratings powerhouse, *Dr Who*. 'The side by side comparison is hardly fair,' said *The Daily Mail*. 'Since a whole season of *Dr Who* probably costs less than a single episode of *Space 1999*.' Barbara Bain was also upset by the channel's dismissive attitude towards the series. 'It is a funny thing to leave the States where *Space 1999* is a hit and find that it is not honoured nearly so much in its own country,' she declared.

Space 1999 sold to practically all corners of the globe, scoring particularly highly in Japan and France. Such success would normally have necessitated a second series, but it was touch and go, according to Gerry. 'I spoke to Abe about a second series and he said, "Gerry, I want you to go and see Barbara Bain, and tell her that if she promises to put some expression in her acting, I'll OK a second series." I was pretty desperate, so I flew to Hollywood and went to her house and explained the situation, and she said, "OK, I understand. If it's going to mean that you're going to get another series, go back and tell Abe I'll move my face all over the place." And so we got the go-ahead.'

Production on another 24 episodes began in January 1976. But there were major changes both in front and behind the cameras. Besides the absence of Sylvia and Morse, the biggest upheaval was a new writer/producer in American Fred Freiberger. In order to further bolster the show's appeal Stateside, Gerry was flown over to stay in the Beverley Hills hotel to find American writers who'd work on the show. 'The agencies had lined up loads of writers, and all day long we were auditioning. It was literally – next! It was one of those. And one guy says, "Yeah, I'd love to do the show." We ask, "Are you prepared to come to Europe?" "Yeah." "We can only offer you that much." "That's fine." And we're pretty much agreed he's the one. "Just as a matter of interest," I ask, "what makes you so keen to come to Europe?" And he said, "Well, you see, I collect wine labels, and I think if I had a year in Europe I could make the most wonderful collection." Next!'

Every night Gerry would call Abe in New York: 'Still no luck.' Then Fred Freiberger walked in and said, 'I was script editor on the first *Star Trek* series.' And that landed him the gig. Freiberger was given virtual *carte blanche* to do what he wanted. Even Grade told him, 'Do it your way.' Freiberger, who'd just come off *The Six Million Dollar Man*, later claimed another producer was offered the job before him, and had suggested the radical step of sacking Martin Landau and Barbara Bain. Freiberger himself was instructed to keep the pair, but at the same time to involve the supporting characters to a greater extent. 'Look, either fire them or let me handle them as stars,' was Freiberger's advice.

At a time when the purse strings were being tightened, Gerry Anderson was reluctant to fire anybody. At one point, Nick Tate faced the axe from ITC's New York office – strangely enough, as he'd proved the most popular actor on the show, receiving 5,000 letters a week. Unsurprisingly, Freiberger and Anderson refused to get rid of him. Back in California, the Landaus were also anxious to return, but equally keen on a raise. 'Look, we can't raise anybody's salary,' announced Gerry.

Martin Landau on one of the many impressive futuristic sets that featured in the series.

'We're lucky if we can get this show on.'

Even though Barry Morse had already decided to jump ship, his days surely would have been numbered with Freiberger around. 'If you're going to have a professor, then have a young kid with a beard in there as the professor,' insisted the American. He got his wish by installing two new young characters: Tony Anholt as first officer Tony Verdeschi and – most significantly – Maya, an alien able to transform herself into different life forms. Perhaps inspired by Nichelle Nichols' seismic impact as *Star Trek*'s Lieutenant Nyota Uhura, Maya was originally written with a black actress in mind. However, Abe Mandell suggested Catherine Schell, who had already appeared in the *Space 1999* episode 'Guardian of Piri', and on the big screen in *The Return of the Pink Panther*. It's not known whether Barbara Bain saw Schell as a rival or not, but the actress had it written into Schell's contract that at no time should she look like she did in real life – hence the dark, heavy makeup she wore as Maya. In one episode, the Tony Verdeschi character was supposed to read a magazine, and become sexually aroused by a picture of a model that resembled Schell. Jealous Maya transforms herself into the actress. Bain went ballistic and ordered that the scene be scrapped. It was.

After screening episodes from the first season, Freiberger came to the conclusion that *Space 1999* was in need of a drastic overhaul. In his opinion there was 'no emotion in the show', and story-lines were poor, with characters just stood around pontificating endlessly. He wanted more action and humour, as the publicity handouts at the time announced it would be 'Bigger, better and more exciting than ever!' Yet not necessarily more interesting – as the majority of new stories proved to be far less thought provoking than their predecessors, and certainly more formulaic. Among the show's hardcore fans, of which there are many, there is a significant split between those who prefer the first season to the second. There was simmering discontent among *Space 1999*'s creative personnel over Freiberger's chosen direction – taking something original and turning it into a programme any television company with enough money could have made. 'Freiberger was a lovable, warm, generous man,' observed writer Johnny Byrne, 'but he should have been kept a million miles away from *Space 1999*.'

Landau particularly missed the presence of Sylvia. He'd liked her openness and her sensibilities, and found it much harder getting on with Freiberger – who, in his view, had far less respect for actors and their creative input. Landau would say, 'Koenig wouldn't do that,' referring to a script where the Alphans, on Koenig's orders, execute a pre-emptive strike at a possible foe. 'It's not within his character, nor his style.' Freiberger just shrugged his shoulders and insisted, 'It doesn't matter. It's a good script and the audience won't notice if it's inconsistent with his character.' Landau raged, 'Of course they will!' The star would argue for hours with Freiberger on such points, usually in vain.

Both Landau and Bain have since spoken many times about their preference for the first series. Landau cites Freiberger as having altered 'the entire essence of the series. I think he brought a much more ordinary, mundane approach to the series. I felt the episodes we started with in the first season were much more along the lines I wanted to go. To some extent, that was corrupted.' Landau also made it known he'd not return for another series if Freiberger remained in charge. Sylvia Anderson has much the same view as her stars. 'The second season went over the top, I think, with people turning into cats and things like that. It didn't have the impact or style of the first series.'

As for Gerry, he got on well with Freiberger on a personal level, 'But his style of writing was not mine at all. He brought in the whole idea of Catherine Schell changing into animals. Whereas my shows, although they were far fetched, I always tried to make everything as believable as possible, but that went out the window here. I know which season of *Space 1999* I prefer.'

Although *Space 1999* continued to prove popular internationally, any thoughts of a third season were scuppered by Lew Grade – who was desperate to channel all available funds toward financing his move into feature films. 'So we got sacrificed,' Landau told *Starlog* magazine in 1986. 'Lew Grade was getting into the movie business and it turned out his advertising budget for his films was our total budget for another season. It would have served them, from a syndication point of view, to have another season, but it came down to economic priorities. I think there was a very good chance of our going another season if he hadn't gotten into movies and needed that money.' The biggest irony of all is that *Space 1999* was cancelled just as *Star Wars* kick-started the sci-fi boom.

Ironically, the fan base for *Space 1999* is arguably bigger today than it was back in the seventies. 'I'm delighted and touched and considerably surprised that the series should have attracted and maintained such a loyal and large bunch of followers over the years,' says Barry Morse. 'But at the same time, it's rather maddening to remember how much better it could and should have been. The writers were doing their damnedest, but they hadn't got the time to sit around and think up all the subtleties that I was longing to incorporate into my character, and the situations.

Starting to shoot as we did, with only one script, the writers were hell-bent to try and keep pace and come up with enough script material for us to shoot tomorrow morning. I can't count the number of times that Martin, Barbara and I spent time trying to make human sense out of this all too frail material that we were being presented with. It's miraculous, really, that such a show should have had the success and appreciation that it has. So it's always seemed to me to be a huge opportunity not fully realised.'

Space 1999 was Gerry's last truly great show. How can you possibly top *Thunderbirds, Stingray* and *Captain Scarlet* anyway? But his later work, such as *Terrahawks* and *Space Precinct*, though entertaining, never even came close. Financially, he was practically wiped out by the end of the seventies. Here was a man who had created some of the most successful TV shows in history, but he never truly benefited from their incredible popularity. First, he'd sold his company to Lew Grade prior to *Stingray*, and, though he was paid a healthy weekly wage, the shows belonged to Lew. Gerry had to make do with ten per cent of the profits. Then disaster struck. A property crash impacted disastrously on Gerry's investments, leaving him in dire need of fast money to stave off financial ruin. 'I went to Lew's chief accountant and I said, "If I give up my ten per cent share on the puppet films," because I thought that they were dead, "would you give me £20,000?" And they said yes. And that was the end of my profit share.'

Today, Gerry Anderson should be one of the richest people in the country. But hardly a penny from the endless TV repeats, or the merchandise from his shows, filters back to the man who created it all in the first place. It's one of the entertainment business's most bitter ironies.

Chapter 8

The Kitsch Squad

- Jason King - The Persuaders - The Protectors -

The 1970s are often derided as 'the decade that fashion forgot', and there is no better example of this sartorial dark age than the new batch of action-adventure series ITC launched at the beginning of the decade. Cravats, medallions, preposterously flared trousers; they're all here, and more. The very height of cool in early seventies Britannia, such flamboyance had the effect of dating these series quicker than their 1960s counterparts.

More importantly, such characters as Jason King and Lord Brett Sinclair represented a major departure from previous ITC action heroes like John Drake and Simon Templar, in that they were played more for laughs, conscious perhaps of the fact that the end was nigh for such shows. By the mid-seventies, the playboy adventurer had become a cultural anachronism, thanks to grittier TV thrillers like *The Sweeney* and *The Professionals*. Whether intentionally or not (both Peter Wyngarde and Roger Moore later confessed to playing the roles with at least a touch of satire), King and Sinclair were ironic pastiches of action series characters.

JASON KING (1971-72)

It was evident very early on during the run of *Department S* that Jason King was the character to whom the public had really latched on. Because of Peter Wyngarde's extravagant star turn, the other two characters scarcely got a look in. It was Wyngarde viewers tuned in to see. It had become his show. 'There is no doubt that, however good the other two actors were, the personality of Peter Wyngarde as Jason King in *Department S* was internationally successful,' observes Cyril Frankel. 'All over the world that character worked.'

Such success arrived to the total bafflement of Lew Grade, who was never a fan of the show, or its star, and was reluctant to resurrect it. Until, that is, pressure from a most unlikely source was brought to bear. 'Two years after *Department S*, we'd not heard anything at all,' recalls Wyngarde. 'It was voted the most popular series in the world at that time. Everybody was raving about it and we'd heard nothing from Lew Grade. And I kept saying to my agent, "Doesn't he want to do another series? It's hot now." Then

Lew Grade sandwiched between the two biggest stars he brought to ITC: Roger Moore and Tony Curtis.

Jason King reading his favourite author – himself.

suddenly I'm summoned to the ATV office in Marble Arch. I go into this extraordinarily plush office with the largest desk you've ever seen, with this little midget sitting behind it with an enormous cigar. Lew got up to greet me and was absolutely charming, and he said, "Listen, we're going to do another series." I said, "Oh wonderful, I'm so thrilled." Then he said, "I've got nothing to do with this. I like a hero to look like Roger Moore. Roger's got these lovely blue eyes, blond hair, nice English smile. You come on and you look like *Viva Zapata*, with this funny moustache and the terrible clothes you wear. But my wife likes you so we're going to do another series."'

Jason King was to solely feature Wyngarde. His two accomplices from *Department S*, Joel Fabiani and Rosemary Nicols, were axed. 'And that was a mistake,' admits Wyngarde. 'Because Jason King was an outrageous character. He was over the top in so many ways, so you don't want to see a lot of him. And the great thing about *Department S* was that the others did all the groundwork, and then you were dying for Jason King to come on to get some light relief. But with *Jason King* the series, they got rid of those two, against my wishes. I kept saying to Monty Berman, "You've got a format which works, don't kill it." He said, "But they're not interested in them, they're interested in you." I said, "The reason why they're interested in me is because of them. Can't you see that?" He said, "No, you'll see. You'll be a huge success. And you get much more money if you go off and do it on your own." I'm afraid that didn't completely convince me, but that's what we did and I think it was a mistake.'

Peter Wyngarde was born in the French port of Marseille. His childhood was anything but conventional. Because his father was in the diplomatic service, the family was constantly on the move from country to country. In Shanghai, during the Japanese invasion of 1941, Wyngarde found himself in a prisoner of war camp. Despite horrendous mistreatment, it was here that Wyngarde discovered his love of performing with appearances in shows for his fellow inmates. When the camp was liberated after the war, Wyngarde was suffering from malnutrition and malaria, and spent two years recuperating in Switzerland before coming to England. Primarily a stage actor, in the 1950s Wyngarde began to gravitate towards film and television with moderate success, before his breakthrough on *Department S*.

Although it would scarcely seem possible, in the new show Wyngarde made Jason King even more of a flamboyant creation – all flares, bouffant hairdo, leather trousers, cravats, chest hair and medallions. The sort of image that would give today's fashion editors seizures. 'Jason King was terribly vain when it came to how he looked,' says Wyngarde. 'He wouldn't carry a gun because it affected the line of his suit.'

Wyngarde's performances sent TV's campometer into the red zone. Just think John Inman or Graham Norton playing James Bond, and you're almost there. 'Peter was a wild enthusiast, very likeable and tremendously charming. And very funny,' recalls Roy Ward Baker, who was drafted onto the series to direct four episodes. 'He contributed a great deal because he developed the character all the time. He was outrageous, but very good. I remember we had a scene where the heroine had been tied up by the villains and put in a cupboard, and she was screaming for help. As King came to the rescue he happened to pass a mirror, and he stopped to try on one or two different cravats. I put that in and Peter said, "Oh marvellous, marvellous. I can do that."'

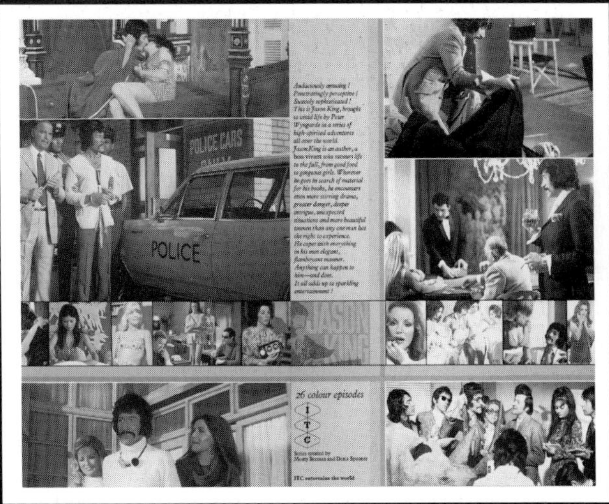

Top: *the front cover of ITC's promotional brochure for the series.* Bottom: *the brochure's stunning inside page.*

Because of the sometimes calamitous rows that went on during *Department S* between Wyngarde and his directors over the interpretation of the King character, Peter had stipulated that only a few be allowed back to work on the new series – principally Cyril Frankel, Jeremy Summers and Baker. 'I loved Roy, he was a nice man. He said, you're the one with the imagination, you fire away and if I don't like it, I won't use it. And it worked.'

Certainly the on-set atmosphere was more congenial than it had been on *Department S*. 'It was collaboration,' explains Frankel. 'Peter would come to me with an idea or I'd go to him with an idea. We were a good team. He was a very good actor. Later on, I fell out with him when we worked together in the theatre. It got to a point where he wouldn't accept direction.'

Despite the promise of higher production values than *Department S*, *Jason King* was shot on economy 16mm instead of 35mm, like the stylish ITC shows of the sixties. This new company policy of using cheaper film stock did not go down well with directors like John Hough. 'All the people on those sixties ITC shows were filmmakers. For example, on *The Saint* we had the cameraman that had shot *Repulsion* with Roman Polanski. So the whole thing was attacked in a film fashion, not a television fashion. And that was the secret. For me it was a golden time in British television history. And I attribute its success to the fact that we had cinema technicians working in the television medium. Plus they were shot on 35mm, and so each episode was a mini-film in its way. We'd go and look at the rushes at a big cinema set up at the studio. The editing was done in the same way it would be for a feature. So everything was geared up as if it was a film. That was the key factor. Then the decision was made to go onto 16mm. After that it was very rare to find a show shot on 35mm. 16mm became the norm. And those earlier days were never recaptured. With 16mm the quality just wasn't there. It was a backward step.'

The series retained the globe-hopping subtext of its sixties cousins. Originally devised as *The World of Jason King*, Wyngarde was desperate that, if a script called for him to be in Paris one week or Venice the next, that they should actually go to these places instead of relying on establishing shots of the Eiffel tower, or obvious back projection. As this would add hugely to the budget, a compromise was reached. Wyngarde, along with Cyril Frankel and a cameraman, visited various cities in order to photograph him wandering into hotels, hailing cabs, trotting down streets, etc. This footage was later inserted into episodes, adding greater authenticity to the stories. Wyngarde has even claimed that some writers looked at the location footage and then created a story around it.

This improvisational and opportunist approach to location shooting was also utilised on another early seventies ITC series, the now forgotten *The Adventurer*. Cyril Frankel recalls that his film crew were passing through Amsterdam on their way back to the UK. 'I phoned our script editor, Dennis Spooner, and said, "What do we do?" And he said, "Cyril, just chose the best locations, go on to rooftops or canals and devise some things, and then we'll build a script around what you do." And it actually worked!'

Guest stars were another feature of *Jason King*, including horror queen Ingrid Pitt, Nicolas Courtney (*Dr Who*'s Brigadier), Felicity Kendal, Roy Kinnear and Burt Kwouk. A veteran of numerous ITC shows going way back to *The Saint*, ask Burt Kwouk about them today and he confesses that they've all rather merged into one blurred mass. '*Jason King*,' he says, straining to remember. 'Was I an assassin in that one? I don't know. I must have had a gun and gone around shooting people. The scripts after a while became a bit interchangeable. It was formula television, really. They were all adventure spy stories, jumping in and out of boats and falling down. But one thing about those shows which was good, they were a great school for me. I learnt how to work fast and how to work efficiently. In a way they were a factory where you went and learnt your bloody trade. Where in the past you'd go out into the provinces and do rep in the theatres, we did these little television movies instead.'

Generally, the ITC shows were criticised for being production line TV, churned out like so many cans of baked beans. Yes, they were made as quickly and as cheaply as possible, but rarely did the standard drop below the acceptable, and often they easily exceeded it. 'One of Lew Grade's unique qualities was that he admired and wanted standards,' George Baker believes. 'He also thought, and rightly, that you could get high standards and you could whip along a bit, but if you put the right ingredients together it worked. You can make a programme quite quickly if it's properly written in the first place, and the production team has had enough time to

Pipe smoker of the year – 1972.

get everything ready. Then you go in, you pitch in and you get it done.'

Unsurprisingly, Burt Kwouk was regularly called upon to play clichéd, inscrutable Red Chinese baddies for ITC. 'Every season there would be two or three episodes with a Far Eastern background, so I got hauled in to do those. I never resented that. A part was a part and I tried to do it as best as I could. It's no good agreeing to do three days on *The Saint* or *Jason King* and expect to play King Lear. If all you want to do is play King Lear then you don't accept jobs like *The Saint*.'

In the new series, Wyngarde was desperate to bring something different to the character this time round. 'I thought, "I must make him more vulnerable," which was the biggest mistake I made. He should never have been vulnerable. I did an episode with Felicity Kendal and I allowed a tear to appear when she was killed, and that finished me. Because Jason must never be vulnerable, he's much too sure of himself and interested in himself to ever get involved with anybody. That was his strength as a character. But I thought we should make him a little more real, because if you're going to carry a film you've got to have tremendous variety, you can't be just one thing going along, you want to see him display different emotions, which was a mistake.'

Despite Wyngarde's sensational star turn, the producers did briefly consider bringing in *UFO*'s Michael Billington as a partner for King. 'Monty Berman came to the studio one day and watched some dailies of *UFO*,' reveals Billington. 'He knew the show was winding down and said, "I want to take Michael over to the *Jason King* set and see if he can be a sidekick for Peter Wyngarde." Because he thought Peter needed somebody to play off. And he got two objections, one was from Gerry Anderson and the other was from Peter Wyngarde. Wyngarde was not happy at all; he wanted to do everything that it was possible to do. He wanted 100 per cent screen time himself.'

Wyngarde also enjoyed doing as many of his own stunts as possible, in spite of being forbidden by his contract. In one *Department S* episode, Wyngarde took a four-day crash course in parachute jumping for a skydiving sequence, making sure the cameraman, jumping with him, filmed it in such a way as to make it clear it wasn't a double. Everyone on the crew knew Wyngarde was doing the jump for real except director John Gilling, who remained none the wiser.

Throughout production *Jason King* continued to grate with Lew Grade, who was disappointed with the series and didn't approve of its high camp aesthetic. Wyngarde himself favours *Department S* over *Jason King*, feeling the new stories weren't up to the previous ones, a feeling shared by Frankel. The show is one of the weakest in the ITC canon, saved only by the ever-watchable presence of Wyngarde.

Conversely, the public loved *Jason King* and made the series a hit. Wyngarde topped a poll that voted him the man most Australian women wanted to lose their virginity to. To exploit his popularity down under, Wyngarde agreed to a promotional trip. He flew to Sydney, not in his familiar exotic garb but in jeans and a T-shirt. Hiding behind sunglasses, he hoped nobody would recognise him. On the same flight was a group of youths Wyngarde presumed was a pop group, and as they were about to land he guardedly looked out of the window and saw crowds of women near the terminal buildings. Naturally he assumed they were waiting for the pop group, and never thought it had anything to do with him. He sat there thinking, 'Those poor little buggers are going to be killed.' He watched as they left the plane, following a discreet distance behind. Suddenly the screaming women surged forward and headed right for him. Wrestling Wyngarde to the ground, they tore at his clothes, cut his hair, even grabbed tufts of his pubic hair! All of which landed Wyngarde in hospital for three days. 'It was as if I was a feast. To be eaten raw. It was terrifying. A similar thing happened in Oslo. I was given the royal suite at this hotel, and when I came out onto the balcony there was this huge crowd screaming and yelling. And you think, "What is the matter. What is it?" You have to question yourself. Why? You're just playing a character. Why have they gone mad for it? You don't understand.'

For a brief time, Peter Wyngarde was the most famous man on television. 'I couldn't go to any country in the world without being mobbed, physically attacked. It was extraordinary. But the thing that really frightened me was that I couldn't even go out of my own front door. I couldn't go to a restaurant, the cinema or the theatre, where you'd think they'd have more respect for you, but you'd find there were twenty people round you. It was very weird.'

Jason King finished its run in May 1972, and Wyngarde's subsequent career never eclipsed what he achieved on those ITC shows. Essentially the King character killed his career stone dead. It was an image so strong that he never truly escaped from it. 'Unfortunately everyone expects Peter to be Jason King,' laments Cyril Frankel. 'Even today, if I go anywhere and I say Jason King, they know who I mean.'

Despite having shaved his head, grown a beard and a tiny moustache, Wyngarde is still recognised today, well over 30 years on. 'Only the other day I drove back to London, and stopped at a Little Chef on the motorway to get a cup of coffee to break up the journey. And there I am, looking as far removed from Jason King as is possible, and this guy came up to me and said, "Mr. Wyngarde, can I have your autograph please?" And I said, "How the hell could you recognise me?" Because one of the things I prided myself in was that I could change my face. And he said, "The moment you walked in, I knew it was you."'

Despite his utter identification with Jason King, Wyngarde never regretted play-

Left: *Wyngarde's pop icon status as King led to him becoming one of the world's sexiest men, getting mobbed at airports.* Right: *Wyngarde off-set, with two runners-up in a Jason King lookalike contest.*

ing the role. 'I loved doing them, I really enjoyed it. But the awful thing is you don't realise how much it takes out of you. You get two hours sleep if you're lucky. And you're writing and rewriting the script all the time, and having to learn the lines and try to make them interesting; never got any sleep.'

Wyngarde was hardly handsomely rewarded for his portrayal of the debonair playboy. Despite *Department S* and *Jason King* being screened around the world endlessly, he has not benefited financially at all. 'I don't get royalties. Nothing. Not a penny. He was great, Lew, but I didn't like how he treated his clients, or victims as I call them. He could have looked after us a little bit better, I think. We earned him a hell of a lot of money. You'd have thought he would have returned the compliment in some way.'

Wyngarde's career was stalling after *Jason King*, so the last thing he needed was a bout of controversy. But that's exactly what happened in 1975, when he was caught and arrested for cottaging in the gents' toilet at Leicester bus station. 'I was appearing with Peter in a play at the time,' recalls actress Sue Lloyd. 'It was awful. And it was worse because he pretended it was somebody else, which was so silly. Peter Wyngarde was a very sexual man at that time. It was the first time I really felt extremely sorry for him, because he was a very arrogant man, always has been, but I really felt for him.'

Each evening Wyngarde used to delight in making a big dramatic entrance onto the stage, waiting at the top of a grand staircase for the applause to stop before

Left: *even a wetsuit looks good on Jason King.* Right: *Wyngarde snuggles up to guest star Ingrid Pitt, famous for her Hammer horror roles.*

waltzing down. 'And this particular night he practically missed his step going down the stairs,' says Sue. 'He was absolutely terrified just walking on the stage. But what I did love was that he tried to go straight into the line as he made his entrance, and there was enormous applause. They'd read all the very nasty press, very personal stuff. When you think that John Gielgud did it like 30 years before, and nothing was made of it. They just felt Peter was arrogant and that he tried to get away with it, too. Peter wasn't open about it. I think he was frightened of his market, the sexy image, the lady-killer. I don't think he thought it helped, in fact in those days it didn't help at all. I really was there to cradle him, because he was feeling very vulnerable. He was frightened about his career, of course he was.'

A quarter of a century before George Michael used a similar situation to revamp his pop profile, for Peter Wyngarde it meant curtains. His career never recovered, and the theatre and television lost one of their brightest lights.

THE PERSUADERS (1971-72)

The premise was devastatingly simple and quite brilliant. A crime fighting duo comprising two bored playboys – American millionaire Danny Wilde and British toff Lord Brett Sinclair, who get into all kinds of scrapes and adventures, just so long as there's a pretty girl at the end of it all. And each show played out against a backdrop of sumptuous European landscapes and the glitzy world of the rich and famous.

It was as *The Saint* was winding down that producer Robert Baker came up with the idea for *The Persuaders*. 'I'd always liked the idea of a buddy movie and I love tongue-in-cheek humour and screwball comedies, and I had this idea of an Englishman and an American playing against each other. So we did a *Saint* episode called "The Ex-King of Diamonds" and brought in actor Stuart Damon as this American oil millionaire to team up with Roger. That was a dummy run for *The Persuaders*, to see if the thing was going to work. And it did. So I took the idea to Lew and he said, "Great – go to America and get an actor."'

Danny Wilde was originally conceived as a Texas oil millionaire, a fledgling J. R. Ewing. Robert Baker flew to America to meet with the networks and to land his man. 'The first guy we tried to get was Rock Hudson, but he didn't want to do television at the time. Then we thought maybe we'd get an older man, like Glenn Ford. And Ford was interested, but didn't want to leave America and come and work in England. So we didn't have a leading man. I had a meeting with ABC, who were going to take the show, and asked for a list of names they'd like, and amongst the names was Tony Curtis. I spoke to Lew that night on the phone and he said, "I know Tony Curtis' agent, he's a friend of mine. Don't worry."'

But there was plenty to worry about. Grade was told that Curtis would never agree to do a television series. 'Everybody's been trying to get him,' said the star's agent. 'But he just doesn't want to do television.' Lew would not be deterred. 'Well at least let me talk to him personally,' he asked. 'Sure,' the agent replied. 'But I know it'll be a waste of time.' A meeting was arranged between the two entertainment giants at the Berverly Hills Hotel. It proved a momentous occasion that Curtis remembers to this day. 'I said, "Excuse me, sir," Lew Grade wasn't a lord back then, "what am I to call you?" He said, "If you do this series you can call me anything you want." So from that day on we just had the best relationship. He enjoyed me a lot. I was a bit of a maverick. I didn't do things according to plan. And he liked that.'

After an hour and a half of discussion, Grade demonstrated yet again his astonishing negotiating skills by managing to pull off what so many network executives had failed to do – sign Curtis for a TV series. It was a major coup. Never before, or since, has a Hollywood star of Curtis' magnitude agreed to do a British television show. 'I may have turned down other shows,' Curtis says. 'But when you present a project like *The Persuaders* to me with Roger Moore, these two razzle dazzle *bon vivants*, how are you going to turn it down? I also liked the idea that I was going to be in Europe for eighteen months. I liked the idea that I could get out of that fucking town Hollywood, and go somewhere else and do this work. Sure, the money was important, but what was more important was it gave me another life in another country. And I was lucky that we almost spoke the same language; they never thought I spoke English.'

With the New York-born Curtis installed, Robert Baker had to totally rethink the Danny Wilde character. Out went the Texan oil millionaire, to be replaced by a wise guy from the Bronx, a self-made millionaire, a wheeler dealer. 'Which actually was better for us because it gave the show more pace, and it suited Tony Curtis. Had it been with Rock Hudson, or someone like that, the pace would have been slower, the repartee wouldn't have been so fast. So having a guy from the Bronx and an Englishman was a better contrast. Why I didn't think of it before I don't know, but events shaped the show.'

Landing Curtis was the least of Grade's problems. Now he faced the even bigger challenge of snaring Moore, who had publicly announced his desire never to return to television after seven years shackled to *The Saint*. Moore had always been Baker's

Moore and Curtis' relationship may have been strained, but their on-screen chemistry was undeniable.

first choice to play Sinclair and together they'd discussed the project, though the actor had since totally forgotten about it and was now hell-bent on pursuing a film career. 'I got a call from Lew one day,' recounts Moore. 'He said, "I want to talk to you. I've sold *The Persuaders*." I said, "But Lew, I don't want to do any more television." "Look," he said, "I'll talk to you tomorrow morning." I said, "Where are you?" "I'm in California." I said, "I can't get to California." He said, "I'll be back in London. I'll see you at seven o'clock in my office." I said, "No, let's make it eight o'clock. You don't sleep, Lew, but I do." So I got there at eight. Lew shoved a great big cigar in my mouth and said, "Right, we're going to do *The Persuaders*." I said, "Lew, I really don't want to do the series." He said, "Listen, the country needs the money. The Queen, think of your queen, she needs the money." He was a man of such enthusiasm that eventually you go along with it. And he made a very generous deal with me. It was very difficult to say no to Lew, because if you started arguing he shoved a cigar in your mouth. And he could always speak faster and louder.'

Although he agreed to make *The Persuaders*, Moore did voice grave concerns about signing a long-term contract that might see him saddled to the show for years. 'At that time Broccoli and Saltzman were tinkering with Roger about James Bond,' Baker reveals. 'And so, Roger was a little bit hesitant that if he went into *The Persuaders* he might lose out on Bond. So Roger had no contract to do *The Persuaders*. Tony Curtis had a contract, but Roger wouldn't sign, so it just became a gentlemen's agreement.'

With his two stars firmly in place, now came the prickly task of settling the billing – would it be Curtis or Moore who received pole position in the opening credits? 'The agents kind of worked it out,' explains Curtis. 'But that's such bullshit. We were above the title, you can't get it better than that, can you? That was never a dilemma, never. They wanted me so badly, and my agent at that time said, "Well, he must have top billing, then give him top billing, what are you giving him, you're giving him bullshit." It's jerking off in Macey's window, that's all it is.'

Lew's nephew Michael Grade, then third partner in a talent agency called London Management, has another view on how the makers got over the billing problem. 'One of our clients was Roger Moore, and we told Lew that Roger wouldn't take second billing to Curtis. Roger went to see Lew who, of course, turned on the charm and made the deal; Roger gets first billing. They start filming and Roger and Tony discover very quickly that they both have a deal to be billed first. Which was very smart of Lew, because if he'd tried to resolve that ahead of time it would have been impossible. Typical Lew.'

Stunning publicity shot taken on location.

Moore's first encounter with Curtis was when he flew to the States with Baker and script editor Terry Nation, for a meeting at the Hollywood legend's Beverly Hills home.

'Lew had said, "Remember – Tony's a spokesman for the anti-smoking lobby in America, so don't smoke,"' recalls Moore. 'Now I smoked cigarettes like a fucking idiot in those days, Bob smoked a pipe and Terry Nation was a smoker. And after about an hour and a half I said, "Listen Tony, Lew said that we're not allowed to smoke but we're all smokers, so do you mind if we have a smoke?" And Tony turned to his wife and said, "Leslie, where's that ashtray?!"'

Curtis then proceeded to open every window in the room, switch on a fan and slap a heavy book on the horrors of lung cancer in Moore's lap. 'Actually, by the time the series started I'd stopped smoking,' Moore reveals. 'I stopped smoking two days after that meeting and never smoked cigarettes again. But when Tony arrived in England he was carrying a little wacky-baccy. I might well have been at the airport to meet him, had it not been for the fact that I had a kidney problem and was in hospital when he arrived. There was an awful lot of press about him having pot. And Bob Hope was doing jokes like, "Tony Curtis was still flying around London airport three months after he was supposed to land." I cut all the press clippings up and put them into a book, because I had nothing else to do, being in hospital. And I gave it to Tony and the book was engraved – "How to sneak into a country without anybody knowing you're there."'

This playful rivalry continued throughout the making of the series, and permeated its way onto the screen. Much has been written about Curtis and Moore's relationship on the *Persuaders* set, that they couldn't stand each other, that they never socialised,

Going for a walk in the countryside – Persuaders *style!*

were never on friendly terms. 'We got along so famously,' asserts Curtis. 'What you saw on the screen is what we were like. Everything worked for us perfectly. And we never fell in love with the same girl; now that's rare. The wonderful thing about working with Roger was that there was no ego involved. So there was never a cross word between us. Never. He liked working with me a lot, and I with him. He thought I was the funniest dude that ever came down the pike. For me, his demeanour and his attitude were excellent. He's the fucking best, man. Nobody better than Roger.'

The truth is both stars were never going to become bosom buddies, as their personalities were so very different: Moore easygoing and laid back, Curtis volatile and temperamental. '*The Persuaders*, that was like a bloody circus that was, but a delightful one,' observes ITC regular Shane Rimmer. 'They certainly respected each other's talents and were a fine mixture, because Curtis was pretty uncontrollable because he knew he could get away with so much. So it was lovely to have Roger, who was very sympathetic to this sort of behaviour but also had this kind of slight reserve. I thought it worked extremely well.'

Actress Sue Lloyd also guested on the show. 'I think professionally they got on, but not really well off. They were totally different. I think that Tony Curtis was fairly free with his pill popping at that time. He was so very different to Roger.' George Baker, another guest star, agrees. 'They weren't great buddies. I think they were poles apart. I remember Tony took a house in Chester Square, and I used to drink at the Plumber's Arms pub which was in Lower Belgrave Street, and quite often he used to come in and spend an hour and chat. Then off he'd go to his grand parties and his coke. But he was a very nice man, and a wonderful actor actually.'

While Curtis' recreational drug use may well have rankled with Moore's traditionalist streak, it certainly impinged on the work itself, as Robert Baker reveals. 'Tony could be a bit prickly, you had to handle him very carefully. For instance, Tony would come in in the morning, black thunder, everyone kept clear of him, and go up to his dressing room. Then he'd come down half an hour later and kiss everybody, after he'd smoked a couple of joints. So as long as Tony was on the joints he was pleasant, but when he wasn't he could be very difficult. You had to handle him with kid gloves.'

Despite their contrasting personalities, as a screen pairing Moore and Curtis were irresistible. 'The chemistry between them was terrific,' says Baker. 'They would ad-lib half the scenes. But we had to be very careful, because Tony would ad-lib and take the story off in the wrong direction. Roger was the stabilising factor – he would

Left: *Moore in drag, clowning around between takes with Curtis.* Right: *Danny Wilde never lost an opportunity to dent Lord Sinclair's establishment credentials.*

always bring the story back into line. We'd do a scene with three or four different takes and each take was different, the dialogue was different, the shape was different. What we would do then was intercut those and take the best from each, which worked beautifully. So the humour on the set, a hell of a lot of it was spontaneous.'

More than anything, the two stars enjoyed bouncing verbally off one another as they developed the light-hearted rapport that became one of the show's trademarks. 'We helped each other setting up the jokes,' explains Curtis. 'We were each other's straight man and that's what made that show successful. The way we behaved toward each other was a perfect marriage between Roger and me, and we were both intelligent enough to see it. We instinctively saw how we were going to contribute to each other.'

Baker doesn't believe there was any element of scene stealing going on; indeed, the fact that both actors were on top of their game undeniably helped the show. Although Curtis' ostentatious acting style may have lent itself to accusations that he was trying to outshine Moore in their scenes together. 'Tony once said to me, "If I have a scene where I walk down a corridor, I won't just walk down the corridor, I'll find something to do while I'm walking down the corridor." That was the kind of actor he was. He'd never do things straight. For instance, the business about his gloves. Tony wore gloves in a lot of the scenes. In fact he washed his hands in one of the scenes with the gloves on. Very clever, because people would say, "Why does Tony wear gloves?" The thing is, you've made the point, and they've noticed it, so they're going to talk about it and watch out for it. So that's a very clever ploy of Tony's. He would always find something to make the scene that much different, just add a little bit of something to each scene. He's a marvellous artist.'

Curtis also insisted, as did Moore, on handling as much of the physical action as he could. 'That was another thing that I enjoyed. I would've been an excellent stuntman, so I just utilised that. I just thought it would help the part and help the picture. And when you see the show you'll see that it's impossible for me to hide from the fact that it was me. God forbid something would happen, I'd sprain a leg or hurt myself and I couldn't shoot for two or three days, that was horror for these film companies. At the beginning they rather enjoyed the fact that I did all these stunts because I saved them some money, but as we started going along they realised that it was a little bit dangerous, and so they tried to calm me down. And I said, "I'm sorry fellas, I'm gonna do what I've been doing since the start of the show and I'm not gonna change anything."'

Curtis' keenness to perform his own stunts didn't go down too well with some of his directors, notably Roy Ward Baker. 'We were filming outside the studio at a very, very tall building. And the plot was that he had to climb up and get inside through a skylight. And we got set up for this and Curtis was hanging about, joking with the crew and talking to the stuntman, and I knew damn well that he was going to do the stunt without telling me. I shouted, "Action," the cameraman started and Curtis went all the way up and did the whole stunt himself. I don't know what his intention was. But I thought it was rather rude, quite frankly.'

It wasn't just that incident which didn't endear Curtis to Roy Ward Baker; the two just didn't get on. It was a clash of personalities. 'He was an oddity, really, Curtis, in many ways. You never got to know him. He was totally reserved. He would lark about; in fact he did too much larking about for my taste. There's a limit to it. Curtis can be very good, of course, and has done some important movies, but as cold as a cucumber. Not my type, because I felt I could never get to know him. There was nothing I could talk to him about. He was the sort of person that you could work with for years and you'd never know him. He wouldn't take direction either. He ignored it. You could talk your head off and he wouldn't take any notice, just do it the way he was going to do it. As a technician though, he was absolutely immaculate. He always knew exactly where the camera was, the lights, the whole thing. You didn't have to tell him any of that.'

The marvellous tongue-in-cheek quality that has made *The Persuaders* such an enduringly popular show was always Robert Baker's intention. This was never going to be a hardboiled, edgy thriller. 'I mean,' says the producer, 'in the very first episode you have these two guys fighting over how many olives you have in a drink; certainly you're not going to take it seriously from that point onwards.' The Brett Sinclair character was originally conceived to have been the more comedic of the two, the stereotypical bumbling British toff. 'But Bob had to rethink the part,' reveals Moore. 'And make Sinclair carry the plot line and Tony do the joke lines.' A development that Curtis instigated himself. 'I think the show needed a comedic touch. The idea was OK but there weren't enough jokes, and I would invent jokes right on the set. Sinclair came out once wearing a velvet robe and a crown, he's gonna go to the House of Lords, and my line was, "Where are you going?" I didn't do that, I said to him, "Will you marry me?" In another scene he showed me the crypt where he was going to be buried. He had twelve or fifteen bodies on the wall and he said, "Danny, when I go that'll be my spot." And he points to the top one on the row, and I said to him, "Well, you've certainly got a good view." So it was these kinds of things that I just threw in there, and they all worked.'

This episode was released theatrically in Turkey.

For Moore, as with Simon Templar, Lord Brett Sinclair was another role that perfectly suited his easygoing style of performing. 'You always take what is right for your personality, and you bring yourself to a part. You're not allowed to wear humps or hooked noses, you're fairly naked as an actor, so it has to be you and your personality and you make what you have fit the character.' In one episode, a neat homage to the Ealing classic *Kind Hearts and Coronets*, Moore famously plays several members of the Sinclair family who are being bumped off by a nutty relative. 'That was a gas. I remember being dressed up as this old Admiral and Johnny Goodman, the associate producer, came in and stood next to me on the set and I said, "You're a very good looking young man," and he got a bit shuffly. And I started leching after him and he was saying, "Who's this bastard actor, get rid of him."' Called 'A Death in the Family', this remains one of Moore's favourite *Persuaders* episodes. 'I was amazed when I played my aunt, I looked just like my mother.'

It was not only the differences between Moore and Curtis as actors and individuals, but also in their characters, that made the show such a treat to watch. Throughout the series, Wilde's brash street savvy and wisecracking American mannerisms, and Sinclair's urbane and extra-dry Britishness, serve as the basis for continual jokes and misunderstandings. 'When I first came out to do *The Persuaders* there was a very distinct line between these two guys,' recalls Curtis. 'They were going to have me playing this slave and Roger was going to be the English lord. The only way I could combat it was that I would play Danny as insolent and arrogant, finding jokes in everything, which I did, and that kind of equalised the part. And finally, by the second and third show, we had a very fine relationship. I think Roger was more concerned, because it was in England, to maintain that English superiority that our darling English friends can have if they're brought up in that environment. And he liked the idea that he was royalty, when in fact his father was a policeman. Roger liked that image of himself, so that's the image he came in to work with, always. "Oh Daniel, please get me my coat." He always had this supercilious attitude towards me.'

These differences are further underlined by the show's now classic title sequence, which displays images from their contrasting upbringings. 'Since we had no explanation of the two characters before they met, we had to explain their backgrounds in the titles,' explains Baker, who devised the memorable opening. 'So you've got the guy from the Bronx playing stick ball in the streets and Sinclair going to Eton, all that stuff. In about 30 seconds it tells you the background of these two guys.' All to the haunting lilt of one of the most famous TV themes in history, courtesy of John Barry.

Much of the appeal of *The Persuaders* also comes from its sheer *elan*; the high living, the staying in the best hotels and eating in the finest restaurants, all so clearly beyond the reach of the majority of its viewers. And of course those two super cars. 'There's this one guy in an Aston Martin and the other guy in a Ferrari,' says Curtis. 'It's better than being in a Volkswagen bus!' The actors were given the chance to choose their own set of wheels. 'I picked the Ferrari,' recalls Curtis. 'I knew that Roger was going to pick some English monster. I was planning to get a Cadillac convertible, but we would have had to have shipped one in from the States, so I decided the Ferrari was the best choice.' Perhaps anticipating his ascension to the role of Bond, Moore chose an Aston Martin for Brett. 'It was sad we couldn't go with the Volvo again, because that was too much associated with *The Saint*, but I think the cars were well chosen, they matched the personalities of both of us. The Aston looked good, it looked classy and was the sort of expensive thing that Lord Sinclair would have.'

Danny and Brett also exhibited an elaborate dress sense, which accentuated their different personalities. Wilde was the non-conformist and affected a very hip, contemporary look. 'My wardrobe reflected the style of the show,' explains Curtis. 'I went down the King's Road and bought leather jackets, trousers, sweaters, boots. I put together a fabulous collection of clothing that I used. There isn't a scene in *The Persuaders* that you see me in the same outfit. I was always changing it and that meant a lot to me, because it gave you a little bit of what that character Danny Wilde was. Clothes make the man. I got that from Laurence Olivier. We were talking about acting and he said, "Clothes make the man. You get dressed up for what you'd like to think you are and you'll become it, looking at yourself in the mirror." Isn't that great advice for an actor? And that's what it was, clothes make the man, both with Roger and with me, and they were so different.'

Sinclair's attire befitted that of an English lord – very formal, albeit with a heavy dash of dandyism, a profusion of wide lapels, frilly shirts and neckerchiefs louder than a Led Zeppelin gig. And all designed by Moore himself. 'I'd discuss with my tailor various things to do, basically classic but trying to bring in an early seventies look. I think it worked. I took a screen credit because we were going to possibly develop it commercially, but I'm so damn lazy I never did anything with it. Who knows, I might have been Beckham before Beckham.'

Besides the nostalgic charm of *The Persuaders*, the show also has enormous camp appeal, particularly when it comes to Moore's flamboyant shirts and the slightly homo-erotic synergy between Sinclair and Wilde. When *The Persuaders* was shown in the mid-nineties on UK television, as part of an ITC season, a *Time Out* scribe wit-

As he did on The Saint, *Moore moved behind the camera to direct a couple of* Persuaders *episodes.*

tily commented, 'Someone walked into my lounge and accused me of watching some ancient gay porn film, such was the puffed up body language and dramatic glances they sparred with. Still, compared to the regency foppism of *Jason King* earlier in the evening, they look like *The Sweeney*.' Of course, the constant cavalcade of beautiful women in every episode of *The Persuaders* was proof enough that they were red-blooded males. As is invariably the case in male 'buddy' TV shows, *The Persuaders* strove to distance itself from any hint of homosexual attraction between its lead characters by constantly entangling them with a stream of hot chicks.

This was achieved by a bevy of female guest stars like Diane Cilento and Joan Collins, who, in those unenlightened days, often served as little more than decoration, relatively incidental plot devices, or as helpless victims to be rescued. After all, with Curtis and Moore you had two of the biggest sex symbols of the age. 'We shared all the women we met,' Curtis playfully quips. 'There was a trade-off at the end of the week. We had a good time.' Annette Andre certainly enjoyed working with Curtis. 'I had a great time on *The Persuaders*. It was fabulous. I liked Tony very much. I thought he was extremely professional and very generous with me as an actress. He rehearsed with me a lot and was very thoughtful. I was amazed. I honestly didn't know he was as serious a person, he was almost too serious. I'm not sure that he and Roger got on all that well. Tony really was a very intense man. But he was a very good actor.'

Valerie Leon has a special reason to remember her guest appearance on the show, because it was Moore himself who directed her episode. 'I was leaping around in a little space car promoting soap. It was a fun episode and I did enjoy making it. For one shot Roger wanted a certain reaction from me, and to get it he gave me an unscripted kiss. I was so surprised, I remember shutting my eyes and enjoying it. And when I opened them I had a big beam on my face, all of which was kept in. So I have good memories of *The Persuaders*. And the loveliest thing of all was I met Roger very recently, and took a photograph of the two of us from *The Spy Who Loved Me*, and without thinking that he would remember me I asked him, "I feel really silly, Roger, but would you mind signing this?" And he wrote, "Dear Valerie. How slim I was then and you still are, love Roger." I was really touched by that, which tells you what a nice guy he is.'

Another female guest star was a very young Susan George, whom director Roy Ward Baker has good reason to remember. 'When she arrived on the set she looked me straight in the eye and said, "You don't remember me, do you?" And I said, "I'm sorry, no, you have the best of me, I don't." "Well," she said, "I was only twelve." She was in an episode of *The Human Jungle* I directed. She played a child. Well, the next time I met her she was no child, I can tell you. She was wonderful.'

Just as Moore had used his union card, obtained when he joined the film industry in 1943 as a trainee animator, to direct episodes of *The Saint*, he took the same opportunity to helm a couple of *Persuaders*. In one he gave his seven-year-old daughter, Deborah, a small role. Her brother Geoffrey, five at the time, also featured in the series. He was the little boy in the credit sequence, playing the young Brett Sinclair. 'Roger was very knowledgeable as a director,' observes Curtis. 'He knew the camera, he knew where the shots should be. And what's more important, he knew how to work in a television environment, which meant he had to work faster than you do in film.'

With his usual panache, Lew Grade announced production of *The Persuaders* at the Monte Carlo TV Festival in February 1970. At two and a half million pounds it was the most expensive British series thus far. 'The budget was very large,' confirms Baker. 'Mainly because we had two stars in it. You could make a series out of their salaries alone. So it had to work.'

Filming began in June in the South of France. 'It sounds great,' says Baker. 'But you're working your arse off all the time.' The unit stayed for close to six weeks in and around Nice and Monte Carlo, shooting exteriors for several of the episodes. Then it was back to England and Pinewood Studios. 'We spent ten to twelve days on each episode and there was always a fun atmosphere, it couldn't have been made any other way,' asserts Curtis. 'But there was always pressure to get it quicker, not spend so much in making them, all of that, but that goes with the territory. Basically we made 24 50-minute movies in about eighteen months. And I loved living in London. I stayed in England for several years after *The Persuaders*. And had my marriage lasted, I'd have been living there now. I got to become a real Anglophile. And I made some fabulous friends there. Paul McCartney and I met and we started going out together with our wives. He'd arrange for us to go to some rock concert. I had the best times.'

To handle the two stars and the high production values involved, the producers followed the same rule as other ITC shows in hiring experienced film directors, including Basil Dearden, who had earlier directed Moore in one of his best cinema outings, *The Man Who Haunted Himself*, 'But there was an odd and tragic coincidence,' explains Moore. 'In the opening sequence of *The Man Who Haunted Himself* my character is involved in a car accident, which was shot off the M4, at the turn-off. Then two years later, Basil Dearden was directing *The Persuaders* and was on his way home from Pinewood, and was killed in the self-same spot that we shot the accident for *The Man Who Haunted Himself*. Very odd.'

Top: *Peter Sellers meets the* Persuaders *team on location in France: Johnny Goodman, Bob Baker and Moore.* Bottom: *Curtis encounters Michael Caine in the gardens of Pinewood Studios. Caine was shooting* Kidnapped *at the time; note the kilt.*

Script supervisor on *The Persuaders* was the famous Terry Nation, the man who created the Daleks. 'You don't have people like Terry Nation anymore,' insists George Baker. 'They don't grow on trees. They're very special.' Nation enlisted his old friend Brian Clemens to come up with the opening episode. 'Terry was a bit lazy and he allowed me to write the pilot which, of course, set the whole style of the series,' explains Clemens. 'I wanted to achieve a sort of buddy movie adventure with *fun*, predating *Romancing the Stone*, etc. But again influenced by Hitchcock. And I loved writing for Roger and Tony. Their creative input was mainly confined to Curtis, who had lots of ideas, mainly on how to avoid Roger upstaging him! On the whole though, it was a happy and relaxed unit, considering the fact that it *could* have been a clash between two prima donnas.' This first episode, by no means the best, does perfectly set up the series. After racing each other to Monte Carlo in their respective sports cars, Danny and Brett continue their rivalry in a restaurant, resulting in a fistfight. Arrested, the pair are surprised to find themselves not in jail, but at the chateau of retired legal eagle turned private crime fighter Judge Fulton. He reproaches the errant playboys for squandering their money and for their lack of social conscience, and offers them the choice of 30 days banged up or helping out in an investigation, which just so happens to involve a beautiful woman. They agree, and soon put paid to a notorious gangland boss. After that, Danny and Brett agree to help the judge in his crusade against top criminals seemingly beyond the reach of the law.

This pilot episode was greeted with mixed reviews when it was screened. 'The two men spent so much time zooming round Monte Carlo in their sports cars that the play seemed like a prolonged commercial for high performance petrol,' derided *The Daily Telegraph*. As the show continued its run the critics weren't any more impressed, but the public lapped it up and turned *The Persuaders* into a ratings winner. The show was a roaring success everywhere except in America – the market for which it had been made in the first place. 'It just didn't happen in America,' says Moore. 'But it did in the rest of the world, particularly Italy, France, and in Germany. They would always say to me in Germany, "My God, we made that so funny, that series." I'd say, "What do you mean, you made it funny? It was funny." "Oh no," they'd say. "The way we dubbed it, we made it funny." I said, "It *was* funny."'

Moore had flown to New York and LA to help launch the series in time for its autumn 1971 debut on ABC, but ratings were disappointing, and only twenty out of the 24 episodes were shown. 'It didn't take off in the States because they didn't put it on at primetime when kids could watch it,' insists Curtis. 'They put it on at nine or ten. See, they were embarrassed by it, those fucking idiots at ABC, they thought they knew everything, they were full of shit. Our series played fabulous all over the place and only in America they stuck it on at an awkward time. This show should have been made available to all the young people that were around. That was ABC's fault, they were short sighted.'

Despite its failure in the States, there was no question of the series being shelved. 'They were ready to go ahead and do more of them,' Curtis reveals. 'Lew came to me and said, "Tony, we thought maybe we'd try and make some more, but we'd have to do it less opulently." I said, "What does that mean?" He said, "Well, we wouldn't have locations." I said, "Wait a minute, those locations are powerful in that first 24 episodes, South of France, places like that. If you're going to do these all in the countryside of England and in sets, you're not going to be able to have that expansive look to it." So Roger and I talked and thought it wasn't really viable, because you weren't going to bring the same *savoir faire* to the series if you were going to cut down on the money. So we respectfully turned around and walked. And when Roger and I decided maybe we didn't want to do it, they were really shocked.'

Robert Baker, however, remembers things a little differently. 'Lew wanted to make more *Persuaders*, but Roger didn't. By that time Roger had the offer to play Bond. He was being groomed by Broccoli and Saltzman. So at the end of the series we knew Roger was going to be Bond. And we had a meeting with Lew and he said, "Let's get another actor to replace Roger." And we said, "Who?" And he said, "What about Noel Harrison?" Who was Rex's son. So we talked about that and said to Lew, "Look, we've made a good show, let's just leave it at that." And Lew said, "Well, I suppose you're right." Otherwise we'd have made much more. It could have gone on for years.'

Curtis is adamant about which direction it should have gone in, had it continued. 'Both Roger and I wanted to do more locations. We wanted to do Hong Kong, we wanted to shoot some in America, South America, in all of these different countries, that's what we thought would be most amusing and amazing, and to introduce all the beautiful girls from around the world. And you know every country's got beautiful girls. But they kiboshed that whole idea. They made a big mistake.'

Since its cancellation, *The Persuaders* has gone on to become one of the most fondly remembered of all TV shows. Its popularity remains undimmed after over 35 years. The show is undemanding escapism. Pure entertainment. '*The Persuaders* hasn't been off the air in France since the bloody thing was made,' declares Baker. 'It's being shown all the time.'

Even more than *The Saint*, *The Persuaders*' cult appeal is massive. Perhaps because there will never be anything like it again. 'That show was unique,' insists Curtis. 'It's such a huge attraction all over the world. These *Persuaders* play anywhere in the world every day. Why is it still so popular? I think it was very European in flavour and that's what I liked about it so much. And the heavies were very defined and you were very aware of their chicanery. It didn't take you twelve reels to find out that he's the murderer.'

Not surprisingly, rumours have persisted over the years about bringing *The Persuaders* back to TV, of a big screen remake, even having Roger's daughter Deborah team up with Jamie Lee Curtis. 'They had a whole number of ideas,' says Curtis. 'At one time, they were going to split up Roger and me, let me work with a younger man, and let Roger work with a younger Danny Wilde. But I'm kind of glad it ended like it did, it makes it unique and different than anything anybody's ever seen, and I like that.'

THE PROTECTORS (1972-74)

After finishing work on *UFO*, Gerry Anderson changed tack completely, turning away from science fiction to embrace the espionage genre. However, it was a move not of his own choosing. '*The Protectors* was not my idea. I went to see Lew, who gave me a piece of A4 paper and there were four paragraphs typed out. He said, "Read that." I did – it was about this international crime fighting agency and its jet-setting operatives who hire out their services to any government, business or wealthy individual that can afford them. He said, "Do you want to make it?" I said, "Um, well." He said, "Gerry, do you want to make it or don't you?" And I went, "Yes." That's how it started. So I had to develop the whole series from those four paragraphs.'

Robert Vaughn was handed the starring role of Harry Rule, an American agent operating out of London. After saying he would never go back to the weekly grind of episodic TV after his long stint in *The Man from UNCLE*, Vaughn (after Chuck Connors, Robert Culp, Ben Gazzara and William Shatner were considered and rejected) had a special reason for agreeing to do *The Protectors*. 'At that particular time in my life, I was so terribly disenchanted with the events of the sixties in America. We had the murders of Dr. King and Robert Kennedy, and there was our continuing involvement in the Vietnam war, which I opposed publicly. So I saw this as a chance to continue to stay away from the United States, which I had kind of subconsciously done since 1968, after the election of Richard Nixon. So this was an offer to live in London for a minimum of eighteen months, which turned out to be three years. And London has always been one of my favourite places in the world.'

The hiring of Vaughn was yet another example of a Hollywood star being cast in a lead role in an ITC series, purely to attract international attention. 'Lew Grade believed in stars,' recounts Marcia Stanton. 'He very much believed in star power. And they were mostly American because we were doing transatlantic deals, so in order to get the series sold you had to have somebody who was known in the States. And he was criticised about it, because he was the first person to do those deals. If

Like a lot of ITC shows, The Protectors *lent itself to the cartoon strip format.*

you're entrepreneurial in any way in this country, it's held against you.'

This ploy of bringing in American actors was not without risk. Obviously, no Hollywood actor on top of his game would ever agree to come over to do a TV series in England, Tony Curtis being the exception. All of which meant that Lew Grade was lumbered with the likes of Steve Forrest and Gene Barry for *The Baron* and *The Adventurer*, forgotten shows today. Both were competent enough actors, but really at the end of their careers. Additionally, American stars found themselves in a totally different working environment. There wasn't the same degree of star pampering that went on back home, and for the most part they never truly came to terms with how the Brits worked, as Sue Lloyd confirms about Steve Forrest. 'It was difficult for him. He was used to the American system. He would click his fingers for his chair and the crew would bring my footstool, if you know what I mean. They didn't like the idea of Steve being like that. But Steve was from the star system. It becomes ludicrous in the States. If your caravan is an inch further forward than the other one, all hell's let loose, whereas here you'd be lucky to get the caravan in the first place. Or you might not get the caravan but the privies at the end of the garden.'

Vaughn was under no illusion as to why he'd been cast in *The Protectors*. 'I didn't see Harry Rule as anything other than a variation of *The Man from UNCLE*'s Napoleon Solo.' Nor was he enamoured of the scripts. 'I couldn't understand them when I read them. I couldn't understand them when I did them. I never understood them when I saw them on air.'

Vaughn's observations certainly hold up under scrutiny. Despite the nostalgia and kitsch factor (some of the fashions would make even Jason King blush), *The Protectors* is very hit and miss. Some episodes are effective, but the majority are leaden affairs, while a few are almost unwatchable. 'It was quite a fraught series,' remembers John Hough, who directed several episodes. 'Robert Vaughn brought over his right-hand man, Sherwood Price, to represent his interests. So there were a lot of demands from Price about the scripts and other things, and he did cause a few traumatic situations. But he wasn't that wrong. He was only interested in making the scripts better. One can't blame him for that. But Robert Vaughn himself was a professional. He wasn't the centre of any of the problems. It really was Sherwood Price trying to represent Robert's interests. And it was too late. The scripts were already written, the thing was cast, the shooting was underway, and it's very diffi-

The Protectors *were an international crime fighting agency whose jet-setting operatives hired out their services to anyone who could afford them.*

cult, once the machine has got going, to alter anything.'

Gerry's first encounter with Price remains vivid even to this day. 'I was in my office reading a script, we hadn't started production yet, and the door burst open and in the doorway was standing a cowboy. I said, "You in the right room?" He said, "Are you Gerry Anderson?" I said, "Yeah." And he threw the script right across the room, and it landed bang in front of me on the desk, and he said, "That is a pile of shit." I said, "Who are you?" He said, "I'm Robert Vaughn's partner, Sherwood Price is the name." Now, I'm fairly placid, but I've got a filthy temper if needs be, and I said, "Well, you just tell me one thing. If this is a pile of shit, why has your partner signed for the series?" And he said, "Baby, the money's good." And he slammed the door shut. And I thought, "This is going to be a really nice series."'

But Ed Bishop, who guest-starred in a *Protectors* episode as a deranged Vietnam vet, thought it poor form on Vaughn's part to denigrate his own show. 'Vaughn went back to America and badmouthed everybody, saying the scripts were lousy, the technicians were lousy, and this was lousy. The series was not *Naked City* or *Kojak*, it didn't reach those elements of success, but it was a good, solid bread and butter series. I think actors who go out and badmouth things, it leaves a very uncomfortable taste. His agent or anybody could've looked through Gerry and Sylvia's record; they're not going to be doing *The Sopranos*. Did he expect anything different?'

Today, Vaughn's opinions about *The Protectors* have mellowed, though he still believes the series was undone by poor quality writing. 'The scripts were the weakest part of the show. It wasn't really the writers' fault so much as the fact that they only had 22 minutes of screen time, and they had three principals in the show which you had to feature, plus there had to be a story and a guest heavy. That's a very difficult thing to put into 22 minutes on the screen. So that was the most difficult aspect of the show for the production team.'

Such views naturally put Vaughn at odds with Gerry Anderson. Today, the actor won't be drawn upon how difficult things became between them, other than to say, 'We didn't have the best of relationships. We didn't have much contact actually, because once he'd cast the show he didn't appear on the set that often. I do remember that he had a monitor in his office so he could watch the activities on the set.' Similarly, Gerry refuses to discuss how bad relations became between himself and Vaughn. 'I can't say too much about Robert Vaughn, except to say that it was a very unhappy series.'

The actor got along much better with Lew Grade, though the tycoon was equally as invisible on the set as Anderson was. Vaughn's business partner saw Grade much more often. 'They used to get together and smoke cigars,' Vaughn recalls. 'And Lew said to him one time, "Sherwood, you know why Robert Vaughn is a good actor? I'll show you why Robert Vaughn's a good actor." And he got up and said, "Take Gene Barry," who had done a series called *The Adventurer* for Lew. "When Gene gets out of a chair he adjusts his tie, adjusts his cufflinks, walks to the door, looks around and then leaves. Now that costs money. That costs film. Vaughn is out of the chair, out the door. Bang. That's an actor."'

Backing up Robert Vaughn in *The Protectors* was New Zealand-born actress Nyree Dawn Porter, as the beautiful and wealthy Contessa di Contini. Nyree first came to the public attention as the strong-willed Irene in the BBC's hugely successful serial *The Forsyte Saga*. (Her *Forsyte* co-star Kenneth More once said of her, 'Nyree Dawn Porter is arguably the worst three actresses in Britain.') It was at an awards banquet where Grade pounced and got her to agree to do the series. Gerry happened to be there too, propping up the bar, as he usually was at such functions, as far away from the dance floor as possible. 'I wouldn't say that I was drunk by any means, but I was fairly tanked up, and suddenly a hand landed on my shoulder – it was Lew. "Where have you been? I've been looking everywhere for you." I said, "Lew, it's twelve o'clock at night, it's my day off." "OK, OK," he said. "I've got some marvellous news. You know Nyree Dawn Porter's been presenting the awards. I've just signed her for the second lead." I said, "But the second lead's a man." He said, "Is it? You'll have to rewrite the scripts, won't you?"'

Unfortunately, Gerry's working relationship with Miss Porter was just as fraught as that with Robert Vaughn. Matters reached a head when the makeup artist he'd signed for the series was unable to join the crew until a week after the first location shoot, in Spain. Gerry simply determined to bring in a temporary replacement. However, Nyree got on so well with the new makeup artist that, when the replacement arrived, the actress sent a message to the production office saying, 'I don't want him.' Gerry went to see her, imploring, 'Nyree, this guy is one of the top makeup men in the country, and I signed him especially for you.' But the actress was adamant. That evening, Gerry was dining alone in a restaurant when Nyree came in, drunk. 'You are a fucking shit bag!' she yelled. 'You are a complete and utter cunt. You're a prick. I hate you.' By this time, everybody in the restaurant had turned round. Gerry managed to keep his cool and said, 'Right, is that it, or have you got anything else to say?' 'No, that's it,' she replied, and stormed out. Luckily, the original makeup man understood the situation and withdrew from the production. 'That was sort of indicative of

Left: *Nyree Dawn Porter brought an icy glamour to the series in her role as a wealthy countess.* Top right: *Robert Vaughn was under no illusions that his* Protectors *character, Harry Rule, was anything other than a variation of* The Man from UNCLE*'s Napoleon Solo.* Bottom right: *dashing Tony Anholt as Paul Buchet,* The Protectors*' 'French connection'.*

how bad things did get,' explains Gerry. 'It was not a happy series.'

Completing the team was young British actor Tony Anholt as Paul Buchet, a French private investigator. Born in Singapore to British parents, Anholt's smooth manner and debonair looks singled him out as a natural for playboy roles. Following *The Protectors*, he appeared in *Space 1999* and BBC drama *Howard's Way*. Tragically, he died of a brain tumour in 2002, aged just 61. 'Tony was my discovery,' says Gerry. 'He was a very nice guy. His death was just terrible.'

The shooting schedule on *The Protectors* didn't help the fraught atmosphere, being one of the most arduous for any ITC series. Conscious that the more sophisticated audiences of the seventies wouldn't accept the studio mock-up sets that were the trademark of *The Saint* and its ilk, Grade gave Anderson a considerable budget to set his stories in some of the most glamorous cities in Europe. So they went to Venice, Rome, Barcelona, Salzburg, Copenhagen and Madrid. In Paris, they filmed inside Napoleon's tomb, a nod towards Vaughn's *UNCLE* character Napoleon Solo. 'The best part of the show was being on location in Europe and staying in top class hotels, living on the highest possible five-star existence you can live on,' Vaughn recalls. 'My wife and I were so indulgent, and fortunately ITC was paying for it. We didn't shoot on weekends at all, and we would take a flight that left London at six pm that got us into

New York 8.15 pm that same day, because of the time difference. We had a car pick us up at the airport and then we'd check into a hotel, have a great restaurant meal, watch the Johnny Carson show and sleep late. Then we'd take a 10 am flight Sunday morning, which got us into London at ten o'clock at night, and I'd then film the next morning. We did that on average once a month. It was grandly self-indulgent.'

Wherever they stopped to film, tourists and crowds flocked to watch. Shooting in a city like Paris, for example, caused numerous problems. Such was the size of the operation that the cast and crew occupied five separate hotels. Gerry Anderson also had to obtain permission to shoot in certain areas. One day, the crew were working without a permit and a local gendarme ordered them to halt. Just then, he spied the shapely figure of Nyree Dawn Porter. It just so happened that this copper was a huge fan, and stood guard while the scene was hurriedly completed.

Venice, though, was a complete disaster. 'The union insisted that we took a union kitchen out with us, so there was this barge going up the Grand Canal with blokes peeling spuds like fury,' remembers Gerry. 'And getting the unit and all the equipment to the various locations at the right time, we had to study the tides because of the bridges being too low at high tide.'

Wherever they were in Europe, Gerry always made sure to be in the next location at least two days before the main unit arrived, to check out everything was fine. In Venice, an Italian production manager had been busily working for six weeks arranging all the locations and filming permits. 'But when I got there this production manager had had a heart attack and was in hospital. And all his notes were in Italian. We got an interpreter in and he was saying, "The rushes, these are things that grow by the river?" It was quite impossible to translate. So we had a terrible time. We had no hotels booked and we had no permissions to film. So we had to do it all on a daily basis. I remember, just as an example, there was this knock on my hotel room door and it was our director, Michael Lindsay-Hogg. It was four o'clock in the morning. He said, "Can we have a conference?" I said, "OK, come in." And he said, "Tomorrow we're due to film at the airport, but the permission's been withdrawn. That's the bad news." I said, "What's the good news?" He said, "The good news is we've got the opera house." So as dawn broke, we rewrote the scene for the opera house.'

Working on a tight schedule, Gerry hired experienced directors like Charlie Crichton, Roy Ward Baker and, of course, Cyril Frankel. Though he liked Gerry personally, Frankel admits to finding the producer difficult to work for. 'Simply because he didn't study the scripts. In the first episode I directed, Nyree Dawn Porter was meant to be drugged, and Gerry Anderson goes into see the rushes and comes running on the set saying, "You're not getting the right performance from Nyree Dawn Porter. She should be more extrovert." He did come back to me afterwards to say, "Oh, I didn't realise she was meant to be drugged." And then when I did one with Eartha Kitt, I told him that something was wrong with the denouement of the script, and he said, "No, the script's perfect, go ahead." Then he sees the rough cut and complains that the ending is all wrong. He hadn't read it! That was my only concern. Otherwise I got on with him very well. But as a director you depend on your producer to have a certain overview, which someone like Monty Berman had.'

Vaughn was also invited to direct one of the episodes, his first excursion behind the camera. 'It was shot in Malta and was written for my wife to be the guest star in. The episode was called "It Could Be Practically Anywhere on the Island", and it referred to the fact that there was a microfilm that a dog ate which then made poo-

poos somewhere, and we had to find the dog's poo-poo. It was the only comedy that we really intended to be a comedy. And I have a copy of it and we run it every couple of Christmases, so we all laugh at how young we were and how [much] thinner and prettier we were.'

Stamina also played a part during the making of *The Protectors*. In Rome, Nyree Dawn Porter's stand-in collapsed from exhaustion after only a week on the job. Vaughn also, through personal choice, did a lot of his own stunt work. 'Whenever I've appeared in an action show, I've usually done most of the stunts that didn't involve water. I can't swim and I'm terrified of water, but almost any other stunt I would do. And the stuntman would also do the stunt, and they'd just look at the film and decide which one looked the best. Most of the time they used me, as I was a fairly good athlete and in pretty good shape.'

One thing that Vaughn never could get his head around was the way crews worked in British television studios, this being his first experience of them. 'The main problem at that time was the union rules. We started at 8.30 every day. Then we had what was called a tea break, which was not supposed to be an actual break. The tea was supposed to be drunk while we were filming. Well that never was the case. A great tea trolley came on the set and the action just stopped for half an hour, sometimes an hour. Then we went to lunch at one and came back to the set at two. Then at 3.30, there was another tea break. And you had to finish at 5.20 according to the union rules, but if we wanted to call an additional fifteen minutes the crew had to vote. But by the time you'd rounded up the crew you'd already wasted fifteen minutes. So the shooting day was seven to eight hours, as opposed to twelve that they do now, and this is why it took so long to do 52 *Protectors* shows, over three years. In America every day was a twelve-hour day. And we shot six days of film per one-hour show. So we went along very rapidly. To give you an example, our cinematographer on the *UNCLE* show, Fred Koenekamp, about once every 90 days he'd be in the hospital from ulcers because the pressure was so great on him.'

Sold by ITC's publicity department as an 'explosive action adventure' and a 'new dimension in nerve-tingling entertainment', *The Protectors* was a solid international hit. And it spawned a top selling record with Tony Christie's rendition of the theme, 'Avenues and Alleyways'. The series also played host to a number of guest stars and faces of the future, including John Thaw, Jeremy Brett, David Suchet and Joss Ackland.

43 SPINE-CHILLING MOVIES

THRILLER

HORROR
AND SUSPENSE
With Stars Like
DONNA MILLS
GEORGE MAHARIS
DENHOLM ELLIOTT
CAROL LYNLEY
HAYLEY MILLS

75-MINUTE MOVIES

BOB HOSKINS
TOM CONTI
CARROLL BAKER
CATHERINE SCHELL
JOANNA PETTET

Chapter 9

The Ultimate Variety Show

- Thriller - The Zoo Gang - The Muppet Show - Jesus of Nazareth - The Return of the Saint - Sapphire and Steel -

The sort of escapist fare ITC had so successfully specialised in, during the whole of the 1960s and early into the 1970s, was slowly becoming passé, as modern TV audiences demanded greater realism from their peak-time drama viewing. For the remainder of its existence, ITC scrambled around looking for an identity and for new trends to latch onto – instead of being at the televisual vanguard as it had been with *Robin Hood*, which had begun the swashbuckler/historical TV genre, the Gerry Anderson shows, and then *Danger Man*, which single-handedly launched the TV spy craze.

But ITC's last years of production were far from inconsequential, as they skipped genres with consummate skill to serve up a dazzling variety of shows – everything from tales of mystery to biblical epics, from comedy to supernatural sleuthing. That was until Lew Grade finally hung up his TV crown and set himself new challenges, one of which would prove his undoing – movies.

THRILLER (1973-76)

The rationale behind this thriller/horror anthology series from the pen of Brian Clemens was simple – to provoke the imagination and allow the viewer's mind to create its own terrors, without resorting to graphic scenes of violence. 'I didn't want gore,' explains Clemens. 'I wanted to scare people. And what does? Not *Elm Street*'s Freddy, but those little things that we all know about, like you are lying in bed late at night, you *know* you locked the back door and yet you hear the familiar squeak as it opens. I have always maintained that violence (and sex) should be taken off the screen and put back where it belongs, in the mind of the audience; they will always make it more scary (and sexier) than any director can *show*.'

In late 1972, Clemens pitched his idea of a series of long-format, one-off thrillers to Michael Grade, who suggested his uncle Lew might be more interested. 'I heard nothing for some months,' Clemens recalls. 'Then Lew called me. Could I write four such thrillers by yesterday? I went to meet him. He said we had a deal and to go away

This promo card for Thriller *highlights the series' use of both British and American guest stars.*

The famous fish-eye lens opening titles of Thriller, *which unsettled viewers before the programme had even started.*

and start writing. I hesitated. "But Lew," I said, "we haven't talked money yet!" Lew grabbed my hand and shook it, "I promise you – you won't be disappointed." I wasn't. I went away, with no formal contract, no idea what I was being paid, and wrote the first four *Thrillers*.'

In all, 43 self-contained dramas were produced, all bearing the unique hallmark of Brian Clemens. 'I wrote all the *Thrillers*, either the whole script or I provided a fully worked-out story to be written by writers of my choice, and whom I could trust. I've always been great at thrillers, and so this series was the easiest and most enjoyable task of my career.'

One of those writers brought in was Dennis Spooner, and it sadly turned out to be his last assignment for ITC. After *Thriller*, Spooner continued working on high-profile TV shows such as *The New Avengers*, *The Professionals* and, in the US, *Hart to Hart* and *Remington Steele*, until his untimely death in 1986. 'Dennis was a man of immense talent and professionalism,' enthused Monty Berman. 'His fertile brain would produce brilliant ideas out of the blue. Quite simply, he seemed to know what audiences would want to watch. And that is a rare gift.'

Clemens also laments the loss of Spooner as, since first collaborating on 1966's *The Baron*, the two writers had become the closest of friends. 'We spoke to each other every day, wrote plays together, and discussed each other's work at length. I miss him every day, and always will. When we wrote comedies he would stomp around my office, sometimes wearing a tea cosy on his head, on the basis that if we couldn't think of anything funny, then at least one of us looked funny! He was a year or so younger than me, so we shared all the same experiences and influences. It became a kind of shorthand for us. I would say, "This scene is a bit *Ben Hur*." He would interject, "But with some *Cruel Sea*." And each of us knew exactly what the other was thinking! It made for a great working relationship.'

Raising finance for *Thriller* proved comparatively simple, as it usually was when Lew Grade was involved. 'Lew went to the States and obtained the sum of $100,000 per showing from the ABC network,' says Clemens. 'Each show was budgeted at $100,000 per episode, so Lew was in the black already and had not yet sold the show anywhere else in the world. There'll never be another Lew.'

With the international market in mind, Grade insisted on a large quota of American actors in leading roles, prompting one irate *TV Times* reader to enquire why the series always featured an American. 'Yes, the series had many guest stars from the States – that was what Lew had agreed with ABC,' explains Clemens. 'Each show would have a star they approved. It could be an American they sent us or a European they considered as a "name". I think it worked very well indeed.' So US actors like Barry Nelson, Stuart Damon and Donna Mills mingled alongside home-grown favourites such as Diana Dors and Richard Todd, plus relative newcomers like Jenny Agutter, Robert Powell and Helen Mirren.

Over the course of its 43 episodes, Thriller *won over the critics and acquired loyal fans. Director Ken Russell never missed an episode. Between 1973 and 1976, the series captured a regular Saturday night audience of around six million – a figure to die for today.*

Perhaps the most irritating aspect of Grade's internationalism was the need to adapt each of the scripts so as to be compatible with American sensibilities. The result was that British members of the cast used words like janitor, apartment, vacation and freeway just as freely as the Americans did. 'We aim to provide good, honest excitement with lots of shots of London and the British scene thrown in. American viewers love that,' trumpeted an ITC spokesman of the day. Perhaps so, but some home-grown viewers and critics resented the idea of having their TV tailored to transatlantic tastes.

Early on, it was decided to produce each *Thriller* story as a 72-minute drama rather than the standard hour, so they could be sold overseas as mini-features. Though this did lead to occasional stories being a touch slow, at least they had the added benefit of more character development. Recording took place at ATV studios, Borehamwood, with ten days allowed for rehearsals and three days for recording. Directors employed included Robert Tronson and Alan Gibson, who'd earlier worked on Hammer's TV anthology series *Journey to the Unknown*. Clemens was usually too busy writing the next episode to spend much time on set, but always made an effort to attend the initial script read-through. His biggest sphere of influence, apart from scripts, was post-production. He also saw to it that his friend, Laurie Johnson, composed the music.

The first season of *Thriller* debuted in the UK in April 1973, running for ten weeks on Saturday nights, and caught the public's imagination, achieving decent ratings despite being up against stiff opposition in the shape of *Kojak*, over on BBC1. But the critics offered mixed opinions; some thought it tense and well plotted, others that it was over the top or unduly formulaic.

Clemens was asked to write further stories to build on the show's popular success. These differed in style to their predecessors by being that little bit more frightening in tone. Because of the increased dramatic content, the series continued to be an audience grabber. Even the press changed their tune. *The Times*, who earlier had dismissed Clemens' efforts, now enthused, 'The programme that continues to catch the eye is *Thriller*.'

In America, the show proved just as popular despite some unexplained tinkering with the format. Most of the episode titles were changed, Laurie Johnson's menacing theme music was cut, and some judicious re-editing went on. Often a brand new teaser sequence was added to the beginning of each episode, using additional scenes recorded in America. Most bizarrely of all, the eerie and highly effective title sequence, comprising various moody locations shot through a fish-eye lens and set upon a blood-red background, was replaced by a piece of unusual artwork based on characters from that particular episode.

With Clemens employed elsewhere, not least with *The New Avengers*, *Thriller* was slowly wound down, the final episodes being transmitted from April 1976. During its last run the press had been totally won over by the series, and duly mourned its loss. 'I was pleased not only by the public response to *Thriller*, some people still come to me and say how I scared them to death, but also within the industry,' says Clemens. 'Ken Russell never missed an episode!'

The 43 episodes of *Thriller* were among the major drama productions of the seventies. The content and style of the series varied dramatically, to give the viewer something different to scare the living wits out of them each week. Clemens ran the whole gamut from murder, witchcraft and supernatural phenomena to straightforward detective and espionage themes. And yet, although those who saw it remember it with huge affection, *Thriller* is today largely a forgotten show. 'I'm sad that they were never re-shown,' Clemens declares. 'I think even today they would still have great power. Thrillers never actually date, although a number of my themes have since reoccurred in mainstream movies. Coincidence? Who knows?'

THE ZOO GANG (1974)

Based on a best-selling novel by Paul Gallico, this adventure series was really a geriatric version of *The Persuaders*. It revolved around four members of the French resistance, collectively known as the Zoo Gang due to their code names (the Fox, the Elephant, the Leopard and the Tiger), who reunite after the war to solve crimes along the glamorous Cote d'Azur.

For television purposes, these brave French fighters were transformed into a mixture of nationalities, presumably to suit the requirements of the global TV market. Certainly, Lew Grade cast the show with astute brilliance. Barry Morse (still fresh in audience's minds as the cop doggedly on the heels of David Janssen's *The Fugitive*) and Brian Keith for the US market, John Mills for Britain and German star Lilli Palmer for the European territories. The tycoon also got personally involved in persuading his veteran stars to take part, incessantly phoning up Mills, who was reluctant to sign on, until the actor finally relented and went to see him. 'Lew lit the biggest cigar I've ever seen,' Mills recalled in his autobiography, 'and did a one-man show for me, playing all the parts from several of the episodes. He sold it to me com-

The stars of The Zoo Gang *toast its success on location in Nice.*

pletely.' It was to be Mills' first ever British television series. Grade did much the same thing to land Lilli Palmer. 'Lew read my role right through for me on the phone,' the actress later recalled. 'I was overwhelmed by his enthusiasm.'

Barry Morse had just finished *The Adventurer* when Grade approached him for *The Zoo Gang* – a project he especially enjoyed, since it meant working with old friends again. 'I knew Johnny Mills and Lilli before, although I didn't know Brian Keith. We all got along very well, and we knew that it was all going to be shot in the South of France. So that was attractive, of course. It all looked very promising.'

Morse played Alec Marlowe (the Tiger), who since the war had been running an auto-repair shop in Vancouver, and still carried the scars of Gestapo torture. American film star Brian Keith was Stephen Halliday (the Fox), a former OSS agent turned successful New York businessman. John Mills played former British commando officer Tommy Devon (the Elephant), who was now living in Nice where he ran his own jewellery shop. The only French group member was Lilli Palmer's Manouche Roget (the Leopard), widow of fellow resistance fighter Claude Roget, who was killed by the Gestapo and whose death the gang swore to avenge.

The pilot episode was adapted by acclaimed writer Reginald Rose from the book, and stuck pretty faithfully to Gallico's original plot. The Zoo Gang are reunited after the unexpected appearance in Nice of the man who had betrayed them to the Gestapo. Capturing the traitor, they put the reward money towards a children's hospital in memory of Claude, their fallen comrade, while also deciding to stay together in order to bring justice to the French Riviera – returning stolen property, combating vice, and so forth.

Never was a show more strategically cast: Brian Keith and Barry Morse for the US market, Lili Palmer for the Europeans and John Mills for the Brits.

While Rose remained as consultant on the series, other writers were brought in, notably John Kruse, who'd written some of the best *Saint* episodes. Lew Grade personally asked Kruse to contribute a story idea, setting him up in an office and making sure he had enough pens and paper to finish the job. Assured Kruse was comfortable, Grade then quietly tiptoed out of the room. After twenty minutes the door opened very quietly, and in Grade came again, smoking a huge cigar and carrying a small cup of coffee which he placed on Kruse's desk, all done in dead silence. He then tiptoed out again.

In the end though, the scripts left a lot to be desired. The stars had all signed their contracts before they ever saw a script, and weren't best pleased with the results – to the point of contemplating strike action, as director John Hough remembers: 'One day on location, John Mills came to me and said, "Look, we're going to strike. Lilli, Brian, Barry and myself, we're all going to strike because the scripts are so awful and we'd like your support." And I said, "Yeah, you've got it, if you feel they're too bad to do." And he said, "We're going to have a meeting with the producer. Will you come?" And I agreed. The meeting was first thing in the morning. And the producer was Herbert Hirschman, a tough American, and a first class producer. So in we went, and John Mills was the spokesman and he said, "None of us want to go and work today because these scripts are so bad." And this producer was brilliant, he knew all our history, and went down the line. "John Mills," he said, "you've been in some wonderful films, but you've done some really bad films too." And he named Lilli Palmer's bad films. And me too. Everybody. He was able to pinpoint all our weaknesses. And he said, "How dare you tell me what a bad script is or not, because you've all made mistakes in your past. Now get back to work!" And we all got up and we all went back to work, and that was the end of the protest.'

Despite the inferior writing, *The Zoo Gang* benefited from the usual high production values. 'We'd all decided among ourselves that we'd get little villas or apartments somewhere around Nice,' Morse remembers. 'But Lew decided that they wanted to have us all under the same roof, so that we could be available for costume and makeup and all that. So they agreed, at no cost to ourselves, to put us all up at a top hotel in Nice. Well, we weren't going to object to that, so we all had suites and it was marvellously enjoyable. I seem to remember, we started to shoot somewhere around the middle of March and it wasn't all that warm at that time, and so instead of it being called the Cote d'Azur, I started to call it the overcoat d'Azur. But we had a wonderful time.'

Thanks immeasurably to the plush locations (interiors were shot at Pinewood) and a theme tune by Paul and Linda McCartney, the series had class by the bucket load. The interplay between the experienced leads also brought gravitas and prestige to the production. And it was all well handled by directors Sidney Hayers and John Hough, both of whom had worked on *The Avengers*. But the critics quickly made their mind up about the show. They didn't like it. 'Oh God, it's awful,' opined *The Guardian*. And this from *The Daily Mail*: 'In the book the Zoo Gang always made their spoils available to charity. This TV series, I suspect, is a pension fund for elderly film stars.'

The show did have potential, with its interesting premise and characters, but the lack of scope for action was a drawback – just how many fistfights could these pensioners realistically get up to each week? In the end only six one-hour episodes were ever made. But it wasn't because of its unpopularity that no more episodes of *The Zoo Gang* were produced. On the contrary, there was a desire among the four leads to carry on, as they'd enjoyed making it so much. Alas, they were all so in demand that it was only possible to do a limited number of episodes. And so, *The Zoo Gang* was unceremoniously put out to pasture.

THE MUPPET SHOW (1976-81)

When the Muppets took the world by storm in 1976, they weren't new to TV audiences. Back in 1969, *Sesame Street* – featuring a host of creations like Kermit, Cookie Monster and Big Bird – became a huge success with both young audiences and their parents. Spurred on by its popularity, its creator, Jim Henson, sought a more adult-orientated show with a primetime slot, but the American networks balked at the idea; to them, Muppets were strictly for kids. 'Jim had been trying to sell the idea for a primetime Muppet show for quite a long time and hadn't been successful,' explains Jane Henson, Jim's widow. 'American TV executives had a pretty clear picture that some entertainment was for children and some was for adults, and they just couldn't really grasp the idea that all ages would enjoy the Muppets. It's not that the networks didn't enjoy it, but they just weren't convinced that all ages would watch.'

Inevitably, it was Lew Grade who saw the potential of the Muppets, perhaps responding to the vaudevillian aspects inherent in its variety show format. And it became a programme that would always hold a very special place in his heart, according to Marcia Stanton. 'Lew was so proud of the Muppets. He loved them all. And they called him Uncle Lew.'

Perhaps the Muppets would never have flourished in America; they needed to come to Britain, the natural home for the broad sense of the absurd that someone like Jim Henson excelled in. 'England has always had that zany, Monty Python kind of humour,' observes Jane. 'In a way, Americans are not quite as willing to say that they think that kind of wacky humour is funny or good. And that's why, when we were designing *The Muppet Show*, we put the old men in the theatre box, Statler and Waldorf, always saying how bad the show was, and they didn't know why they would watch it. We sort of did that so people back in America could sit on their sofas and say, "I don't know why we watch this!"'

In what was a large and risky financial undertaking, Grade brought Henson and his entire puppet company over to England, setting them up at Elstree Studios. It was a little bit of Hollywood in Hertfordshire, as the core of the Muppet team were all Americans: Jim and his long time collaborator, Frank Oz, plus executive producer David Lazer. The move to the UK was also a big gamble for Henson, who had worries and demands of his own. 'We wanted good enough budgets and very high production values,' says Lazer. 'That was critical to us and to Jim. And we wanted creative independence, nobody could come in and say, "Let's do it this way," or, "Do it that way." And Lew kept his word. His word was the strongest bond you could ask for. Unbelievable. I don't think he ever read a script; he just had such blind faith in us, and Jim Henson in particular. Lew had such reverence for Jim. He never wanted to bother him with any problems of any kind. I was kind of the buffer. At least three times a week I'd get wakeup calls from Lew; "How's it going, my dear? Do you need any help?" And the fact that he kept his word was so important, especially in show business. He was from the old school, where your word was everything. And he was the ultimate entertainer himself. He was pure showbiz. It was such an honour and a pleasure and fun to be with him.'

Besides Henson, Oz and Lazer, all the principle puppeteers were also American, as were the writers (with the exception of Chris Langham, who would later write and appear in *Not the Nine O' Clock News*). But the crew was British. Part of the home-grown talent was Martin Baker, who'd been with Lew Grade's ATV since he left school in 1966. 'I got a job in the post room at ATV house. I'd always wanted to get into television. And people used to say, "Oh, Lew will be there in the morning to help you sort out the mail." I thought they were winding me up. But if you were on the early shift and got into the mail room at 6.30 in the morning, Lew would appear at the door, his first cigar of the day already lit, "Good morning, boys." It was the most extraordinary thing; there he was, looking for the deals from the States. I also remember getting his lunch from the Cumberland hotel across the street and taking it up to his office. Then he would have a nap in the afternoon, because he'd already had a long day, and then he'd get his second wind so he could be on the phone to the States in the late afternoon. Amazing man.'

To the impressionable young Baker, Grade was a great influence, and his apprenticeship with ATV probably the best grounding in television he could have had. 'I started in the mail room at the corporate offices, then I moved out to the studio centre at Elstree as a gofer and a tea boy, so I grew up learning the business from the studio floor upwards. And I loved every minute of it. I think it's sad today that people in the business don't get those opportunities. People today, I find, don't want to learn how to get there, they just want to be there.'

Baker worked on a host of variety shows that Lew Grade churned out in the late sixties, such as *This Is Tom Jones* and some Julie Andrews specials. Massive Hollywood stars were coming over to appear in them all the time; Sammy Davis Jr., Burt Bacharach and Gene Kelly. And it was on one of these specials that Baker first met Jim Henson. 'In 1968, Jim and Frank Oz came over to England as guests on the Tom Jones show. It just said "the Muppets" on their paperwork, and nobody knew who the Muppets were. I called Jim, who was staying at the Dorchester, to say I was going to send a limousine to pick him up, and he said, "Frank and I were thinking

Arguably the greatest cast of characters in TV history.

maybe we'd take the train out." I said, "Well, if you go to Kings Cross you get the train straight out to Elstree and Borehamwood, but it'll take you an hour or more. So if you want to do that I'll meet you at the station." And indeed that's what Jim did and that was typical, as I learnt Jim to be just this ordinary guy that, rather than have a big fancy limousine pick him up at the hotel, he liked the sound of the adventure of going on the train. And so he and Frank arrived at the station with a couple of black puppet boxes, and I whisked them down to the studio, which was five minutes away. And that was my first encounter with Jim Henson. Little did I know that I would end up working with the guy.'

Baker and Henson just seemed to make a connection, and when *The Muppet Show* started production in January 1976, Baker was installed on the production side. 'We did two shows in January, which served as two pilots if you like. Then Jim went back to the States, and we weren't sure whether it was going to happen or not. Then we got the go-ahead, and Jim came back in March or April, and we went into production on 24 shows that year. And the rest, as they say, is history.'

The Muppets became an international phenomenon, the like of which television has barely seen before or since. 'I think Jim always felt that it would be successful,' muses Jane. 'He just didn't know how successful. I think it took all of us by surprise, how it took off round the world. We used to joke that it played in more countries than existed.' In fact, the series was sold in something like 102 countries, and had an estimated world audience of 250 million. In the US it was seen on 150 stations, and became one of the top-rated syndicated shows in history. 'I think it worked because it was a show that you could see the whole family sitting down to watch,' observes Baker. 'The kids got something out of it, because the Muppets were fun and colourful, but the adults equally got something out of it, because the humour was always skewed up rather than down. It wasn't crude or offensive, but it was just skewed enough to tweak the older audience's appeal.'

The format itself was perfection. Essentially it was a variety show, incorporating comedy sketches and musical numbers rounded off with a guest star. And what stars. No other show in history can compete with the Muppets' guest list, which included legendary figures from movies, theatre, dance, TV and music, the likes of Elton John, Steve Martin, Diana Ross, Roger Moore, John Cleese and Liza Minnelli. The only show one can compare it to today, for the amount of stars vying to appear, is *The Simpsons*. But while that's just vocal talent, on *The Muppet Show* these stars actually performed in the flesh. But at the beginning, it was very, very tough getting anybody of any note to appear. 'Nobody wanted to do a puppet show,' confirms Lazer, whose job it was to hire the stars and look after them. 'So our first guests were not really A-list people. But as soon as we booked Peter Ustinov, Lena Horne and Candice Bergen – and this was as favours that we'd pulled in from friends – that upgraded it immediately. And then the show started getting popular and people clamoured to be on it.'

Both Jim Henson and Lazer believed the guest stars were critical to the show's appeal. 'It was a reason, we thought, for viewers to tune in to see what someone like Rudolf Nureyev would do with the Muppets. That was our toughest catch. I worked to get Nureyev for six months, calling him all over the world. And finally I booked him. That's probably one of our best shows. Nureyev danced "Swine Lake". And he said, "I can't be upstaged by a pig," and put a hand in front of Miss Piggy's face. He was the star.'

It's incredible that the Muppet team had the gall to ask the world's greatest ever dancer to perform a ballet on television with a pig! 'But he had a good sense of humour and we did kind of a trade-off,' recalls Lazer. 'We took him to his favourite London restaurant and said, "What is it that you would love to do?" And he said, "I would like to tap dance and sing." Now Nureyev saying that, it's fabulous. People want to see something out of context. And in exchange we offered him "Swine Lake", and he loved the idea. He loved it.'

Often, it was the notion that these stars could do something on television that

The one and only Miss Piggy.

they'd never done before, but secretly always wanted to do, that acted as one of the inducements for coming on. 'We always said to the guest star, "Is there anything that you wished you could've done in your career, but never had a chance to do?"' Jane remembers. 'And different people would say different things. And each guest star made the show a different experience each week.'

Besides Nureyev, another big star that left an impression on Lazer was Peter Sellers. 'Peter Sellers, and this is awful to say, had no sense of humour. He was so serious and withdrawn. But the minute he was on screen this brilliance shines. He said, "I will do any character, but I will not be myself." We wanted him to do Inspector Clouseau in one scene, and he refused. And Jim said to me, "Talk to him, we need Clouseau for that scene." So I had to convince him to do Clouseau. And he did, reluctantly. Some of the comedians that appeared on the show surprised me. They were as funny as hell on screen, but they were totally different off, like Sellers. Danny Kaye, he was very subdued off camera. They were plagued with sorrow, or something, I don't know what it was. I found that a little depressing, because you expected them to be on all the time. But Milton Berle was fantastic. He came with three index boxes filled with thousands of jokes, and stayed up until 2 am with us sharing them. I remember that for one scene he gave Statler and Waldorf, the old guys in the box, the best lines, and I said, "Milton, I thought you would want the laugh?" And he said, "No, if the situation is funny, we all come off good."'

Still going strong, the Muppets are now part of the Disney family.

Even more amazing is that these huge stars, many of them legends, were paid exactly the same nominal fee to appear. 'But the pampering was always good,' explains Baker. 'First class air travel, staying at the best hotels, a limousine to and from the studio, wined and dined. I credit Jim and David Lazer, they did everything with style, and that was what the Muppets were about. I wouldn't say the pampering was excessive, it was just done stylishly. These were stars and they were treated as stars.'

And they were all great. Some fitted in more comfortably than others, but the vast majority of them got into the spirit of the show and ended up loving the experience. 'These were unique people,' says Lazer. 'They were a little bit intimidated, coming to another country and working with – felt! But Jim and Frank and the puppeteers had a way and a sense of humour that could unravel their nerves. And after a few rehearsals, they would forget the puppeteer was there and go right head on with the puppet character. I remember Raquel Welch and Miss Piggy did a dance routine, and it was breathtaking. And Raquel treated Miss Piggy like another woman!'

On average, each show took a week to produce. A day to rehearse, a further day for the music recording, and then three days of actual shooting in the studio, with one day put aside for the guest star. Purely from a technical standpoint it was a gruelling schedule, with 24 shows produced a year. As for the Muppets themselves, they were mostly hand and rod puppets, made out of foam rubber, where the operator had one hand inside the puppet's head, manipulating the mouth, while the other hand controlled a rod attached to one or both of the puppet's hands. The rods were painted to blend into the background, and were so skilfully manipulated that audiences were often completely unaware of them. 'I think one of the reasons the show worked in all cultures was because the guys making the puppets, but mostly the people performing them, worked very hard for believability,' asserts Jane. 'Each character was worked on until it was believable as a character. You felt that you really knew somebody like that, you knew a Miss Piggy, these are people you knew.'

A major part of the success of *The Muppet Show* was the strength of its characters. Even today, Kermit and Miss Piggy remain instantly recognisable TV icons. Jim Henson himself operated Kermit, and some commented that it was difficult to tell where the personality of the puppeteer left off and where the mind of the frog began. They shared the same voice, the same gentle personality, and the same relaxed, unaffected manner of getting things done. While Kermit rarely lost his temper running things at the Muppet Theatre, Henson never lost his composure even under the most arduous pressure. 'People often ask me, "What was it like to work for Jim Henson?"' says Baker. 'I reply, "You didn't work for Jim Henson, you worked with Jim Henson." And that to me was the sign of who he was. It was never, "I'm the boss and you're the employee." Jim was the most extraordinary man to work with.'

The wonderful Kermit, the first puppet Jim Henson ever made.

What Mickey Mouse is to Disney, Kermit is to the Muppets. He is the face of the company and Jim Henson's first creation, conceived not long after he'd first started as a puppeteer, aged seventeen. Not far behind Kermit in popularity is Miss Piggy, who in the beginning was merely one of several pig characters on the show. 'But she had this quality that just came forward and wanted to be the star, demanded to be the star,' recalls Jane. 'And then she started playing up to Kermit and then falling for him, and always being very brazen and yet very vulnerable at the same time. And much of that is Frank Oz's performing. And Jerry Juhl's writing. And Kermit and Miss Piggy's love affair was built on the way Frank Oz and Jim worked together, they had a pretty special working relationship.'

Frank Oz, who also operated and lent his voice to Fozzie Bear, established a formidable working team with Henson. 'Who they are and were as individuals was reflected in their marriage of Kermit and Miss Piggy,' explains Baker. 'And Kermit and Fozzie Bear, and *Sesame Street*'s Ernie and Bert. They were all Jim and Frank. They were extensions of who they were, and their chemistry and timing were great. Jim and Frank to me were alongside those other classic comedy duos like Laurel and

Hardy. The audience don't know Jim and Frank in the same way, but they certainly know their characters.'

Despite overwhelming public demand, it was decided to end production on *The Muppet Show* in 1980, after 120 shows. There was a general feeling that it had run its course. Although it was still doing well, both Jim Henson and Lew Grade agreed that it was better to go out on top. Already Henson was setting his sights on movies. To cash in on the success of the Muppets, Grade financed two features – *The Muppet Movie* (1979) and *The Great Muppet Caper* (1981). Henson then diversified further, directing fantasy epics such as *The Dark Crystal* and *Labyrinth* starring David Bowie, with George Lucas as executive producer. Ultimately, Henson wanted to do what Oz has since achieved, become an accomplished and respected Hollywood director. 'He really did not think that he would go on and stay a puppeteer,' reveals Jane. 'He felt that he would like to be a movie director. But even though Jim wanted to direct films, it was obvious that what he did exceptionally well was bring these puppets to life.'

Irrespective of the success of the films and Jim Henson's other ventures, there was something so particularly special about *The Muppet Show* that was hard to match. 'I think it touched the innocence in all of us,' observes Lazer. 'Because the characters are innocent. They would always stick together and they would always help out one another. And there was never a bias. I never heard Jim or any of his family commit a racial slur or show any sign of bigotry, and that reflected in his work. All the characters were all different colours, and different species; the world was in perfect harmony. And that's why I think it touched everyone around the world. And Jim was one of the nicest people I've ever known in my life. It was the closest I've come to genius in my life, truly. And I've been round some important people. This was a visionary. And he had a love for harmony. He hated confrontations. He couldn't deal with it. And he had a magnificent sense of humour. He was so much fun to be with. He was truly a special, special person.'

What Jim Henson may have subsequently achieved, in what was already a career filled with dazzling originality, will never be known, as he died in 1990, aged only 54. 'It was very sudden and a huge shock,' recalls Baker. 'Jim was the healthiest guy in the world. I could count on one hand the times he was ill. But he got this viral infection and sadly didn't treat it. It all happened very quickly, and within a matter of days we lost him. That was a huge trauma. And the impact of his passing around the world hit me hard. I'd known him for 25 years, it was like working with your best friend, and I don't know that I had an appreciation for what he meant out there in the world. When you started seeing the massive media coverage surrounding his death, only then did it really hit you as to how big he was, and how big the Muppets were. I think we'd just taken it for granted, he was just the guy you went to work with every day.'

With Jim's passing, not only did the heart and soul of the company vanish overnight, but its creative force too. Jim's family, in particular his son Brian, stepped in to run the organisation. But people within were left wondering, could the company survive without Jim Henson? 'I would have said absolutely not,' admits Baker. 'Forget it, he's too powerful a figure, it's all built around Jim. But extraordinarily, in the aftermath of losing Jim and Brian stepping in, there was a group of us, and I like to think of myself as being part of that group, who rallied together and had this commitment that we were going to keep this company alive. We couldn't let it slip away from us. It was a real testament to everybody, because it could so easily have crumbled. My assessment was that you don't replace a Jim Henson. Jim was a one of a kind, a true genius, and you can't replace him. But what I believe kept us going was that there was a little bit of Jim in a lot of us, and together somehow we could keep the flag flying.'

In 2004, after over a decade of on-off negotiations, Disney bought the Muppets. 'Jim always felt that Disney offered the best home for the characters on a go forward basis,' says Baker. 'That they would live on in the theme parks, and on video, and all the various businesses that Disney are in. Jim had always realised that there isn't a better place than Disney.' Only time will tell if the Disney Corporation will do justice to Jim Henson's truly magical and unique legacy.

JESUS OF NAZARETH (1977)

Despite an incredible track record of hit shows like *The Saint*, *Thunderbirds*, *The Prisoner*, *The Muppet Show* and *The Persuaders*, Lew Grade was never more proud of anything he achieved than he was of *Jesus of Nazareth*.

One could say that the show was commissioned by the highest source possible. 'Lew had an audience with the Pope,' confirms Marcia Stanton. 'And the Pope had said, "I hope one day you will do the story of Jesus." And Lew was so overwhelmed by the meeting that he said yes.'

Lew had long been an admirer of director Franco Zeffirelli, notably his lyrical version of *Romeo and Juliet* and *Brother Sun, Sister Moon*, about the life of Francis of Assisi. To Lew he seemed the obvious choice for his Jesus project. But RAI television in Italy, who were joint financiers, wanted Ingmar Bergman. 'They gave Bergman something like $50,000 to write a draft script,' Zeffirelli recalls. 'But fortunately for me, and everybody I think, he did a fuck up. I have great respect for him, a great director, but he did not approach it properly. Actually, what he did was the controversial approach of Kazantzakis, the book that later was done by Scorsese for *The Last Temptation of Christ*. And Italian television when they read it, they felt very, very desperate. So Lew Grade didn't even read it, he said, "My choice is Zeffirelli. Either him or we won't do it." So if it wasn't for a Jewish British man, I would never have done *Jesus of Nazareth*, which I still rank as the highlight of my career.'

But Zeffirelli's initial instinct was to turn it down. He'd already made his religious film on Francis of Assisi, and that's why he'd earlier declined an offer to direct *Jesus Christ Superstar*. 'But my agent kept nagging me and said, "Franco, if you don't do it, somebody else will do it and you'll regret it later." So I finally said yes, because in every director's mind there is a hope one day to do a film of Jesus, the greatest tragedy ever told.'

Ever the entertainer, Lew Grade envisaged the film as packed with stars, realising, of course, that it would mean upping the budget far higher than he had originally anticipated. He decided to pursue Laurence Olivier for the cameo role of Nicodemus, assuming that once he'd landed the theatrical lord every other star would follow. He telephoned Olivier's agent, Laurence Evans, only to be told bluntly, 'Larry doesn't play cameos.' Lew was the last person in the world to give anything up without a fight, so he countered with, 'Look, tell Larry I'd very much like him to do it. Just remind him about the National Theatre's production of *Saturday, Sunday, Monday* which I put on at the Lyric Theatre, guaranteeing them all salaries, all the costs of the production, and then gave them an advance of £5,000.' A few hours later, Evans phoned back with the news that Olivier would be happy to play Nicodemeus.

As Lew anticipated, every major star he approached next was eager to sign on, once they heard Olivier was involved. Lew's nous and perseverance had guaranteed the greatest cast ever assembled for a TV production, including Ralph Richardson, James Mason, Michael York (as John the Baptist), Anthony Quinn, Rod Steiger and Olivia Hussey as a luminous Mary.

Now the search was on for the toughest role to fill, that of Jesus himself. Zeffirelli thought the task almost impossible, so he put a clause in his contract that he would not commit himself totally unless he found the right actor. 'And that was quite an extraordinary sequence of events. I saw Robert Powell in a play in London and thought he was a wonderful and intriguing actor, so I cast him for Judas and brought him to Rome. Then, when we saw his screen test, we were absolutely blinded by the strength of his eyes. And my cameraman said, "If you have a Judas with those eyes, what eyes must Jesus have?" So I grabbed Robert Powell at the airport, he was going back to London, and I said, "You must do another test." So we made him up to look like Jesus, and he worked instantly. And the next day I phoned Lew and said, "We've found the man for us. We've found our Jesus."'

There was just one small problem. Powell wasn't married at the time, but living with his girlfriend, former Pan's People dancer Babs Lord. It was a 'godsend' for the tabloids, recalls Michael Grade. 'Within a few days of Lew announcing that Robert Powell had been cast, *The Sun* or *The Mirror* had got hold of the story and came up with the headline: "Jesus living in sin with Pan's People dancer." And when the paper came out, Lew buzzed the head of the press office at ATV and sent for him, and said, "What the hell is this? What are they trying to do, crucify him?"'

For the pivotal role of John the Baptist, Zeffirelli personally chose Michael York – an actor he'd worked closely with on two previous films, *The Taming of the Shrew* and *Romeo and Juliet*. 'Playing John the Baptist was much less daunting a prospect than the task that Robert Powell faced in playing Jesus,' explains York. 'Although John figures prominently in religious literature and art, he seems not to be as well established in the collective unconscious as Jesus. Everyone has a very personal image of Christ, whereas John is a more shadowy figure. All I knew is that he had to be a blazingly charismatic figure. Obviously long hair and a beard were requisite for the role, so I grew my own. I hate having to stick on false hair. One other thing I had to do was white out any modern tooth fillings, so that, what with all that crying in the wilderness, everything looked authentically "biblical", even in close-up!'

After Lew Grade announced he was making a film about the life of Christ, a modicum of scepticism was voiced within the industry. At one business party, Lew was approached by writer Ted Willis, who asked playfully, 'Lew, I bet you can't name the twelve disciples?' 'I certainly can,' countered Lew. 'Well, name them,' Willis replied. 'Peter, Paul, Mark, Thomas . . .' And then he stopped. Willis said, 'Go on. Name the others.' Lew answered, 'I haven't finished reading the script yet.'

Despite his commercial approach to television, and the criticism levelled at him over the years for his formulaic programming, Grade was determined that *Jesus of Nazareth* would be of the highest possible quality. Personally hiring the much respected Anthony Burgess to write the screenplay was a clear demonstration of his intent. 'Although, when you think about it, Burgess wasn't an automatically safe choice to write *Jesus*,' posits Zeffirelli. 'Because he had done quite different material, *A*

Despite hit shows like The Saint, Thunderbirds *and* The Prisoner, *Lew Grade was never more proud of anything he achieved than* Jesus of Nazareth. *Originally considered to play Judas, it was his startling blue eyes that won Robert Powell the role of his career.*

Clockwork Orange, that kind of subject. But Lew Grade knew that Anthony was a Catholic, and he brought an extraordinary input into telling this story. In fact he wrote the whole script in sixteen days. He hid himself out in a place in France and after sixteen days he came out with this script. Actually, I can't believe it, but the six parts were all there. He was incredible; it was like an eruption of a volcano that he created this thing in a little over two weeks. And Lew said to me, "You see, you didn't believe in him." But it was a big jump from *A Clockwork Orange* to *Jesus of Nazareth*.'

One of Zeffirelli's main concerns when Burgess was writing the script was to prevent it turning into an anti-Jewish statement. 'That was naturally very important for Lew Grade as well. So I was very careful with Anthony Burgess not to turn this story of Jesus into an anti-Semitic affair, which has not been observed recently, by somebody who will remain nameless.'

Lew's faith in Zeffirelli was reciprocated tenfold, and the two men formed a strong union for the duration of the pressurised shoot. 'Lew had a wonderful relationship with Zeffirelli,' remembers Marcia. 'When they worked out the first budget Zeffirelli came back afterwards, having realised all the complications of the location filming and the actors' salaries, accommodation and travel, and told Lew the budget needed to be doubled. Lew sort of swallowed and said yes, because he had confidence in Zeffirelli.'

Zeffirelli himself claims that Lew Grade was perhaps the most remarkable person he ever worked with. 'He couldn't have been nicer. He kept looking at the dailies and sending me cables, every day, saying wonderful things. He was genuinely enthusiastic. And a tireless man, day and night he was available, always answered your calls and pushed you in the right direction. And he had great respect for the artist. But he managed sometimes to have an iron hand in a velvet glove. He was so positive and communicated confidence and enthusiasm to everybody.'

Zeffirelli likes to tell of one incident that seems to sum up Lew, when the TV mogul said to him, 'Franco, remember you are a movie director, but this is television. How many people can you put in a television screen? You better cut down the numbers.' Zeffirelli swore that Lew had considered asking him to cut down the number of the apostles!

To get the funding needed for so large an enterprise, Lew Grade had made a dynamite deal with TV giant NBC, and secured a sponsorship arrangement with the equally massive General Motors. 'But there was a row,' explains Michael Grade. 'The bible belt in America got exercised about the portrayal of Jesus on television, and General Motors started to wobble and backed out. Lew then had to go and find a new sponsor.'

Lew told his people in New York that he wanted to see the top man, not the advertising executive, but the top man at Procter & Gamble. 'Just give me ten minutes with him,' he urged. 'With some difficulty, they eventually fixed for Lew to see the president of Procter & Gamble,' Michael continues. 'So Lew flies to their head office in Cincinnati and walks into this pristine, mirror glass, brand new building. He's been told he's only got fifteen minutes, they've managed to squeeze him in. And everywhere there were signs saying, "Thank you for not smoking," "This is a non smoking building." And Lew said, "I was gasping for a cigar." So finally he gets in to see this man, whose desk is clear, there's no ashtray. They did a little bit of small talk, and Lew's conscious of the time. And the company president said, "What can I do for you, Lord Grade?" So Lew starts his sales pitch, and he said to me later, "As a salesman, you know when you're dying on your feet, and I was gasping." It wasn't coherent, so he stopped. And the company president said, "Are you all right, Lord Grade?" Lew said, "Actually, no, I'm not. I cannot do this project justice unless I'm allowed to smoke a cigar." So the fella said, "Of course." He presses his intercom; "Miss Jones, bring in an ashtray for Lord Grade." Now, there isn't an ashtray in the building. So this takes another ten minutes. Eventually she comes in with a saucer or something, and says, "I hope this is all right." "Yes, fine." And Lew told me, "I went to my pocket and I pulled out one of my cigars, and it was like a foot long. And the guy looked at me and said, 'Lord Grade, you're not going to smoke that, are you?'" And Lew said, "No, I'm going to hit you over the head with it if you don't buy this show." At which point the fella just fell apart, they bonded and he made the sale. Lew loved to tell that story.'

In many ways, *Jesus of Nazareth* became something of an obsession for Lew, taking over his life in a way no other programme had done before. Cyril Frankel recalls one meeting he had with Lew during this time. 'I had an open door to Lew, and he was really remarkable. And I remember one day, going up in the lift to see him, and as the doors opened there he was, with a cigar at 7.30 in the morning, and he said, "Cyril, I can only give you 30 seconds because I'm up to here in Jesus Christ."'

Most of *Jesus of Nazareth* was shot in Tunisia and the Middle East. 'My abiding memory of filming was how cold it was,' recalls Michael York. 'Dressed only in my designer rags in Tunisia during springtime. I remember icy dungeons where the film crew wore ski outfits, and baptising in a chilly River Jordan. But I had great words to speak and the fiery rhetoric kept me warm, as did the lashings of pasta from the Italian crew. By this time, Zeffirelli and I had established a good working relationship and could rely on each other. When he needed some extra words in a scene where John was speaking, he trusted me to go to the Bible and find an appropriate passage. He was passionately serious about this project, but there was always a prevailing sense of humour and irony that lightened the workload and relaxed the atmosphere.'

The inevitable end.

To validate every aspect of the production, a panel of religious experts was hired to act as advisers. Zeffirelli even brought in a rabbi as a bar mitzvah teacher, despite the fact there were no bar mitzvahs during the period, as the rabbi tried explaining to the director. 'Nonsense,' insisted Zeffirelli, 'I've already built the synagogue.' So the bar mitzvah scene went ahead, but the boy playing Jesus stumbled at the important moment. 'Cut!' Zeffirelli glared at the rabbi, who excused himself by saying, 'Franco, every Jewish boy stumbles on his bar mitzvah.' To which Zeffirelli replied, 'Not the son of God.'

It was a strenuous shoot and the pressure was enormous for Zeffirelli, but he wasn't fazed by it at all. 'I studied for two years, and then after that you have to trust yourself and dive into it with no fear, and just hope that God's hand is guiding you. But most of all I was impressed by Robert Powell. What he went through, how much he studied; he gave his blood. There were scenes that were not physically bearable for a man who played that role. There were no special effects, everything was for real. And he was there with strong conviction, day by day, doing these incredibly difficult scenes, the last supper, or the resurrection of Lazarus, the crucifixion. The demands on him were incredible. He was a tremendous professional.'

Not only was *Jesus of Nazareth* one of the television events of the 1970s, but, at over six and a half hours long, it remains one of the greatest ever entertainment achievements. Universally praised by critics, it was also a ratings smash around the world, and today has been seen by over two billion people. 'Lew knew it was going to be good,' says Marcia. 'I mean, that cast and Anthony Burgess writing. It was an incredible team. You just don't see that sort of thing anymore. It was a masterpiece. I remember the Pope made a speech on the balcony overlooking St Peter's Square, saying everybody should go home and watch *Jesus of Nazareth* on television that evening. You couldn't have better PR than that.'

THE RETURN OF THE SAINT (1978-79)

After a break of almost a decade, and with the original shows still drawing strong ratings around the world, *Saint* producer Robert Baker believed the time was right to resurrect Simon Templar for the late seventies audience. 'I suggested *The Return of the Saint* to Lew, and he didn't need any persuading. I then spoke to Leslie Charteris, and suggested to him that the time was right for it to come back, and he agreed too. We set up a deal and took it to Lew and he said, "OK, now find an actor to play the Saint."'

Baker already had someone in mind, a young actor by the name of Ian Ogilvy who had appeared in the cult horror films of director Michael Reeves, notably *Witchfinder General*. 'It was Bob's wife actually, that got me the part,' reveals Ogilvy. 'The story is that his wife was watching me on television – it might have been *Upstairs, Downstairs* – and she said, "Come and have a look at this chap, wouldn't he make a good Saint?" And Bob agreed.'

The two met over lunch, and Baker asked Ogilvy if he would consider starring as the Saint, should the series return. 'Not only would I consider it,' replied the eager young actor, 'but I'd almost certainly agree.' After that Ogilvy heard nothing for years, presuming the idea had quietly withered and died, until he got a call from his agent. 'Did you ever hear of a man called Bob Baker?' Ogilvy sat bolt upright in his chair. 'Yes, why?' His agent continued, 'He wants you to do this television programme.' 'So it was really rather an easy way of getting a job,' Ogilvy explains. 'I didn't have to audition for it or anything. I wish all jobs were like that.'

Ogilvy was perfectly cast; few, if any, other British actors in the seventies could have played the part of Simon Templar and made it their own. He possessed the proper upper-crust bearing and dashing good looks. More importantly, Baker saw in Ian Ogilvy an actor who would keep the series' continuity going, in that physically he was a similar type to Roger Moore. 'Although he didn't have the charisma of Roger, I'm afraid,' admits Baker. 'Ian's a good actor, probably a better actor than Roger, and a nice guy, excellent to work with, but he didn't quite have that presence Roger had.'

Putting pen to paper, Ogilvy was under no illusion that this was a star-making opportunity, that overnight he'd become a household name. 'I was in my mid-thirties, so I'd been round the block a few times, I wasn't some little raw beginner. I knew perfectly well that it would make me very well known. But it didn't give me any pause at all. I agreed to the series immediately.' There was also the pressure of taking over from such a huge personality as Roger Moore, whose portrayal of the Saint had entered television legend. 'Ian was nervous about taking over from Roger.

Perfect casting – what other British actor of the late seventies could have played Simon Templar other than Ian Ogilvy?

Very nervous,' confirms Baker. 'I remember on one occasion we were filming in Italy, and Roger came to visit us on the set and to spend the evening with us, and Ian was very reluctant to meet Roger, he felt embarrassed. I think Ian was a little unsure of himself, because Roger had been such a big success.'

As originally conceived, Ogilvy was to have played Simon Templar junior and the series, rather uninspiringly, was to be called *The Son of the Saint*. Thankfully, Baker scrapped that idea. After all, a host of other fictional heroes, like James Bond and Sherlock Holmes, had survived being played by different actors, so why not the Saint? As for Ogilvy, he was left pretty much alone to come up with his own interpretation of the character. 'I always used to say that there were two expressions with the Saint, smiling and not smiling. Basically I saw him as a fun character. I liked the fact that he never took life himself particularly seriously. I have a theory about the Saint, which was like Bond and all those other characters, and it's that these hero roles don't actually have much character, so therefore it's your personality that you're putting across. So I knew that Roger did Roger and I did Ian. People were either going to like Ian or not like Ian. They liked Roger a lot and I just hoped they'd like me.'

Like most of its predecessors, *The Return of the Saint* had to be sold stateside to recoup its considerable budget. And so, a Hollywood producer by the name of Anthony Spinner, who'd worked on shows like *The Man from UNCLE* and *Cannon*, was brought in for the sole purpose of tailoring the stories for US consumption. He'd hover in the background and say things like, 'Better not do that, because that won't work in America.' Or, 'Let's do this, that will work in America.' Ogilvy bemoaned his presence and the all-powerful American influence that, in his opinion, was to the detriment of the series. As the TV critic of *The Daily Express* remarked, 'The show has been castrated to comply with what the American network deemed acceptable fodder, with the result that it was the worst of both worlds.'

Spinner also demanded that scenes of excessive violence be cut, a decision that caused further friction. 'I kept telling them, you just can't have ten murders and five rapes in each episode,' he complained to *The Hollywood Reporter*. 'Sometimes they believe me and sometimes they don't. It all depends on the day.' Spinner was aware that the prevailing televisual climate in America was staunchly anti-violence. However, in Britain tastes tended toward harder edged shows like *The Sweeney*, and so, by comparison, the new *Saint* looked a bit tame and timid. 'I always used to think it was crazy that two enormous, hulking brutes would come towards me, and I'd hit them once and they'd just fall over,' remembers Ogilvy. 'I always wanted to say, "Can I maybe have an iron bar in my hand or something?" But no, I wasn't allowed to do any of that. Really, a lot of the guts went out of the show, I think, because of this.'

The biggest irony is that the political climate of the late seventies lent itself to introducing a tougher Saint, although the series did tackle some hard-hitting contemporary issues like terrorism and drugs. 'I don't think what Spinner was saying was wrong for the time,' muses Ogilvy. 'It was just I don't think it helped the show very much. And also, this was a family show that they thought kids ought to be able to see at seven o'clock in the evening. I just felt it took some of the edge out of it.'

The final straw for Ogilvy came when Spinner wrote an episode that had the Saint fighting assorted vampires, and brandishing crucifixes like a male version of Buffy. 'He wanted to take the character of the Saint in a direction that nobody had ever gone before, and to be honest I thought it was a terrible mistake. And in a panic I went to Leslie Charteris, with whom I'd become quite good friends. We would discuss with each other the latest script that was coming our way, because Leslie used to get all the scripts and expressed a lot of strong views on them, good and bad, but sometimes really terrifically, wonderfully bad. And Leslie managed to squash that particular episode, and it was never made. I know the Saint is a bit of a fantasy figure, but that's really a major departure and we just thought it was demented, and not at all what the character was about.'

As a link to the past, Robert Baker hired most of the original production crew from the sixties *Saint*, as well as a lot of the same directors and writers, including ITC veteran Tony Williamson. Sadly, this was to be Williamson's last ITC credit. The man who contributed to *Danger Man*, *The Champions*, *Randall and Hopkirk (Deceased)*, *The Persuaders* and more died in 1991. Shortly before his death, Williamson lamented the

Left: *ex-Bond girl Britt Ekland guest-starred in one episode.* Top right: *as good as any film poster of the time; how the new* Saint *series was sold to the world.* Bottom right: *it was a tough job being the new Saint, but somebody had to do it.*

fact that the kind of shows he made his name on were just not being made anymore by British TV. 'We no longer have entrepreneurs such as Lew Grade with vision and imagination prepared to back producers and writers to make series that are both popular and inventive. These days too many decisions are taken by accountants.'

Bringing back so many of the old writers didn't fit particularly well with Anthony Spinner, who complained bitterly to his colleagues back in Hollywood that Lew Grade was living in the sixties, 'And surrounds himself with people who still think that an adventure show needs a lot of big breasted females with spike heels zooming around in motorboats.'

Ogilvy had his own concerns about some of the writing. 'I would get these scripts and some of them were kind of cobbled together, I thought. And some of my lines I'd find really hard to say, they were a bit corny and clichéd.' Today, the actor admits it was a bit presumptuous of him to alter his own dialogue, and it led to a tricky encounter with director Leslie Norman. 'Les had lost his vocal chords, he had the same operation Jack Hawkins had, so he spoke with that belch speaking. Everybody was terrified of Les, he was one of those very short-tempered directors who was like a dictator on the set. And I was warned about this. And on the first day I had rewritten the scene quite extensively, and I met him and said, "Les, this scene, I've rewritten it." He said, "Why?" "Les, because it's fucking horrible. It's a terrible, terrible scene. It's really badly written and I've just changed the dialogue, because the dialogue sucks." And he went, "I wrote it." And I went, "OK, I can't take any of that back now, can I? But I still think it sucks." "Well, what do you want to say?" So I told him and he said, "Well, that's crap too." So we looked at each other and I said, "Maybe we could meet in the middle, how about that?" And he grinned at me, and we became the best of friends after that. I mean, it was presumptuous of me to rewrite anything. I believe Roger never rewrote a word. Roger said, "Where do I stand? What do I say?" I'm sure that's what made Roger very popular with Bob Baker. I'm not sure my fiddling with the scripts was all that popular.'

Another veteran asked by Baker to contribute was Cyril Frankel, who, despite being ITC's most prolific director, had never before helmed a *Saint*. 'The reason was Roger Moore,' Frankel reveals. 'I regarded Roger as a friend and, as he'd been playing the part for years, and as I regard myself as an actor's director, I didn't feel I could be of any help and I would be just doing a technical job. So although I was offered it, I declined.' Frankel was asked to direct a special two-part episode of *Return*, but his unusual working methods didn't find favour with some members of the crew. 'I allow intuition to tell me what to do. This caused problems on *The Saint* with the production manager, who came to me and said, "What are your next three shots?" And I said, "I really don't know." And he said, "But you must know, you must tell me." I said, "No. I take each scene as it comes and find a way."'

Frankel hadn't worked for ITC since the early seventies, when his patience had finally snapped over the dearth of quality scripts on *The Adventurer*. 'I got one script, "Icons Are Forever", and I found some passages which I thought needed a rewrite, so I made an appointment with our producer, Monty Berman, and Dennis Spooner to go over these points. And poor Dennis, who had obviously reached the end of his patience with all this rewriting, said to me, "Cyril, why are you always finding faults, why don't you just shoot it, it's only for television?" So I said, "Right!" And I went away and thought, "Do I resign now?" This was episode nineteen out of 26, and I was contracted to direct two or three more. I decided not to resign but to find a way of shooting it. So I made it very stylistic, creating unusual camera angles, and then, of course, when they had the rough cut, Dennis said, "I told you it would be alright." But I said to my agent, "No more production line television, I didn't come into this industry for bad writing." And he said, "Cyril, are you sure?" He then rang me up soon afterwards, saying that they wanted me for *The New Avengers*, and I said, "No."'

Another veteran was Roy Ward Baker, who since the original series had alternated between television and films with huge success, notably with Hammer, directing the classics *Quatermass and the Pit* and *The Vampire Lovers*. Raymond Austin too was invited back to work on what would be his last show for ITC, before landing his big break, a contract in the United States. He'd just finished his *Saint* episode, and was prepping the next one, when the call from Hollywood came. Having given him his first shot at directing, Robert Baker wasn't about to stand in his friend's way now. 'I went to see Bob,' Austin recalls. 'And said, "I've got a deal with you on *The Saint* and I'm going to stick to it." And he said, "You've got to be crazy. You've got a chance like this. Go." And I said, "What about our contract?" He said, "Forget it. I can get another director. Go. You'll be crazy not to." So I got on the plane and went. That's the sort of nice guy Bob Baker is.'

In the States, Austin carved out a hugely successful TV career directing episodes of *Charlie's Angels*, *Hart to Hart*, *Quincy* and *Magnum*, among many others. But at first it was something of a culture shock. 'When we shot an *Avengers* or a *Saint* we had ten days. My first show in America was *Hawaii Five-0* and we had five days. Over in the States crews shoot much faster. In England, in the days of those ITC shows, after I'd say, "Cut," the first assistant would say, "Check the gate," meaning check there's no hairs in the gate, or you'd have to go again. In America you didn't check for hairs in the gate, if there was a hair in the gate, that's life, you'd just use another shot or cut round it in the editing room. Because in America it was about numbers and money, not about the ethics and the quality of the show.'

Like Roger Moore before him, Ogilvy looked into the possibility of moving behind the camera and directing the odd episode. 'I proposed this to Bob and he said, "Next series." But there never was a next series.'

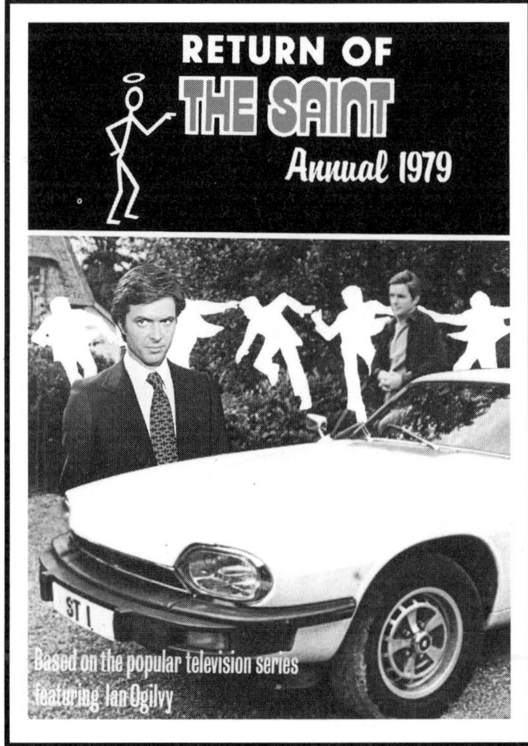

As compensation for not providing a car for the Roger Moore series, Jaguar presented Ogilvy's Templar with a gleaming XJ-S.

One obvious advantage the new *Saint* enjoyed over its predecessor was the use of exotic locations. As opposed to somewhere like Monte Carlo being replicated – sometimes laughably badly – on the studio lot, Bob Baker was determined to shoot for real in places as diverse as the South of France, Venice and Rome. In authentic surroundings, Ogilvy was able to get a handle on the role and get stuck into the physical requirements dictated by such an action series, but not to the extent of handling his own stunt work. 'Actors do not do their own stunts – period. A stunt by definition is something that is so dangerous that if an actor did it, it could easily incapacitate him. So no actors do their own stunts, because the insurance companies don't allow it. What actors are allowed to do is what is called action, which is fight scenes. So I always said publicly, when asked, "No, I don't do my own stunts, I'm not stupid." First of all, the stuntman does it better than I can, and secondly, the hard fact of the matter is, if a stuntman hurts himself or gets killed, it's terrible but the show goes on. If I get hurt or killed the show stops.'

While shooting one episode, a director asked if Ogilvy could jump off a ten-foot wall, to which the actor replied that he could but might break his ankle on landing. But if the director pulled the camera back twenty feet his stunt double could do it. 'I got over the whole macho business of wanting to show everybody how brave I was very quickly indeed,' Ogilvy confesses. 'My stunt double, Les Crawford, came to me and said, "Ian, every time you do one of these stunts you're taking money out of my mouth. Quite honestly, don't you occasionally want to sit down and let somebody else do the fucking work?" And I went, "OK, yeah." I was actually told off by my stunt double. You learn.'

Guest star Burt Kwouk, however, had no hesitation about taking his role to the limit. 'I remember sitting in one of those little four-seater Cessna planes in my episode, and somebody came up and said, "This is what you do. We'll switch it on, these are the pedals, you hold on to this and you move the pedals and it will go along the ground slowly, but don't let it get off the ground because you're not insured." Well, I couldn't resist that, could I? So, I took it off the ground a few feet and let it drop again. I don't think they were very happy about that.'

As with the earlier shows, guest stars were another feature of the new series, and Ogilvy was given a complement of stunning seventies sex goddesses to rival Moore's sixties harem: the likes of Britt Ekland, Diane Keen, Judy Geeson, Kate O'Mara, Jenny Hanley, Susan Penhaligan, Gayle Hunnicutt and Rula Lenska.

As shooting continued, Ogilvy began to feel the strain. The press interest, from the day he was announced as the new Saint, was enormous, and the production schedule was gruelling, as he was pretty much required for every scene. 'I've always said that the *Saint* show was quite tough, because you are on your own. There are very few shows that I can think of where the leading character is completely alone; there are no other regulars at all. So the burden of the work was on me very heavily, and on Roger. I was always the first called and the last to go at night. My wife at the time used to sometimes ask Bob to try and find a way of letting me sleep in an hour or so. "Couldn't you use the guest actor or something and let the poor man rest occasionally?" she'd say. It was a hard grind. But it was terrific. And you never complain. You're working.'

The ITV network saw *The Return of the Saint* as the perfect vehicle to launch its entire Sunday night schedule, and gave it a 7.15pm slot. 'When the children are still up and television executives believe their parents do not want to be mentally stimulated,' as one critic pointed out. *The Sun* was even more vindictive: 'What a disappointment the first episode turned out to be. The character of the new Saint has been as thinly drawn as his matchstick man trademark. No actor could do much with it and Mr. Ogilvy is no exception. As Dorothy Squires might say – come back Roger Moore, all is forgiven.' This was par for the course as far as reviews went. 'I thought the critics were going to have a field day,' recalls Ogilvy. 'Which they did, they all ripped the show to pieces. They were reasonably kind to me, but they weren't very kind to the show. But that was alright. People who watch *The Saint* don't actually read the critics. It wasn't a show that critics really needed to bother with. I haven't seen them for

Ian Ogilvy confessed to being anxious in taking on the role of Simon Templar. 'The public liked Roger a lot and I just hoped they'd like me.'

a long time, but I thought they looked very good, I thought they were quite stylishly done. Let's face it, this wasn't great art we were doing, it was entertainment. And of their type and of their period I think they were entertaining.'

The public agreed and watched the show in their millions, making their own minds up as to whether Ogilvy was a worthy successor to Moore. 'Taking over the role of the Saint was going to be difficult for Ian, because they were always going to compare him with Roger,' insists Baker. 'So, until you get over the initial acceptance of the new Saint, you're going to have problems. We made one series. Had we made a second series I think he would've probably been accepted. The same as Roger had difficulty in being accepted initially as Bond. So I think Ian had the slight disadvantage of following Roger.'

In London one evening, during the show's run, Ogilvy bumped into the American Broadway star Elaine Stritch, who was in residence at the Savoy Hotel. 'It's great to meet you,' she said. 'But when I first saw your show I thought you were terrible. I thought the show was terrible, I hated the show, it was godawful. But my goodness, you have just got better and better and now I'm hooked.' Ogilvy smiled before pointing out, 'Miss Stritch – they weren't shown in the order they were filmed. All that's happened is you've got used to it.'

Alas, Lew Grade never did. Despite being sold to 73 countries, the tycoon cancelled the show to the utter amazement of everyone concerned. 'I was contracted to six series of *The Saint*,' reveals Ogilvy. 'And there was no question about it; we were going to make more, because we were a huge hit. So it came as rather a surprise. As far as I understand it, Lord Grade didn't like the show. He particularly didn't like the fact that it was the most expensive show he had on his books. And at the time he was taking a lot of the profits from his television shows, and plying them into his very unsuccessful film ventures. So the first thing he was going to cut was an expensive show like *The Saint*, which was costing him far too much money as far as he was concerned. And anyway, I don't think he ever liked us. I'm pretty sure he didn't like me. I never met him. This was my big boss and I never met the guy. I'm told that his accountant said to him, "But Lord Grade, we have sold all over the world, and next time round we don't actually have to spend so much money. We could shoot the whole thing in England." But he wasn't interested. He just wanted to get rid of it. I think he was very short-sighted.'

Maybe the timing was all wrong. The golden age of the playboy adventurers was dead and buried. Swinging bachelors like Simon Templar and Jason King had pioneered a masculine credo of leisure and materialism, but, by the mid-seventies, they looked positively prehistoric alongside more current TV action heroes like Carter and Regan from *The Sweeney*. 'The new *Saint*s were well made shows,' says Baker. 'But I think the timing was wrong. The glorious sixties were over and we were in the seventies, and the world was altering very rapidly, we were beginning to get terrorism, drug-related crime, you had to take a slightly more serious view. And the character was a little more serious; he didn't have the flippancy of Roger. So we had Templar get involved in stories with terrorists, and that sort of thing, which was right for the period, but it didn't have the tongue-in-cheek quality of *The Saint*. It didn't have quite the same magical quality. So I think the time was wrong. Successes are entirely due to the right thing at the right time, that's the secret, and you can't double guess that, you've got to be lucky.'

In the era of punk rock, Ian Ogilvy's version of the Saint represented slightly hackneyed, if pleasingly nostalgic, viewing. 'Anachronistic, I would call it,' says the actor. 'I mean, I hated the early clothes that we had. I kept saying, "This is going to date us. In two years time these really hip clothes I'm wearing now are going to look ridiculous!"'

Most significantly of all, *The Return of the Saint* proved to be the last of ITC's big-budget adventure series. Yet it's fondly remembered, and Ogilvy, certainly in England, is still heavily associated with it, even though it was a quarter of a century ago. 'I have to be honest that *The Saint* was what put me on the map. I was not unknown before, but I became really rather famous after that, but really rather poor, and there's absolutely no fucking point being famous if you're also poor, the two do not go together. And one of the reasons why I like America is that the two can't go together. In America if you're famous, you are rich, period, because people pay you for fame. People go, "We made him a star, let us now capitalise on it." And the English situation was, "We've made him a star, now he can piss off." I sound angry, but it was far too long ago for me to be angry about. Looking back it was wonderful, absolutely wonderful making that show. It was the best time. I was king. The crew called me "guvnor", which was a mark of respect and affection, which was terrific. We all got along very well. It was a very professional team. I enjoyed it enormously.'

Ogilvy moved out to the States in 1989 because, after *The Saint* was cancelled, he'd found work very hard to come by. Within the industry, there was a feeling of,

'No, no, we can't use you – you're the Saint.' So he went back to the theatre until he secured roles in numerous American television series. Finding the work enjoyable, Ogilvy decided to set up permanent home in the States, where he has embarked upon a successful second career as an author.

Ogilvy's *Saint* connection almost landed him the most coveted role in movies; that of James Bond himself. 'There was a period when Roger was going to stop. And every time the tabloids had a blank page to fill they would always do, "Who's going to be the new Bond?" and they'd put my picture up with a lot of other actors. I just thought it was terribly funny. And then, during that period, I was invited to lunch, and one of the guests was Jerry Juroe, head of publicity with the Bond company Eon. And after lunch he said, "Look, I don't know really whether I should tell you this, but you're a nice guy so I think I will. We've been looking at lots of people and your name was very seriously considered, because of the whole Roger Moore/*Saint* connection. But the decision has been made, and if we wanted another Roger Moore type you'd have got the part, but we don't, we want another Sean Connery." And the relief I felt, I swear to you, was, "Thank God for that," because I don't really think I was right for Bond. I don't think Roger was right for Bond either, by the way. I didn't have a hard enough edge to play Bond.'

Despite its unceremonious cancellation, rumours persisted of further *Saint* series. One did turn up in the late eighties, a fairly insipid collection of made-for-TV movies with Simon Dutton that made the Ogilvy version look like *Ben Hur* by comparison. There were also plans for a film, backed by Paramount and originated by Charteris and Baker. 'It was going to be Saint and son of the Saint,' Baker reveals. 'This was an idea that Leslie Charteris and I had that the Saint has a bastard son from a former girlfriend, and it's this relationship between father and son. The idea was to introduce this young character and then the old man would bail out, leaving the young character as the Saint and to do more films. We buggered around for a year with scripts. It was developing slowly. Then Paramount brought in a new director who had his own concept of the Saint, and that's when it went off the rails.' The project eventually metamorphosed into the Val Kilmer *Saint* movie that totally misunderstood what the character was all about, and bombed spectacularly. 'Val Kilmer met Roger in Los Angeles after that film opened,' says Baker. 'And told him, "We certainly fucked up *The Saint*, didn't we?"' Quite.

SAPPHIRE AND STEEL (1979-82)

Nominated as 'Perhaps the most enigmatic fantasy series of all time' by sci-fi journal *Starburst*, *Sapphire and Steel* was the brainchild of P. J. Hammond – a prolific television writer, mainly in the field of police thrillers like *Z Cars* and *The Sweeney*. He'd been watching the 1960 George Pal movie *The Time Machine* on television with his family, when the idea of a time travel series for children struck him. But instead of going backwards and forwards in time, he thought, what if time was a malevolent force able to break into the present, snatch people and cause disruption? He hit upon the concept of a pair of time detectives from another dimension, who arrive at the scene of a time disturbance to restore the natural order. 'I wanted to write a sci-fi series that I hoped would be different,' explains Hammond. 'And one that would appeal to all age groups and both sexes. And a series that relied upon character and atmosphere rather than chases and threats of physical violence. I also felt it important to write about ordinary people who find themselves caught up in strange circumstances, and are then helped by extraordinary beings.'

Having previously worked for Thames TV, Hammond pitched his idea – then called *The Time Menders* – to one of the station's prominent producers, Pamela Lonsdale. 'She liked the idea and commissioned the first episode,' Hammond recalls. 'Hoping to whet the appetites of those reading the script, I left the episode open-ended. This seemed to work and, while there was some concern about which age group to aim at, the children's drama department liked the pilot episode very much. Unfortunately, the then head of Thames drama felt that the idea had no mileage as a series, and [it] was dropped.'

Hammond still believed in his project, and sent it to the children's drama department of Southern Television. There it aroused some interest, and Hammond was invited down to their offices in Southampton to talk about it. 'But in the meantime, David Reid at ATV had read the pilot episode, and was excited enough to commission a six-part series without the need of story-lines. It was also his idea to change the title to *Sapphire and Steel*. And he was right.' Apparently, Reid found Hammond's script and ideas so intriguingly disturbing he'd had trouble sleeping afterwards.

Reid's first act was to hire Shaun O'Riordan as producer/director. A former actor in series like *The Adventures of Robin Hood* and *The Larkins*, O'Riordan moved behind the camera in the sixties, directing episodes of *Emergency Ward 10*. He also forged a reputation as an effective director of atmospheric suspense dramas, notably by helming episodes of Brian Clemens' *Thriller*. Hammond met with O'Riordan and, after some useful discussions, set about writing the remaining episodes. At this point, *Sapphire and Steel* was still planned as a children's series. Then things started to get very ambitious. Adhering to ATV/ITC's policy of stellar casting, Reid insisted the roles of *Sapphire and Steel* be played by 'name' actors, thus lifting the show firmly out of a children's slot and into primetime. The scripts were sent to Glasgow-born David McCallum, still a cult idol for his portrayal of Ilya Kuryakin in *The Man from UNCLE*, and Joanna Lumley, who had recently scored big as Purdey in *The New Avengers*. Both actors were intrigued enough by the unusual nature of the premise to commit to the project.

Hammond was especially pleased with the choices of McCallum and Lumley. 'They matched the characters I had had all along in my mind's eye. Both were wonderful to work with. They brought depth to the characters and added extra touches, such as humour and a feeling of friendly rivalry between them. And they were not acting simply for the sake of it. They believed in those characters. Even though the plots were pure fantasy they always played it straight, and I believe that was part of its charm.'

The success of *Sapphire and Steel* owes much to the performances of its two stars. Joanna Lumley especially enjoyed working on the series after the strain of The *New Avengers*, where she'd sometimes handle scenes from anything up to four different episodes in a single day. McCallum was equally enthusiastic, involving himself as much as he could in production matters – from wardrobe to makeup to the writing – which led to occasional conflicts with his directors. It was this serious approach that informed much of the way he played Steel, with a hard, sometimes cold edge, a man who had little time for anything save the mission. Joanna commented that young fans of the show told her they were afraid of Steel, but felt they could come up and hold Sapphire's hand and everything would be alright.

Throughout the series, Sapphire and Steel remained enigmatic characters. We

The two charismatic stars of Sapphire and Steel: *Joanna Lumley and David McCallum.*

know Steel is mentor and intellectual guide to Sapphire, and the team's organiser, trained to deploy her far greater paranormal powers to the optimum level. But almost nothing of who, what or where they came from is ever revealed. 'I always wanted the origins of the characters to be a mystery,' Hammond explains. 'I believe that it is somehow rewarding if we do not know everything, and I had no intention of boring the audience with too much science. I also believed that viewers should have the opportunity of making up their own minds about where the duo came from.'

Years later, Joanna Lumley put forward the interesting theory that both Sapphire and Steel were in fact ghosts. 'We died a long time ago, which is why we are able to disappear and flash in and out of walls and turn time backwards and forwards.'

On set, both actors enjoyed a good relationship, despite having wildly different personalities and habits. McCallum was a fastidious health nut, while Joanna was a voracious smoker. Inevitably, there were rumours that the pair either detested each other or were lovers. 'I could never work out if they were having an affair or not, because they used to have breakfast together occasionally,' recalled O'Riordan. 'But I never found out.'

In all, 34 half-hour episodes were produced between 1979 and 1982 at the ATV studios in Elstree. Most of the stories were studio-bound, which added to the claustrophobic feeling and eeriness of the show. 'The stories were deliberately atmospheric and scary,' confirms Hammond. 'I did not want to write about ray guns and knives and monsters, but about things that go bump in the night and our own inherited fears, plus the terror that can be found in everyday objects. In other words, things off-centre, things not as they seem. And I think that's scary enough, because

The Avengers *meets* The Man from UNCLE.

part of it all is the ability to scare ourselves.'

Each story is notable for its high level of imagination and esoteric qualities. Hammond's stories were grandly ambitious for a show aimed at a family teatime audience, an almost unique blend of sci-fi, ghost story and thriller. Plots included a faceless form that traps people in old photographs, a black entity that feeds on the resentment of dead soldiers, and a country house party that is gradually slipping back in time to the 1930s, and where the guests are being bumped off one by one. Like the show's multitude of fans, Hammond has his favourite stories and is also not averse to criticising his own work. 'I'm very fond of the eight-part railway station story, even though I would have preferred it as a six-part. This would have tightened it up. However, my favourite is "Adventure Four", with the shape that lives in photographs. In retrospect, I felt that "Adventure Three" – the time capsule – could have been less complicated. This story would also have benefited from, say, computer graphics, which were not around at the time.'

Sapphire and Steel also required a great deal of intellectual engagement on the part of the viewer, at times perhaps too much. McCallum and Lumley were constantly wary of the stories becoming overly confusing. 'My mother used to have a cleaner, Mrs. Puttock,' McCallum recalled. 'She saw the first episode and said, "I loved it, but I didn't understand it." So we always tried to make the stories Puttock-proof.' Joanna particularly felt that excessive complexity would make viewers switch off. Mystery was fine and exciting, but not when it was too dense. On one episode, in mid-scene, she walked off-set declaring, 'For fuck's sake, I can't do this. I don't understand it. I really don't fucking understand it.'

The critics were mostly in sympathy with Joanna. 'I was thinking of running a competition for the best description of what exactly is going on in *Sapphire and Steel*,' pondered *The Sun*'s TV critic. 'But I suspect the only entry would come from P. J. Hammond who must have a plausible explanation up his sleeve since he wrote this load of old rubbish.' Others revelled in its complex nature, particularly *The Daily*

Telegraph: 'I haven't got a clue what's going on, but it is still gripping enough for me to make sure I'm around when the final part is shown next week.'

To complicate matters further, none of the stories had an official title, being referred to simply as 'Adventure One', 'Adventure Two', etc. 'Giving the stories separate titles was something that I never considered at the time,' Hammond admits. 'I suppose I saw Sapphire and Steel's assignments as one long story divided by changes in location.'

Aiding O'Riordan behind the camera and directing alternating stories was David Foster – a staff director at ATV. His toughest assignment was auditioning child actors for one episode, and getting some 60 brats turning up all accompanied by their 'theatre mums'. These were notoriously competitive on behalf of their children, bleating out things like, 'My daughter goes first!' One very young girl came in with her mum and Foster gently asked, 'If I tell you to cry, do you think you could cry, is that possible?' The mother immediately interjected, 'Of course she can cry,' and slapped her hard across the face. 'There you go.'

Hammond always made sure that he personally attended all the recording sessions. 'And I have lots of good memories from those frantic but inspired days. The lighting man worried about having to light absolute darkness, yet managed to do it. And I shall never forget the eerie sight of children, wearing sepia clothes and sepia makeup, queuing for food in the studio restaurant.'

Almost immediately, *Sapphire and Steel* proved popular with audiences, especially amongst the young, generating its own comic strip in *Look-In* which ran for almost two years. 'I was very pleased with the reaction of both the audience and the critics,' says Hammond. 'There were a few angry protests because we showed supernatural goings-on so early in the evening, and others were concerned about Steel's callousness, especially in the episode where he sacrifices the life of a ghost hunter.' To prove his point, Hammond sent this author two contrasting letters he received from the public, one for the show, the other very much against:

For: *This is the first time I've ever written to any TV people concerning any TV programme, but having just watched the first episode of* Sapphire and Steel *I dropped the washing up, the ironing and the sewing to write and say Congratulations. Best thing since* Dr Who.

Never thought I'd see this kind of quality on ITV – it's riveting. I couldn't drag myself away to make a cuppa and my six-year-old son refused to finish his chips till it was over.

Well done to all involved – lots more please.

Against: *I feel that I must protest at the timing of the new series* Sapphire and Steel.

My two children, aged six and eight, were looking forward to a new enjoyable programme to watch before they went to bed but, after watching just a few minutes of this programme, were terrified and begging not to be left upstairs alone.

As soon as I realised that the programme was totally unsuitable I switched it off and then had to spend quite a considerable time calming them sufficiently to go to sleep.

The public momentum the show had earned was almost derailed when, a quarter way through 'Adventure Two', there was a technician's strike that took the entire ITV network off the air. When the station returned to normal it was wisely decided to show the story again from the start, rather than resuming where it left off. But the damage had already been done. 'The TV strike was a bit of bad luck, and I felt that it did affect things. It meant that the viewers were made to wait until the stories could be picked up again,' recalls Hammond. 'The series had been received with both interest and surprise, and it's a pity that it was not allowed to maintain its momentum at the time.'

Sapphire and Steel did maintain sufficient popularity for David Reid to commission new stories from Hammond. Then, in 1981, a crisis emerged. With a production date looming for the fifth adventure, Shaun O'Riordan found himself without any scripts from Hammond. The show's creator had suddenly dried up. 'I was more or less writing them while they were still in production. This was a creatively rewarding but very draining experience, and I needed to take a break.'

O'Riordan met with David Reid and was pointed in the direction of writer Anthony Read, then story editor on *Hammer House of Horror*. 'Look, I've got this problem,' O'Riordan explained. 'I need six scripts almost instantly.' Read was given two past episodes to watch and, despite his heavy commitments, needed little persuading to agree, seeing the show as a challenge, something he could have fun with. Because of the limited time factor, Read thought it advisable to have a partner and engaged Don Houghton, whom he'd never worked with and only knew vaguely, but had long admired. Houghton, he thought, was an inventive guy, utterly professional, with a great sense of humour. They also shared a Hammer connection, Houghton having written *Dracula AD 1972* and *The Satanic Rites of Dracula*.

Within 24 hours, a story was mapped out. They then split the writing chores for the episodes between them. O'Riordan was amazed and delighted to receive the first script within just a week. Not surprisingly, Read and Houghton had their own approach to *Sapphire and Steel*, and so their tone is different and far less enigmatic than Hammond's. Given the two writers' Hammer backgrounds, it's hardly surprising that this story is an example of the show at its most horrific, especially the scene where one character is infected with a disfiguring disease, complete with repulsive makeup. O'Riordan was all for such bravura terrors, knowing that kids loved monsters. 'They love the horror of a good nasty,' he asserted.

Hammond penned the next adventure, which turned out to be the last for *Sapphire and Steel* in more ways than one. Set in a service station café where time is at a standstill, director David Foster faced a highly unusual technical problem. One of his actors, Edward de Souza, had to walk through a door as if it wasn't there. Foster was very specific with the instructions to his effects team: 'It must be so flimsy that when he walks into this thing it just shivers around him and he doesn't notice it.' Foster checked two or three times to see how they were getting on. 'I think this glue looks a bit strong to me,' he observed. But the effects boffins just said, 'Oh no, it'll be alright, guv.' On set Foster assured de Souza everything would be fine. 'You just walk straight through that door and it'll go away like a puff of wind.' He did and bounced off it. Being a real old pro, de Souza merely blinked and walked straight at it again, only to bounce off a second time. Foster had to return the door to the effects shop and have it remade.

The *Sapphire and Steel* production team were always fighting to come up with sufficiently credible effects on a limited budget. Often the series was innovative out of pure necessity rather than choice, as the money simply wasn't there. On screen, the show's lack of finances was sometimes painfully obvious, such as in the episode where a character wrestles with a locked door only for the surrounding wall to wobble. Another gaffe occurs in the final episode of the fourth story, when the hacking cough of a crew member can clearly be heard in the background of a scene. Ever the professionals, McCallum and Lumley gamely carry on as if nothing's happened.

'Adventure Six' controversially ends with Sapphire and Steel trapped in space and time. The final haunting image is of the couple looking out from a café window, floating amid a sea of blackness and stars. It was a deliberately ambiguous ending that didn't find favour with everyone. In her 1989 autobiography, Joanna Lumley wrote, 'It was an absorbing show that I was sad to finish. To our dismay the last episode had us banished in a time lock. We were assured we'd be released in the next series. There never was another series and our characters are still up there, waiting to break free and continue the fight.'

In the end, *Sapphire and Steel* were killed off by television politics. Hammond was working on other story ideas and had a 'get out of jail' card up his sleeve for his heroes, by having one of their time detective colleagues come in and rescue them. But then ATV lost its television franchise to the recently formed Central, and the executives there, with typically short-sighted corporate mentality, swept out all but the most popular of ATV's shows. It was then that *Sapphire and Steel* was snapped up by ITC to form part of it's back catalogue, the show finding its true home amongst similar generic programmes like *The Prisoner* and *Randall and Hopkirk*. Hammond took the cancellation of his pet project surprisingly well. 'I felt that there was little left to say as far as stories were concerned anyway. I did not want the series to outstay its welcome or become a parody of itself.'

Since it went off the air, *Sapphire and Steel*'s popularity has steadily grown and today it's regarded as one of the best examples of British TV fantasy. In 2001 it was voted seventh in a Channel 4 poll of the top ten sci-fi shows of all time. Unsurprisingly, rumours do sometimes emerge about the possibility of a new series, but it doesn't look very likely. 'Sadly, TV companies are no longer interested in producing sci-fi and fantasy programmes,' laments Hammond. 'Even though the viewing public is obviously all for them. I have been asked to write audio scripts for Sapphire and Steel, but have declined because I feel the show can only work visually. If it were to be remade as a TV show or film, it would be interesting to see how present-day effects would assist the production. Then again, I feel that this can sometimes be overdone.'

Maybe *Sapphire and Steel*, like so many other cult shows, is best left alone and spared the ignominy of a modern make-over. As Hammond so eloquently puts it, 'Someone said to me recently, "Sapphire and Steel was a series that flared just once and has never been forgotten." I can't agree with him more.'

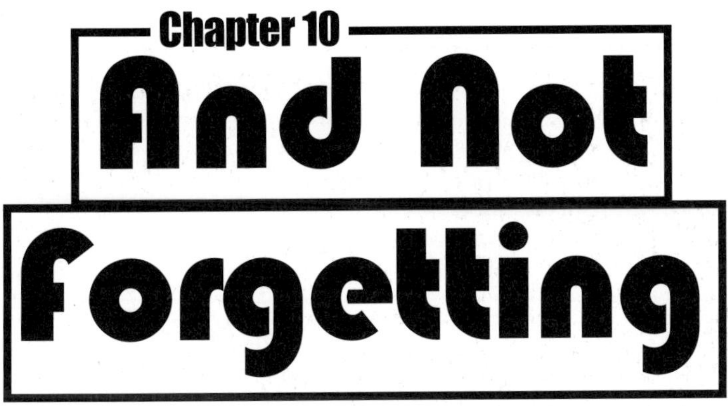

- Sir Francis Drake - Gideon's Way - The Baron - Strange Report -
The Adventurer - Hammer House of Horror -

The wonderful shows you've been reading about in this book are, of course, the most famous from the ITC catalogue. But Lew Grade was responsible for so much more, as the full list that concludes this celebration amply demonstrates. But some of them, although undeserving of a section of their own, do warrant a little closer scrutiny.

Sir Francis Drake (1961) was the last of ITC's historical swashbucklers, and probably the least remembered. Terence Morgan starred as the daring captain who plundered his way across the Atlantic, wreaking havoc on the dastardly Spanish, while ex-Gainsborough starlet Jean Kent sat on a throne a lot as Queen Elizabeth.

Although accurate in period detail (the Golden Hind was reported to be an exact replica of the original vessel), a great deal of poetic licence was taken with Drake's adventures for dramatic effect. *The Sunday Times* described the show as 'For those who like their history unhistorical, not to say jazzed up to the knocker.' Clive Donner, then fresh from directing for *Danger Man*, believes, 'It's probably rather camp if you saw it now. And Terence Morgan was a nice guy and a good actor, but he had no real charisma at all. Instinct told me that the producers had a lot less money and a lot less time than on *Danger Man*. They still wanted quality, but they wanted it quick, they wanted it cheap.'

Gideon's Way (1965) was a police drama series featuring the cases of old school Scotland Yard copper George Gideon, played by amiable British character actor John Gregson. Shooting on 35mm film, rather than videotape, gave the show much higher production values than other contemporary cop shows, like *Z Cars* and *Dixon of Dock Green*. *Gideon's Way* possibly inspired the police dramas of the future, as it was the first British cop series to escape the confines of a studio and get out onto the gritty streets themselves, filming around London's East End.

Produced by the *Saint* team of Monty Berman and Bob Baker, the series featured guest stars aplenty, like Donald Sutherland and John Hurt. Future ITC stars George Sewell, Annette Andre and Mike Pratt also made early appearances. ITC's most prolific director, Cyril Frankel, made his debut for the company with *Gideon's Way*. 'It was probably the best written television series I was ever associated with,' he declares.

Hollywood actor Steve Forrest as The Baron

The Baron (1966) was based on a series of books by John Creasey (author of the source novels for *Gideon's Way*), and featured a reformed jewel thief who becomes an antique dealer and amateur sleuth. *Saint* producers Monty Berman and Bob Baker ditched the original stories, feeling they were a little out of date for swinging sixties audiences, and turned Creasey's character into a bored Texan rancher living in London as an antiques dealer, while doing a bit of secret agenting on the side. Sort of Lovejoy meets James Bond.

Steve Forrest and Sue Lloyd, the stars of The Baron.

Cast as John 'the Baron' Mannering was American film actor Steve Forrest, who sought to base his portrayal on Patrick McGoohan. 'I'm sure I made myself a pain in the ass to all those writers,' he says now. 'Because I admired *Danger Man* very much, there was always a quality of the unknown with McGoohan. I was so influenced by him and I thought that it would work very well in *The Baron*. But they didn't want to write the part that way, and so the stories didn't focus on Mannering in the way that *Danger Man* had done on Drake. But that was the direction I wanted to take *The Baron* in.'

Despite these creative differences, Forrest loved his time working and living in England. 'London was the centre of everything at that time. One night my wife and I went to the premiere of *Alfie*, and sat right with the Beatles. I was not familiar with the Beatles, but when I came back home and told the kids they went out of their minds.'

Sadly, Forrest was much lambasted by critics when the show aired. 'Hollywooden hero Steve Forrest has the healthy and virile good looks of a man who's filled to the ears with Wacko, the wonder loaf,' howled *The Daily Mail*. Guest star George Baker wasn't too enamoured of Forrest either. 'He was a funny fella. He was brother to the absolutely impeccable actor, but I think rather a drunk, Dana Andrews. But not in the same league, I'm afraid. He was a very wooden actor.' Director Robert Tronson can't help but agree. 'It's rather sad in a way, because I think Steve would've liked to have been a better actor and he knew he wasn't. He also had this immense respect for British actors. I directed one episode and George Baker – who had been with the Royal Shakespeare Company – was in it, and that produced in Steve a dog-like devotion. And George treated him appallingly, just treated him like dirt.'

The cosmopolitan cast of Strange Report:, *Kaz Garas, Anthony Quayle, Anneke Wills.*

The usual glossy production values associated with ITC were brought to bear upon *The Baron*, but the critics didn't fall in love with the show. This from *The Sun*'s TV critic: 'I asked a chap in ATV [ITC] if he recommended *The Baron*. "I have one recommendation," he said, "duck!" I didn't duck low enough and got this custard pie full in the puss last night.' A little unfair.

'It got a pretty bad reception,' remembers Sue Lloyd, who had a regular role in the series. 'The critics made some real snide comments about Steve's wooden acting, but my God, was it popular?'

Not popular enough, it seems, since only one season was ever made. 'I had hoped that we would do more,' laments Forrest. 'I don't quite know why they didn't go ahead with it, because the minute that the show went on I couldn't go to the drug store, people recognised me wherever I went.'

Strange Report (1968) was an offbeat ITC series, produced by London-born Norman Felton, producer of the long running series *Dr Kildare* and *The Man from UNCLE*. The highly respected actor Anthony Quayle, making his first TV series, played Adam Strange, a retired Scotland Yard commissioner, now a private sleuth called in to tackle cases too baffling for the authorities. Set in 'swinging London', Strange employed the latest techniques in forensic science and used his psychological skills, rather than a gun or his fists, to bring the villains to book.

The wacky plots incorporated black magic, kidnapped diplomats and brainwashing – leaving some critics scratching their heads. The *Sunday Times* reviewer found it 'pretty well incomprehensible and wholly barmy. This series is well down on inventiveness compared with some of its predecessors.' Others regretted that, due to its pursuit of export dollars, Quayle was saddled with an American assistant. His other assistant was more home-grown, as played by Annette Wills, famous as Polly in *Dr Who*.

The series' impressive line-up of guest stars included Bernard Lee, John Thaw, Ed Bishop, Richard O'Sullivan, Ian Ogilvy and Martin Shaw.

For *The Adventurer* (1972), Lew Grade cast yet another American actor, Gene Barry, to play a wealthy government agent who poses as a movie star to travel the globe, carrying out secret missions. Most famous for his role in the original *War of the Worlds* film, Barry's Hollywood manner did not impress the British crew. 'Gene was not widely popular, because he was very much full of himself,' claims Barry Morse, who appeared in the series. 'He seemed to feel that he was omniscient, omnipotent and infallible. He had the illusion that he knew everything about everything, and would tend to tell anybody in any department what they ought to be doing, usually in relation to how best to show him off.'

When Morse was offered the chance to direct some episodes, having kicked around the business as long as he had, he knew how to deal with such difficult people. 'I realised all he really wanted was a good deal of buttering up. So I would butter poor Gene up quite shamelessly. First thing in the morning I'd say, "Oh Gene, how wonderful you look. Your hair's so well done. Is that your own suit, wonderful!" All that stuff, which of course he took to very kindly. He wasn't particularly a pleasant person to work with, frankly.'

Part of Barry's contract entitled him to script approval, which created friction with story editor Dennis Spooner. 'Gene was always criticising the scripts and wanting improvements,' recalls Cyril Frankel. 'He and Dennis clashed on the scripts.' To be fair, most of the crew were only too painfully aware of the thinness of the material. 'The quality of the writing was pretty poor and never got much better,' confirms Morse. 'So the show was doomed.' Despite this, *The Adventurer* had an impressive roster of guest stars like Alexandra Bastedo, Stephanie Beacham, Ingrid Pitt, Jane Asher, and an early appearance from Ben Kingsley.

ITC did have high hopes for the series, lavishing enough money on it for location shooting in Europe. 'The funny thing about *The Adventurer* was the very first episode,' Frankel recalls. 'We had a location in the south of France, which was very nice, but there was no script. I think I got the script the day I got on the plane. After that we tended to get the scripts late. You were lucky if you had a week, and in that week you had to cast it, discuss sets with the art director, all that.'

Critical and public reaction to *The Adventurer* was muted. 'It didn't set the world alight,' says Morse. 'The quality of the writing was not good enough. All too few people in our business, especially those in the higher reaches of it, who control the money, understand that what makes good drama is the interchange of thoughts and feelings between human beings. It doesn't have to do with car chases or explosions, as so many producers seem to think nowadays.'

Hammer House of Horror (1980) was both the final hurrah for the famous studio that dripped blood, and for ITC itself, being the last significant television series commissioned by the company. Hammer was on its knees by the close of the seventies, when a new management team headed by Roy Skeggs took over. Skeggs believed that the studio's future lay in television, and set about developing scripts for a fear-filled series. A chance encounter with Lew Grade on a plane trip to Los Angeles led to ITC agreeing to back the entire project. But a US sale was harder to achieve, due

Gene Barry as The Adventurer.

to Hammer's traditional blood and boobs ethos that Skeggs would not compromise over. 'We are going further in the way of gore and nudity than anyone has gone before for a television series,' he proudly announced.

While a lot of *Hammer House of Horror* is of varying quality, the series' claim to fame is the episode 'The Silent Scream', which featured the great Peter Cushing's last ever role for the studio which had made him a star. Skeggs was also right about the violence, which came in for its fair share of criticism. *The Sun*, in prudish mode, complained, 'Couldn't they see it was a tasteless, badly written load of gratuitously gory rubbish?' Others were more predisposed towards it, like *The Daily Mail*: 'With its canny mixture of sex and the supernatural, Hammer may have hit the nail on the head.'

The public also enjoyed the series, with ratings increasing on a weekly basis. Not surprisingly, ITC asked for another thirteen episodes, but the deal ultimately fell through. It took Skeggs another three years to find backing from elsewhere for *Hammer House of Mystery and Suspense*, but that series didn't live up to its predecessor.

Chapter 11

Mr Television A Final Tribute

During the mid-seventies, ITC began a film division which churned out a steady stream of major movies like *The Boys from Brazil*, *Capricorn One*, *The Eagle Has Landed*, *The Dark Crystal* and *The Return of the Pink Panther* – along with several very high class projects such as *On Golden Pond* and *Sophie's Choice*. 'Lew had become involved with so many film people that he suddenly thought here was an area that he hadn't explored before,' explains Marcia Stanton. 'And he was fascinated by it.'

Moving into film production was almost a natural progression for someone of Lew's talents. But the real reason behind his gradual shift away from TV into cinema was quite straightforward. He had no choice. 'What happened was, when he reached the age of 70, under the then rules of the regulator, the IBA, he had to remove himself from any day to day involvement in his television company,' says Michael Grade. 'It was a stupid rule because he still had all his faculties and contacts and energies.'

According to Marcia Stanton, Lew never resented what the IBA made him do. 'But he did believe that retirement should be struck out of the English language. To have that reason to get up in the morning, to go out and be involved in an office, really kept him going because he was so bright. He never forgot any fact. He could look through a balance sheet and he could spot any inaccuracy in a second. He just had that kind of memory.'

And so Lew switched to movies, 'But I think his enthusiasm got a little bit the better of him at some point,' observes Michael Grade. 'And he overextended and hit a cash flow difficulty.' Along with the critical successes and hits were a string of ripe turkeys and box office disasters like *The Cassandra Crossing*, *The Legend of the Lone Ranger*, *Saturn III* and *Voyage of the Damned*. But Lew was really hit for six by the notorious failure of his pet movie project, the mega-expensive *Raise the Titanic*, for which the retort, 'It would have been cheaper to have lowered the Atlantic,' has passed into movie folklore. Even if Lew claimed he never said it, he probably wished he had.

One of Grade's best movies as a film producer was *Capricorn One*, about a fake manned space mission to Mars. 'Lew was absolutely wonderful,' recalls its director, Peter Hyams, who went on to make *Outland*, *2010* and *End of Days*. 'He was bigger than life, although not quite as big as his cigars. He had the attention span of a fruit fly and I don't think he read stuff very carefully. Right before *Capricorn One* started shooting, he called me up and said, "Hey, my boy, you're going to make a wonderful film." I said, "Thank you sir." And then he said, "If you're interested, I've got an idea – when the men get to Mars they could meet Martians and we can have a big special effects

Lew in typical pose, clutching an award.

sequence." And I said, "They don't actually get to Mars, that's what the whole movie's about." He said, "Oh yes, quite right, quite right. Make a wonderful film." And hung up. That's when I realised, I don't think he ever read the script. He was just great, Lew.'

Many feel that Lew's decision to go into movies was very much to the detriment of his TV shows. 'It's strange,' muses Ian Ogilvy. 'Here was this brilliant businessman who'd created this marvellous entertainment empire, suddenly has this rush of blood to the head that he was going to be Louis B. Mayer, and he wasn't. He was a brilliant television man, but it turned out that his choice of film subjects was absolutely disastrous. And the sad thing about it was that the crew of *Return of the Saint* and I suffered from it, because our show was cancelled because Lew needed the money for his films. Bob Baker, I think, was heartbroken, because there was no reason why we couldn't have gone on for at least seven years.'

Space 1999 was another series that was cancelled because Lew diverted funds away from his TV projects, to put into film production. It was only a matter of time until ITC itself ceased producing for the small screen. A part of television history was at an end. But Lew Grade's legacy lives on today, thanks to numerous repeats of his shows on TV and availability on DVD, bringing nostalgia to people of a certain age and creating successive generations of new fans.

It's an incredible and almost unique achievement. What's even more remarkable is that it was overseen by just one man, albeit an exceptional man. In 1967, when ATV was awarded the Queen's Award to Industry, it was so indicative of Lew Grade not to see it as a personal salute, nor even as a wonderful acknowledgement of his sales efforts, but more a tribute to all the elements concerned with the production of his programmes – the producers, directors, writers, artists and technicians. 'He was adored and people loved doing business with him,' asserts Michael Grade. 'He was very straight. He delivered what he said he was going to deliver. He always kept his word. He relied entirely on his instincts. That was his training, he was an agent, face to face, get the booker on the phone; "This is a great act" or "You've got to buy this show" – "All right Lew, I'll take your word for it." And his judgement was very good. He wouldn't have lasted two minutes if he had no judgement, or if he was selling crap all the time. He picked good people and let them get on with it. He trusted the creative people. The difference now is that everything is done by committee, they squeeze the life out of creativity.'

Lew knew the value of talent, and had that fabulous gift of making the people that worked with him feel they were special and wanted. 'He was a remarkable man,' declares director Robert Tronson. 'A very good employer. He loved his people, his workers. I'd never actually met him, and I was in the casting director's office at the ATV studios one day, and suddenly there was a tap at the door, and it was Lew, there to see someone else. I excused myself and left. As I was walking down the corridor to the lift, I heard this pitter-patter of feet and it was Lew running after me, and he said, "Mr. Tronson, I'm sorry we've never actually met." He'd obviously asked who I was. And he said, "I'm so grateful for the stuff you've done." It was wonderful. I was so moved, because there was no need for it. He did have that very real consideration for his staff and workers. Unique, I think, in the world of television and film.'

ATV and ITC were very special places to work in. 'There was this magic in the air,' insists director John Hough. 'And the people cared. Instead of asking you to do it quicker and with less quality, they'd push you to excel yourself. And when they showed the rushes in the morning, if a director had done anything particularly creative they would applaud it. You knew that they wanted something special from you. I don't think that kind of working environment has ever been repeated. But the discipline was there too. So it was creative and interesting, but very strongly disciplined. It was like Michelangelo painting the Sistine Chapel on a nine to five contract.'

And Lew himself was a very special kind of boss. Few people knew him better than Marcia Stanton, who worked side by side with the man for over 40 years. 'I considered him like a father figure, and we really were a family and I loved him very, very dearly. He was always a very happy person. And he always saw the best side of everybody and the best side of every deal. He was a tremendous optimist. And every day, he used to wander all round the ATV office and say hello to everybody in the organisation. It was tremendous working there. And all sorts of guests used to come and visit him. He had everybody from Sidney Poitier to Bing Crosby and Julie Andrews. I particularly remember the day that Warren Beatty came in to see him. Somebody got wind of it in the reception, and the girls stopped the lift at every floor so that they could look at him.'

Most of all, Lew was a deal maker. 'He loved what he did,' says Michael Grade. 'He'd walk into a room at a party and he'd look around to see if there was anybody he could sell something to.' Was it the thrill of the chase that he loved? A gambling instinct? The money? Yes, of course it was the money, Lew revelled in the high life, but it was also something far deeper than mere materialism that kept him going. As David Lazer, *The Muppet Show*'s executive producer, explains, 'Why did Lew take on the Muppets? I think when he saw the characters, without even realising it, he saw the innocence of them. And he saw the entertainment value. Money is always there, but I don't believe in my heart that Lew was driven by money. I think he was driven by success. Just like Jim Henson, he never thought of the money, it was always the best possible show we could make, and then the money came. It's a by-product.'

Right up to his death in 1998, the great Lew Grade was still making deals, as if he felt that if he stopped his passion for life would wither away too. 'One of the last deals that Lew did was on his film called *Something To Believe In*,' Michael Grade recalls. 'He wanted very badly to get Tom Conti to play a Vatican official in the movie, and rang Tom's agent, Ross Chato. He said, "I want Tom to do this movie, I'm sending the script over." Ross sent the script to Tom Conti and back came the message, "Love the script, but sadly the part's not really big enough for me." It was only three pages. Lew phoned Ross; "It's money, isn't it?" Ross said, "No, it's nothing to do with money, Lew, he just doesn't feel the part's big enough." So Lew said, "Well, make him an offer." So the offer went off, and back came the same reply, "Sorry, the part's not big enough." Ross gave Lew the news, and Lew said, "I suppose I'll have to see him. Send him up to see me." Now, many an actor before has had to make this trip, sure that they're not going to do it, but knowing they're going to do it when they get there. And Tom Conti was not the first. And Tom sat there and Lew did a performance; "My boy, this is a cameo. It's only three pages. But it's an Oscar for Best Supporting Actor. Everybody in the picture talks about you when you are off the screen, the picture can't happen without you, this is the key role, the whole emotional thrust of the picture hangs on *you*." Tom says, "I'll think about it, Lew." He went back to the office and said to Ross, "OK, I surrender." So Ross rings Lew and she says, "Lew, he'll do it." "Thank goodness," says Lew. "There's only one thing," says Ross. "It's not the money?" said Lew. "No, it's not the money. He's worried about the billing." "Billing?" said Lew. "It's three pages. What does he want billing for?"'

Lew, you are sadly missed.

Gerry Anderson: 'Probably the nearest Britain has ever come to producing a children's myth maker on the level of Walt Disney.' – New Statesman.

AFTERWORD BY GERRY ANDERSON

1959. I had just completed a puppet cowboy Western, *Four Feather Falls*, for Granada. The budget for each show was £250, and on completion of each episode the black and white 35mm print was dispatched to Granada. A few days later, a cheque arrived with a compliment slip.

When we completed it and it was successful, I naïvely expected Granada to ask us to make either more episodes or another series. However, I heard nothing further from them until 2004, when they took over Carlton Television and, by default, became the owners of most of my television series.

My fledgling production company, AP Films Ltd., had now run out of money, and I took the decision to put it into voluntary liquidation. Fortunately, a friend suggested I should see Lew Grade, with a brochure of another property we had developed, *Supercar*. Much to my surprise, Lew agreed to back 26 half-hour episodes.

As I left his office, I turned and said to Lew, 'We really need to start immediately, so could I have a letter of intent?' Lew responded angrily, 'You've got to understand one thing, Gerry, my word is better than any legal agreement.' Eighteen years later, Lew's words were proven beyond any doubt.

Supercar was made, and had a huge success in America. When production was nearing its end, Lew called me to his office, at what would become a traditional 7.30 meeting in the morning, and asked me if I had another series for him. I said, 'Yes, it's called *Fireball XL5*.' He poured me a coffee and gave me some biscuits. We discussed it for five minutes and he said, 'Go ahead.'

Fireball XL5 was sold to NBC America and, soon after, Lew bought my company and financed a specialised film studio with the latest gear and all the equipment we needed. Our first project under Lew's wing was *Stingray*.

Stingray was the first colour television series to be made in this country. Although it was in colour for its sale to America, at that time we were still transmitting in black and white in the UK. A few years later, when colour first came here, the British fans were amazed when they suddenly saw the repeats in colour. Unaware of the situation, many thought we had by some magic turned black and white into full colour.

My next visit to Lew, after the success of *Thunderbirds*, was rather special. As soon as I arrived in his office, he said, 'Come with me,' and took me down to the basement where there was a gleaming, brand new, blue Rolls Royce. 'Here's a present for you, Gerry,' he said.

A new production company called Century 21 was formed, which had a dedicated puppet studio, merchandising company, recording company and toy company.

Two puppet feature films were made, followed by the television series *Captain Scarlet*, *Joe 90* and *The Secret Service*. Lew then switched me to live action. There followed *UFO*, which led the ratings in New York and Los Angeles for seventeen consecutive weeks, *Space 1999*, and finally *The Protectors*, with Robert Vaughn.

For some time I had seen the writing on the wall. There were people in the organisation plotting against Lew, and a while later he was deposed.

He continued working from his Bond Street office until he died, at the age of 92. He was, and still is to my memory, the greatest impresario this country has ever seen.

Thank you, Lew, and God bless you.
April 2006

ITC – TV-OGRAPHY

The Adventures of Robin Hood (1955-1959)
Regular Cast: Richard Greene, Bernadette O'Farrell, Patricia Driscoll, Alan Wheatley, Alexander Gauge, Archie Duncan, John Arnatt, Rufus Cruickshank.
Guest stars: Jane Asher, Ian Bannen, Alfie Bass, Geoffrey Bayldon, Wilfrid Brambell, Bernard Bresslaw, Patrick Cargill, Kenneth Cope, Harry H. Corbett, Graham Crowden, Nigel Davenport, Anthony Dawson, Roger Delgado, Paul Eddington, Charles Gray, Nigel Green, Irene Handl, Thora Hird, Gordon Jackson, Sid James, Jennifer Jayne, Lionel Jeffries, Geoffrey Keen, Sam Kydd, Desmond Llewelyn, Leo McKern, Francis Matthews, Edward Mulhare, Lawrence Naismith, Richard O'Sullivan, Bill Owen, Nicholas Parsons, Conrad Phillips, Leslie Phillips, Donald Pleasence, Michael Ripper, Norman Rossington, Joan Sims, John Schlesinger, Patrick Troughton, Zena Walker, Douglas Wilmer, Billie Whitelaw.
Directors: Lindsay Anderson, Daniel Birt, Terry Bishop, Don Chaffey, Arthur Crabtree, Robert Day, Terence Fisher, Bernard Knowles, Peter Maxwell, Ralph Smart.
Writers: Arthur Behr, Raymond Bowers, John Cousins, John Dyson, Eric Heath, Ring Lardner Jr., Ian Lartain, Robert Lees, Ian McLellan Hunter, C. D. Phillips, Leslie Poynton, Anne Rodney, Milton Schlesinger, Adrian Scott, Ralph Smart.
143 episodes x 25 minutes (b/w)

The Scarlet Pimpernel (1955)
Regular Cast: Marius Goring.
Guest Stars: Alfie Bass, Ivor Dean, Roger Delgado, Yvonne Furneaux, Christopher Lee, Peter O'Toole, Conrad Phillips, Michael Ripper, Robert Shaw, Patrick Troughton,
Directors: David MacDonald, Michael McCarthy, Wolf Rilla, Dennis Vance.
Writers: Marius Goring, Michael Hogan, John Moore, Diana Morgan.
18 episodes x 25 minutes (b/w)

Fury (1955-1960)
Regular Cast: Peter Graves, William Hudson.
Directors: Ray Nazarro, Sidney Salkow, Lesley Selander.
Writers: Robert B. Bailey, Melvin Levy, Nat Tanchuck.
116 episodes x 25 minutes (b/w)

The Count of Monte Cristo (1956)
Regular Cast: George Dolenz, Nick Cravat, Fortunio Bonanova, Robert Cawdron.
Guest Stars: Ian Bannen, Robert Brown, Adrienne Corri, Finlay Currie, Nigel Davenport, Walter Gotell, Stratford Johns, Charles Lloyd Pack, Conrad Phillips, Patrick Troughton, Rita Webb, Douglas Wilmer.
Directors: Charles Bennett, Budd Boetticher, David MacDonald, Sidney Salkow, Dennis Vance.
Writer: Sidney Marshall.
39 episodes x 25 minutes (b/w)

The Adventures of Sir Lancelot (1956-1957)
Regular Cast: William Russell, Jane Hylton, Ronald Leigh-Hunt, Cyril Smith, Robert Scroggins.
Guest Stars: Alfie Bass, Martin Benson, Wilfrid Brambell, Michael Caine, Nigel Green, Robert Hardy, Jennifer Jayne, Edward Judd, Patrick McGoohan, Derren Nesbitt, Yvonne Romain, Leonard Sachs, Zena Walker.
Directors: Terry Bishop, Arthur Crabtree, Desmond Davis, Lawrence Huntington, Bernard Knowles, Peter Maxwell, Ralph Smart, Anthony Squire.
Writers: H. H. Burns, Selwyn Jepson, Harold Kent, Peter Key, Robert Lees, Peggy Phillips, Leslie Poynton, Leighton Reynolds, John Ridgley.
30 episodes x 25 minutes (b/w)

The Buccaneers (1956-1957)
Regular Cast: Robert Shaw, Alec Clunes, Peter Hammond, Terence Cooper.
Guest stars: Jane Asher, Alfie Bass, Earl Cameron, Adrienne Corri, Hazel Court, Anthony Dawson, Roger Delgado, Paul Eddington, Sid James, Andrew Keir, Ferdy Mayne, Andre Morell, Bill Owen, Richard Pasco, Eric Pohlmann, John Schlesinger, Joan Sims.
Directors: Terry Bishop, Bernard Knowles, Peter Maxwell, C. M. Pennington-Richards, Ralph Smart.
Writers: Neil R. Collins, Basil Dawson, Terence Moore, Peter Rossano, Thomas A. Stockwell, Zachary Weiss.
39 episodes x 25 minutes (b/w)

O.S.S (1957)
Regular Cast: Ron Randell, Lionel Murton, Robert Gallico.
Guest Stars: Geoffrey Bayldon, Roger Delgado, Anton Diffring, Ronald Fraser, Walter Gotell, Gerald Harper, Christopher Lee, Francis Matthews, Lois Maxwell, Conrad Phillips, Leslie Phillips, Michael Ripper.
Directors: Allan Davis, Peter Maxwell, Robert Siodmak.
Writers: Paul Dudley.
26 episodes x 25 minutes (b/w)

Hawkeye and the Last of the Mohicans (1957)
Regular Cast: John Hart, Lon Chaney Jr.
Directors: Sam Newfield, Sidney Salkow.
Writers: Robert B. Bailey, Hugh King, Louis Vittes, Louis Stevens.
39 episodes x 25 minutes (b/w)

Sword of Freedom (1957)
Regular Cast: Edmund Purdom, Adrienne Corri, Martin Benson.
Guest Stars: Jane Asher, Geoffrey Bayldon, Wilfrid Brambell, Nigel Davenport, Paul Eddington, Bill Fraser, Charles Gray, Andrew Keir, Jean Kent, John Le Mesurier, Richard O'Sullivan, Luciana Paluzzi, Joan Plowright, William Russell, Patrick Troughton, Kenneth Williams, Peter Wyngarde.
Directors: Terry Bishop, Terence Fisher, Bernard Knowles, Peter Maxwell.
Writers: George Baxt, Leighton Reynolds, William Templeton.
39 episodes x 25 minutes (b/w)

The New Adventures of Charlie Chan (1957)
Regular Cast: J. Carrol Naish, James Hong.
Guest Stars: Maxine Audley, Honor Blackman, Lisa Daniely, Strother Martin, Francis Matthews, Conrad Phillips, Douglas Wilmer.
Directors: Leslie Arliss, Don Chaffey, Alvin Rakoff.
Writers: Leon Fromkess, Homer McCoy, Ted Thomas, Gene Wang.
39 episodes x 25 minutes (b/w)

William Tell (1958-1959)
Regular Cast: Conrad Phillips, Jennifer Jayne, Nigel Green, Willoughby Goddard.
Guest stars: James Booth, Wilfrid Brambell, Michael Caine, Kenneth Cope, Adrienne Corri, Roger Delgado, Frazer Hines, Sid James, Edward Judd, John Le Mesurier, Christopher Lee, Warren Mitchell, Derren Nesbitt, Donald Pleasence, Robert Shaw, Frank Thornton, Patrick Troughton, Richard Vernon.
Directors: Terry Bishop, Quentin Lawrence, Peter Maxwell, Ernest Morris, Anthony Squire, Ralph Smart.
Writers: Ian Stuart Black, John Kruse, Doreen Montgomery, Rene Wilde.
39 episodes x 25 minutes (b/w)

White Hunter (1958)
Regular Cast: Harry Baird, Rhodes Reason, Tim Turner.
Guest Stars: Earl Cameron, Clifford Evans, Eunice Gayson, Christopher Lee, Andre Morell, Arnold Ridley, Robert Shaw, Barbara Shelley.
Directors: Peter Maxwell, Ernest Morris, Joseph Sterling.
Writers: Lee Loeb, Kenneth Taylor.
39 episodes x 25 minutes (b/w)

H. G. Wells' Invisible Man (1958-1959)
Regular Cast: Lisa Daniely, Deborah Watling, Johnny Scripps, Tim Turner.
Guest Stars: Honor Blackman, James Booth, Robert Brown, Hazel Court, Anton Diffring, Ronald Fraser, Walter Gotell, Charles Gray, Irene Handl, Edward Hardwicke, Ian Hendry, Joan Hickson, Jennifer Jayne, Geoffrey Keen, Desmond Llewelyn, Andre Morell, Conrad Phillips, Leslie Phillips, Dennis Price, Michael Ripper, Peter Sallis, Barbara Shelley, Patrick Troughton, Douglas Wilmer, Mai Zetterling.
Directors: Quentin Lawrence, Peter Maxwell, C. M. Pennington-Richards, Ralph Smart.
Writers: Leslie Arliss, Ian Stuart Black, Brenda Blackmore, Brian Clemens, Michael Connor, Michael Cramoy, Leonard Fincham, Lindsay Galloway, Stanley Mann, Doreen Montgomery, Michael Pertwee, Ralph Smart.
26 episodes x 25 minutes (b/w)

The Four Just Men (1959)
Regular Cast: Richard Conte, Dan Dailey, Vittorio De Sica, Jack Hawkins.
Guest Stars: Jane Asher, Alan Bates, Honor Blackman, Kenneth Connor, Jess Conrad, Roger Delgado, Judi Dench, Paul Eddington, Charles Gray, Patricia Hayes, Lionel Jeffries, Richard Johnson, Geoffrey Keen, Warren Mitchell, Richard O'Sullivan, Donald Pleasence, Eric Pohlmann, Michael Ripper, Robert Shaw, Frank Thornton, Patrick Troughton, Mai Zetterling.
Directors: Anthony Bushell, Don Chaffey, Basil Dearden, William Fairchild, Harry Watt.
Writers: Marc Brandell, Leon Griffiths, Louis Marks, Jan Read.
39 episodes x 25 minutes (b/w)

Interpol Calling (1959)
Guest Stars: Robert Brown, Hazel Court, Bernard Cribbins, Anthony Dawson, Ursula Howells, Stratford Johns, John Le Mesurier, Donald Pleasence, Leonard Sachs, Patrick Troughton, Peter Vaughan.
Directors: Charles Frend, C. M. Pennington-Richards, Jeremy Summers.
39 episodes x 25 minutes (b/w)

Danger Man (1960-1961)
Regular Cast: Patrick McGoohan.
Guest Stars: Honor Blackman, Earl Cameron, Jackie Collins, Hazel Court, Wendy Craig, Finlay Currie, Roger Delgado, Patricia Driscoll, Fenella Fielding, Walter Gotell, Charles Gray, Nigel Green, Kenneth Haigh, Edward Hardwicke, Percy Herbert, Jennifer Jayne, Burt Kwouk, Moira Lister, Terence Longdon, Jean Marsh, Lois Maxwell, John Le Mesurier, Warren Mitchell, Kieron Moore,

Lawrence Naismith, Derren Nesbitt, Donald Pleasence, Nyree Dawn Porter, Michael Ripper, Patsy Rowlands, Peter Sallis, Robert Shaw, Barbara Shelley, Frank Thornton, Patrick Troughton, Sam Wanamaker, Richard Wattis, John Woodvine, Patrick Wymark, Mai Zetterling.
Directors: Julian Amyes, Terry Bishop, Anthony Bushell, Clive Donner, Charles Frend, Seth Holt, Patrick McGoohan, C. M. Pennington-Richards, Peter Graham Scott, Ralph Smart, Michael Truman.
Writers: Ian Stuart Black, Marc Brandell, Oscar Brodney, Brian Clemens, Lew Davidson, Jo Eisinger, Doreen Montgomery, Michael Pertwee, John Roddick, Ralph Smart, Robert Stewart, Jack Whittingham.
39 episodes x 25 minutes (b/w)

Supercar (1960-1962)
Regular Voice Cast: Graydon Gould, David Graham, George Murcell, Sylvia Anderson.
Directors: David Elliott, Bill Harris, Alan Pattillo, Desmond Saunders.
Writers: Hugh Woodhouse, Martin Woodhouse.
39 episodes x 25 minutes (b/w)

Whiplash (1960)
Regular Cast: Peter Graves, Anthony Wickert.
Guest Stars: Annette Andre, Guy Doleman, Jennifer Jayne.
Directors: Peter Maxwell, John Meredith Edwards.
Writers: Michael Plant, Gene Roddenberry.
34 episodes x 25 minutes (b/w)

Ghost Squad (1961)
Regular Cast: Ray Austin, Ray Barrett, Angela Browne, Donald Wolfit.
Guest Stars: Tom Adams, Norman Bird, Honor Blackman, Hazel Court, William Gaunt, Nigel Green, William Hartnell, Jill Ireland, Gordon Jackson, John Junkin, Bill Kerr, Lois Maxwell, Barbara Shelley.
Directors: Phil Brown, James Ferman, Peter Sasdy, Don Sharp, Dennis Vance.
Writers: Julian Bond, Brian Clemens, Tudor Gates, Richard Harris, Robert Holmes, Malcolm Hulke, Gerald Kelsey, Philip Levene.
52 episodes x 50 minutes (b/w)

Sir Francis Drake (1961-1962)
Regular Cast: Terence Morgan, Jean Kent, Patrick McLoughlin, Richard Warner, Roger Delgado, Michael Crawford.
Guest Stars: Francesca Annis, Nigel Davenport, Glyn Edwards, Barry Foster, Susan Hampshire, Andrew Keir, David McCallum, Victor Maddern, Zena Marshall, Kieron Moore, Barry Morse, Lawrence Naismith, Nanette Newman, Warren Mitchell, Michael Ripper, Patrick Troughton, Edward Woodward, Patrick Wymark.
Directors: Terry Bishop, Harry Booth, Anthony Bushell, Clive Donner, David Greene, John Lemont, Peter Maxwell, Peter Graham Scott.
Writers: John Baines, Ian Stuart Black, Brian Clemens, John Keir Cross, Larry Forrester, Lindsay Galloway, Tudor Gates, David Giltinian, David Greene, Margaret Irwin, Doreen Montgomery, John Roddick, Paul Tabori, Gordon Wellesley, Cedric Wells, Hugh Ross Williamson.
26 episodes x 25 minutes (b/w)

Fireball XL5 (1962)
Regular voice Cast: Paul Maxwell, John Bluthal, Sylvia Anderson, David Graham, Gerry Anderson.
Directors: Gerry Anderson, David Elliott, Bill Harris, John Kelly, Alan Pattillo.
Writers: Gerry Anderson, Sylvia Anderson, Alan Fennell, Anthony Marriott, Dennis Spooner.
39 episodes x 25 minutes (b/w)

The Saint (1962-1969)
Regular Cast: Roger Moore.
Guest Stars: Dawn Adams, Patrick Allen, Annette Andre, Francesca Annis, Jane Asher, Ronnie Barker, Ray Barrett, Alexandra Bastedo, Geoffrey Bayldon, Stephanie Beacham, Steven Berkoff, Ed Bishop, Honor Blackman, Peter Bowles, Robert Brown, Tony Britton, Veronica Carlson, John Carson, Julie Christie, Carol Cleveland, Jackie Collins, Nicholas Courtney, Howard Marion Crawford, Stuart Damon, Lisa Daniely, Nigel Davenport, Ivor Dean, Roger Delgado, Angela Douglas, Gabrielle Drake, Shirley Eaton, Samantha Eggar, Sandor Eles, Susan Farmer, William Gaunt, Eunice Gayson, Julian Glover, Michael Gough, John Gregson, Robert Hardy, Doris Hare, Imogen Hassal, David Hedison, Ian Hendry, Percy Herbert, Peter Jeffrey, Freddie Jones, Yootha Joyce, Alexis Kanner, Geoffrey Keen, Alexander Knox, Burt Kwouk, Alan Lake, Valerie Leon, Fiona Lewis, Jeannie Linden, Cec Linder, Sue Lloyd, David Lodge, Philip Madoc, Jean Marsh, Francis Matthews, Lois Maxwell, Jane Merrow, Warren Mitchell, Kate O'Mara, Andre Morell, Barry Morse, Fulton Mackay, Barbara Murray, Derren Nesbitt, Nanette Newman, Anthony Nichols, Cecil Parker, George Pastell, Conrad Phillips, Nyree Dawn Porter, Nosher Powell, Mike Pratt, Dave Prowse, Anthony Quayle, Oliver Reed, Shane Rimmer, Michael Ripper, Anton Rogers, Yvonne Romain, Andrew Sachs, Barbara Shelley, Vladek Sheybal, Sylvia Sims, Victor Spinetti, Yutte Stensgaard, Nigel Stock, Donald Sutherland, Dudley Sutton, Patrick Troughton, Peter Vaughan, Wanda Ventham, Richard Vernon, Edward Woodward, Peter Wyngarde,.
Directors: John Ainsworth, Robert Asher, Ray Austin, Roy Ward Baker, Robert S. Baker, Anthony

Bushell, John Paddy Carstairs, David Eady, Gordon Fleming, Freddie Francis, John Gilling, David Greene, James Hill, Pat Jackson, John Krish, Robert Lynn, Roger Moore, Ernest Morris, John Moxey, Leslie Norman, Jim O'Connelly, Alvin Rakoff, Jeremy Summers, Robert Tronson, Michael Truman, Peter Yates.
Writers: Ian Stuart Black, Julian Bond, Norman Borisoff, Paddy Manning O'Brien, Philip Broadley, Michael Cramoy, Lewis Davidson, Basil Dawson, Brian Degas, Marcus Demain, Ronald Duncan, Paul Erickson, Terence Feely, Larry Forrester, John Gilling, John Graeme, Leonard Graham, Richard Harris, Kenneth Hayles, Robert Holmes, Norman Hudis, Donald James, Harry W. Junkin, Gerald Kelsey, John Kruse, Ian Martin, Terry Nation, Michael Pertwee, John Roddick, Roy Russell, Jack Saunders, Dick Sharples, Robert Stewart, Bill Strutton, Leigh Vance, Michael Winder.
114 episodes x 50 minutes (b/w and colour)

Man of the World (1962)
Regular Cast: Craig Stevens, Tracy Reed, Graham Stark.
Guest Stars: Ray Barrett, Finlay Currie, Nigel Davenport, Shirley Eaton, Peter Jones, Geoffrey Keen, John Laurie, Paul Maxwell, Juliet Mills, Warren Mitchell, Derren Nesbitt, Anthony Quayle, Patrick Troughton, Sam Wanamaker, Patrick Wymark.
Directors: Harry Booth, Anthony Bushell, Charles Crichton, Charles Frend, David Greene, John Llewellyn Moxey, Jeremy Summers.
Writers: Ian Stuart Black, Julian Bond, Marc Brandell, Brian Clemens, Lindsay Galloway, Tudor Gates, Michael Pertwee.
20 episodes x 50 minutes (b/w)

Espionage (1963-1964)
Guest Stars: Martin Balsam, Stanley Baxter, Bernard Bresslaw, Diane Cilento, Anthony Dawson, Bradford Dillman, Barry Foster, James Fox, Julian Glover, John Gregson, Dennis Hopper, Michael Hordern, Arthur Kennedy, Bernard Lee, Roger Livesey, Millicent Martin, Sian Phillips, Donald Pleasence, Anthony Quayle, Nigel Stock, Sam Wanamaker, Robert Webber, Billie Whitelaw.
24 episodes x 50 minutes (b/w)

Forest Rangers (1963-1966)
Regular Cast: Graydon Gould, Rex Hagon.
Directors: Paul Almond, Leslie Arliss, George Gorman.
Writers: Lindsay Galloway, George Salverson.
104 episodes x 25 minutes (colour)

The Sentimental Agent (1963)
Regular Cast: Carlos Thompson, Burt Kwouk.
Guest Stars: Annette Andre, Peter Arne, Carol Cleveland, Imogen Hassall, Walter Gotell, Sue Lloyd, Patrick Magee, Warren Mitchell, Dennis Price, Diana Rigg, Donald Sutherland, Anneke Wills.
Directors: Harry Booth, John Paddy Carstairs, Charles Frend.
Writers: Ian Stuart Black, Julian Bond, Brian Clemens, Tudor Gates.
13 episodes x 50 minutes (b/w)

Stingray (1964-1965)
Regular Voice Cast: Don Mason, Robert Easton, Lois Maxwell, Ray Barrett.
Directors: David Elliott, John Kelly, Alan Pattillo, Desmond Saunders.
Writers: Gerry Anderson, Sylvia Anderson, Alan Fennell, Dennis Spooner.
39 episodes x 25 minutes (colour)

Danger Man – second series (1964-1966)
Regular Cast: Patrick McGoohan.
Guest Stars: Dawn Addams, Francesca Annis, Amanda Barrie, Martine Beswick, Peter Bowles, Bernard Bresslaw, Ray Brooks, Peter Butterworth, Adrienne Corri, Wendy Craig, Howard Marion-Crawford, Graham Crowden, Lisa Daniely, Maurice Denham, Patricia Driscoll, Paul Eddington, Denholm Elliott, John Fraser, Yvonne Furneaux, Eunice Gayson, Judy Geeson, Nigel Green, Joan Greenwood, Kenneth Griffith, Susan Hampshire, Ian Hendry, Joan Hickson, Donald Houston, Alf Joint, Burt Kwouk, Wilfrid Lawson, Bernard Lee, Mark Lester, Moira Lister, Desmond Llewelyn, Terence Longdon, Kate O'Mara, Roy Marsden, Jane Merrow, Warren Mitchell, Andre Morell, Margaret Nolan, Nicola Pagett, Jacqueline Pearce, Eddie Powell, Mike Pratt, Wendy Richard, Shane Rimmer, Anton Rodgers, Nadim Sawalha, Johnny Sekka, Vladek Sheybal, Sylvia Sims, John Standing, Barbara Steele, Nigel Stock, Richard O'Sullivan, Yoko Tani, Wanda Ventham, John Woodvine.
Directors: Stuart Burge, Don Chaffey, Charles Crichton, Robert Day, Pat Jackson, Quentin Lawrence, Patrick McGoohan, Ralph Smart, Jeremy Summers, Michael Truman, Peter Yates.
Writers: Raymond Bowers, Marc Brandell, Philip Broadley, Norman Hudis, Malcolm Hulke, Jesse Lasky Jr., Quentin Lawrence, Louis Marks, Michael Pertwee, Jan Read, John Roddick, Pat Silver, David Stone, Ralph Smart, David Weir, Tony Williamson.
47 episodes x 50 minutes (b/w and colour)

Court Martial (1965)
Guest Stars: Martine Beswick, Diane Cilento, Mark Lester, Sal Mineo, Cameron Mitchell, Eric Pohlmann, Anthony Quayle, Shane Rimmer, Donald Sutherland.
Directors: Lewis Allen, Seth Holt, Peter Medak,

Alvin Rakoff, Peter Graham Scott, Robert Tronson, Sam Wanamaker.
Writers: Julian Bond, Leon Griffiths, George Markstein.
26 episodes x 50 minutes (b/w)

Gideon's Way (1965)
Regular Cast: John Gregson.
Guest Stars: George Baker, Ray Barrett, Ray Brooks, George Cole, Suzan Farmer, Donald Houston, John Hurt, Gordon Jackson, Sue Lloyd, Jean Marsh, Lois Maxwell, Ray McAnally, Jane Merrow, Geoffrey Palmer, Mike Pratt, Michael Ripper, George Sewell, Donald Sutherland.
Directors: Roy Ward Baker, Cyril Frankel, John Gilling, James Hill, Quentin Lawrence, Leslie Norman, Jeremy Summers, Robert Tronson.
Writers: Norman Hudis, Malcolm Hulke, Harry W. Junkin, Jack Whittingham.
26 episodes x 50 minutes (b/w)

Thunderbirds (1965-1966)
Regular Voice Cast: Peter Dyneley, Shane Rimmer, Sylvia Anderson, David Holliday, Matt Zimmerman, David Graham, Christine Finn, Ray Barrett.
Directors: Brian Burgess, David Elliott, David Lane, Alan Pattillo, Desmond Saunders.
Writers: Gerry Anderson, Sylvia Anderson, Tony Barwick, Martin Crump, Alan Fennell, Donald Robertson, Dennis Spooner.
32 episodes x 50 minutes (colour)

Seaway (1965)
Regular Cast: Austin Willis, Stephen Young.
Guest Stars: Faye Dunaway, Cec Linder, Sally Kellerman, Barry Morse.
Directors: John Berry, Harvey Hart, Daniel Petrie, Harrison Starr.
Writers: Lindsay Galloway, Alvin Goldman, Abraham Polonsky.
30 episodes x 50 minutes (colour)

The Baron (1966)
Regular Cast: Steve Forrest, Sue Lloyd, Colin Gordon, Paul Ferris.
Guest Stars: Terence Alexander, Patrick Allen, Annette Andre, Peter Arne, George Baker, Peter Bowles, Jeremy Brett, Lisa Daniely, Anton Diffring, Sandor Eles, William Franklyn, Yvonne Furneaux, Walter Gotell, Robert Hardy, Freddie Jones, Bernard Lee, Valerie Leon, Philip Madoc, Lois Maxwell, Jane Merrow, Geoffrey Palmer, Nosher Powell, Mike Pratt, Vladek Sheybal, Sylvia Sims, Dudley Sutton, James Villiers, Kay Walsh, Sam Wanamaker, Douglas Wilmer, John Woodvine, Edward Woodward, Peter Wyngarde.
Directors: Robert Asher, Roy Ward Baker, Don Chaffey, Gordon Flemying, Quentin Lawrence, John Moxey, Jeremy Summers, Robert Tronson.
Writers: Brian Clemens, Michael Cramoy, Brian Degas, Harry W. Junkin, Terry Nation, Dennis Spooner.
30 episodes x 50 minutes (colour)

Captain Scarlet and the Mysterons (1967-1968)
Regular Voice Cast: Francis Matthews, Ed Bishop, Donald Grey, Cy Grant, Elizabeth Morgan.
Directors: Brian Burgess, Leo Eaton, David Lane, Robert Lynn, Alan Perry, Desmond Saunders, Ken Turner.
Writers: Gerry Anderson, Sylvia Anderson, Tony Barwick, Bryan Cooper, Peter Curran, Ralph Hart, Bill Hedley, David Lee, Alan Pattillo, Shane Rimmer, David Williams.
32 episodes x 25 minutes (colour)

The Prisoner (1967-1968)
Regular Cast: Patrick McGoohan.
Guest Stars: Annette Andre, George Baker, Michael Billington, Peter Bowles, Angela Browne, Earl Cameron, Patrick Cargill, John Castle, Finlay Currie, Guy Doleman, Paul Eddington, Mark Eden, Clifford Evans, Colin Gordon, Kenneth Griffith, Alexis Kanner, Leo McKern, Jane Merrow, Angelo Muscat, Derren Nesbitt, Conrad Phillips, Eric Portman, Anton Rodgers, Donald Sinden, Nigel Stock, Wanda Ventham, Richard Wattis, Zena Walker, Peter Wyngarde.
Directors: Don Chaffey, Pat Jackson, Patrick McGoohan, Peter Graham Scott, David Tomblin.
Writers: Terence Feely, Gerald Kelsey, Frank Maher, Patrick McGoohan, George Markstein.
17 episodes x 50 minutes (colour)

Man in a Suitcase (1967-1968)
Regular Cast: Richard Bradford.
Guest Stars: Patrick Allen, Michael Bates, Rodney Bewes, Ed Bishop, Colin Blakely, Patrick Cargill, Carol Cleveland, Howard Marion-Crawford, Stuart Damon, Roger Delgado, Mark Eden, Edward Fox, Judy Geeson, Marius Goring, John Gregson, Donald Houston, Ursula Howells, Jennifer Jayne, Felicity Kendal, Sam Kydd, Bernard Lee, George Leech, Ray McAnally, T. P. McKenna, Philip Madoc, Ferdy Mayne, Jane Merrow, Derren Nesbitt, Dandy Nichols, Anthony Nicholls, Bill Owen, Nicola Pagett, Jacqueline Pearce, Mike Pratt, Anton Rodgers, Norman Rossington, George Sewell, Barbara Shelley, Donald Sutherland, Robert Urquhart, Peter Vaughan, James Villiers, Simon Williams.
Directors: Don Chaffey, Charles Crichton, Peter Duffell, Freddie Francis, Charles Frend, John Glen, Pat Jackson, Gerry O'Hara, Jeremy Summers, Robert Tronson.
Writers: Philip Broadley, Bernie Cooper, Stanley R. Greenberg, Richard Harris, Francis Megahy, Robert

Muller, Roger Parkes, John Stanton, Dennis Spooner, Edmund Ward.
30 episodes x 50 minutes (colour)

Strange Report (1968)
Regular Cast: Anthony Quayle.
Guest Stars: Tom Adams, Keith Barron, Ed Bishop, Lisa Daniely, Anton Diffring, Kenneth Haigh, Robert Hardy, Anthony Higgins, Saeed Jaffrey, Bernard Lee, Ray McAnally, Jane Merrow, Zienia Merton, Ian Ogilvy, Martin Shaw, Vladek Sheybal, John Thaw.
Directors: Robert Asher, Charles Crichton, Peter Duffell, Peter Medak, Daniel Petrie.
Writers: Brian Degas, Moris Farhi, Tudor Gates, John Kruse, Jan Read, Leigh Vance.
16 episodes x 50 minutes (colour)

Joe 90 (1968-1969)
Regular Voice Cast: Len Jones, Rupert Davies, Keith Alexander, David Healy.
Directors: Peter Anderson, Leo Eaton, Brian Heard, Alan Perry, Desmond Saunders, Ken Turner.
Writers: Gerry Anderson, Sylvia Anderson, Tony Barwick, Pat Dunlop, Donald James, David Lane, John Lucarotti, Shane Rimmer, Keith Wilson.
30 episodes x 25 minutes (colour)

The Champions (1968-1969)
Regular Cast: Stuart Damon, Alexandra Bastedo, William Gaunt, Anthony Nicholls.
Guest Stars: Terence Alexander, Patrick Allen, Peter Arne, Felix Aylmer, Steven Berkoff, Colin Blakely, Jeremy Brett, John Carson, Adrienne Corri, Nicholas Courtney, Roger Delgado, Gabrielle Drake, Paul Eddington, Clifford Evans, Julian Glover, Hannah Gordon, Walter Gotell, Michael Gough, Gerald Harper, Imogen Hassall, Donald Houston, Bernard Kay, Burt Kwouk, Andrew Keir, Bernard Lee, Jennie Linden, David Lodge, Kate O'Mara, Patrick Magee, Paul Maxwell, Donald Pickering, Mike Pratt, Dave Prowse, Anton Rodgers, Vladek Sheybal, Donald Sutherland, Frank Thornton, Robert Urquhart, Patrick Wymark, Peter Wyngarde.
Directors: Robert Asher, Ray Austin, Roy Ward Baker, Paul Dickson, Freddie Francis, Cyril Frankel, John Gilling, John Moxey, Leslie Norman, Don Sharp, Sam Wanamaker.
Writers: Ian Stuart Black, Philip Broadley, Brian Clemens, Donald James, Gerald Kelsey, Terry Nation, Ralph Smart, Dennis Spooner, Tony Williamson.
30 episodes x 50 minutes (colour)

The Secret Service (1969)
Regular Voice Cast: Stanley Unwin.
Directors: Peter Anderson, Leo Eaton, Brian Heard, Alan Perry.
Writers: Gerry Anderson, Sylvia Anderson, Tony Barwick, Pat Dunlop, Donald James, Shane Rimmer.
13 episodes x 25 minutes (colour)

Department S (1969-1970)
Regular Cast: Peter Wyngarde, Joel Fabiani, Rosemary Nicols.
Guest Stars: Dawn Addams, Anthony Ainley, Alexandra Bastedo, Norman Bird, Isla Blair, Peter Bowles, Veronica Carlson, John Carson, Iain Cuthbertson, Edward de Souza, Michael Gothard, Jenny Hanley, Anouska Hempel, Anthony Hopkins, Bernard Horsfall, Donald Houston, Stratford Johns, Ronald Lacey, Alan Lake, Fiona Lewis, Sue Lloyd, Kate O'Mara, Jean Marsh, Lois Maxwell, Kieron Moore, Patrick Mower, Anthony Nicholls, George Pastell, Nosher Powell, Dave Prowse, Anton Rodgers, Tony Selby, Dudley Sutton, Robert Urquhart, Anthony Valentine, Wanda Ventham, Richard Vernon.
Directors: Ray Austin, Roy Ward Baker, Paul Dickson, Cyril Frankel, John Gilling, Leslie Norman, Gilbert Taylor.
Writers: Philip Broadley, Leslie Darbon, Donald James, Harry W. Junkin, Gerald Kelsey, Terry Nation, Tony Williamson.
28 episodes x 50 minutes (colour)

Randall and Hopkirk (Deceased) (1969-1970)
Regular cast: Kenneth Cope, Mike Pratt, Annette Andre.
Guest Stars: Felix Aylmer, Keith Barron, Alexandra Bastedo, Norman Bird, Brian Blessed, Ray Brooks, Veronica Carlson, Carol Cleveland, Adrienne Corri, Nicholas Courtney, Ivor Dean, Roger Delgado, John Fraser, Liz Fraser, Michael Gothard, Doris Hare, David Healy, David Jason, Freddie Jones, Peter Jones, Ronald Lacey, Valerie Leon, Sue Lloyd, David Lodge, Philip Madoc, Lois Maxwell, Paul Maxwell, Jane Merrow, Kieron Moore, Nosher Powell, Michael Ripper, Anton Rodgers, Andrew Sachs, George Sewell, Dudley Sutton, Nigel Terry, Peter Vaughan, Timothy West, Frank Windsor.
Directors: Ray Austin, Roy Ward Baker, Paul Dickson, Cyril Frankel, Leslie Norman, Jeremy Summers, Robert Tronson.
Writers: Ray Austin, Donald James, Gerald Kelsey, Mike Pratt, Ralph Smart, Tony Williamson, Ian Wilson.
26 episodes x 50 minutes (colour)

UFO (1970-1971)
Regular Cast: Ed Bishop, George Sewell, Michael Billington, Gabrielle Drake, Grant Taylor, Dolores Mantez, Wanda Ventham, Peter Gordeno.
Guest Stars: Tom Adams, Stephanie Beacham, Steven Berkoff, Shakira Caine, George Cole,

Adrienne Corri, Roland Culver, Stuart Damon, Windsor Davies, Suzan Farmer, Anouska Hempel, Michael Jayston, Alexis Kanner, Philip Madoc, Jean Marsh, Lois Maxwell, Paul Maxwell, Jane Merrow, Patrick Mower, Derren Nesbitt, Conrad Phillips, Mike Pratt, Tracy Reed, Shane Rimmer, Vladek Sheybal, Christopher Timothy, David Warbeck, Douglas Wilmer, Tessa Wyatt.
Directors: Gerry Anderson, Cyril Frankel, David Lane, Alan Perry, David Tomblin, Ken Turner.
Writers: Gerry Anderson, Sylvia Anderson, Tony Barwick, Alan Pattillo, Dennis Spooner, David Tomblin.
26 episodes x 50 minutes (colour)

Shirley's World (1971)
Regular Cast: Shirley MacLaine.
Guest Stars: Joss Ackland, Rodney Bewes, Brian Blessed, James Booth, Cyril Cusack, Stuart Damon, Nigel Davenport, Murray Head, Nicky Henson, Burt Kwouk, Jeremy Lloyd, Ron Moody, John Neville, Dandy Nichols, Bill Owen, Una Stubbs, Sally Thomsett, James Villiers, Akiko Wakabayashi.
Directors: Ray Austin, Ralph Levy.
17 episodes x 25 minutes (colour)

Jason King (1971-1972)
Regular Cast: Peter Wyngarde.
Guest Stars: Tony Anholt, Felix Aylmer, Alexandra Bastedo, Ralph Bates, Stephanie Beacham, Norman Bird, Nicholas Courtney, Roger Delgado, Michele Dotrice, Sandor Eles, Liz Fraser, Paul Freeman, Julian Glover, Nigel Green, Imogen Hassell, Anthony Higgins, Donald Houston, Freddie Jones, Yootha Joyce, Felicity Kendal, Roy Kinnear, Burt Kwouk, Ronald Lacey, Dinsdale Landen, Jane Lapotaire, John Le Mesurier, Fiona Lewis, Sue Lloyd, T. P. McKenna, Alfred Marks, Kieron Moore, Patrick Mower, Kate O'Mara, Lance Percival, Ingrid Pitt, Mike Pratt, Denis Price, Milton Reid, Clive Revill, Anton Rodgers, Pamela Salem, Madeline Smith, Yutte Stensgaard, Patrick Troughton.
Directors: Roy Ward Baker, Paul Dickson, Cyril Frankel, Jeremy Summers.
Writers: Philip Broadley, Donald James, Harry W. Junkin, Gerald Kelsey, Dennis Spooner, Robert Banks Stewart, Tony Williamson.
26 episodes x 25 minutes (colour)

The Persuaders (1971-1972)
Regular Cast: Tony Curtis, Roger Moore.
Guest Stars: Joss Ackland, Tom Adams, Annette Andre, George Baker, Ralph Bates, Peter Bowles, Diane Cilento, Carol Cleveland, Joan Collins, Roland Culver, Sinead Cusack, Denholm Elliott, Susan George, Peter Gilmore, Hannah Gordon, Nigel Green, Jenny Hanley, Anouska Hempel, Ian Hendry, Geoffrey Keen, Andrew Keir, Suzy Kendall, Bernard Lee, Valerie Leon, Jennie Linden, Sue Lloyd, David Lodge, Alfred Marks, Lois Maxwell, Deborah Moore, Laurence Naismith, Derren Nesbitt, Patrick Newell, Margaret Nolan, Kate O'Mara, Jean Marsh, Nicola Pagett, Arnold Ridley, Shane Rimmer, Willie Rushton, Peter Sallis, Catherine Schell, Madeline Smith, Terry-Thomas, Patrick Troughton, Peter Vaughan, Richard Vernon, Thorley Walters.
Directors: Roy Ward Baker, Basil Dearden, Val Guest, James Hill, Peter Hunt, Peter Medak, Roger Moore, Leslie Norman.
Writers: Tony Barwick, Brian Clemens, Terence Feely, Val Guest, Donald James, Harry W. Junkin, John Kruse, Terry Nation, Michael Pertwee.
24 episodes x 50 minutes (colour)

The Adventurer (1972)
Regular Cast: Gene Barry, Barry Morse, Catherine Schell, Stuart Damon.
Guest Stars: Dawn Addams, Anthony Ainley, Jane Asher, Alexandra Bastedo, Stephanie Beacham, Ed Bishop, Adrienne Corri, Gabrielle Drake, Paul Eddington, Eunice Gayson, Judy Geeson, Sheila Gish, Anouska Hempel, Donald Houston, Freddie Jones, Ben Kingsley, Roy Kinnear, Burt Kwouk, Alan Lake, John Levene, Fiona Lewis, Jennie Linden, Alfred Marks, Andre Morrell, Kieron Moore, Patrick Mower, Anthony Nicholls, Lance Percival, Ingrid Pitt, Dennis Price, Pamela Salem, Angela Scoular, George Sewell, Sylvia Sims, Peter Vaughan.
Directors: Paul Dickson, Cyril Frankel, Val Guest, Barry Morse.
Writers: Monty Berman, Philip Broadley, Brian Clemens, Donald James, Gerald Kelsey, Dennis Spooner, Tony Williamson.
26 episodes x 25 minutes (colour)

The Protectors (1972-1974)
Regular Cast: Robert Vaughn, Nyree Dawn Porter, Tony Anholt.
Guest Stars: Joss Ackland, Patrick Allen, George Baker, Ralph Bates, Stephanie Beacham, Tom Bell, Ed Bishop, James Bolam, Peter Bowles, Jeremy Brett, Robert Brown, Sinead Cusack, Lisa Daniely, Peter Firth, Brian Glover, Hannah Gordon, Michael Gough, Nigel Green, Georgina Hale, Don Henderson, Ian Hendry, Prentis Hancock, Donald Houston, Saeed Jaffrey, Paul Jones, Freddie Jones, Eartha Kitt, Ronald Lacey, Alan Lake, Dinsdale Landen, Laurence Naismith, Patrick Magee, Kieron Moore, Patrick Mower, Christopher Neame, Kate O'Mara, Shane Rimmer, Bruce Robinson, Vladek Sheybal, Anthony Steel, David Suchet, John Thaw, Patrick Troughton, Lalla Ward, Douglas Wilmer, Stuart Wilson.
Directors: Roy Ward Baker, Don Chaffey, Charles Crichton, Cyril Frankel, John Hough, Jeremy

Summers, David Tomblin, Robert Vaughn.
Writers: Sylvia Anderson, Tony Barwick, Brian Clemens, Terence Feely, Donald James, Jesse Lasky Jr., Ralph Smart, Dennis Spooner.
52 episodes x 25 minutes (colour)

Thriller (1973-1976)
Guest Stars: Jenny Agutter, Patrick Allen, Tony Anholt, Francesca Annis, Alun Armstrong, Carroll Baker, Ian Bannen, Keith Barron, Ralph Bates, Edward Bishop, Brian Blessed, Peter Bowles, Jeremy Brett, Christopher Cazenove, George Chakiris, Diane Cilento, Gary Collins, Tom Conti, Sinead Cusack, Stuart Damon, Kim Darby, Windsor Davies, Anton Diffring, Bradford Dillman, Diana Dors, Gabrielle Drake, Denholm Elliott, Suzan Farmer, Jan Francis, Pamela Franklin, Judy Geeson, Julian Glover, Charles Gray, Susan Hampshire, Edward Hardwicke, Gerald Harper, Nigel Havers, Don Henderson, Ian Hendry, Bob Hoskins, Gayle Hunnicutt, Michael Jayston, Peter Jeffrey, Richard Johnson, Freddie Jones, Jean Kent, Michael Kitchen, Ronald Lacey, Dinsdale Landen, Leigh Lawson, John Le Mesurier, Jennie Linden, Cec Linder, Maureen Lipman, Patrick Magee, Donna Mills, Hayley Mills, Helen Mirren, Patrick O'Neal, Joanna Pettet, Ingrid Pitt, Nyree Dawn Porter, Robert Powell, Stephen Rea, Angharad Rees, Catherine Schell, Anthony Steel, Dudley Sutton, Linda Thorson, Oliver Tobias, Richard Todd, Patrick Troughton, Anthony Valentine, Peter Vaughan, Max Wall, Dennis Waterman, Stuart Wilson.
Directors: Robert D. Cardona, John Scholz-Conway, John Cooper, David Cunliffe, Ian Fordyce, Alan Gibson, Bill Hays, Peter Jeffries, Don Leaver, Peter Moffatt, Shaun O'Riordan, James Ormerod, John Sichel, Malcolm Taylor, Robert Tronson, Dennis Vance.
Writer: Brian Clemens.
43 episodes x 65 minutes (colour)

The Zoo Gang (1974)
Regular Cast: John Mills, Brian Keith, Lilli Palmer, Barry Morse.
Guest Stars: Vic Armstrong, Earl Cameron, Peter Cushing, Walter Gotell, Alf Joint, Bill Kenwright, Philip Madoc, Kieron Moore, Jacqueline Pearce, Ingrid Pitt.
Directors: Sidney Hayers, John Hough.
Writers: William Fairchild, John Kruse, Reginald Rose.
6 episodes x 50 minutes (colour)

Space 1999 (1975-1977)
Regular Cast: Martin Landau, Barbara Bain, Barry Morse, Prentis Hancock, Nick Tate, Zienia Merton, Catherine Schell, Tony Anholt.
Guest Stars: Vic Armstrong, Geoffrey Bayldon, Brian Blessed, Peter Bowles, Joan Collins, Bernard Cribbins, Peter Cushing, Stuart Damon, Roy Dotrice, Sarah Douglas, Lynne Frederick, Judy Geeson, Julian Glover, Cassandra Harris, Lisa Harrow, Gareth Hunt, Richard Johnson, Freddie Jones, Paul Jones, Barbara Kellerman, Jeremy Kemp, Leigh Lawson, Christopher Lee, Margaret Leighton, Rula Lenska, Valerie Leon, Ian McShane, Philip Madoc, Roy Marsden, Vicki Michelle, Patrick Mower, Anthony Nicholls, Dave Prowse, Shane Rimmer, Pamela Stephenson, Patrick Troughton, Anthony Valentine, Billie Whitelaw, Douglas Wilmer.
Directors: Ray Austin, Tom Clegg, Kevin Connor, Charles Crichton, Val Guest, Peter Medak, Dave Tomblin.
Writers: Gerry Anderson, Sylvia Anderson, Tony Barwick, Johnny Byrne, Terence Dicks, Fred Freiberger, Donald James, Christopher Penfold.
48 episodes x 50 minutes (colour)

The Muppet Show (1976-1981)
Guest Stars: Julie Andrews, Joan Baez, Shirley Bassey, Harry Belafonte, Candice Bergen, Milton Berle, Victor Borge, George Burns, Dyan Cannon, Johnny Cash, Petula Clark, John Cleese, James Coburn, Alice Cooper, Dom DeLuise, John Denver, Marty Feldman, Bruce Forsyth, Mark Hamill, Debbie Harry, Bob Hope, Glenda Jackson, Elton John, Madeline Kahn, Danny Kaye, Gene Kelly, Kris Kristofferson, Cheryl Ladd, Liberace, Steve Martin, Ethel Merman, Spike Milligan, Liza Minnelli, Dudley Moore, Roger Moore, Zero Mostel, Rudolf Nureyev, Vincent Price, Christopher Reeve, Kenny Rogers, Roy Rogers, Diana Ross, Leo Sayer, Peter Sellers, Brooke Shields, Paul Simon, Sylvester Stallone, Twiggy, Peter Ustinov, Raquel Welch, Andy Williams.
Directors: Philip Casson, Peter Harris.
Writers: Jack Burns, Jim Henson, Jerry Juhl, Chris Langham.
120 episodes x 25 minutes (colour)

Jesus of Nazareth (1977)
Cast: Robert Powell, Anne Bancroft, Ernest Borgnine, Claudia Cardinale, James Farentino, Ian Holm, Olivia Hussey, James Earl Jones, Stacy Keech, James Mason, Ian McShane, Laurence Olivier, Donald Pleasence, Christopher Plummer, Anthony Quinn, Fernando Rey, Ralph Richardson, Rod Steiger, Peter Ustinov, Michael York.
Director: Franco Zeffirelli.
Writer: Anthony Burgess.
Running Time: 371 minutes (colour)

The Return of the Saint (1978-1979)
Regular Cast: Ian Ogilvy.
Guest Stars: Joss Ackland, Annette Andre, Alfie Bass, Helmut Berger, George Cole, Maurice Denham, Sarah Douglas, Britt Ekland, Mel Ferrer, Prunella Gee, Judy Geeson, Brian Glover, Prentis

Hancock, Jenny Hanley, Murray Head, Anouska Hempel, Ian Hendry, Donald Houston, Gayle Hunnicutt, Stratford Johns, Diane Keen, Geoffrey Keen, Burt Kwouk, Rula Lenska, Kate O'Mara, Paul Maxwell, Michael Medwin, Laurence Naismith, Derren Nesbitt, Susan Penhaligon, Donald Pickering, Shane Rimmer, Anton Rogers, Nadim Sawalha, Catherine Schell, Anthony Steel, Linda Thorson, Christopher Timothy, Sam Wanamaker, Stuart Wilson, Tessa Wyatt.
Directors: Ray Austin, Roy Ward Baker, Tom Clegg, Kevin Connor, Charles Crichton, Cyril Frankel, Peter Medak, Leslie Norman, Peter Sasdy, Jeremy Summers, Sam Wanamaker.
Writers: Philip Broadley, Morris Farhi, Terence Feely, John Goldsmith, Leon Griffiths, John Kruse, George Markstein, Michael Pertwee, Tony Williamson.
24 episodes x 55 minutes (colour)

Sapphire and Steel (1979-1982)
Regular Cast: Joanna Lumley, David McCallum.
Directors: David Foster, Shaun O'Riordan.
Writers: Peter Hammond, Don Houghton, Anthony Read.
34 episodes x 25 minutes (colour)

Hammer House of Horror (1980)
Guest Stars: Nicholas Ball, Norman Bird, Pierce Brosnan, Christopher Cazenove, Warren Clarke, Brian Cox, Peter Cushing, Suzanne Danielle, Paul Darrow, Diana Dors, Denholm Elliott, Jon Finch, Julia Foster, Prunella Gee, Barbara Kellerman, Leigh Lawson, Simon MacCorkindale, Peter McEnery, Conrad Phillips, Sian Phillips, Dinah Sheridan, Gareth Thomas, Anthony Valentine.
Directors: Tom Clegg, Alan Gibson, Don Leaver, Joe McGrath, Peter Sasdy, Don Sharp, Robert Young.
Writers: Jeremy Burnham, David Fisher, David Lloyd, Nicholas Palmer, Anthony Read.
13 episodes x 50 minutes (colour)

Shillingbury Tales (1981)
Regular Cast: Robin Nedwell, Diane Keen, Lionel Jeffries, Bernard Cribbins, Jack Douglas, Linda Hayden.
Director: Val Guest.
Writer: Francis Essex.
6 episodes x 50 minutes (colour)